Unhealthy Times

Unhealthy Times

Political Economy Perspectives on Health and Care

Edited by

Pat Armstrong,
Hugh Armstrong,
and David Coburn

70 Wynford Drive, Don Mills, Ontario M3C 1J9
www.oupcan.com

Oxford University Press is a department of the University of Oxford.
It furthers the University's objective of excellence in research, scholarship,
and education by publishing worldwide in

Oxford New York

Athens Auckland Bangkok Bogotá Buenos Aires
Cape Town Chennai Dar es Salaam Delhi Florence Hong Kong Istanbul
Karachi Kolkata Kuala Lumpur Madrid Melbourne Mexico City Mumbai
Nairobi Paris São Paulo Singapore Taipei Tokyo Toronto Warsaw

with associated companies in Berlin Ibadan

Published in Canada
by Oxford University Press

First published 2001

Canadian Cataloguing in Publication Data

Main entry under title:

Unhealthy times : political economy perspectives on health and care in Canada.

Includes bibliographical references and index.
ISBN 0-19-541509-4

1. Health care reform—Economic aspects—Canada. 2. Medical policy—
Economic aspects—Canada. I. Armstrong, Pat, 1945– . II. Armstrong, Hugh,
1943– . III. Coburn, David, 1938– .

RA395.C3U53 2001 362.1'0971 C00-933070-4

Cover Image: Steve Taylor
Cover Design: Peter Barata

1 2 3 4 - 04 03 02 01

This book is printed on permanent (acid-free) paper ∞.
Printed in Canada

Contents

INTRODUCTION

The Political Economy of Health and Care

Political economy has its roots in both liberalism and Marxism, but the branches have spread well beyond the work of either John Stuart Mill or Karl Marx. In Canada, Harold Innis led the way with his analysis of how staples such as fish and fur shaped Canadian social, political, and economic life. Later, C.B. Macpherson challenged the dominant liberal interpretation of democracy and Stanley Ryerson reinterpreted history to reveal the integral relations among ideas, economics, politics, and social relations. More recently, scholars such as Wallace Clement and Leo Panitch have documented the powerfully linked economic and political forces that help structure social life in this country, as well as the forms of resistance to these same forces. More recently still, feminists and post-modernists have pushed political economy approaches beyond an exclusive focus on classes, formal economies, ideologies, and politics to include households, differences within classes, social movements, discourses, subjectivities, and power relations that extend far beyond the paid workplace. In short, political economy is a dynamic field of inquiry. It is constantly shifting boundaries and core concerns in response to theoretical debates, research, and changes both within and across societies. At the same time, political economy in all its variety shares basic assumptions that not only distinguish this approach from others but justify this frequently conflict-laden evolution.

First, as the term suggests, 'political economy' understands politics and economics as integrally related. For a political economist an adequate study of the whole cannot be developed from the separate study of individual parts. Nor can it be developed without attention paid to the people who are the subjects of history. States, markets, ideas, discourses, and civil society are not independent variables but interrelated parts of the same whole. This whole is shaped, but not determined, by the mode of production, that is, by the means of producing and reproducing for socially determined needs. In Canada today, the dominant mode is a particular form of capitalism. This mode of production, like the markets central to its structure and representation, is seen as a social construct, not as a natural, neutral, or inevitable mechanism governed by immutable laws. Its particular construction and the relations among its parts change over time and within particular contexts. So, for example, in the period following World War II, the various levels of Canadian states could be described as relatively autonomous from corporations and as seeking to limit the negative consequences of markets. Today, the state openly arranges partnerships with corporations and works to enshrine markets through international agreements. Nevertheless, there is a logic to capitalist modes of production, albeit a logic that works out in a wide variety of forms and one about which there is considerable theoretical dispute. This logic reflects the drive for profit and has a profound influence on the conditions and relations of work.

Largely in response to feminist critiques, the political economy is now defined to include households and communities as well as formal economies, the social relations of gender as well as paid and unpaid work. The search for profit influences what is done in and out of markets, in and out of homes. It conditions what is sold and what is paid for, what is commodified and what is not. At the same time, the particular form of the relationship between states and markets creates different patterns of commodification and distribution.

The political economy also includes the cultural and ideological—the ideas, discourses, and practices that dominate, and those that subvert, existing relations of ruling. The increasing emphasis on these aspects of analysis results in part at least from the critiques developed by feminists and post-modernists. But in political economy, these ideas and subjectivities are not free-floating. Nor can they be understood in isolation. Rather, they need to be explained with reference to material conditions, in terms of their mutual, and often contradictory, relationship.

Second, political economy is historical. This means much more than examining change over time. And it means more than focusing on the material aspects of politics and economics. It assumes that people collectively and individually make their own history, although not under conditions of their own choosing or simply as a result of ideas that spring independently to their minds. People are social, actively formed within particular social locations and relations, rather than pre-existing autonomous individuals. Ideas and discourses are central components of this active formation. Ideas and ways of seeing can serve to reinforce or disrupt the existing order, although the common-sense understanding of the world is strongly influenced by those with economic and political power.

Equally important, these relations are relations of inequality and of ruling. Initially, political economy concentrated on inequalities related to class and defined history strictly in terms of class. Although political economy has been slow to incorporate consideration of gender, of culture/'race'/ethnicity, of age and sexuality, many of the most exciting developments in political economy are focused on understanding the intersections among these and with class. Increasingly, the daily and pervasive practices that constitute governance are also part of the analysis as the notion of ruling is extended far beyond politics into households, communities, and workplaces. Now, the central question of 'who benefits?' goes far beyond class, and no longer are classes seen as the sole agents of change. However, class, gender, 'race', and other differences are still understood as relationships, and as relationships that change over time and with place, rather than as fixed categories that can be easily measured through indicators such as socio-economic status.

Political economists grapple with the tensions between structure and agency, between ideas and material conditions, between class and gender, class and race, and between the tendency to separate aspects of these for the purposes of analysis and the need to unite them in order to understand the whole. What this means in terms of health and health care is the purpose of this book.

Some lines of analysis in the political economy of health have been clearly established. The emphasis on the whole resulted in what is now called 'the determinants of health'—the idea that health is determined by food, shelter, jobs, and joy as well as by the care received and delivered.

The historical approach to the question of who benefits helped reveal the medical dominance in health-care delivery, a dominance facilitated by overlaps in those delivering care and those within the state establishing a public system. The notion of class forces made the role of unions in creating medicare visible at the same time as the focus on class for many years rendered organized women's groups invisible. Similarly, the literature on labour process that defined work in factory terms often ignored the female-dominated health-care sector, although it did draw attention to the importance to health of control over work. Paradoxically, the transfer of care work to the home has revived interest in a political economy approach that links paid and unpaid work not only to each other and to gender but also to the search for profit. Indeed, as health and health care become increasingly defined by both politicians and corporations as business enterprises, and even more frequently as profitable, the relevance of a political economy approach is more and more obvious.

In the last decade, health care has become an enormously profitable business. The interrelationship between states and corporations has become closer and more visible. Yet most Canadians remain stubbornly resistant to calls for privatization in health care. They cling to the egalitarian principles set out in the Canada Health Act. In groups that only sometimes follow class lines, they are protesting the commodification of care. At the same time, state withdrawal from services is leaving many women conscripted into unpaid care work. New forms of decision-making are altering governance, in terms of where and how decisions are made and who is making them. Meanwhile, the transformation of work in and out of the market is fundamentally altering the conditions for health.

A political economy approach has only begun to be applied to these developments in health and health care. To meet this challenge, political economy as a discipline must continue to evolve in ways that take the new conditions and relations into account. We invited such analysis for inclusion in this book. The purpose is not to provide a comprehensive or integrated view of health care in Canada. Instead, the contributions are intended to stimulate further development of a political economy approach, to demonstrate how this way of viewing our health-care system continues to evolve in order to understand the forces, conditions, ideas, practices, and relations that are central to health and care.

The emphasis in this book is on the political economy as the context for change. It is organized around locating within this context, first, health-care reforms and then two major themes within these reforms—evidence and risk. Each section begins with an outline of how political economy can help us understand the issues. The various chapters each use a somewhat different interpretation of political economy to explore particular aspects of the overall theme. Together, they demonstrate both how political economy can make health and health-care reforms more transparent and how political economists are exploring various paths towards understanding current social transformations.

PART ONE

Locating Health Care

In the first years of the twenty-first century we are entering a new era. Nation-states are in the process of a world transformation from modernism to late modernism or to post-modernism, from Fordist to post-Fordist modes of production, from organized to disorganized capitalism or from monopoly to global capitalism. In this new global era states play a lesser role than they have previously. The workings and logic of nations have been thrown open to the enhanced power of transnational corporations. What had previously seemed solid and inevitable now appears fragile and contingent. Nowhere is this more true than in regard to health-care systems. These are now at the centre of debates about their viability, their appropriateness, their efficiency, and their utility. Canadian newspapers daily record challenges to the basic principles underlying national health insurance, the centrepiece of Canadian health care. These challenges emanate from neo-liberal attempts to commodify health care, to make public health care more and more like a market, but also from those who want to save medicare by making it more effective and efficient. These forces collide with collective movements struggling to preserve approximately equal access to health care for all Canadians.

The health-care system involves much more than formal methods of helping those with health problems to finance their care. Health care is not only part of markets but also part of the household or domestic sphere. There are both formal and household-centred forms of caring. Formal health-care systems are at the centre of a huge health industry that is one of the largest economic sectors in Canada, ranging from enormous drug companies that produce both prescription and over-the-counter drugs to sprawling health science centres. Despite these vast institutions, which employ a significant fraction of the Canadian labour force, health status has a rather uncertain relationship with the formal health-care system. The majority of the evidence available today indicates that, among the advanced capitalist countries, national levels of health (as measured by longevity) are at least as highly related to prevailing general social conditions as they are to the size of the health-care system. Nevertheless, health care is crucial for the cure of acute conditions and injuries and is important regarding chronic conditions. Moreover, the amelioration of symptoms, pain, and suffering, quite apart from curing illness, is a valuable goal. Access to health care is also a basic human right.

Though most policy discussions on health care in Canada emphasize costs and payment mechanisms (medicare), health systems themselves cannot simply be equated with methods of paying for health care. National health insurance is just one mode of organizing health systems. Other forms include national health systems (as in the United Kingdom) in which the state owns and manages (or used to own and manage) all health-care institutions. At the other end of the spectrum, and standing more or less alone among the advanced industrialized countries, is the United States, which provides state medical aid for the elderly and the poor but has mainly a privately run health-care system. Most other countries show some variation on these three basic types.

In international public opinion polls, the Canadian system of medicare is not only favoured by Canadians over other forms, but Americans and even the British would prefer the Canadian system over their own (Blendon et al., 1990). Medicare has been a success in making doctor and hospital care available under standard conditions to Canadians; indeed, medicare has almost come to define what it means to be Canadian. It is immensely popular politically, which makes for political difficulties for those who wish to dismantle it.

While health care in Canada has been partially decommodified, that is, access to health care does not depend on how much money one has, all of the papers in this section imply that within a capitalist society there will always be powerful pressures towards privatization. These pressures will not go away. Many of the current debates about health care in Canada not only focus on the supposed deficiencies of the present system, but also revolve around privatizing or recommodifying health care. Though the present Premier of Alberta, Ralph Klein, assures Albertans that his most recent proposals to fund private hospitals would not bring 'two-tier' health care, there are many reasons for believing otherwise. Once private (and most likely American) health-care corporations have their foot in the door, the North American Free Trade Agreement contains provisions that would hinder any attempt thereafter to 'discriminate' against them or to favour public delivery. NAFTA and the World Trade Organization (WTO) are biased against the public provision of goods and services. With private corporations entrenched there would be tremendous pressure to allow them to provide additional private services to those willing to pay. As Williams et al. and Leys suggest in this section, the introduction of private interests in health care brings us to the top of a slippery slope. There are, however, a number of different movements for change, one to privatize, another to 'preserve through reform', and popular and professional social movements are resistant to both of these processes.

In fact, since the introduction of medicare in the late 1960s an increasing proportion of health care in Canada has been financed from private sources. Initially, private health insurance companies rushed in to cover anything medicare did not and to supplemented medicare coverage. Dental insurance, eye-care insurance, insurance for prescription drugs, private health insurance covering the upgrading of hospital rooms and various devices or procedures not covered by medicare, and out-of-country health insurance all flourished. The proportion of private funding in health care increased from 23.6 per cent in 1975 to 25.4 per cent in 1990, and then to an estimated 30.4 per cent in 1999. In Ontario, the home of an aggressively neo-liberal government, it is estimated that private funding accounted for over one-third of all health-care expenditures in 1999 (CIHI, 1999).

Currently, with the underfunding of medicare there are pressing issues regarding waiting lists for diagnosis and treatment. This situation has become so serious that patients in Ontario and other provinces are now sent to the United States for radiation or other therapies. Complaints are increasing that patients are not receiving appropriate and timely care or that the care received is not patient-focused and compassionate. Cutbacks on federal health funding to the provinces, and not only provincial actions, have been a major factor in creating a fiscal crisis in health care. Some governments and their media and private-sector supporters also find it ideologically useful to 'create' health-care crises as an excuse to push for privatization.

Attacks on medicare by private corporations and by right-wing governments are part of the larger movement to undermine the welfare state. Yet, cutbacks in government spending do not mean cutbacks in societal spending. Costs are not avoided by transferring these from the state to the private domain—they are simply more hidden from public scrutiny. The United States pays 15 per cent of its massive gross national product (GNP) for health care, as compared to about 9 per cent in Canada (CIHI, 1999). The percentage of GNP the US pays is much more than that for any other nation, and this is for a system in which about 40 million people are not insured and most of the others are underinsured. Certainly, contrary to the prevailing business wisdom, state systems for providing health care are more efficient than private ones. Much of the difference in costs between Canada and the United States is made up of huge administrative bills incurred by a complex American 'non-system' involving thousands of insurers, payers, and providers and immense volumes of paperwork and auditing (Drache and Sullivan, 1999).

A potential coincidence of interests exists between patients and providers in helping to save medicare. Yet, the role of providers in aiming to preserve health care is somewhat contradictory, for at the same time they benefit from state spending on care. In health care as in other areas, incomes and cutbacks are not spread evenly among the upper and lower echelons of the workforce. Substantial incomes are largely expropriated by the more powerful groups, such as the medical profession. Women workers in particular tend to be lower in the provider hierarchy within the system and, in addition, bear the brunt of providing unpaid care outside of the system.

In this section three of the four chapters concentrate on medicare. The major theme underlying these chapters is the assault on government-financed services through the rise of globalization and neo-liberalism. Governments are being shrunk or hollowed out. Neo-liberalism, that is, a single-minded emphasis that markets are the most efficient and effective producers of goods and services, is now almost hegemonic as policy and ideology even in purportedly 'liberal' political parties. Free trade among nations is now an official orthodoxy and is supported by the huge corporations, which benefit from escape from national controls. Nevertheless, these doctrines face popular resistance.

All of the chapters contain somewhat the same message. That is, they note the continuous pressures to commodify health-care services in an era of global markets, a globalized health-care industry, and the dominance of neo-liberal ideology, parties, and policies. If states were once responsive to working-class interests and to those of the poor under the particular conditions of nation-based monopoly capital, in a global era the interests of business are paramount and there are attacks on many 'citizenship rights'. The role of the state in enhancing the well-being of all has been weakened and undermined. While the power of corporations has been vastly enlarged, divisions still exist between health care corporations and non-health corporations and between small and large business. These divisions provide some openings for opposition to the downsizing or privatization of health care. Yet, the traditional opposition to business interests provided by unions, left-wing parties, or working-class movements has also been weakened and fragmented. What has sustained medicare so far is an immense general public support that politicians of whatever stripe cannot ignore.

Because health care is the largest item on provincial budgets the 'New Right' likes to portray medicare as bleeding governments of revenue and promotes 'private money' or private markets as the solution. Certainly there is an element of 'rationing' in public systems through the allocation of resources to health care. Still, these decisions are public and open to debate. Markets do not eliminate rationing, they simply hide it. In private systems one's place in the queue is decided on the basis of income. Yet, politicians can openly tamper with medicare only at their peril. As Williams et al. (Chapter 1) and Leys (Chapter 4) note, a series of vested interests—organized medicine, hospitals, and some health-care businesses—in addition to broad social movements, provide support for medicare in Canada and for the National Health Service in Great Britain. Because of its public popularity in Canada, medicare is never directly attacked but is more subtly undermined. Health-care funding is cut, resulting in long lineups for various procedures. Programs and services are pushed outside the medicare envelope and thus are no longer covered by medicare. Rather than being totally dismantled, medicare is being 'hollowed out'.

The chapters in this section indicate that the analysis of health care in Canada needs to be multi-levelled. There are interest groups inside and outside of health care. The health-care system is difficult to change in part because of the entrenched power of medicine and that of other large health-care institutions. Recently shaping the interaction of all of these groups, however, have been changes in the 'rules', i.e., change in the power structures within which health-care systems are embedded so that corporate power is greater and state control is weakened. While the political spectrum has become decidedly skewed to the right, there has been resistance to complete marketization.

Although medicare has so far survived attacks on it, as long as it operates within a predominantly free-enterprise economy it will be subject to pressures towards commodification. Moreover, as these chapters suggest, our health-care system results from a complex of factors and forces seemingly far removed from the doctor-patient relationship. Joel Lexchin, for example, notes in Chapter 2 that the drug industry powerfully shapes both what is studied in medical research and what is done for patients in the health-care system itself. Hundreds of researchers in public institutions spend much of their time carrying out drug trials, while there is a general neglect of other (non-drug) forms of cure or care. The powerful medical profession, the other health-care professions, and hospitals, while acting to protect health expenditures—expenditures for some are income for others (Evans, 1997)—in other respects serve to prevent necessary changes that might enhance access and the quality of care. Reforms become distorted in ways that benefit existing powerful groups.

Not much is said by any of these authors, however, about the quality of care. Many reformers have focused their energies on the virtues of medicare in attempting to prevent it from being dismantled. In this process the quality of health care in Canada and the speed, effectiveness, and compassion with which care is given are not often analysed. It can be argued that many of the delays that now afflict those seeking diagnosis, or therapy, are due to the fiscal undermining of care. It is also clear that health care can be made more efficient and effective. There are major problems within medicare, including delays in diagnosis and treatment, a lack of responsiveness to community and patient concerns, and the continuing power of medicine and hospitals to shape reforms in their own interests. The question is thus raised about how to make health care more directly responsive to patients, more effective and more humane without losing equality of access.

Moreover, in the focus on medical care or on the social determinants of health, there is a neglect of services that lie somewhere between the two, namely public health services. A tradition within Canada focuses on the prevention of disease through immunizations, pure water, and food regulations, as well as on the provision of preventive services such as prenatal and postnatal care. Canada also leads the world in the area of health promotion, that is a focus on attaining and maintaining 'wellness', although this is rapidly being superseded by a 'population health' approach, which is more easily co-opted. Nevertheless, both health promotion and population health have focused attention on inequalities in health, if not on why and how these inequalities are produced and reproduced (the task of political economy).

Critiques of health care show similarities to critiques of the welfare state. The welfare state provided benefits, often on the simple basis of citizenship, yet it also occasionally developed into a system of bureaucratic or welfare dominance over 'clients' or consumers. Thus, we need not necessarily return to the welfare state of the 1970s, nor should health care necessarily remain static and unchanging; rather, a more democratic form of state and a more responsive form of social citizenship and health-care service are required. There may indeed be a movement from the mass provision of care under traditional welfare systems to more individually tailored access to health-care resources. The challenges involved in this shift are to preserve equity in access, to improve the fit between individual needs and health care, and to avoid falling into the trap of a private system that simply privileges those with money. We do need vigorous debates about health care in Canada, but not debates restricted by the narrow ideological blinkers of those whose major claim to voice is corporate ownership.

Clearly, a focus on health is not only important in itself but provides the basis for a trenchant critique of neo-liberalism in general. A focus on health and health care forces attention to human well-being rather than only to an economistic fixation on gross economic statistics as measures of how well nations are functioning. The measure of Canadian society is not how high our GNP is but the well-being of Canadians and the care we provide for those in need. The role of a political economy of care is to help us to understand caring systems in all their complexity and to stimulate us to do something about this understanding.

References

Alford, R.R. *Health Care Politics.* 1995. Chicago: University of Chicago Press.

Blendon, R., R. Leitman, I. Morrison, and K. Donelan. 1990. 'Satisfaction with health systems in ten nations', *Health Affairs* 9, 2: 185–92.

Canadian Institute for Health Information (CIHI). *National Health Expenditure Trends (1975–1999) Report.* www.cihi.ca/medrls/execnhex.htm

Drache, D., and T. Sullivan, eds. 1999. *Market Limits in Health Reform: Public Success, Private Failure.* New York: Routledge.

Evans, R.G. 1997. 'Going for the gold: The redistributive agenda behind market-based health care reform', *Journal of Health Politics, Policy and Law* 22, 2: 427–65.

CHAPTER 1

From Medicare to Home Care: Globalization, State Retrenchment, and the Profitization of Canada's Health-Care System

A. Paul Williams, Raisa Deber, Pat Baranek, and Alina Gildiner

Introduction

Universal government health insurance (medicare) is widely regarded as a triumph of the postwar Canadian state. And clearly it is a triumph. Compared to the medical free market of the US, where a fifth of the population remains uninsured and where overall costs are the highest in the world and continue to rise, health-care expenditures in Canada have been relatively contained, and all Canadians have access to medically necessary hospital and doctor services without regard to their economic means (General Accounting Office, 1991; Woolhandler and Himmelstein, 1991, 1998; Mhatre and Deber, 1992; National Forum on Health, 1997a, 1997b).

Yet Canadian medicare faces tremendous challenges. Like other elements of the postwar state, medicare is confronted by an array of political forces aimed at restructuring, reinventing, or otherwise shrinking the public sector (Shields and Evans, 1998). Such forces are evident in the ascendancy of neo-liberal, free-market ideologies that oppose public intervention in areas of perceived private concern and prescribe a greatly reduced role for the state. They are also evident in the push towards economic and political globalization that proponents use to justify demands for tax reductions and the harmonization of domestic social policies with international (primarily US) norms (Bennett, 1991; OECD, 1995). If the expansion of the postwar state was motivated by perceptions of 'market failure', an inability on the part of market economies to achieve economic growth and social goals, current demands for state retrenchment are justified by perceptions of 'government failure', an inability on the part of governments to maintain growth and provide services on a responsive, cost-effective basis (Boyer and Drache, 1996; Peters, 1995).

Such forces fuel an antagonistic political assault on medicare. Because it is publicly funded and regulated, medicare is portrayed by adherents of neo-liberal free-market ideologies as a source of inefficiency, waste, and abuse in an era of increasingly competitive global markets. Since it remains the single largest expenditure category for provincial governments, medicare is viewed as a barrier to expenditure control, deficit reduction, and tax cuts. And because it does not permit publicly insured health-care services to be provided in private markets on a for-profit basis, medicare is criticized as an arbitrary limitation on choice and on the freedom of individuals to purchase any services they can afford (Day, 1998; Deber, 1991, 1998; Fuller, 1998; Saunders, 1997). While noted health economists in Canada and other countries continue to point out that health markets are not like other markets and that single-payer, publicly administered health-care systems are optimal on both efficiency and equity grounds (Evans, 1984; GAO, 1991; National Forum on Health, 1997a, 1997b; Reinhardt, 1996; Royal Commission on Health Services, 1964), the political assault on medicare intensifies.

In this chapter we analyse the politics of medicare in a period characterized by mounting pressures to dismantle the postwar state. Our first objective is to assess the contradictory factors that have precipitated attempts to reduce the scope of government health insurance in favour of private markets, yet, at least to this point, have also sheltered medicare from the direct assaults experienced in other areas, including labour rights, public education, and social welfare. In spite of an increasingly loud chorus of criticisms from rightist political organizations such as the Canadian Alliance, influential business groups such as the Business Council on National Issues, conservative think-tanks such as the C.D. Howe and Fraser Institutes, and hostile elements within the organized medical profession, medicare remains the best-protected social program in Canada (McBride and Shields, 1997; Weller, 1996: 124–5).

We suggest that medicare's endurance is due in large part to sustained support among the general public; medicare remains a defining characteristic of Canadian identity and the top issue of concern among Canadians (Ekos Research Associates, 1998; Fuller, 1998; Northrup, 1998; LeBlanc, 1999). However, the endurance of our health-care system is also due to the fact that it serves an array of vested private interests, including those within the organized medical profession, hospitals, employers, and the pharmaceutical industry.

For its part, organized medicine strongly opposed the introduction in 1966 of the Medical Care Insurance Act, the legislative basis of the Canadian system, and it continues to oppose government intrusions into areas of perceived medical control and dominance (Fuller, 1998; Taylor, 1987; Williams, Vayda et al., 1995). However, professional opposition to publicly funded health insurance in Canada has been tempered by the fact that physicians gain enormously from a system that solidifies medical dominance by covering doctors' services to the exclusion of services rendered by other health-care providers. Because medicare guarantees payment for virtually every service that physicians themselves deem to be medically necessary, physicians reaped windfall economic benefits following medicare's introduction and continue to have incomes averaging between three and five times those of other working Canadians (Armstrong and Armstrong, 1994; Coburn et al., 1983; Fuller, 1998;

Naylor, 1986; Williams, Vayda, et al., 1995). Professional opposition to medicare is also tempered by a growing awareness of the extent to which physician autonomy in the medical free market of the US is being eroded by rising corporate control (Fuller, 1998; Williams, Vayda et al., 1995; Woolhandler and Himmelstein, 1995).

Hospitals also have strong vested interests in publicly funded health care. Hospitals rose to dominance in the Canadian health system largely as a result of public initiatives to increase hospital capacity. These included postwar federal grants-in-aid for hospital construction, the Hospital Insurance and Diagnostic Services Act of 1957, which offered the provinces shared funding for services provided in hospitals, and medicare itself, which continued to cover hospital services while extending coverage to medical services provided by doctors outside of hospitals (Taylor, 1987). In 1998 hospitals and physicians accounted for 34 per cent and 14 per cent respectively, of national health-care expenditures, which totalled more than $75 billion (CIHI, 1998). Medicare also continues to shelter Canadian hospitals from the need to compete with other providers and from the need for costly management and accounting infrastructures, which in the US contribute to overhead costs exceeding 25 per cent for large for-profit Health Maintenance Organizations (Fuller, 1998; Woolhandler and Himmelstein, 1998).

As the free trade debate has made clear, many elements of business also have strong interests in maintaining a high-quality, publicly funded health-care system. Heavily unionized, labour-intensive industries like the automotive industry continue to benefit substantially from a program that protects them from the high costs of private health insurance experienced by their US counterparts. Because public health insurance shares the costs of illness across the entire population, instead of assessing costs directly to employers or to workers who might in turn seek to recover them through higher wages, business coalitions such as the Employer Committee on Health Care-Ontario (ECHCO, 1995) have argued for maintaining public medicare, while also advocating for cost containment through hospital closures, wider use of lower-paid health professionals, various user charges, and a bonus system for doctors who discourage overuse of the system and encourage health promotion (Fuller, 1998). The pharmaceutical industry also benefits because ready access for the public to hospitals and physicians results in huge numbers of prescriptions, and drugs provided in hospitals, as well as many covered by provincial drug plans, are paid for by the public purse (Williams, Cockerill, and Lowy, 1995). Prescription drug expenditures now rank as the third largest category in Canadian health budgets, accounting for 14 per cent of all expenditures (CIHI, 1998).

Such private interests, along with strong public support, have thus far blunted the capacity for sustained, overt political attacks against medicare. In Alberta and Ontario, for example, where in other respects state retrenchment has been most marked, neo-liberal governments have been compelled by intense political opposition to limit health-care spending cuts and to put additional money into such high-visibility programs as cancer treatment and cardiac and emergency care. For its part, the federal government, itself bent on a course of fiscal constraint and deficit reduction and the author of substantial cuts to cash transfer payments to the provinces in recent years, now seems intent on portraying itself as the defender of universal medicare against the forces of incipient privatization and health system decline in the provinces (Gherson, 1998; Thanh Ha, 1999). Responding to mounting public concerns about an erosion of medicare, the 1999 federal budget included an additional $11.5 billion over the next five years that provincial governments have promised to spend on health care, although what exactly this entails remains vague (Health Canada, 1999).

Nevertheless, we want to stress that we are *not* arguing that medicare remains unscathed; far from it. Rather, our second major objective in this paper is to analyse ways in which public health care *is* being undermined. This includes an ongoing erosion of the five principles of the Canada Health Act through the emergence of private clinics, the delisting of certain insured services, limits to portability, and so on (Fuller, 1998). But more importantly, we contend that medicare is also being eroded by what amounts to a massive, though less visible, hemorrhaging of programs and services *outside* of public coverage. Stymied politically in their attempts to reduce health-care costs but under increasing pressures and their own agenda for tax cuts, debt reduction, and a general shrinking of the postwar state (McCarthy, 1999), neoliberal governments such as that of Ontario are now engaged in massive health-care reforms that shift the locus of care outside of hospitals and doctors' offices, and, in the process, outside of the 'rules' and universal entitlements of medicare. In the less visible, less politically mobilized, and highly fractioned terrain of the society as a whole, governments wishing to do so are relatively free to avoid their fiscal and moral obligations to universal access without the intense political confrontation that any forthright assault on medicare would inevitably provoke. While medicare remains a conspicuous symbol of commitment to the public interest, it is progressively 'hollowed out' (Jessop, 1993; Shields and Evans, 1998).

As a concrete example, we analyse the case of Ontario, where a much anticipated reform of community-based long-term care has been implemented alongside the restructuring (downsizing) of hospital services. This reform promises to meet the increasing need for high-quality, cost-effective health and support services in the community through the introduction of 'managed competition'. We argue, however, that in addition to changing the *locus* of care from hospitals to the community, reforms of this type also fundamentally change the *conditions* under which care is provided. In contrast to medicare, which *guarantees* all citizens access to medically necessary services regardless of where they live or work, Ontario's reform guarantees only that people will be *assessed* for services; it does not guarantee that they will receive them. In consequence, access to care in the community, including many of the same services that hospitals have provided in the past (e.g., nursing care, rehabilitation, drugs, and personal support), is no longer an established entitlement. It depends instead on the judgement of local boards using variable criteria to assess needs and eligibility, and on provincial willingness to provide adequate funding.

An additional concern is the introduction of competition as a principle of service provision and its effects on a 'marketplace' populated by a diversity of relatively small not-for-profit providers and by some of the most vulnerable groups and individuals in society, including the acutely and chronically ill, the frail elderly, and those with disabilities. In contrast to other markets where consumers may exercise a significant amount of choice and control, consumers of health and long-term care services may have few options since care is often not discretionary and since many lack the ability to voice their interests politically or to 'exit' from services or providers that do not meet their needs (Evans, 1984; Hirschman, 1970; Rachlis and Kushner, 1994; Williams et al., 1999). In this connection, we emphasize that our primary focus is not *privatization* per se, since doctors and hospitals have always remained private providers under medicare. We are concerned with the *profitization* of health care, that is, the provision of health services as a profit-making business.

We begin by examining key contradictions and conflicts characteristic of Canadian medicare. These conflicts and contradictions place important limits on the capacity of the publicly funded health system to respond to a rapidly changing and increasingly hostile political environment. Subsequently, we analyse Ontario's recent reform of community-based long-term care. We conclude by reflecting on the implications of the continuing shift out of medicare; in Ontario, we suggest, health care is deliberately being 'put to market', and the provincial government, as a matter of policy, is about to ensure that business is booming.

Inherent Contradictions and Conflict

Like the larger postwar state of which it is part, the Canadian health-care system is characterized by fundamental structural contradictions and political-ideological conflicts that need to be understood before we can begin to analyse the nature and implications of ongoing health policy 'reforms' (Burke and Stevenson, 1993).

A first major contradiction lies in an increasing awareness that health systems do little to produce health; rather, they provide *medical treatment for illness*. Numerous papers, reports, and studies over the past 25 years in Canada and internationally have emphasized that health-care systems fail to resolve social and economic problems that cause illness. These problems include income inequality and poverty, poor housing, poor sanitation, poor nutrition, lack of education, unemployment, and unsafe work (Daly et al., 1998; Evans et al., 1994; Lalonde, 1974; Mustard and Frolich, 1995; Syme, 1998; Wildavsky, 1979). Indeed, it has even been suggested that by directing massive resources to illness treatment, and therefore away from health promotion and social problems causing illness, health systems may inadvertently mitigate against health (Evans and Stoddart, 1990). But this is not unlike other major programs of the postwar state, such as unemployment insurance, which does little to create work, welfare programs that fail to address the root causes of poverty and economic inequality, and social security programs that ignore the causes of dependency among the elderly.

Nevertheless, and this is at the heart of the contradictory nature of the postwar state, universal medicare plays a major progressive role in redistributing the costs of illness. In contrast to economic markets, which work on the basis of price and the ability to pay, universal health insurance provides access on the basis of need. As the American economist Uwe Reinhardt observes, health systems are in essence redistributive mechanisms, with different national systems building upon different assumptions about how the costs of illness should be paid. While public systems share these costs broadly across society, market-based systems concentrate costs on the ill, who are also among those least likely to be able to pay (Reinhardt, 1996). Canadian researchers have similarly concluded that user fees and other forms of private payment for health services redistribute the costs of illness: the rich and healthy gain; the poor and sick lose (Rachlis and Kushner, 1994; Evans et al., 1994; Williams and Lum, 1997).

These are important conclusions in the context of a growing international literature that suggests that social and economic inequalities, even more than absolute levels of economic development, impact negatively on health. Because inequalities may be exacerbated by market-based health-care systems that place the burden of illness on those who are ill, an erosion of public entitlements to health care, particularly when it coincides with a more general erosion of the redistributive mechanisms of the postwar state, may result in 'lowered health status or a health status which is not as high as it might otherwise have been' (Coburn, 1999).

A second major contradiction has to do with the extent to which medicare reinforces historically dominant political interests and relationships. Although it is often thought of as a reform of health-care *delivery*, medicare was and remains primarily a reform of health-care *funding*. As emphasized earlier, by defining health and health care almost solely in terms of doctor and hospital services and by funding those services to the exclusion of similar services delivered by other providers in locations outside of hospitals and physicians' offices, public medicare consolidated a curative, symptom-oriented approach to illness, as well as medical and hospital dominance over health-services delivery, health policy and health expenditures (Armstrong and Armstrong, 1994, 1996; Coburn et al., 1983; Naylor, 1986; Tuohy, 1999; Williams, Vayda et al., 1995).

Of course, such consolidation is not unique to Canadian medicare. As Navarro (1973) has observed, while extending coverage to entire populations, national health insurance systems in the industrialized nations have often served to solidify rather than transform existing relationships. In and of itself, national health insurance has not been an impetus for reform; indeed, by entrenching dominant political interests, it may even constitute a barrier to meaningful reform. This is a key point, since we contend that by defining health care in terms of hospital and doctor care and by guaranteeing public payment for services that doctors deem to be medically necessary, medicare solidified the political power of the medical profession, which it continues to wield to block state attempts to initiate reforms. Indeed, as a number of observers have noted, medicare contributed to the emergence of what amounts to a private government in the health field (the medical profession) alongside and in competition with the public government of the state (Taylor, 1987, 1992; Williams, Vayda et al., 1995; Stevenson and Williams, 1985; Stevenson et al., 1988). Moreover, medicare also continues to shelter the profession from the same economic market forces rapidly undercutting physicians' clinical and economic autonomy in the US (Woolhandler and Himmelstein, 1995). Under 'socialized' health care, the vast majority of Canadian physicians continue to work in private, fee-for-service practices, and with the exception of voluntary guidelines issued by provincial medical associations, there are currently few state intrusions into clinical decision-making. As the results of surveys conducted over the last decade reveal, the real issue for most Canadian physicians is not the demise of medicare—an increasingly large majority oppose a return to a medical free market—but control over private practices and incomes *within* a publicly funded system (Williams, Vayda et al., 1995).

However, this juxtaposition and blurring of public and private interests is also the source of continuing political struggles between governments and the medical profession that immobilize medicare politically and leave it vulnerable to neoliberal assaults (ibid.; Burke and Stevenson, 1993; Naylor, 1986; Ruggie, 1996). Beginning with the Saskatchewan doctors' strike in 1962, the history of medicare is a history of escalating profession-government conflict in which successive attempts by governments to manage medical services, control costs, or reorient the system away from a single-minded reliance on hospitals and doctors have been met by concerted opposition from provincial medical associations, including militant job action to defend their interests. It has been argued that the tide of professional power peaked and is now in decline, yet the profession's capacity to resist unwanted government intrusion remains substantial (Coburn et al., 1997; Tuohy, 1988; Heiber and Deber, 1987).

Ontario provides a good example. Faced with the need to fulfil an election promise of deficit reduction *and* a 30 per cent income tax cut, one of the earliest actions of the Progressive Conservative government of Mike Harris, first elected in 1995, was to pass omnibus legislation giving it sweeping powers across a range of policy fields. In the health field, elements of this legislation unilaterally terminated all previous agreements between the government and the provincial medical association, absolved the government from responsibility for breaches of those agreements, removed control of the schedule of insured fees from the profession, and ended government subsidies to malpractice insurance premiums. Under the legislation the Minister of Health could set professional fees, restrict the granting of billing privileges to individual physicians, and control where physicians could practise in the province (OMA, 1995). Subsequently, the provincial government reduced income ceilings for individual physicians beyond which their fees would be progressively discounted, increased income 'clawbacks' or penalties to be assessed to individual physicians as total physician payments exceeded a cap set by government, and introduced plans to limit the ability of physicians to establish practices in geographic areas deemed by the province to be 'over-doctored'.

However, rather than capitulating to state power, militant groups of physicians including family practitioners, orthopedic surgeons, and obstetricians, began a series of 'practice adjustments', including a refusal to provide insured services to new patients except in emergencies. Confronted by a defiant profession and by growing public concerns about a decline in access to medical care, the government capitulated and signed an agreement to increase the fee-for-service payment pool for physicians, lift the income clawbacks assessed against individual practitioners, prohibit the diversion of funds from the fee-for-service pool to finance payments to other professions such as midwifery and nurse practitioners, and give the provincial medical association an effective veto over future health care reforms involving physicians (OMA, 1997; OMA and Government of Ontario, 1997).

An additional complicating factor in Canada, which further limits the capacity for extending universal coverage to new fields such as home and community care, is the constitutional division of powers that gives the provinces primary jurisdiction over health care while providing the federal government with the economic resources needed to fund it. In recognition of the imbalance between responsibilities and resources and of fiscal disparities between the provinces, transfer payment programs were established in the postwar period to provide federal funds to cover part of the costs of 10 different provincial insurance plans, first just for hospitals and then for physicians' services as well (Taylor, 1987; Deber et al., 1998). To the 'carrot' of federal funding was affixed the 'stick' of the federal threat to withhold funds should the provinces fail to comply with five national conditions: universality, accessibility, comprehensiveness, portability, and public administration. To qualify for federal funds, provincial plans had to provide coverage to all Canadians, on uniform terms and conditions, for all medically necessary services delivered in hospitals and by physicians, with no charges to insured persons for insured services. With widespread public support, the federal government has used this stick to force provinces to ban user fees. However, the federal government cannot force the provinces to implement reforms that would change the way care is provided or extend public coverage beyond hospitals and doctors' services, although it was assumed at the inception of medicare that such an extension would eventually take place (Royal Commission on Health Services, 1964).

However, in attempts to deal with its own deficit, the federal government over time cut back on the cash contributions to the provinces for health, in the process whittling down the federal government's financial 'stick' (Mendelson, 1995). By 1998 in Ontario, for instance, it was calculated that only 11 per cent of total provincial health spending was derived from federal cash transfers; this sparked fears that the province, led by the neo-liberal Harris government, might choose to exit from public medicare in favour of private health-care markets (Gherson, 1998). Such fears were heightened by a provincial move, spearheaded by an alliance of the separatist government in Quebec and neo-liberal governments in the richer provinces of Ontario and Alberta, seeking a 'social union' that would reduce the federal government's power to launch new programs in areas of provincial jurisdiction such as health and education (Greenspon, 1998; Mahoney, 1998a, 1998b). A social union agreement between the federal government and the provinces was struck in early 1999, made possible by a federal budget which, as noted earlier, promised an infusion of $11.5 billion to the provinces over the next five years. The provinces, for their part, promised to spend these additional funds on health. However, the federal government also stepped back from its earlier advocacy of national programs for home care and pharmaceutical care. As it now stands, the provinces may choose to extend public coverage in this manner, but the federal government has little capacity to force such a move or to restrain the onset of market forces outside of the mainstream of hospital and doctor services.

Neo-Liberal Ideology and Globalization

As Starr's concept of the 'conservative assimilation of reform' reminds us, state actions presented as fundamental policy reforms resulting in a redistribution of power may in fact serve to solidify the power of dominant groups and interests (Starr, 1982). The shift from hospitals to home and community provides an excellent example of Starr's concept. Such a shift has long been advocated by consumers and health-care analysts as a means of reforming the health system and redressing a range of historical problems, including an overreliance on expensive high-tech, bed-based, expert-driven illness care. A shift from hospitals, it has been argued, could provide an effective counter to expert dominance and devolve decision-making to consumers and communities most familiar with their own health needs and the appropriate ways of addressing them. In addition to facilitating the more efficient and rational use of scarce health care resources, this shift would allow individuals, families, and communities to take back control over their own health. Thus, groups and interests disempowered by the rise of medical and hospital dominance could be re-empowered, and cost savings achieved through the more efficient use of health services could be reinvested in new or more appropriate health services, or allocated to the social determinants of health (Burke and Stevenson, 1993; Rachlis and Kushner, 1994).

However, it is important to acknowledge that current policy reforms aimed at downsizing the hospital sector and shifting care to home and community have been controlled, for the most part, not by progressive reformers intent on a more equitable society, but by governments intent on curbing public expenditures and introducing a greater reliance on economic market forces. Examples of other such 'reforms' in Ontario include substantial cuts to social welfare benefits to those in the lowest income categories matched by tax cuts for those in the highest income categories; the reduction or withdrawal of perceived barriers to free markets such as rent controls, environmental protection, employment equity, and labour rights; and the sale of public utilities. This period has been characterized by economic growth, but also by a dramatic increase in the number of families, including children, living below the poverty line and a rapidly growing gap between rich and poor (National Council of Welfare, 1998; Carey, 1998).

Theoretical explanations for the rise of neo-liberal ideology remain incomplete, and are beyond the scope of this chapter. However, the links of neo-liberalism to the politics of economic globalization have been widely noted (e.g., Coburn, 1999). A perceived need to free capital from the constraints of public policy in order to ensure competitiveness in global markets is cited by neo-liberal ideologues as justification for the rapid dismantling of all perceived barriers to trade, including tariffs and other regulatory restrictions on the movement of capital across national boundaries. Labour legislation that protects the rights of workers is seen to increase labour costs and decrease labour market 'flexibility'; public services are seen to squeeze the private sector out of potentially lucrative markets; and a range of social programs, together with the tax structures that finance them, are seen as factors encouraging a general decline in the work ethic and put domestic capitalist enterprises at a disadvantage vis-à-vis competitors in jurisdictions with lower labour costs and tax rates (Teeple, 1995). In addressing the relationship between neo-liberal ideologies and globalization, and the oft-stated corollary that the latter is 'inevitable', it has been observed not only that the two are mutually supporting but that they are intimately intertwined and that, to a large extent, economic globalization is as much a *product* as a *source* of such ideologies (Doern et al., 1996; Shields and Evans, 1998).

Over the last decade, Canada has become signatory to an array of international agreements that place restrictions on the policy instruments that governments can apply to address domestic issues (Reinicke, 1998). These include the Free Trade Agreement (FTA) between Canada and the United States and the subsequent North American Free Trade Agreement (NAFTA), which includes Mexico. More recently, Canada has been a willing participant in international negotiations initiated behind closed doors by the Organization for Economic Co-operation and Development (OECD) aimed at achieving a Multilateral Agreement on Investment (MAI), which would establish a global investment regime and, in the words of one proponent, the 'constitution of a single global economy' (Clarke and Barlow, 1997).

While it is not possible to examine such agreements in the detail they deserve here, it is important to point out that they generally restrict the capacity of governments to give preferential treatment to local providers, restrict governments' ability to make domestic policy, and make public governments accountable to private foreign corporations, all of which have important implications for health and health care. Under Annex II of NAFTA, governments have the ability to list health as an unbounded reservation, that is, a social policy established or maintained for a public purpose outside the limits of the trade agreement. However, neither 'social policy' nor 'public purpose' are defined. Compared to Canada, the other two parties to this agreement (the US and Mexico) have much more restrictive views on the appropriate role of government in health. Indeed, the US has taken the position that where for-profit services exist, that sector no longer constitutes a social service for a public purpose (Appleton, 1999). While NAFTA does not prevent a government from re-entering a field with a commercial presence, private investors are entitled to claim compensation for harm to their property (market share or goodwill), which under the terms and conditions of NAFTA is likely to be substantially more generous than under domestic law (ibid.). Moreover, under NAFTA, foreign corporations (but not their domestic counterparts) have the right to make claims against any Canadian government (including provincial and local levels) on the basis of any legislation, policy, or practice and to have such claims adjudicated by an international tribunal.

What are the implications of such agreements for the shift from medicare to home and community? As more and more care moves from under the umbrella of medicare, it is open to private financing and for-profit delivery. In community-based long-term care in Ontario, recent government policy reforms deliberately promote the expansion of for-profit enterprises as a means of increasing competition with not-for-profits and driving down costs. International trade agreements such as NAFTA, and potentially the MAI, make it increasingly difficult and potentially expensive to reverse this trend. Even if public health care remains, by continuing to restrict coverage to 'medically necessary' services, while pushing care outside of hospitals through bed closures and by refusing to cover new drug therapies that reduce the need for invasive surgery and hospitalization, neo-liberal governments can ensure that a growing portion of the health field, like any other commercial field, is 'open for business' to global competitors.

Under such conditions it seems simplistic and perhaps a bit naïve to assume that the ongoing shift in the locus of care out of hospitals to the home and community will necessarily produce the sorts of public benefits and social equity that health reformers and promoters have long wished for (Burke and Stevenson, 1993; Rachlis and Kushner, 1994). While resources are now being drawn away from hospitals in Ontario and in other provinces, they will not necessarily be reinvested in the determinants of health or in health care at other sites. Even more importantly from our perspective, the collective public entitlements associated with hospital and doctor services under the mainstream of medicare may be superseded in home and community by the logic of global competition. Thus, the discourse of health system reform and restructuring, supported ironically by legitimate criticisms of hospitals, physicians, and the medical model, is open to assimilation by neo-liberal governments bent on state retrenchment, tax cuts, and economic globalization.

Ontario's Health System Reforms

An early initiative of the Harris government in Ontario was to establish the provincial Health Services Restructuring Commission, an arm's-length expert panel that has ordered large-scale amalgamations, mergers, and closings of hospitals and hospital beds across the province as a means of achieving efficiencies in care delivery. These actions, together with hospital budget cuts made by the province, have produced significant reductions in hospital bed capacity and in average length of stay (ALOS). Between 1990 and 1997, even before the impact of the latest round of hospital closings had been felt, ALOS dropped from 8 to 6.5 days, while day surgery increased from 63 per cent to 69 per cent of all surgery done in Ontario (Ministry of

Health, 1998). As in other jurisdictions experiencing hospital downsizing, this has stimulated rapidly rising demands for home and community care (Thompson et al., 1998; *Maclean's*, 1998).

On the surface, at least, such actions and outcomes may appear as a logical and long overdue step. Mounting evidence after all, suggests that many procedures done in hospitals can be done just as effectively on an out-patient basis and that convalescing in hospitals is costly, ineffective, and undesirable compared to discharging patients to more appropriate care settings (Thompson et al., 1998; Metro Toronto District Health Council, 1995). However, since hospital restructuring does not assume that rates of illness or the need for illness care have decreased (indeed, because of an aging population alone one might expect overall needs to increase), access to appropriate care in home and the community is essential.

However, while Ontario's Commission was mandated to *order* hospital closings, it was specifically restricted to *making recommendations* for a parallel restructuring of services outside of hospitals. In its public statements, the Commission, along with other local planning agencies, duly emphasized that before hospital bed closures took place substantial funding had to be put into home and community care (Metro Toronto District Health Council, 1995; Ontario Community Support Association, 1999). As the Commission has become more aware of the impact of the hospital bed closures it has ordered, it has substantially increased its estimates of the funding required to ensure that adequate care is available outside of hospitals and that the burden of illness is not transferred onto individuals and families (Health Services Restructuring Commission, 1998). While the Commission's directives for hospital amalgamations and closings are now being implemented, albeit with considerable pain, its recommendations for a substantial 'reinvestment' outside of hospitals have generated less support from the provincial government. For instance, although the province has made multiple announcements of 'new' money to flow into community-based long-term care, this money is to be phased in over a period of six to eight years. Even then, new money appears to fall short of the immediate reinvestment called for by the Commission (Government of Ontario, 1998a, 1998b; Health Services Restructuring Commission, 1998; Ontario Community Support Association, 1999).

As hospital restructuring has proceeded, Ontario's Ministry of Health has been engaged in a parallel but separate reform of community-based long-term care (Deber and Williams, 1995; Williams et al., 1999). Such care goes well beyond substitutes for acute care in hospitals to encompass a wide range of social services and personal supports necessary to maintain functional independence and to prevent or delay institutionalization. Nevertheless, community-based long-term care also includes many professional services, such as nursing, physiotherapy, occupational therapy, speech pathology, and nutrition, as well as related services such as drugs, assistive devices, and personal care, which are covered by the Canada Health Act when they are provided in hospitals but not necessarily covered when they are provided elsewhere.

Ontario's reform of community-based long-term care has had two major publicly stated aims. The first has been to systematize the 'patchwork quilt' of services, programs, providers, eligibility requirements, funding mechanisms, and quality standards that had grown up willy-nilly in a field where government has historically had little direct involvement. As a result, many seniors, children, and people with disabilities 'fell though the cracks' and did not get adequate care (Deber and Williams, 1995; Williams et al., 1999).

A second major aim has been to introduce competition into the field as a means of driving down costs and achieving cost efficiencies. Under the current reform 43 local Community Care Access Centres (CCACs) assess needs and purchase services for particular regions throughout the province on a competitive basis from not-for-profit and for-profit providers. This is an important shift in policy direction since prior to the reform most professional services in Ontario were delivered by not-for-profit organizations. In general, the not-for-profits were more likely to have unionized workforces and what are euphemistically referred to as higher 'cost structures' as a result of better wages and benefits that may not apply to for-profit competitors entering the marketplace (Ontario Community Support Association, 1999).

Reflecting this aim, Ontario's reform presents a 'managed competition' model imported from the US, which assumes that a 'crisis' in health care exists because of a lack of competition among providers (Fuller, 1998; Ministry of Health, 1997a, 1997b). Under this model a single intermediary organization (not the provincial government) in a local area (the CCAC) is given responsibility for purchasing services from providers on behalf of consumers under guidelines set by the province. Competition between providers is promoted, with for-profit providers seen as a means of increasing competition with the existing not-for-profit providers and driving down prices, which in this labour-intensive field means driving down wages. The criteria for selecting providers balance objective considerations of cost against more subjective and difficult-to-quantify considerations such as innovation, provider diversity, and service quality (Williams et al., 1999). In Ontario the CCACs purchase services within fixed budgets set by government; they have no ability to raise funds, and individual consumers have no guarantee, even if they are judged eligible for services, that services will be available.

Like governments in other parts of the world that have chosen to contract out services, the current government in Ontario insists that competition among providers can be 'managed' in the interests of consumers and the taxpaying public. Yet, evidence of such benefits in other jurisdictions is equivocal, particularly for 'softer' human services where outcomes are difficult to measure and where unprincipled organizations could skimp on quality, training, and wages as a means of winning contracts and maximizing profits. Thus, the risk arises that for-profit providers will seek to maximize profits by refusing services to consumers with greater needs or by providing poorer-quality services (Bendick, 1989).

Compounding these risks is the fact that rising demands generate substantial pressures to reduce unit costs and to contain service volume. On the demand side, because the population is aging and because hospitals are now discharging patients 'quicker and sicker', more individuals require community-based care and more require more intensive and specialized care. In their first year of operation CCACs in many areas of the province experienced substantial budget overruns, due in large part to rapid increases in referrals from hospitals (Kushner, 1997). Although the provincial government has subsequently announced increases to CCAC budgets, it has also moved to restrict guidelines used by CCACs when determining service eligibility. First priority for services is now given to people 'at risk of dying, or suffering the breakdown of an essential bodily function'. Until recently, the bulk of the clients in this category would have been cared for in hospitals (Toronto District Health Council, 1999). This has caused Ontario's CCACs to spend a growing proportion of their limited budgets on treatment of acute illness, thus displacing 'well' seniors and other individuals who require services to delay or prevent institutionalization (Havens, 1995).

Here, it is important to stress that under Ontario's reform, consumers have limited capacity to choose either among providers or among intermediary organizations, and little recourse against poor-quality or inadequate services. CCACs are, in effect, regional monopolies with consumers obliged to seek home-care services from the centre in their area. Further, in response to a consumer who sought to appeal a decision of his local CCAC, provincial government lawyers recently argued that there was no right of appeal. CCACs, they argued, were 'creatures of government policy' and thus not covered under the provincial Long-Term Care Act, which specifies a basket of mandatory services and includes a patient's bill of rights as well as a statutory appeal mechanism. Although the province's quasi-judicial Health Services Appeal Board subsequently ruled against the government, finding that the CCACs was obliged to meet legislative requirements, the provincial government first ignored this ruling and then introduced regulations to limit the authority of the Appeal Board in this connection (Care Watch Toronto, 1999; Health Services Appeal Board, 1999; Daly, 1999).

The reform has also had major implications for workers. As noted above, in a field as labour-intensive as community-based long-term care, substantial cost savings cannot be achieved without reducing labour costs. However, until now, there have been barriers to across-the-board reductions since most workers in hospitals and many workers in established not-for-profit provider organizations have been protected by collective agreements. One result is that established not-for-profit providers such as the Red Cross, St Elizabeth Health Care, and the Victorian Order of Nurses have experienced strikes and lockouts as workers have tried to resist reductions of wages and benefits, which management has claimed are necessary to be competitive in an increasingly competitive marketplace (Ontario Nurses' Association, 1998a, 1998b).

Meanwhile, for-profit companies such as Comcare (Canada) Incorporated and Olsten have won CCAC contracts. Both hire nurses on a casual basis, without the wages or benefits provided by not-for-profit companies, which in any event pay considerably less than hospitals. This led to a well-publicized strike by nurses in Kingston, Ontario, seeking a first contract with Comcare (Chamberlain, 1998; Landsberg, 1998). By hiring nurses on what it calls an 'elect-to-work' basis, Comcare avoids having to pay staff not needed on a particular day by calling only those nurses for whom they have work. This approach is defended by the company as a way of maintaining staffing flexibility and providing nurses who have lost jobs in hospitals with the choice to work. However, the Ontario Nurses' Association (ONA) sees it as an aggressive means of eroding wages, benefits, and working conditions with potentially adverse effects for the continuity and quality of patient care. The ONA has warned that unrestrained competition could also result in larger companies underbidding smaller companies to gain first contracts, and then raising prices once they force their competitors out of the marketplace (Ontario Nurses' Association, 1998a, 1998b).

Whether or not such developments lead to domination by global health-care corporations or to a precipitous decline in access to or quality of care, they highlight the fact that the 'rules' and principles governing care outside of hospitals are fundamentally different from those governing the mainstream of hospital and doctor services under medicare. Under medicare, reasonable access to services is universal, and services cannot be denied, although patients may have to queue up to receive them; in the community, services *may* be provided. Under medicare, Canadians have access on 'uniform terms and conditions' regardless of where they live or work; under Ontario's managed competition reform, access to care is subject to local eligibility requirements and budget constraints, and any local entitlements to home-care treatments are not 'portable' from one region to another even within the province. And while under medicare incipient privatization and commercialization of care have been aggressively opposed by the federal government, in Ontario, outside of medicare and outside of federal influence, competition and the commercialization of care are now enshrined as principles of service delivery.

Discussion

At this juncture it is important to reaffirm that the publicly financed health-care system remains a leading political success of the postwar Canadian state: under medicare, all Canadians, regardless of where they live or work, have access to medically necessary hospital and doctor services without regard to their economic means. While medicare continues to be limited to hospital and doctors services, its basic principles remain sound on grounds of both equity and efficiency, and it continues to draw strong public support.

Nevertheless, medicare now faces considerable challenges tied to the rise of neoliberal ideologies and globalization, both of which push to substitute private market mechanisms for the public mechanisms of the postwar state. And such challenges are all the more pressing because of medicare's political immobility. In the process of providing universal access to medical care, Canadian medicare also solidified the political power of hospitals and the organized medical profession; this juxtaposition of public and private interests continues to fuel a cycle of conflict over control of the health system that restricts the possibilities for progressive reform *within* universal coverage. Thus, medicare is made vulnerable to neo-liberal politics (Williams, Vayda et al., 1995).

Here, we want to stress that medicare should be conceptualized as more than just a program; it is the reproduction within the institutions of the state of a particular set of structural interests and relationships that existed at the historical point at which the system was created (Tuohy, 1999). Even as other sectors of the Canadian economy have experienced a transition from competitive to monopoly to global capitalism (Ross and Trachte, 1990), medicare has ensured that the mainstream of Canada's health system remains dominated by relatively small not-for-profit hospitals (and regional boards) and physicians working as autonomous entrepreneurs. This compares to a US health-care market increasingly dominated by huge global health-care corporations with budgets larger than those of most Canadian provinces (Fuller, 1998; Woolhandler and Himmelstein, 1998).

However, medicare does little to impede the more general advance of neo-liberalism and globalization in other areas of state activity, as evidenced by the continuing political assaults on social welfare, labour rights, environmental protection, public education, and so on. Nor is medicare completely immune. One line of ideological assault has been to argue that health care is not different from other market commodities, and thus, that it should be opened up to the discipline of market forces. This line is bolstered, paradoxically, by the recognition that health has many determinants, most of which, such as poverty, are outside of the direct influence of the health-care system. While the political left, including social activists and health promoters, had hoped that this recognition would lead to income redistribution, better housing, and greater social equality in addition to universal health care, the neo-liberal right has been able to argue that since we already admit to multiple levels of access to food, clothing, and shelter, health care should be treated no differently (Deber, 1991; Deber et al., 1998; Evans, 1984).

This brings us back to our central argument—because medicare is immobile politically, neo-liberal governments wishing to introduce market forces into health care have considerable leeway to do so at the boundaries of hospital and doctor services. By shifting care out of hospitals, by failing to cover drug therapies that can be substituted for costly in-patient procedures, and by shifting primary responsibility for whole groups or categories of patients (e.g., workers' compensation clients, automobile accident victims) to other programs, governments can rapidly erode the public system without risking the political confrontation that any forthright assault on that system would generate. While the federal Health Minister recently recognized the need for national home-care and pharmaceutical-care programs, such programs have been thwarted by factions within the federal cabinet wishing to pursue an agenda of spending restraint and debt reduction in order to maintain Canada's competitiveness in a global economy. In addition, the new 'social union' agreement in effect allows provincial governments to escape federal funding conditions (Greenspon, 1998).

In the meantime, the profitization of health care moves ahead. In Ontario, much care has now been 'restructured' out of hospitals onto the much more complex and less visible terrain of the community, where it is not subject to the rules of medicare. Besides the moral, ethical, and social issues this raises, Ontario's managed competition reform is producing additional, if predictable, problems that emphasize its underlying ideological bent towards less, rather than more, public regulation of private markets. For instance, the Provincial Auditor concluded that, in spite of promises that competition can be managed in the interests of consumers and taxpayers, there are few mechanisms for ensuring that this is actually the case (Office of the Provincial Auditor, 1998). The report indicates that there are inadequate performance indicators for Community Care Access Centres, little inspection of provider organizations to ensure cost-effectiveness or contract compliance, and no plan for training workers who will provide services—often in consumers' homes—beyond conventional supervision and peer review. In addition, no system exists for gathering information about the costs of services provided to individuals, no standard procedures are in place for verifying if services paid for were actually provided, and management information systems are inadequate for planning and managing service delivery.

As we suggested earlier, the key issue here is not private provision of services per se, since the majority of providers under medicare have always been private, but the potential conflict between private profits and the public interest. Where not-for-profit providers may invest service efficiencies in care, for-profit providers may be inclined to capture them as profits even at the expense of service access and quality (Social Planning Council of Metropolitan Toronto, 1997; Wright, 1990). This is suggested by numerous American media reports of private, for-profit HMOs reducing costs through 'cream-skimming' (i.e., enrolling only healthy or low-risk patients for whom costs are likely to be minimal, while refusing to take the sickest in most need of care) or 'under-servicing' (i.e., delaying or limiting access to services even when they are required, as a means of reducing costs and increasing profits) (Williams et al., 1999; DeCoster et al., 1997). In this connection the province of Manitoba recently reversed its plan to profitize the provision of community care services in response to escalating conflict with public-sector unions and in light of evidence that private for-profit providers could not provide services more cheaply than the public sector (Shapiro, 1997).

Major factors in this connection are profits and administrative overhead. Recent data reveal that the largest for-profit American HMOs, such as Aetna/US Healthcare, take up to 26 per cent of revenues on profits and overhead. Notably, private plans that insure Canadians for services not covered under medicare have roughly the same overhead as their US counterparts (Woolhandler and Himmelstein, 1998). Such high estimates are similar to those provided by the Royal Commission on Health Services (1964) prior to the institute of universal health care, which found that overhead costs for private prepayment and commercial health insurance carriers then operating in Canada ranged between 18 and 44 per cent, figures that made the prospect of publicly funded health insurance look all the more attractive.

Competition has other costs as well. Ontario's reform pits providers against one another in the competitive process, and it forces CCACs to work at a distance from providers to ensure a degree of objectivity in purchasing decisions. As such, the reform produces negative incentives to co-operation and transforms information about service provision from a public resource into a private commodity. Providers are increasingly reluctant to reveal gaps in their service capabilities or to give details of their operations for fear of losing a 'competitive edge'. Moreover, because the managed competition process takes place at the local level and because much of the adjudication process is being conducted 'in camera' as a matter of standard business practice, reports on the implementation of reform in Ontario are mostly anecdotal. The result is that a reform ostensibly meant to increase public accountability has in fact made access to information more difficult. It also presents global health-care corporations with the opportunity to enter the marketplace without public scrutiny or awareness (Williams et al., 1999).

Conclusion

In conclusion, we want to emphasize again the challenges to public medicare presented by the rise of neo-liberalism and globalization, which push to substitute free-market forces and private profits for the collective public good. In spite of sustained public support for medicare and opposition to the emergence of a health-care system tiered by economic class, governments pursuing neo-liberal agendas are now taking advantage of medicare's political immobility to shift care beyond its boundaries. Outside of public entitlements and outside of the public eye, health care is being put to market.

Note

The authors were supported by grants from the National Health Research Development Program, and the Social Sciences and Humanities Research Council of Canada.

References

Appleton, B. 1999. 'International agreements and national health plans: NAFTA', in D. Drache and T. Sullivan, eds, *Market Limits in Health Reform: Public Success, Private Failure*. London: Routledge.

Armstrong, P., and H. Armstrong. 1994. 'Health care in Canada', in Armstrong, Armstrong, J. Canaria, G. Feldberg, and J. White, eds, *Take Care: Warning Signals for Canada's Health System*. Toronto: Garamond.

——— and ———. 1996. *Wasting Away: The Undermining of Canadian Health Care*. Toronto: Oxford University Press.

Bendick, M., Jr. 1989. 'Privatizing the delivery of social welfare services: An ideal to be taken seriously', in S.B. Kamerman and A.J. Kahn, eds, *Privatization and the Welfare State*. Princeton, NJ: Princeton University Press.

Bennett, C.J. 1991. 'Review article: What is policy convergence and what causes it?', *British Journal of Political Science* 21: 215–33.

Boyer, R., and D. Drache. 1996. *States Against Markets: The Limits of Globalization*. London: Routledge.

Burke, M., and H.M. Stevenson. 1993. 'Fiscal crisis and restructuring in Medicare: The politics and political science of health in Canada', *Health and Canadian Society* 1, 1: 51-82.

Canadian Institute for Health Information (CIHI). 1998. 'Canada to spend more on health care in 1998 says Canadian Institute for Health Information', press release, 19 Nov.

Carey, E. 1998. 'Rich get richer as wage gap widens', *Toronto Star*, 22 Oct., A1.

Care Watch Toronto. 1999. 'Does long term care have any legal status in Ontario?', *Who Cares? A Newsletter About Community Care* (Spring): 1.

Chamberlain, A. 1998. 'Home care nurses strike for contract with private firm', *Toronto Star*, 21 Jan., A8.

Clarke, T., and M. Barlow. 1997. *MAI: The Multilateral Agreement on Investment and the Threat to Canadian Sovereignty*. Toronto: Stoddart.

Coburn, D. 1993. 'Professional powers in decline: Medicine in a changing Canada', in F.W. Hafferty and J.B. McKinlay, eds, *The Changing Medical Profession*. Oxford: Oxford University Press.

———. 1999. 'Income inequality, lowered social cohesion and the poorer health status of populations: The role of neo-liberalism', unpublished manuscript, Department of Public Health Sciences, University of Toronto.

———, S. Rappolt, and I. Bourgeault. 1997. 'Decline vs. retention of medical power through restratification: An examination of the Ontario case', *Sociology of Health and Illness* 19, 1: 1–22.

———, G.M. Torrance, and J.M. Kaufert. 1983. 'Medical dominance in Canada in historical perspective: The rise and fall of medicine?', *International Journal of Health Services* 13, 3: 407–32.

Daly, M.C., G.J. Duncan, G.A. Kaplan, and J.W. Lynch. 1998. 'Macro-to-micro links in the relation between income inequality and mortality', *Milbank Quarterly* 76, 3: 315–340.

Daly, R. 1999. 'Province moves to thwart mother's home care appeal', *Toronto Star*, 16 Sept., A8.

Day, B. 1998. 'How the private sector can save Medicare', *Hospital Quarterly* (Spring): 64–8.

Deber, R. 1991. 'Philosophical underpinnings of Canada's health care system', *Canada-US Outlook* 2, 4: 20–45.

———. 'Public and private places in Canadian healthcare', *Hospital Quarterly* (Spring): 28–31.

———, L. Narine, P. Baranek, N. Sharpe, K.M. Duvalko, R. Zlotnik-Shaul, P. Coyte, G. Pink, and A.P. Williams. 1998. 'The public-private mix in health care', in National Forum on Health, *Striking a Balance: Health Care Systems in Canada and Elsewhere*, vol. 4. (SainteFoy, Qué.: Editions MultiMondes, 423–545.

———. and A.P. Williams. 1995. 'Policy, payment and participation: long-term care reform in Ontario', *Canadian Journal On Aging* 14, 2: 294–318.

DeCoster, C., M. Smoller, N.P. Roos and E. Thomas. 1997. 'A comparison of ambulatory care and selected procedure rates in the health care systems of the province of Manitoba, Canada; Kaiser Permanent Health Maintenance Organization; and the United States', *Healthcare Management Forum* 10, 4 (Winter): 26–34.

Doern, G.B., L.A. Pal, and B.W. Tomlin. 1996. 'The internationalization of Canadian public policy', in Doern, Pal, and Tomlin, eds, Toronto: Oxford University Press.

Ekos Research Associates. 1998. 'Rethinking government', presentation to National Conference on Home Care, 9 Mar.

Employer Committee on Health Care—Ontario (ECHCO). 1995. *A Perspective on Health Care*. Toronto, July.

Evans, R.G. 1984. *Strained Mercy: The Economics of Canadian Health Care*. Toronto: Butterworths.

———, M.L. Barer, and T.R. Marmor. 1994. *Why Are Some People Healthy and Others Not? The Determinants of Health of Populations*. New York: Aldine de Gruyter.

——— and G.J. Stoddart. 1990. *Producing Health, Consuming Health Care*. CIAR Population Health Working Paper No. 6. Toronto: Canadian Institute for Advanced Research.

Fuller, C. 1998. *Caring For Profit: How Corporations Are Taking Over Canada's Health Care System*. Ottawa and Vancouver: The Canadian Centre for Policy Alternatives and New Star Books.

General Accounting Office, US. 1991. *Executive Summary: Canadian Health Insurance*. GAO Report HRD–191–90, June.

Gherson, G. 1998. 'Ottawa tries to prevent exit from Medicare', *National Post*, 3 Nov., A1.

Government of Ontario. 1998a. 'Government invests $1.2 billion to improve long-term care in largest-ever expansion of health services', press release, 29 Apr.

———. 1998b. 'Jackson announces $19.1 million in increased funding to expand long-term care community services', 14 July.

Greenspon, E. 1998. 'Rock hopes to tie new health funds to home care', *Globe and Mail*, 6 Oct., A1.

Havens, B. 1995. 'Long-term care diversity with the care continuum', *Canadian Journal on Aging* 14, 2: 245–62.

Health Canada. 1999. 'Health initiatives in the 1999 budget', fact sheet, Feb.

Health Services Appeal Board. 1999. Order, in the Matter of Ian Strathern and Community Care Access Centre Niagara and Douglas Jackson. File I.C. 6149. 6 Jan.

Health Services Restructuring Commission. 1997. *A Vision of Ontario's Health Services System*. Jan.

———. 1998. 'Commission calls for reinvestment of $266 million for capital and $263 million for services in Toronto', news release, 27 Apr.

Heiber, S., and R.B. Deber. 1987. 'Banning extra-billing in Canada: Just what the doctor didn't order', *Canadian Public Policy* 13, 1: 62–74.

Hirschman, A. 1970. *Exit, Voice and Loyalty*. Cambridge, Mass.: Harvard University Press.

Jessop, B. 1993. 'Towards a Schumpeterian workfare state? Remarks on post-Fordist political economy', *Studies in Political Economy* 40 (Spring).

Kushner, C. 1997. *Laying a Firm Foundation: A Response from Ontario's CCACs*. Toronto. Oct.

LeBlanc, D. 1999. 'Canadians rank health care as top priority for leaders' attention: Poll finds 43 per cent of respondents put issue first on list of concerns', *Globe and Mail*, 2 Feb., A4.

Lalonde, M. 1974. *A New Perspective on the Health of Canadians*. Ottawa: Government of Canada.

Landsberg, M. 1998. 'Home care privatization squeezes sick to ensure profits', *Toronto Star*, 3 Jan., L1.

McBride, S., and J. Shields. 1997. *Dismantling a Nation: The Transition to Corporate Rule in Canada*. Halifax: Fernwood.

McCarthy, S. 1999. 'PM rejects cutting taxes to U.S. levels: Average Canadian family $28,000 poorer, opposition critics say', *Globe and Mail*, 4 May, A12.

Maclean's. 1998. 'The Health Report', 15 June, 14–43.

Mahoney, J. 1998a. 'Provinces seek speedy solution on social-union arrangement', *Globe and Mail*, 3 Oct., A9.

———. 1998b. 'Alberta proposals on clinics amended, minister says', *Globe and Mail*, 11 Nov., A6.

Mendelson, M. 1995. *Looking for Mr. Good-Transfer: A Guide to the CHST Negotiations*. Ottawa: Caledon Institute of Social Policy, Oct.

Metro Toronto District Health Council. 1995. *Implications of Metro Hospital Restructuring on Community-Based Health Services*. Toronto, Aug.

Mhatre, S.L., and R.B. Deber. 1992. 'From equal access to health care to equitable access to health: A review of Canadian provincial health commissions and reports', *International Journal of Health Services* 22, 4: 645–68.

Ministry of Health, Ontario. 1997a. *Provincial Requirements for the Long-Term Care Request for Proposals Process*. Toronto: Long-Term Care Division, July.

———. 1997b. *RFP Guide: Tips for Conducting an RFP (Request for Proposals)*. Toronto: Long-Term Care Division, Sept.

———. 1998. 'A healthier Ontario: Progress into the 90s', presentation notes, 8 June.

Mustard, C., and N. Frolich. 1995. 'Socioeconomic status and the health of the population', *Medical Care* 33, 12: DS43–DS54, Supplement.

National Council of Welfare. 1998. *Poverty Profile 1996*. Ottawa.

National Forum on Health. 1997a. *Canada Health Action: Building on the Legacy*, vol. 1, Final Report of the National Forum on Health. Ottawa.

———. 1997b. *Canada Health Action: Building on the Legacy*, vol. 2, Synthesis Reports and Issues Papers. Ottawa.

Naylor, C.D. 1986. *Private Practice: Public Payment: Canadian Medicine and the Politics of Health Insurance, 1911–1966*. Montreal and Kingston: McGill-Queen's University Press.

Navarro, V. 1973. *Medicine Under Capitalism*. New York: Prodist.

Northrup, D. 1998. 'The Canadian legislator study', *Institute for Social Research News Letter* (York University) 13, 2: 1–2.

Organization for Economic Co-operation and Development (OECD). 1995. *Governance in Transition: Public Management Reforms in OECD Countries*. Paris: OECD.

Office of the Provincial Auditor, Ontario. 1998. *1998 Annual Report*. Toronto: Queens' Printer.

Ontario Community Support Association. 1999. *Key issues and positions*. Toronto, Apr.

Ontario Medical Association (OMA). 1995. 'Members' summary of Bill 26, the Savings and Restructuring Act', *Ontario Medical Review* 62, 12: 14–17.

———. 1997. 'OMA membership accepts interim agreement', press release, 11 Jan.

——— and Government of Ontario. 1997. *Agreement*. 14 May.

Ontario Nurses' Association. 1998a. 'Ontario Nurses' Association Blacklists Comcare, Kingston', media release, 4 Feb.

———. 1998b. 'VON branches locked out; St. Elizabeth workers continue their job action', *News* (Sept.-Oct.): 7–8.

Peters, S. 1995. *Exploring Canadian Values: Foundations for Well-Being*. Canadian Policy Research Networks Study No. F-01. Ottawa.

Rachlis, M., and C. Kushner. 1994. *Strong Medicine: How To Save Canada's Health Care System*. Toronto: HarperCollins.

Reinhardt, U. 1996. 'Economics', *Journal of the American Medical Association* 275, 23: 10–11.

Reinicke, W.H. 1998. *Global Public Policy: Governing Without Government?* Washington: Brookings Institution Press.

Ross, R.J.S., and K.C. Trachte. 1990. *Global Capitalism: The New Leviathan*. Albany: State University of New York Press.

Royal Commission on Health Services. 1964. *Report*, vol. 1. Ottawa: Queen's Printer.

Ruggie, M. 1996. *Realignments in the Welfare State: Health Policy in the United States, Britain, and Canada*. New York: Columbia University Press.

Saunders, J. 1997. 'Private health services in Canada: The potential, the politics and the propaganda', *Hospital Quarterly* (Winter): 16–23.

Shapiro, E. 1997. *The Cost of Privatization: A Case Study of Home Care in Manitoba*. Ottawa: Canadian Centre for Policy Alternatives, Dec.

Shields, J., and B.M. Evans. 1998. *Shrinking the State: Globalization and Public Administration 'Reform'*. Halifax: Fernwood.

Social Planning Council of Metropolitan Toronto. 1997. 'Merchants of care? The non-profit sector in a competitive social services marketplace'. Toronto, Apr.

Starr, P. 1982. *The Social Transformation of American Medicine*. New York: Basic Books.

Stevenson, H.M., and A.P. Williams. 1985. 'Physicians and Medicare: professional ideology and Canadian health care policy', *Canadian Public Policy* 11, 3: 504–21.

———, ———, and E. Vayda. 1988. 'Medical politics and Medicare: professional response to the Canada Health Act', *Milbank Quarterly* 66, 1: 65–104.

Syme, S.L. 1998. 'Social and economic disparities in health: Thoughts about intervention', *Milbank Quarterly* 76, 3: 493–506.

Taylor, M.G. 1987. *Health Insurance and Canadian Public Policy: Seven Decisions that Created the Canadian Health Care System*. Montreal and Kingston: McGill-Queen's University Press.

———. 1992. 'Medicare turns 30', *Canadian Medical Association Journal* 147, 2: 233–7.

Teeple, G. 1995. *The Global Economy and the Decline of Social Reform*. Toronto: Garamond.

Thanh Ha, T. 1999. 'Chrétien tosses aside productivity as focus of Liberals' economic policies: Health care the basis of both productivity and standard of living, PM says', *Globe and Mail*, 4 May, 12.

Thompson, L., B. Brassard, J. Hader, R. White, and S. Lewis. 1998. 'Can I go home today? The hospital and home care study'. Health Services Utilization and Research Commission, Province of Saskatchewan.

Toronto District Health Council. 1999. Letter to the Ministers of Health and Long-Term Care, Ontario, Mar.

Tuohy, C.H. 1988. 'Medicine and the state in Canada: The extra-billing issue in perspective', *Canadian Journal of Political Science* 21, 2: 267–96.

———. 1999. *Accidental Logics: The Dynamics of Change in the Health Care Arena in the United States, Britain, and Canada*. New York: Oxford University Press.

Weller, G.R. 1996. 'Strengthening society I: Health care', in A. Johnson and A. Stritch, eds, *Canadian Public Policy: Globalization and Political Parties*. Toronto: Copp Clark.

Wildavsky, A. 1979. *Speaking Truth to Power*. Boston: Little, Brown.

Williams, A.P., J. Barnsley, S. Leggat, R.B. Deber, and P. Baranek. 1999. 'Long-term care goes to market: Managed competition and Ontario's reform of community-based services', *Canadian Journal on Aging* 18, 2: 126–53.

———, ———, J. Tanner, and R. Cockerill. 1997. 'Organized medicine and the Canadian state: The intensification of political conflict over the future of public Medicare', paper presented to the annual meeting of the Canadian Political Science Association, St John's, Nfld.

———, R. Cockerill, and F. Lowy. 1995. 'The physician as prescriber: Relations between knowledge of prescription drugs, encounters with patients and drug companies, and prescription volume', *Canadian Health and Society* 3, 1–2: 135–66.

——— and J.M. Lum. 1997. 'Women in Canada's health system: Prospects for the future', *Proceedings*, 5th Simposio sobre de la Salud de las mujeres, Fundacion Felisa Rincon de Gautier, San Juan, Puerto Rico, 3 Dec., 73–101.

———, E. Vayda, M.L. Cohen, C.A. Woodward, and B.M. Ferrier. 1995. 'Medicine and the Canadian state: From the politics of conflict to the politics of accommodation?', *Journal of Health and Social Behaviour* 36, 4 (Dec.): 303–21.

Woolhandler, S., and D.U. Himmelstein. 1991. 'The deteriorating administrative efficiency of the US health care system', *New England Journal of Medicine* 324 (May): 1253–58.

——— and ———. 1995. 'Extreme risk—The new corporate proposition for physicians', *New England Journal of Medicine* 333: 1706–8.

——— and ———. 1998. *For Our Patients, Not For Profits: A Call to Action*. Cambridge, Mass.: Center for National Health Program Studies, Harvard Medical School/The Cambridge Hospital.

Wright, D.A. 1990. 'An analysis of privatization and commercialization: The argument in favour of maintaining a strong voluntary sector in Canada'. Toronto: Ontario Association of Visiting Homemaker Services, Feb.

CHAPTER 2

Pharmaceuticals: Politics and Policy

Joel Lexchin

Introduction

Traditionally, the pharmaceutical industry was in a strong position vis-à-vis its relationship with the Health Protection Branch (HPB), the arm of Health Canada in charge of drug monitoring and approvals, but it was unable to play a dominant role in determining the federal government's industrial strategy as it affected the industry. Over the past decade and a half, the industry has further strengthened its influence in the HPB, but it has also acquired a formidable role in shaping government industrial policy. The objective of this chapter is to review the historical relationship between the industry and government, then to describe the factors of the last 10–15 years that have led to the expansion of the industry's power, and finally to discuss some of the consequences on the use of pharmaceuticals in Canada.

Lack of Influence in Industrial Policy

The best example of the industry's historical lack of influence over the political process comes from the battle around Bill C-102 and compulsory licensing to import. A compulsory licence is essentially a permit that effectively negates a patent. Theoretically, the company owning the patent on a drug would be a monopoly seller until the patent expired. However, if other companies apply for and are granted a compulsory licence against a drug, they can then market their own version of that drug before the patent has expired. The compulsory aspect means that the company owning the patent cannot block the licence from being granted.

Compulsory licensing for drugs in Canada dated back to 1923, when the Patent Act was amended to allow individuals or corporations to apply to the Commissioner of Patents for a compulsory licence to use a patented process to manufacture a drug in Canada. The intention behind this legislation was to encourage multiple companies to manufacture the same drug. In a marketplace with many sellers, it was hoped that the companies would engage in competitive pricing in order to gain market share. The amendment was largely unsuccessful in its goal, however, mainly because of the requirement that the drug be manufactured in Canada. The Canadian market was simply too small to support a manufacturing facility (Gorecki, 1981).

During the 1960s three reports pointed out that drug prices in Canada were among the highest in the world and all three reports identified patent protection as one of the major reasons for this situation (Canada, House of Commons, 1967; Restrictive Trade Practices Commission, 1963; Royal Commission on Health Services, 1964). The decision of the Liberal government was to extend compulsory licensing and allow companies to receive a licence to import a drug into Canada rather than having to manufacture it here. The Pharmaceutical Manufacturers Association of Canada (PMAC) mounted a campaign against the legislation, which cost $200,000 to $250,000 annually (Lang, 1974). Each PMAC official was given a list of the top 100 companies in Canada, along with the names and curricula vitae of their chief executive officers, and urged to contact these people with the message that Bill C-102 was bad for Canadian business. When the bill was in the committee stage, the PMAC supplied the opposition Conservatives with ammunition to use against antiindustry witnesses (ibid.). However, despite this intensive lobbying and propaganda effort Bill C-102 was passed by the House of Commons.

Lang believes that the determination of the civil service was ultimately responsible for the government's success in securing passage of Bill C-102. Equally important was the relatively marginal position of the pharmaceutical industry in the Canadian economy: there were (and still are) no multinational pharmaceutical companies based in Canada, and employment in the pharmaceutical industry was low, as was the overall value of production by the industry. Therefore, it was relatively easy for the government to pass a bill antithetical to the drug companies since the political consequences were minimal.

Clientele Pluralism

The industry has exercised its influence in the HPB through a method of interaction—a policy network—termed 'clientele pluralism' (Atkinson and Coleman, 1989). This is a situation where the state has a high degree of concentration of power in one agency (the HPB), but a low degree of autonomy. With respect to pharmaceuticals, in Canada, government regulation of drug safety, quality, and efficacy is almost solely the responsibility of the HPB. But the state does not possess the wherewithal to undertake the elaborate clinical and preclinical trials required to meet the objective of providing safe and effective medications. Nor is the state willing or able to mobilize the resources that would be necessary to undertake these tasks. Therefore, a tacit political decision is made to relinquish some authority to the drug manufacturers, especially with respect to information that forms the basis on which regulatory decisions are made.

On the other hand, the association representing nearly all of the multinational companies operating in Canada, the PMAC, is highly mobilized to assume a role in the making and implementing of drug policy through an elaborate committee structure, the ability to act on behalf of its members, and the capacity to bind member firms to agreements. (There is an association of domestically owned generic pharmaceutical manufacturers, the Canadian Drug Manufacturers Association, but its members are responsible for less than 15 per cent of drug sales in Canada.) In clientele pluralism, the state relinquishes some of its authority to private-sector actors, who in turn pursue objectives with which officials are in broad agreement (ibid.).

Not only does the state turn over some of its authority in clientele pluralism, but the objectives being pursued are often jointly developed between industry and the relevant state bureaucracy, in this case the PMAC and the HPB. Two examples serve to show concretely how a clientele pluralist policy network operates in the field of drug policy. Since the Food and Drugs Act of 1953, an inspection program has existed for all drug plants to ensure cleanliness and requirements such as dosage accuracy. Representatives of the PMAC worked with government officials in drawing up the standards for manufacturing and a number of PMAC member companies helped to train the inspectors who apply them (PMAC, 1966). As a further refinement in regulating manufacturing practices a joint industry and government committee was struck, which led to the development of good manufacturing practices (GMPs) and these came into effect in 1981. The companies continue to be provided with a regular opportunity for input into refinements of GMP regulations in the form of an annual meeting between HPB officials and the PMAC. While there are guidelines for inspectors to use to assess compliance with GMPs, they are published 'by the authority of the Minister of National Health and Welfare' and carry no legal force. However, membership in the PMAC is conditional upon acceptance of GMPs and so the association acts to enforce compliance with the guidelines. If companies break them they can be threatened with expulsion from the PMAC (Atkinson and Coleman, 1985).

A second example of delegation of government authority to the industry is control of promotional practices. This area has had a long and contentious history, but also a long history of co-operation between government and industry. Governments in nearly all industrialized countries, including Canada, have ceded day-to-day control over some or all aspects of pharmaceutical promotion to voluntary national industry associations. In turn, these associations have developed codes of marketing that their member companies are expected to adhere to. Promotion in Canada is regulated by two codes, one developed and administered by an independent organization, the Pharmaceutical Advertising Advisory Board (PAAB), and the second the Code of Marketing Practices from the PMAC. Despite apparently reasonable provisions, both codes suffer from serious enforcement problems (Lexchin, 1997a) that result in a significant amount of deceptive promotion (Lexchin, 1994a).

The joint state-industry development and implementation of GMPs appears to be relatively successful, as opposed to the control of promotional practices, but the issue here is not how well these examples of the operation of a clientele pluralist policy network are functioning. The point is that in both cases the state and industry are co-responsible for the formulation of policy, and the state has largely ceded its responsibility for the implementation and enforcement of policy to the PMAC (Atkinson and Coleman, 1989).

The Growth of the Political Influence of the Industry

A potent convergence of three factors led to the growth of the influence of the industry over Canadian pharmaceutical policy: the ascendancy of intellectual property rights to the top of the United States trade agenda; Canadian participation in bilateral and multilateral trade agreements; and the ever-present question of Canadian unity.

In the early 1980s the United States had a large trade imbalance. One of the factors that was seized on as a significant contributor to this problem was lost sales due to 'piracy' in the entertainment and pharmaceutical industries. Piracy here means that countries with 'weak' intellectual property rights were copying American goods and selling them at prices that undercut those being offered by American companies.

In 1981 US President Ronald Reagan appointed Ed Pratt to head that country's top private-sector trade advisory panel. Pratt was also president of Pfizer Inc., an American multinational drug company, and with his help the issue of intellectual property rights and patent protection for pharmaceuticals became the top priority of the US trade agenda (McQuaig, 1991). As a result, Canadian policies around patent protection and compulsory licensing became a major issue in US-Canada relations. When Reagan met with Prime Minister Brian Mulroney at the 'Shamrock Summit' in Quebec City in March 1985 one of the key items discussed was drug patents. In October of that year the annual report of the US Trade Representative on trade irritants with US trade partners listed Canada's drug legislation as one of the irritants. The chief US Trade Representative, Clayton Yeutter, rebuked the Conservatives for failing to make the long awaited changes in Canada's drug patent laws. George Bush, US vice-president at the time, publicly complained about the delay in the changes when he visited Ottawa in June 1986 (Sawatsky and Cashore, 1986).

At the same time that patent protection moved to the fore of US interests, the Conservatives fixated on a policy of free trade with the US. The federal government continually and vigorously denied that there was any connection between the Canada-US Free Trade Agreement (FTA) and changes in compulsory licensing (Crane, 1986; Howard, 1987), but the facts make their denials hard to credit. Bill Merkin, the US deputy chief negotiator in the free trade talks, said:

> Ottawa didn't want it [intellectual property] to be in the free trade negotiations. They didn't want to *appear* to be negotiating that away as part of the free trade agreement. Whatever changes they were going to make, they wanted them to be *viewed* as, quote, 'in Canada's interest.' . . . It was a high priority issue for us. We were not above flagging the importance of resolving the issue [to the Canadian negotiators] for the success of the overall negotiations. (McQuaig, 1991: 136)

The Americans gave conclusive evidence of the linkage between the two issues the day after the successful conclusion of the FTA. A US summary of the agreement said it contained a clause 'to make progress toward establishing adequate and effective protection of pharmaceuticals in Canada by liberalizing compulsory licensing provisions' (Auerbach, 1987: G2). It was only after Conservative politicians demanded the removal of that section that it was dropped from the final text of the agreement.

In return for free trade with the Americans the Conservatives produced Bill C-22 and eventually passed it in December 1987. In essence the bill gave companies introducing new drugs a minimum of seven years of protection from compulsory licensing. One senior official in the US administration said that 'We want better than that [bill] in a free-trade agreement', while to another senior official it was 'barely acceptable'. The US Pharmaceutical Manufacturers Association (PMA) was willing to support the bill, but said that the American industry 'would like to see a similar level of protection as in Western Europe and the U.S. . . . Canada's out of sync' (Lewington, 1987: A1).

The third factor in this equation that led to the erosion of compulsory licensing was the geographical location of many of the multinational companies. Companies such as Merck had long had their offices, manufacturing, and research facilities in the Montreal area and promised further investment in return for changes in Canadian patent legislation. Although Canadian unity was not as strong a force in the mid-1980s as it was to become, the Conservatives dominated the seats in the House of Commons from Quebec and did not want to risk alienating their soft-nationalist Francophone support by opposing the industry and its allies in the Quebec government.

This same grouping of interests once again came into play in the early 1990s. This time the fight was over Bill C-91, which abolished compulsory licensing and gave the multinational companies 20 years of patent protection for their products. In this case, instead of the FTA it was the Canadian eagerness to sign the North American Free Trade Agreement (NAFTA) and to stay in line with the General Agreement on Tarrifs and Trade (GATT) that coincided with the interests of the drug industry. Although there is an argument that compulsory licensing would be theoretically possible under these agreements (Dillon, 1997), the Canadian government used them as the grounds for completely eliminating compulsory licensing.

Ed Pratt, the Pfizer chairman, systematically went about putting intellectual property rights onto the GATT agenda. He first formed alliances with the US motion picture and computer industries and helped form the 'Intellectual Property Rights Committee' (IPC), which consisted of 13 major US corporations. Then, with the encouragement of Clayton Yeutter, Pratt sought allies in Europe and Japan and eventually won over the two major umbrella industrial organizations—UNICE (the Union of Industries of the European Community) in Europe and Keidanren in Japan (Ostry, 1990). What made the GATT and NAFTA ideal candidates for enforcement from the IPC's point of view was their jurisdiction over trade. Implicit in the choice of enforcement through the GATT was its threat of 'cross-retaliation', that is, the withdrawal of market access for exports of goods from countries that break GATT rules, in this case the enforcement of a standard of intellectual property rights sought by the IPC (Dillon, 1997).

The most recent example of how industry objectives have triumphed over consumer interests comes from the review of Bill C-91 in the spring of 1997 and some of the aftermath of that review. From 1987 to 1993, the average price per prescription (excluding the dispensing fee) in Ontario went from $12.48 to $24.09, a rise of 93 per cent compared to an increase in the consumer price index of 23.1 per cent. Over half of the rise in prescription costs was due to the introduction of new drugs, specifically new (since 1987) patented medications. Prices for prescriptions containing new patented medications rose at a rate of 13.4 per cent per annum since 1988 compared to 7.6 per cent for prices for prescriptions using non-patented drugs (Green Shield Canada, 1994).

The prescribing of newer, more expensive drugs in place of older, less expensive (but not necessarily less effective) ones was not something that started in 1987. The practice was well entrenched when Canada had compulsory licensing. What was different was that there were no generic competitors for these new patented medications. Prior to 1987 generics were coming on the market within five to seven years after the appearance of the originator product. The first generic would typically be priced about 25 per cent lower than the brand-name product, and when there were three or four generics then the price differential would be 50 per cent (Lexchin, 1993). In the absence of compulsory licensing the originator product typically is in a monopoly situation for about 12 years.

The Patented Medicine Prices Review Board (PMPRB) was established in the wake of Bill C-22 to protect consumer interests with powers to limit the introductory prices for new patented drugs and prevent prices for existing patented drugs from rising by more than the rate of inflation. However, as the figures above show, the consumer interest is not being protected because the PMPRB can only control one aspect of drug prices, the factory gate price that the companies charge. Companies can and have overcome that minor obstacle by increasing the promotional pressure on physicians to use the newer, more expensive products, thereby driving up the price of a prescription and in the process maintaining the profit levels of the companies even during the recession of the early 1990s. Even prior to Bill C-22 the industry in Canada was among the most profitable industries in the country. Over the eight years ending in 1987 the pre-tax rate of return on equity for drug manufacturers averaged 36.8 per cent compared to an average for all manufacturing industries of 14.0 per cent. Since the enactment of Bills C-22 and C-91 the pharmaceutical industry, if anything, has been even more profitable relative to all manufacturing industries than it was before, with pre-tax profit margins on equity of 29.6 and 10.7 per cent, respectively (Lexchin, 1997c).

In anticipation of this sort of cost and profit outcome, the Liberals had vehemently opposed Bill C-91 while they were in opposition; but by 1997 their attitude had changed. During the debate over Bill C-91, Liberal MP David Dingwall claimed that 'The Tory agenda is clear, one primary objective, which is to put money in the multinational corporations at any cost. Consumers be damned, research and development be damned, the health care system be damned, the objective is the bottom dollar of the multinational corporations who happen to be driving the agenda of the neo-Conservatives who are opposite this House [of Parliament]' ('Drug Patent Law', 1997). When the Liberals were elected in 1993, Dingwall became Minister of Health and by 1997 his attitude had changed: 'we are now part and parcel of the international community in terms of our commitments to NAFTA. And I don't want to raise a false expectation that with the review of Bill C-91, which is coming up in 1997, that we are going to flush the intellectual property rights which Canada has supported from day one and will continue to support' (ibid.).

Examples of the Liberal reluctance to tamper with the new patent regimen are not hard to find. The initial draft of the report on C-91 from the Standing Committee on Industry contained a recommendation that the government 'ask the World Trade Organization [set up after the conclusion of the GATT negotiations] to re-evaluate 20 year patents for drugs' (Standing Committee on Industry, 1997). By the time the final report was issued a few weeks later that recommendation had been dropped.

A second example of the industry's growing power concerns what have come to be known as the 'NOC linkage regulations'. These arrangements link the marketing approval, or notice of compliance (NOC), for a generic drug to the patent status of the original brand. Specifically, they provide for an automatic stay of the NOC for generic drugs until it is demonstrated that all relevant patents on the innovator product have expired, or until a court has determined that sale of the generic would not infringe the innovator's patent or that the patent is invalid. If the innovator company alleges patent infringement, approval of the generic can be delayed for up to 30 months or in some cases even longer (Rhein, 1998). Although there were expectations that these regulations would be eased in the wake of the C-91 review, in fact, in the view of the generic industry they were strengthened. While the Canadian Drug Manufacturers Association calls the amendments to the NOC regulations 'another sell-out', the PMAC takes the position that the amendments 'would appear to reconfirm the existing regulatory environment of patent protection in Canada' (ibid.).

Canadian obligations under the GATT and NAFTA were not the only factor influencing the government in favour of the multinational companies. In the wake of the passage of Bill C-91 the pharmaceutical industry made a number of high-profile large capital investments in the Montreal area (PMAC, 1995). A key feature of the industrial strategy of the Quebec government was, and is, the development of the pharmaceutical industry (Boards of Trade of Metropolitan Toronto and Metropolitan Montreal, 1996); in fact, the Quebec government has gone so far as to obtain affiliate membership status in the PMAC. Therefore, any perceived threat to the economic viability of the multinational pharmaceutical industry is also an implicit attack on the Quebec government, something that would give the Quebec separatists further ammunition in their fight for an independent Quebec and consequently something that all federal parties are loath to undertake.

In the areas of trade agreements and national unity, political ideology expressed through elected politicians appears to have been decisive. The senior bureaucrats, primarily in the Department of Industry, Trade and Commerce, played a secondary, supportive role. The activist position of the civil service, which Lang (1974) believed had a major role in the passage of Bill C-102, was abandoned.

Beyond Clientele Pluralism

In recent years there has been a fundamental change in the relationship between the Health Protection Branch and the multinational pharmaceutical industry. Not only does the state still relinquish some of its authority to private-sector actors, but the private sector, i.e., the drug companies, is now the major source of funding for the branch of the HPB, the Therapeutic Products Program (TPP), that regulates the industry.

This deepening of the ties between the private and public sectors has its roots in the prevailing ideology of cutting back on the role of public institutions. Federal and provincial governments have gone from providing full funding in a variety of sectors to tying grants to the ability of organizations to raise money from the private sector. The University of Toronto accepted money to establish a business centre and a centre for international relations and, until student and faculty protest forced a change in policy, was willing to allow the donors unprecedented influence in the running of these centres. Hospitals like Toronto's Hospital for Sick Children look to the pharmaceutical industry to fund their research centres.

Downsizing the role of government played into the obsession with the federal deficit. The government saw nothing wrong with decreasing funding to the HPB from \$237 million in 1993–4 to \$136 million in 1996–7, with a projection for 1999–2000 of just \$118 million (Kennedy, 1997). As resources for the HPB were progressively cut, the agency turned to the drug companies themselves for funds to keep operating, a process termed 'cost recovery'. Companies now pay an annual fee for each drug they market and fees for the evaluation of drug submissions, for licensing manufacturing establishments, and for a number of other services. Industry contributed 70 per cent of the \$49 million in revenue that the TPP expected to receive in 1997–8 (TPP, 1997).

The move to private-sector funding and more co-operation with industry is also reflected in the selection process of some of the civil servants at the TPP. In 1991 when the Drugs Directorate, the predecessor of the TPP, was looking for someone to head its Bureau of Nonprescription Drugs, Judy Erola, then president of the PMAC and formerly the federal Minister of Consumer and Commercial Services, was invited to sit on the hiring committee (Regush, 1991). While the government maintained that the best person was hired and there was no conflict of interest, another interpretation is that the government was looking for people who were acceptable to industry.

There are signs in a couple of areas that this combination of industry funding and a civil service with a bias for uncritical co-operation with industry is leading to a reorientation of HPB policy that is even more favourable to industry than in the past.

Up until March 1997, government controlled advertising of over-the-counter products to consumers. All promotion through radio or television had to be pre-cleared by HPB staff, and print advertisements were reviewed if there were complaints about them. As of April 1997, those functions have been turned over to a private-sector agency, the Advertising Standards Council of Canada, a move that will probably lead to a loosening of standards for promotion of this set of products. Government is not just weakening the controls on over-the-counter promotions. Currently, regulations ban direct-to-consumer advertising (DTCA) of prescription drugs, but for the past couple of years industry has been pushing the HPB to give up that restriction. Merck Frosst, one of the largest multinationals operating in Canada, has gone so far as to assert that the industry has a legal right to advertise prescription drugs directly to the public (Merck Frosst Canada, 1996). There are strong grounds for believing that DTCA would lead to inappropriate prescribing, greater overall expenditures on prescription drugs, and adverse health outcomes for consumers (Lexchin, 1997b). In 1996 the HPB held a workshop on the topic of DTCA, and apparently only provincial worries that DTCA would drive up the cost of provincial drug programs are stalling further moves in this direction.

Besides control over promotion, priorities involving the actual drug approval process may have been influenced. For over a decade the pharmaceutical industry has been pushing for more rapid regulatory approval and for eliminating the backlog of drugs awaiting approval (Lexchin, 1994b). This whole question of approval times and backlogs has largely been driven by industry interests. There is no good evidence that delays in the Canadian regulatory process have deprived Canadians of any important new drugs. From January 1991 to December 1995 a total of 404 new patented drug products were marketed in Canada for human use. Out of that number only 33, or just over 8 per cent, were felt to be either 'breakthrough' medications or substantial improvements over existing therapies (PMPRB, 1996). The conclusion of a study team that looked into the Canadian Drug Safety, Quality, and Efficacy Program was that there was 'no compelling evidence that delays in the approvals of New Drug Submissions pose significant hazards to the health of Canadians' (Overstreet et al., 1989: 46). On the other hand, it is decidedly in the companies' interest to get their products to market faster. The more rapidly they are approved and available for purchase the longer the monopoly period that the companies enjoy and therefore the greater the sales potential of the drugs.

If recent documents from the HPB are any indication, the government has adopted the industry's priorities on this issue. One aspect of 'visioning the ideal [regulatory] system' in a 1990 paper was 'improv[ing] the business climate'. Also the system should not 'impose a burden on the pharmaceutical manufacturer which makes it less competitive' (Drugs Directorate, 1990: 10). A working group from the TPP looked at ways of efficiently managing the limited resources and came up with a series of recommendations for moving submissions through the system more rapidly. However, the working group admitted that 'the pharmaceutical industry is looking for dramatic improvement in service' and 'the implementation of the proposed changes may not result in the level of improved performance desired by our industry clients.' This pressure prompted the working group to recommend that Canada consider relying more on foreign drug reviews in its approval process (Working Group on Backlog Assessment, 1994). The recommendation was subsequently approved by senior management in the TPP.

Perhaps the most revealing statement about this reorientation of the relationship between the HPB and the industry came from Dann Michols, the director general of the TPP. In an internal bulletin distributed to HPB staff in February 1997 he discussed the question of who is the HPB's client. In the context of cost recovery Michols advised staff that 'the client is the direct recipient of your services. In many cases this is the person or company who pays for the service.' The one-page document focused on service to industry, relegating the public to the secondary status of 'stakeholder' or 'beneficiary' (Michols, 1997).

The growing convergence between the goals of the HPB and the pharmaceutical industry means it is unlikely that the HPB will have the political will to tackle the longstanding problems of excessive secrecy in and a lack of public input into the regulatory process. The ideological blinkers on senior staff in the TPP in these areas are apparent in looking at the response, or non-response, to the recommendations in the Gagnon report (Gagnon, 1992). This report, released in July 1992, contained 152 recommendations for reforming the operations of the TPP, but none referring to improved public accountability. No one in the TPP senior management commented on the lack of any recommendations about improving public access or transparency. Neither of these is a priority for the pharmaceutical industry since the industry benefits from less transparency and public access. As it currently stands, the industry has preferred access into the regulatory process, which means that policy formulation often reflects the interests of the industry. Opening the system up to other groups would dilute the influence of the industry (Lexchin, 1990). Similarly, the industry benefits from excessive secrecy. As it currently stands all of the information about the efficacy and safety of products that companies submit to the HPB as part of the regulatory approval system is deemed confidential, and access to this information by anyone else is denied unless the company agrees to release it.

Abraham (1995) thoroughly analysed what went on in the US Food and Drug Administration and its British equivalent in regard to approval of five drugs for arthritis in the 1970s and 1980s. His conclusion, backed up by persuasive research, was that regulators consistently gave the benefit of scientific doubts about safety and effectiveness to the commercial interests of drug manufacturers at the expense of the best interests of patients. If biases are present in these two countries it is naïve to think that they are absent in Canada. But without access to what goes on behind the closed doors of the regulatory system we have no means of exposing these biases and little hope of correcting them.

Conclusion

Public policy in regard to drug products should focus on three areas: drugs should be safe, effective, and of high quality; they should be affordable; and they should be used in a rational manner. What has happened over the past decade has seriously weakened the government's power in all three of these areas. By yielding to political pressure both from within and outside the country the federal government has let the interests of the pharmaceutical industry prevail over consumer interests when it comes to deciding about drug prices.

Cost-cutting in the Health Protection Branch has forced it to become reliant on the industry for the majority of its funding. Even before this happened there was a close relationship between these two bodies, but this has been accentuated by the institution of cost recovery, and as a result the HPB sees the industry as its client. This has meant that measures to protect public health have become secondary to keeping the industry satisfied with the performance of the HPB. There has already been a weakening of an already inadequate system of controlling drug promotion and there are signs that health and safety issues are taking a back seat to the priorities of the industry, such as speeding up the approval process. If this influence of the industry is not countered, initiatives will not be forthcoming on such issues as public input and secrecy.

With excessive prices for prescriptions and declining health and safety standards, drugs cannot be prescribed or used appropriately. These conclusions have serious implications for the entire health-care system. From 8.4 per cent of total health-care spending in 1980, by 1996 drugs consumed 12.5 per cent of the health-care dollar (Dingwall, 1997). This sort of growth is tolerable and even justifiable if spending on drugs represents a cost-effective use of money. Up until now, arguments could be made in favour of using drugs over more costly hospitalization; for example, although drugs for HIV/AIDS may be overpriced they still are cheaper than putting people in hospital for extended periods of time. But what will happen in the scenario that I have sketched out, as spending continues to escalate and safety standards decline?

To begin with, Canada will probably price itself out of any chance for a national pharmacare program. In the early 1990s, Canada, along with the US, ranked at the bottom of the list of the 24 Organization for Economic Co-operation and Development countries on three measures of public drug spending:

1. the public expenditure on prescribed medicines as a percentage of total expenditure on medicines;
2. the percentage of the population eligible for pharmaceutical benefits under a public scheme;
3. the average percentage of a beneficiary's prescribed medicines paid by a public fund. (OECD, 1993)

Since then the situation may have deteriorated even further as provinces have increased deductibles and patient co-payments in their public drug plans.

As safety declines, we can anticipate increasing costs in other parts of the health-care system. Direct-to-consumer advertising, should it become a reality, will lead to some physicians prescribing in response to patient demand for specific drugs. A body of work shows that under these circumstances prescribing deteriorates (Schwartz et al., 1989; Macfarlane et al., 1997). At a minimum, less appropriate prescribing is more expensive, but the costs are usually measured in more than just money. If patients receive the wrong products their illnesses are likely to become more serious, necessitating either further trips to physicians or hospitalization. These risks will be compounded if less is known about the safety of the drugs being prescribed. Based on figures showing that about 15 per cent of hospitalized patients experience an adverse drug reaction (Lexchin, 1991) and a death rate of 1.5 per cent from drug reactions (Brennan and Gowdey, 1989), at present there could be as many as 2900 deaths annually in Ontario hospitals from adverse drug reactions. With less safe drugs being used this figure will increase.

While there are other forces tearing away at the Canadian health-care system, changes that have occurred and are ongoing in the area of prescription drugs bring it even closer to the precipice.

References

Abraham, J. 1995. *Science, Politics and the Pharmaceutical Industry. Controversy and Bias in Drug Regulation*. London: UCL Press.

Atkinson, M.M., and W.D. Coleman. 1985. 'Corporatism and industrial policy', in A. Cawson, ed., *Organized Interests and the State*. London: Sage.

——— and ———. 1989. *The State, Business, and Industrial Change in Canada*. Toronto: University of Toronto Press.

Auerbach, S. 1987. 'U.S. bowed to Canadian demands to change pact', *Washington Post*, 17 Oct., G2.

Boards of Trade of Metropolitan Toronto and Metropolitan Montreal. 1996. *A Prescription for Success*. Mar.

Brennan, M., and C.W. Gowdey. 1989. 'Adverse drug reactions: A review of fatalities reported in Ontario', *Ontario Medical Review* 56 (Aug.): 23–6.

Canada, House of Commons. 1967. *Second (Final) Report of the Special Committee of the House of Commons on Drug Costs and Prices*. Ottawa: Queen's Printer.

Crane, D. 1986. 'Drug bill concessions seem tied to trade talks', *Toronto Star*, 7 Dec., B1.

Dillon, J. 1997. *On Feeding Sharks: Patent Protection, Compulsory Licensing, and International Trade Law*. A study prepared for the Canadian Health Coalition. 4 Mar.

Dingwall, D.C. 1997. *Drug Costs in Canada*. Submitted to the House of Commons

Standing Committee on Industry for the Review of the Patent Act Amendment Act, 1992.

'Drug Patent Law'. 1997. *The House*, CBC Radio, 25 Jan.

Drugs Directorate. 1990. *Drug Product Licensing*. Ottawa: Health and Welfare Canada, Oct.

Gagnon, D. 1992. *Working in Partnerships . . . Drug Review for the Future*. Ottawa: Health and Welfare Canada.

Gorecki, P.K. 1981. 'Regulating the price of prescription drugs in Canada: Compulsory licensing, product selection, and government reimbursement programmes', *Technical Report No. 8*. Ottawa: Economic Council of Canada.

Green Shield Canada. 1994. *A Report on Drug Costs*. Toronto, Oct.

Howard, R. 1987. 'MPs say Tories made deal on drug bill', *Globe and Mail*, 16 Oct., A13.

Kennedy, M. 1997. 'Fears raised over cuts to health protection', *Montreal Gazette*, 15 Sept., A1.

Lang, R.W. 1974. *The Politics of Drugs*. Lexington, Mass.: Lexington Books.

Lewington, J. 1987. 'Drug-patent bill not enough to satisfy U.S. on free trade', *Globe and Mail*, 13 Aug., A1.

Lexchin, J. 1990. 'Drug makers and drug regulators: Too close for comfort. A study of the Canadian situation', *Social Science and Medicine* 31: 1257–63.

———. 1991. 'Adverse drug reactions: Review of the Canadian literature', *Canadian Family Physician* 37: 109–18.

———. 1993. 'The effect of generic competition on the price of prescription drugs in the Province of Ontario', *Canadian Medical Association Journal* 148: 35–8.

———. 1994a. 'Canadian marketing codes: How well are they controlling pharmaceutical promotion?', *International Journal of Health Services* 24, 1: 91–104.

———. 1994b. 'Who needs faster drug approval times in Canada: The public or the industry?', *International Journal of Health Services* 24, 2: 253–64.

———. 1997a. 'Enforcement of codes governing pharmaceutical promotion: What happens when companies breach advertising guidelines?', *Canadian Medical Association Journal* 156: 351–7.

———. 1997b. 'Consequences of direct-to-consumer advertising of prescription drugs', *Canadian Family Physician* 43: 594–6.

———. 1997c. 'After compulsory licensing: coming issues in Canadian pharmaceutical policy and politics', *Health Policy* 40: 69–80.

Macfarlane, J., W. Holmes, R. Macfarlane, et al. 1997. 'Influence of patients' expectations on antibiotic management of acute lower respiratory tract illness in general practice: Questionnaire study', *British Medical Journal* 315: 1211–14.

McQuaig, L. 1991. *The Quick and the Dead*. Toronto: Viking.

Merck Frosst Canada Inc. 1996. *Direct-To-Consumer Advertising of Prescription Pharmaceuticals. A Merck Frosst Position Paper on How to Use Comprehensive Patient Information to Deliver Improved, Cost-Effective Health Outcomes*. 17 July.

Michols, D. 1997. 'Drugs and Medical Devices Programme Quality Initiative Bulletin #2'. Ottawa: Health Protection Branch, Feb.

Organization for Economic Cooperation and Development (OECD). 1993. *OECD Health Systems: Facts and Trends 1960–1991*, vol. 1. Paris: OECD.

Ostry, S. 1990. *Governments and Corporations in a Shrinking World*. New York: Council on Foreign Relations.

Overstreet, R.E., J. Berger, and C. Turriff. 1989. *Summary Report: Program Evaluation Study of the Drug Safety, Quality and Efficacy Program*. Ottawa: Health and Welfare Canada.

Patented Medicine Prices Review Board (PMPRB). 1996. *Eighth Annual Report for the Year Ended December 31, 1995*. Ottawa: Supply and Services Canada.

Pharmaceutical Manufacturers Association of Canada (PMAC). 1966. *Submission to House of Commons Special Committee on Drug Costs and Prices*. Ottawa: PMAC.

———. 1995. *Promises Made . . . Promises Surpassed!* Ottawa, Sept.

Regush, N. 1991. 'Top industry lobbyist helped choose federal drug watchdog', *Montreal Gazette*, 5 Dec., B1.

Restrictive Trade Practices Commission. 1963. *Report Concerning the Manufacture, Distribution and Sale of Drugs*. Ottawa: Queen's Printer.

Rhein, R. 1998. 'Patent passions run high in Canada', *Scrip Magazine* 67 (Apr.): 37–9.

Royal Commission on Health Services. 1964. *Report*. Ottawa: Queen's Printer.

Sawatsky, J., and H. Cashore. 1986. 'Inside dope', *This Magazine* 20, 3: 4–12.

Schwartz, R.K., S.B. Soumerai, and J. Avorn. 1989. 'Physician motivations for non-scientific drug prescribing', *Social Science and Medicine* 28: 577–82.

Standing Committee on Industry. 1997. *Draft Report. Review of Section 14 of the Patent Act Amendment 1992*. Apr.

Therapeutic Products Program (TPP). 1997. *Overview of Product Licensing Framework II*. Ottawa, Sept.

Working Group on Backlog Assessment. 1994. *Backlog Assessment—Final Report*. Ottawa: Drugs Directorate, Sept.

CHAPTER 3

Health, Health Care, and Neo-Liberalism

David Coburn

Introduction

Medicare is so important to Canadians that our system of national health insurance almost defines what it means to be Canadian as opposed to American. Yet, the beginnings of medicare and its subsequent history have often been surrounded by controversy. Today, medicare is the focus of constant newspaper headlines and health-care policies are central to the platforms of all political parties. Some want the existing system strengthened, others argue for more privatization, and some feel that medicare can only be preserved if it is reformed or transformed.

Somewhat less attention is paid to what medicare is supposed to do—to improve the health of Canadians. In that area we are confronted with relatively high rates of longevity (as one measure of health) in Canada as compared with other countries. Yet there are large and persistent inequalities in health status between higher- and lower-income Canadians—the rich live longer and are healthier than the poor.

How can recent developments in the health care and the health of Canadians be understood? The ferment surrounding medicare and health inequalities is occurring at a time of broader social, economic, and political change, often captured by the term 'globalization'. In this chapter I join these apparently disparate topics—medicare, health inequalities, and globalization—in a political economy analysis of health and health care. Political economy would insist that there are links between broader social structures, such as globalization, and more immediate and practical concerns such as the fate of medicare. Of course, there are a variety of 'political economies'. Here I present a structurally oriented class-based perspective. My intention is not to describe events but to attempt to understand, or, in other terms, to theorize them.

A political economy approach is particularly fruitful because it analyses events within a larger context and through time, and it has as much to do with the choices people are presented with as with the choices they make from those available. The emphasis here is on understanding how economic, political, and social change, in Canada and internationally, can help us to explain current events in the health field.

The focus is on the post-World War II era to the end of the century, a period recently characterized by the onset of globalization and neo-liberalism. The major facets of globalization examined here are the internationalization of capital, the rise of transnational corporations, and the spread of a set of ideas and policies supporting and being reinforced by this process, that is neo-liberalism. Neo-liberalism is conceptualized here as an emphasis on the market as a source of wealth and justice. Neo-liberals tend to assume that a 'free-enterprise' economy will produce the greatest good for all (for a more detailed analysis of neo-liberalism in the context of health inequalities, see Coburn, 2000). Economic globalization, then, is national free enterprise on a global scale (Stubbs and Underhill, 1994). While I will allude to the problems inherent in neo-liberalism, a full critique is not given here. Nevertheless, a major difficulty with neo-liberalism is that the economy neo-liberals desire cannot coexist with the kind of society that most people seem to want. Neo-liberal economies tend to bring dysfunctional societies.

Following Ross and Trachte (1990), Esping-Andersen (1990, 1999), and Navarro (1986, 1988, 1989, 1999), I contend that changes in health care and in health inequalities in Canada (and elsewhere) in the contemporary era can be understood through a framework based on the rise of globalization and neo-liberalism, changes in class structure, and the decline of the welfare state. In analysing health care within this broader context we need to know something about the general pressures on nation-states brought about by multinational corporations and international trade. In addition, there has to be an account of differing national responses to globalization, as noted by Esping-Andersen regarding welfare state types as well as by Navarro's accounts of national differences in class structures. While globalization presumably presents nations with a range of constraints, countries still vary in their responses to such pressures, and these often are reflected in different types of welfare states and health-care systems and in socio-economic and health status. As Gough (1978) has noted, an adequate analysis requires explanations of both international similarities and national differences.

In this chapter I first briefly consider the background literature regarding medicare and health inequalities in Canada then describe the theoretical basis for understanding the pressures of globalization. This framework is then applied to the two areas of medicare and health status. Finally, I discuss possible objections to, or qualifications of, the explanations offered.

Medicare and Health Inequalities: Background Literature

Medicare

Many analysts in Canada have explained the introduction of medicare in pluralist interest group terms. Health insurance came about, it is claimed, partly because powerful interest groups supported it and secured state sanction in coercing a recalcitrant medical profession into concessions (Taylor, 1978). In this view, other events—recessions, war, the rise of third political parties and protest movements—are used to explain the actions of interest groups, but these disparate forces are not linked within some overall framework, nor are the choices of some explanatory factors or forces over others explained.

Pluralist interest group approaches of this type suffer from serious defects. Empirically, it has been shown that business is by far the predominant interest group (see, e.g., Banting, 1986; Coleman, 1988; Useem, 1984). Moreoever, the state is not a neutral, unbiased referee but is influenced by business interests: structurally, through its reliance on the adequate functioning of the economy; instrumentally, through the flow of personnel from business to the state and vice versa and through the more general power of the business class as a lobby group and as a source of political funds and ideology. Hence, there is considerable doubt about the 'plural' in 'pluralism'. How, given business power, was the struggle to implement medicare successful in the 1960s in the face of much right-wing opposition, while medicare now faces attacks from many factions within the business community?

Theoretically, pluralist interest group theory, while useful at one level (no one would doubt the existence of groups focused on immediate interests), tends to be more descriptive than explanatory, often verges on tautology, or fails to specify why the interests of some are realized and the interests of others are not. Even in modified form (as élite theory) pluralist interest group theories are, if not incorrect, at least radically incomplete.

Political economists are more likely to point to what they view as basic structural factors within the capitalist mode of production as explaining how, why, and when health insurance was finally implemented across Canada in all provinces by 1971. The emphasis is thus as much on how the social environment elicits particular responses from social groups as it is on the agency or internal structure of these groups themselves. Swartz (1977), for example, feels health insurance only came about because of a prolonged working-class struggle for access to health-care services. Walters (1982), on the other hand, contends that the state's own interests were more important. Today, with the welfare state in Canada under attack (McQuaig, 1992, 1995), the changing economic context of recession or international competition is often given as explanation for the contemporary restructuring or downsizing of health care or for threats to the principles of medicare from forces pushing for privatization. Yet the links between such broad factors as globalization and current events in health care are seldom explained. For example, it seems to be currently assumed that particular political or bureaucratic actions are direct responses to obvious fiscal crises, hence, presumably, do not need explanation. This, however, simply ignores what should be explained about the relationships between economics and politics. Political change cannot simply be 'read off' directly from government budgetary documents. What is a fiscal crisis for some is not so for others. A class-based political economy analysis also faces somewhat the same issue regarding changes over time, as do pluralist interest group perspectives. That is, why was the working class successful in gaining health insurance in the face of business opposition at one point, yet now the same groups seem in retreat in the face of right-wing attacks on the principles of medicare?

What is meant by a class-based approach? In this chapter I assert that the capitalist mode of production—and the classes arising within this mode of production—

conditions and shapes all institutions and actions within it, including in the health sphere. For example, one characteristic of capitalism, the attempt to turn products or services into commodities to be sold, produces pressure at all times to privatize health care for profit. A specific focus on class, however, further implies that our society is characterized, in its 'deep structure', by conflict between classes defined in terms of their relationship to ownership of the means of production or productive forces generally. In common-sense terms there is conflict between capital and labour or between business and workers because generally what is in the interests of one is not necessarily in the interests of the other. Lower pay immediately benefits employers but not workers. Of course, the class picture of Canada is much more complex than two classes facing one another. There are often said to be 'old middle classes', i.e., small business, and 'new middle classes' of professionals and managers, which confound the overly simple notions of a two-class system. Moreover, 'class fractions', or status groups within classes, and class differences intersect in complex ways with gender, 'race', ethnic, and other differences. Nevertheless, a class-based approach would ultimately contend that a basic conflict exists between those who own or control the means of production (the business class) and those who do not. From this perspective class conflict underlies a good deal of what happens regarding health and health care because health care is viewed as one aspect of the rise (and recent fall?) of the welfare state. The welfare state itself is seen as a partial outcome of the conflict between classes, with the dominant or ruling or business class generally opposing welfare state measures (because they interfere with profits or control over production) and workers and the poor generally supporting these. In fact, many of the references cited in this paper attest to the cogency of such an argument.

A class-based analysis promises a coherent explanation both for long-term historical changes in health and health care and for contemporary differences among various nations in their health status and health-care systems. Such explanations, however, have often neglected the series of links between broad changes in capitalism and the class structure and changes in various societal institutions, such as in the health field (for an exception, see Navarro's writings). Thus, while pluralist interest group approaches are inadequate, current explanations from a political economy class perspective require further development. I suggest here, and have noted earlier (Coburn, 1999), that changes over time in medicare can be understood through changes in the relationships among classes and class fractions within different phases of capitalism, first monopoly capitalism (at the time of medicare's formation) and now in the current phase of global capitalism.

Health Inequalities

There have always been major health inequalities in Canada. That is, the poor have tended to be sicker and to die younger than the rich. However, developments in the post-World War II era were supposed to ameliorate this problem in two ways. First, the social inequalities brought by the market were to be reduced through various welfare state measures. Second, the introduction of national health insurance, it was assumed, would reduce any remaining health inequalities by eliminating problems of differential access to medical services for groups of higher or lower socio-economic statis (SES). Yet, as Manga (1987) has noted, there is a 'Medicare Paradox'—while medicare did improve lower-class access to care, health inequalities still remain and the wealthier are still healthier. This paradox, reinforced by international comparisons of health-care systems and national longevity data, the stress literature, and developments linking social and psychological states with physiological events, has led to the now predominant idea that health care does not produce health (Amick et al., 1995; Evans et al., 1994; Evans and Stoddart, 1990). Attention is again being devoted to the social determinants of health in a revival of concerns first begun in the middle of the nineteenth century. In Canada this movement has been termed 'population health', and a particular rather narrow version of population health (Evans and Stoddart, 1990) is now more or less official orthodoxy in policy circles in the federal and provincial governments. While the population health program as currently envisaged has problems (for a critique, see Poland et al., 1998), there is widespread agreement on the core proposition—that health is at least as much determined by social factors such as SES or income as it is by access to doctors, hospitals, and nurses.

Much health research is thus now focused on the social determinants of health, with most attention on the relationships between general social position or socio-economic status (SES) and health status. The SES component of most recent interest has been that of income and income inequality. This interest has been largely stimulated by the work of Richard Wilkinson. Wilkinson's hypothesis focuses on international or regional differences in health and longevity rather than on differences within a single country. Evidence over the last century has indicated that, within nations, SES differences are universally associated with differences in health status, although both variation in SES and the linkage between SES and health status vary over time and among nations. Wilkinson shows that, among the developed countries, income inequality rather than level of gross national product per capita (GNP) is the strongest correlate of national levels of longevity (Wilkinson, 1996, 1999; Coburn, 2000; Lynch et al., 2000; Muntaner and Lynch, 1999). In other words, the degree of spread in income, or the extent of difference in income between the richest and poorest in a society is a better predictor of average national health status than is the overall wealth of the nation as determined by GNP. Wilkinson and others often contend that social fragmentation is the factor linking income inequalities with lower health status. That is, income inequality leads to social fragmentation (loss of social cohesion or social supports, increased crime rates, etc.), which in turn produces lowered health status.

A key fact is that those of higher SES are in better health than those below them, even at very high levels of SES. High-level executives show somewhat poorer health status than those even higher in the hierarchy. Thus, much of the attention has turned not to material inequalities but to various psychosocial mechanisms linking SES to health status (Wilkinson, 1996; Kawachi and Kennedy, 1997). Social inequalities or social hierarchies are said to produce poorer health because of the lowered self-esteem or lowered perceived control of those lower in SES—the negative psychological impact of inequality. This psychosocial emphasis, however, is disputed by other analysts, who argue that underlying social conditions and the social infrastructure, rather than invidious (psychological) status comparisons, underlie the relationship of social inequalities, social fragmentation, and health status (Coburn, 2000; Lynch et al., 2000; Muntaner and Lynch, 1999; Navarro, 1998, 1999). International relationships between national income inequality and lowered health status reflect the differences in basic social conditions affecting the different social strata rather than simply the psychological (as opposed to the material) effects of income inequality per se. The rich simply have 'easier' and less stressful lives. Here, no claims are ventured about the virtues of either argument; rather, both of these mechanisms may be operative.

My specific concern is with something long neglected in the population health literature: What produces social inequalities in the first place? While numerous researchers have explored methods of ameliorating the effects of poor social conditions on the health of the underprivileged, primarily through focusing on children's health, hardly any have asked about the possible causes of inequality itself. Yet, examining the causes of social inequalities, and not simply their effects, changes our understanding of the causal sequences involved in the income inequality/health status relationship (Coburn, 2000). Moreover, if Wilkinson is correct in viewing inequalities and general social conditions as explanatory of differences in average health status among nations, understanding social and income inequalities can also help us understand differences in the health status of both rich and poor.

In this analysis of the contextual structural changes shaping medicare and health inequalities in Canada, I draw heavily on the work of Ross and Trachte on globalization, welfare state theorists such as Esping-Andersen, and class theorists such as Navarro. Globalization and the rise of neo-liberalism have produced profound changes in the direction of market-oriented ideology and politics (Stubbs and Underhill, 1994, 2000). Globalization, as a real force and as ideology, reinforced the re-emergence of business to a dominant position in Canadian society. Business dominance, in the market and regarding the state, led to attacks on working-class rights in the market and on citizenship rights as expressed even in the liberal (market-dependent) version of the welfare state in Canada. With the decline of the relative autonomy of the state came a business-state coalition to rationalize health care. This brought the state, with business backing, into territory previously occupied solely by the medical profession. At the same time medicare, as part of the welfare state, began to be restructured and hollowed out. Labour's lessened market power and the shredding of the welfare state because of the new-found power of business also led to major increases in social inequality, income inequality, and social fragmentation. Thus, the forceful enactment of neo-liberal ideologies and politics has exacerbated differences among rich and poor Canadians and, at the same time, undermined those institutions, such as universal medical insurance, that might have buffered the effects of increasing income inequalities on poor health.

Theoretical Framework

Ross and Trachte (1990) help us to understand the common pressures of globalization in effecting national class structures and social inequalities; Esping-Andersen (1990, 1999) and Navarro (1988, 1989, 1998, 1999) are relevant in explaining the reasons for national differences in reaction to common international pressures. All of these formulations are congruent with a classical political economy focus on capitalism as a changing mode of production and class structure as a fundamental influence on all social and health events within a particular social formation.

Global Capitalism

In *Global Capital: The New Leviathan* Ross and Trachte (1990) argue that capitalism has developed through competitive, monopoly, and now global phases. The resolution of contradictions and crises in one phase leads to a qualitatively different kind of capitalist regime. Each phase is characterized by different labour-state-capital relationships.

In competitive capitalism labour is subordinate to capital primarily because much of the population is unemployed or underemployed. Businessmen more or less directly control the state. The working class is unorganized and weak. Tendencies within competitive capitalism towards concentration lead to a new phase, monopoly capitalism. Smaller firms merge with or are swallowed by larger companies. The economy segments into monopoly and competitive fractions. The monopoly sector is dominant and exploits both its own workers and competitive-sector capitalists (who have to sell to monopoly firms and who face fierce competition within their sector) and workers.

Workers' struggles under monopoly capitalism produce an 'enfranchisement' of labour through labour unions and the organization of working-class political parties. Monopoly firms do not have to engage in ferocious competition among themselves regarding prices, as is the case for competitive capital. The monopoly sector is thus relatively amenable to affording concessions to its increasingly organized working force, whose wage increases it can pass on to the competitive sector or to consumers through price increases.

In monopoly capital the state becomes relatively autonomous from the capitalist class because, though monopoly capital is dominant, the capitalist class is divided. Moreover, because of the increasing organization of labour, the state has to secure a minimal loyalty of labour under terms not necessarily completely in capital's favour—hence the rise of the welfare state during the period of national monopoly capitalism.

The major focus in this chapter, however, is on the transformation of monopoly to global capitalism. This change is brought about by increased global competition and is accompanied and facilitated by improved production techniques, communication technologies, and transportation. Corporations compete on a worldwide scale and exploit various factors of production, particularly labour, throughout the globe. Capital mobility, or the strategic use of the threat of mobility, gives capital an immense advantage over labour and over national or local governments. The power of labour is effectively undermined because of the threat of capital flight. The relative autonomy of the state decreases as states or regions are manipulated or coerced into acceptance of the doctrine that prosperity is contingent on concessions to business.

The increase in the power of capital accompanying globalization brought back views long since thought confined to the nineteenth-century competitive phase of capitalism. The welfare state, and particularly anything to do with labour market policy, came under fierce attack from a newly united right and its international and national agents in the business community.

Welfare State Regimes

Previous to Esping-Andersen's description of welfare state types, theories about the welfare state classified nations according to the amount of funds spent by the state on social welfare measures, resulting in a gradational classification of nations into 'more or less' of a welfare state. Esping-Andersen's (1990, 1999) major insight is that types or groups of welfare states show quite different forms and not only amounts of welfare state expenditure. These can roughly be aligned according to the degree to which the welfare state regime in question 'decommodified' citizens' relationships to the market, that is, the extent to which citizens have a public alternative to complete dependence on the labour market in order to have a socially acceptable standard of living (O'Connor and Olsen, 1998). Three major empirical types were noted: the social democratic welfare states, showing the greatest decommodification and emphasis on citizenship rights; the liberal welfare state, which is the most dependent on markets and emphasizes means and income testing; and an intermediate group, the corporatist welfare states, characterized by class- and status-based insurance schemes and a heavy reliance on the family to provide support.

The major examples of the social democratic welfare states are the Scandinavian countries, particularly Sweden and Norway. The liberal welfare states include the Anglophone nations, such as Australia, Canada, the United Kingdom, and the United States (with Britain earlier being on the verge of being a social democratic welfare state). The corporatist/familist states include such countries as Germany, Austria, France, and Italy.

Much of the literature on the welfare state is based on some form of class or class coalitional perspective as an explanation for the production or maintenance of different welfare state types (Korpi, 1989; O'Connor and Olsen, 1998). Greater working-class strength and/or upper-class weakness and various combinations of class coalitions produce stronger welfare states and preserve these in the face of attack.

The importance of Esping-Andersen for our model is that medicare can be viewed, not in isolation, but as the last key in the enactment in Canada of the

Keynesian welfare state, in however an attenuated form (Wolfe, 1984, 1989). Medicare is one segment of a long historical process of struggle for access to health care and social services by working-class parties and movements (Swartz, 1977). Any explanation for medicare has to account for the similarities between its fate and that of other welfare state measures (such as education and social welfare).

Class and Health Systems

Navarro (1988, 1989) is useful because he has applied class analysis to national differences in health system types. Navarro views the various types of health-care system—national health care, health insurance, or private health care—as reflecting national differences in the strength of the organized working class. National health systems are generally the product of strong working-class movements or of a working-class/rural coalition along with a weaker bourgeoisie. Health insurance reflects a somewhat weaker working class and/or a stronger upper class. More privately oriented systems, currently almost confined to the United States, reflects weak working-class organization and a powerful, almost hegemenous, business class.

The arguments noted above have oversimplified the work of the theorists mentioned. Nevertheless, all of these analysts note the importance of class structure. Ross and Trachte provide a way of tracing historical *changes* in class structure through changes in the capitalist mode of production, from its monopoly form to its global form. The work of Esping-Andersen and Navarro is useful in its examination of different national reactions to these pressures.

These perspectives can now be applied to help us to understand developments in health and health care in Canada: the increasing role of the state in medicare, current attacks on the system, and increasing inequality (and health inequalities).

The Contemporary Era: Globalization, Neo-Liberalism, Medicare, and Health Inequalities

I argue that: (a) globalization was accompanied by and helped foster changes in the Canadian class structure characterized by the rise of the power of business with its accompanying ideology of neo-liberalism; (b) neo-liberalism and economic globalization are associated with the decline of the welfare state and attacks on the role of the state generally; (c) neo-liberalism is associated with greater socio-economic and health inequalities. The essence of neo-liberalism is a thoroughgoing adherence to the virtues of a market economy and, by extension, a market-oriented society. While some neo-liberals appear to assume that one can construct any kind of society on any kind of economy, the position taken here is that the economy, the state, and civil society are inextricably interrelated.

Globalization and neo-liberalism helped produce a decrease in the relative autonomy of the state vis-à-vis business. Business attacks on the state were associated with a decline of the welfare state. In particular, medicare became the object of state cutbacks and attempts to rationalize the health-care system. In effect, a business-state coalition sought to make health care less costly, and some segments of the business community lobbied for privatizing health care. Part of these 'reforms' were aimed at reducing the ability of the powerful medical profession to shape health care in its own interests. The push to rationalize health care came about not only because of a desire to see a 'smaller state' but also because of the drive by neo-liberals to break or undermine the strength of unions in the public sector. Medicare was restructured and rationalized.

At the same time workers lost power in the market, i.e., an undermining of unions gave workers less power vis-à-vis employers, and cutbacks were made even to the liberal or market-dependent form of the welfare state in Canada. This attack on the welfare infrastructure was associated with an increasing income polarization and social fragmentation. These are the very conditions that have been closely linked to the health and illness of populations.

The Political Economy of Neo-Liberalism in Canada

In Canada, business influence increased greatly in the 1980s and 1990s, due partly to the threat of capital mobility, partly to the influence of such institutions as the International Monetary Fund and the World Bank in pushing notions towards neo-liberal policies, and partly to the new ideological unity between large and small business (Allen, 1992). The (re)uniting of the right made domestic capitalists much more powerful agents of the global interests of capital. Within Canada, foreign, mainly American, subsidiaries had a powerful influence, for example, in the newly formed Business Council on National Issues (BCNI). Foreign holders of Canadian government debt or bonds or equities—again, chiefly Americans—could threaten Canadian governments with a reduced credit rating, with higher interest rates, or with withholding business investment unless particular market-oriented policies, were put in place (McQuaig, 1992, 1995).

During the 1970s Canadian capitalists and those representing American interests formed and/or supported organizations and foundations such as the BCNI, the C.D. Howe Institute, and the Fraser Institute. Business sponsored or supported apparently popular movements, such as the National Citizens' Coalition and the Canadian Taxpayers Federation, to spread the market-oriented message. The BCNI, composed of the CEOs of 150 of the largest corporations in Canada, was particularly influential (Clarke, 1997). Free trade with the United States, and later with Mexico, was justified as the only option that Canada had in the face of increasing international competition and the formation of other trade blocs, such as the European Community, from which Canada was excluded. The 1980s mark a significant turning point in which Canada became heavily committed to market-oriented policies.

The relative autonomy of the state significantly decreased. Federal and provincial governments, whatever their political leanings, were forced (or felt they were forced) into slashing government expenditures, reducing deficits, and paying down the debt. Many of the provinces cut government employment and undermined labour rights. So radical was the cutting of state expenditures that a highly fiscally conservative liberal Federal government went from over a $40 billion deficit to a predicted surplus within three years (1994–7). Right-wing parties were the political expression of increased business influence. In the 1980s and 1990s neo-liberal parties gained power in Alberta, British Columbia, Saskatchewan, and Ontario. A right-wing party, the Reform Party (later the Canadian Alliance), became the official opposition in Parliament. Business attained a virtual ideological hegemony, partly through its control of the media. One extreme right-wing businessman, Conrad Black, owns over 50 per cent of the daily newspapers in Canada and all of the daily newspapers in three provinces. Moreover, international trade agreements, whether with the United States and Mexico or on a more worldwide basis, were viewed by many conservatives as 'disciplining democracy'. It was openly claimed that trade agreements and international competition were needed to prevent national governments from 'interfering' in markets increasingly dominated by multinational corporations.

Neo-Liberalism, the Welfare State, and Inequality

The rise of neo-liberalism and of inequality since the 1970s is tied to the decline of the welfare state. While markets produce inequalities, these may be prevented (through labour market policies of full employment, retraining programs, etc.) or ameliorated (through social welfare measures or the decommodification of education, health, and welfare). Decommodification meant that access to social resources was not completely determined by market criteria (i.e., income or wealth) or by power in the market (the ability of some groups to bargain for 'private' welfare benefits—see Esping-Andersen, 1999). Both health, through the effects of the welfare state on the social determinants of health, and health care, through various forms of national health-care systems, are tied to the fate of the welfare state.

In the nineteenth century, inequality had been viewed as legitimate or perhaps inevitable, but within the welfare state issues of inequality seemed no longer a major concern. The welfare state had solved the problem of market-produced difficulties (1) because inequalities in the market were ameliorated through the notion of social citizenship (the idea that citizenship or residency alone entitled one to access services); and, (2) because fluctuations of 'boom and bust' were reduced by Keynesian counter-cyclical economic policies (demand stimulation in times of downturn; restriction of demand in times of boom) (Esping-Andersen, 1990; O'Connor and Olsen, 1998; Korpi, 1989; Quadagno, 1987).

The welfare state, however, is not a unitary phenomenon. As Esping-Andersen has indicated there are various 'types' of welfare state. The ones involving the least state action and the greatest dominance of market-related solutions were the liberal welfare states of the Anglophone industrialized democracies. Within liberal welfare states social policies were most generally designed to supplement market provision, to reflect participation in the market, or to be targeted or 'means-tested' rather than universal in application. There were differences even within liberal welfare states, as American/British/Canadian differences attest, with a major difference between Canada and the US being that of health care.

In the 1980s and 1990s the undermining of the welfare state took many forms. All union or labour 'privileges' were attacked. Increasingly tough laws were enacted regarding barriers to union recognition. The right to strike was taken away from various categories of workers, including public-sector workers, wage freezes or rollbacks were forced on public-sector workers, and the numbers of workers in the public sector, and in government generally, were reduced. Various universal social measures, such as family allowances, were cut or made contingent on income/contribution. Even universal old age pensions were attacked. The Canadian version of the Keynesian welfare state, a product of monopoly capitalism, was shrunk, shredded, or restructured (Johnson et al., 1994; Moscovitch and Drover, 1987; McQuaig, 1992; Teeple, 1995; Wolfe, 1984). But conservative governments seldom directly attacked some of the more popular social welfare measures. Rather, these were first undermined at the same time that an unending barrage of publicity radically weakened public expectations of what governments should provide (Clarke, 1997; Mishra, 1990).

Medicare and Health Inequalities in a Neo-Liberal Era

Medicare

Health care and education are central components of the welfare state. In the 1970s and 1980s, increasing costs had made health care the largest item in all provincial budgets, consuming about one-third of provincial government expenditures. But health care and education were not as radically under fire as were social welfare and labour force measures (see, e.g., Johnson et al., 1994; Moscovitch, and Drover, 1987). The latter were changed, more or less unilaterally. Health care, however, was somewhat different. Health care and education were partly functional for business. Health care is also the site of powerful business, professional, and patient interests. And, just as other big business interests had seen some advantages in socializing the costs of care at the time of the origins of health insurance in the 1960s, in the 1980s and 1990s business saw some benefit in preserving it. The absence of health-care costs to individual firms was a competitive advantage vis-à-vis United States corporations (Coburn and Fynes, 1995). Yet, at the same time, pressures from the 'New Right', plus the traditional free-enterprise message from small business, reinforced by the new 'logic of international competition', produced a focus on a leaner and meaner state. The analytical emphasis then shifts from being solely focused on the struggles of labour versus capital to the implications in the health field, of changes within classes, the importance of 'class fractions'. Here we point to differences in interests between health and non-health-care business as well as continuing differences between big corporations and small business. The changing balance of power of these groups has significance for health and health care.

In an era of neo-liberalism, medicine lost its once dominant position in the face of an even more powerful opponent, the state. But state actions were initiated and facilitated by a business push to roll back the welfare state generally, to rationalize government services specifically, and to undermine the role of public-sector unions. The relationships between labour, the state, and capital in a global era were radically different from what they had been under monopoly capitalism. These changed class relationships had their consequences in controversies over the fate of medicare.

The public popularity of medicare meant that at least the first impulse was to try to make medicare more co-ordinated, effective, and efficient rather than simply to privatize it. This 'corporate rationalizer' movement, supported by an implicit state-business coalition, produced massive pressures on the medical profession because medical control of health care, and of the health-care division of labour, was seen as a major obstacle to rationalization.

There are, however, somewhat ambiguous relationships among medicine, the New Right, and big business. The big-business objective of cost savings through socializing the costs of health care within medicare and a free enterprise ideology make poor bedfellows. Though capital is more united than it was, regarding the financing of health care at least, it still contains contradictory aims. Big business and small business are not always in accord, with the former tending to favour at least some form of national health insurance, though possibly reduced in its scope.

Change was not confined to Canada. In Britain, Margaret Thatcher brought about massive changes in health care towards 'an internal market' within the National Health System (see Chapter 4) by establishing a policy committee without any medical members, a policy later partially rolled back by a Labour government. In the United States implicit and explicit state-business coalitions were formed to control costs at the same time that provider corporations and insurers industrialized and reaped huge profits from health care and sought to rationalize care on a business pattern (Bergthold, 1990; Brown, 1993; Martin, 1993; Salmon, 1990, 1994). While medicare was challenged in various countries a struggle continued, as evidenced in current debates over the fate of medicare.

Health Inequalities

In the new global era neo-liberals claim that higher degrees of inequality are inevitable or that inequalities are an inescapable adjunct to economic growth or to the 'realities' of international competition. Inequality is also viewed as a key motivational factor aiding a productive economy, i.e., through lowering the costs of (some) labour. And it is argued that any measures to alter market-produced motivations simply deform the operation of markets and, furthermore, are unjust or at least inefficient. Inequality, then, is more to be welcomed or at least accepted than it is to be prevented or ameliorated by state or other forms of welfare (see Kenworthy, 1998, for a summary and rebuttal of many of these arguments). Much contemporary neo-liberal policy, in fact, involves recommodifying aspects of society that were decommodified or taken out of the market during the rise of the welfare state.

The suggestion is that there has been a general international rise in inequality, although this rise has been less dramatic in some countries than in the liberal welfare state regimes. The most recent evidence from the United States, Britain,

Australia, Canada, New Zealand, and the other OECD countries indicates that neo-liberalism in action, while obviously a far from perfect neo-liberalism, is associated with rapidly increasing inequality. The US and the UK, countries recently dominated by highly neo-liberal regimes, show particularly rapid increases in income inequality (Atkinson, 1995; Gottschalk and Smeeding, 1997, forthcoming; Korpi and Palme, 1998; Smeeding, 1997). Social inequalities are also increasing in Canada (Brink and Zeesman, 1997). Moreover, linking inequality with welfare state types, the liberal Anglophone countries show higher inequality than do such corporatist nations as Switzerland, Germany, and the Netherlands which, in turn, show higher inequality than do the social democratic Scandinavian countries (Atkinson, 1995; Gottschalk and Smeeding, forthcoming; Kenworthy, 1998; Korpi and Palme, 1998; Smeeding, 1997). Inequalities certainly existed before recent neo-liberal regimes or doctrines, but inequality was and is exacerbated under neo-liberalism. Inequalities are thus related to the class structure because class pressure tends to reduce the degree to which markets predominate.

Any consideration of the social determinants of health would have to take account of welfare state dynamics. Whether or not the effects of welfare state measures are direct and material or indirect and psychosocial is a matter of dispute. There may well be critical periods in the life cycle in which the buffering effects of the social wage or of social policies generally are crucially important (Bartley et al., 1997; Bartley et al., 1998; Daly et al., 1998; Popay et al., 1998). Bartley et al. (1997: 1195) feel that the welfare state has both material and psychosocial effects 'by preventing dramatic falls in living standards and by a wider effect on the degree to which citizens experience a sense of control of their lives'. Redistributive policies are important both materially and psychosocially. 'Cross nationally, higher levels of both social expenditure and taxation as a proportion of gross domestic product are associated with longer life expectancy, lower maternal mortality, and a smaller proportion of low birthweight deliveries' (Davey Smith, 1996: 988; see also Kaplan et al., 1996; Kennedy et al., 1996). There are thus numerous suggestions that the welfare state provided the material base for a more equal and presumably a more cohesive society and that this more or less directly influences health status (Lynch et al., 2000).

With a widening and polarization of social inequalities we can expect increasing degrees of health inequalities within Canada (Raphael, 2000; Raphael, this volume). Internationally, the liberal welfare states tend to show lower overall health status than do the social democratic welfare states. Canada, however, is, or perhaps was, something of an exception. Canada has a mean health status, as measured by longevity, closer to those of Sweden and Norway than it is to the United States, the United Kingdom, or Australia. Canada is thus an anomaly in having higher overall general health status than its social welfare type would have predicted. The question, though, is how long this anomaly will last. A study by Brink and Zeesman (1997), for example, indicates that in Canada prior to about 1980 an index of 'social health' largely paralleled the rising gross domestic product. After that time, there is a rapidly increasing gap, with the index of social health remaining static relative to an increasing GDP. Though the social health index comprised a large number of measures ranging from infant mortality to unemployment, the findings do point to a widening gap between gross economic performance statistics and well-being.

The UK presents a particularly startling example of the rise of inequality, beginning with the first Thatcher government in 1979 and producing degrees of inequality not seen for generations. Recent evidence from the United Kingdom indicates that, for men between ages 25–39, there has been an unprecedented increase, rather than decrease, in mortality rates. This is particularly true for poor men under 40 (*The Economist*, 11 Jan. 1997).

Is there a lag between increasing inequality in Canada and longevity? If social welfare measures and equality have their effects on health mainly through their effects in childhood, as a good deal of evidence suggests, Canada's relatively high international standing in health status is threatened by continued neo-liberal economic policies in two ways. First, increased social and income inequality is likely to be associated with widening health differences between different groups of Canadians. Second, a variety of social welfare measures, including medicare, which might have buffered the effect of increasing social and income inequalities on health status, are being undermined. The international evidence suggests that continued increases in inequality in Canada will result in lower overall longevity rates than would have been expected, and actually may result in decreases in health status or increases in mortality for particular income groups, and perhaps for the population as a whole. Neo-liberal policies thus both widen the differences in health between poor and rich Canadians and threaten the average health status of rich and poor alike.

Discussion

Drawing linkages between such broad processes as the international spread of neo-liberalism, medicine, health care, and health status raises a host of conceptual and empirical issues. There are always alternative ways of viewing specific events. A few of the complexities that have been ignored here in presenting the thread of an argument tying broad structural movements to events in health care should be noted.

Globalization, said by Ross and Trachte to be the latest 'variant' of capitalism, is itself a contested concept. Some argue that globalization is little more than the return of a cyclical trend evident previously, while others feel that globalization is more political rhetoric than reality (Hirst and Thompson, 1996). Yet, some factors in the mix today were not present previously. The prominence of capital flows and the technical facility to speed up the flow of capital around the world at the click of a computer keyboard are obviously more important now than previously. The formation of trade blocs and of international agencies to promote freer trade, as well as the increased dependence of national budgets and financial policies on international financial bond markets, seem specific to today's world.

It might also be claimed that globalization really is a New Right ideology. Is the increased power of capital 'real' or simply an ideology used to suppress struggles against business hegemony? I would argue, both. That is, competitive pressures on corporations, plus technological change, have increased capital mobility, for some forms of capital more than others. Yet this process is also used ideologically and politically by international and national class agents in attempts to make citizens powerless within their own countries. Thus, we now have the doctrine of 'we have no choice' and the inevitability of following the interests of corporations or of instituting or reproducing a more market-oriented society or international economy. The market, and now the international market, is viewed as a force of nature it would be foolish to resist. Nevertheless, there are economic, political, and cultural aspects of the spread of neo-liberalism on a worldwide basis. There are also 'degrees of freedom' and openings for resistance to neo-liberal doctrines.

The term 'globalization' is itself something of a misnomer. Neo-liberal economics and the New Right have managed to appropriate the term for their own purposes. Globalization obviously has cultural and political elements. Few would argue, for example, with the idea that there should be more international interaction and contact, and it is increasingly obvious that all of humanity shares the fate of 'spaceship earth'. Yet, too often by 'globalization' is simply meant the spread of market ideology around the globe. In that sense the term is misleading. It might be better termed the internationalization of capital or worldwide neo-liberalism.

How global is globalism? At least some of the effects of globalization are filtered through three major trade blocs, in Europe, North America, and the Pacific region (Morales-Gomez and Torres, 1995; Nef, 1995). In the case of contemporary Canada many pressures are less those of a global nature and more those of harmonizing downward towards the practices of Canada's dominant bilateral trading partner, the United States (Banting, 1995; Berry, 1995; Nef, 1995). Nations differ in the nature of their location within processes of globalization, and in Canada's case we are tied to continentalism. Much of Canada's history in the twentieth century can thus be read in terms of its struggles to maintain some national control over its own economy, polity, and society in the face of tremendous pressures from the US. In some respects global free trade was the lever used by the United States to pry open the Canadian nut. From this perspective globalization facilitated the integration of Canada into a continental, and not only a global, economy.

There have been trends towards the internationalization of capital, the rise of neo-liberalism, and the strengthening of the capitalist class both outside and inside Canada. Still, these trends are not complete, and in a sense they never are because we are speaking of dynamic processes and not end states. There are always countervailing powers. Pressures to downsize and restructure the Keynesian welfare state and medicare met both still-powerful providers and public defenders of medicare embodied in working-class and other social movements. It is the rather ambiguous position of big business regarding medicare, and the tremendous public support for medicare, that has so far helped preserve national health insurance in the face of attacks from the New Right, despite the quickly crumbling structures of other aspects of what now seems to have been a Utopian era of state welfare provision.

My contention is that viewing recent events as involving a movement from monopoly to global capitalism enables us to understand not only previous developments in health and in health care, but also their current transformation. The beginnings of medicare and current debates over its fate reflect basic changes in class structure. Such an analysis also points to increasing inequality within Canada as a source both of differences in how long different groups of Canadians live and of how healthy they are. It also suggests that the health of the rich is linked with the health of the poor because greater income inequality is associated with lower health status for everyone, not only those living in poverty.

Note

I owe thanks to Susan Rappolt for her collaboration on an earlier paper on this topic and for her work on an SSHRC research project, which provided some of the inspiration for this paper. Thanks also to Ivy Bourgeault, Jan Angus, Mary Fynes, and Olga Kits for their collaboration on the same project. The Critical Social Science and Health Group in Public Health Sciences at the University of Toronto, particularly Joan Eakin, Rick Edwards, Rhonda Love, Blake Poland, and Ann Robertson, prompted a number of the ideas on which this paper is based. Dennis Raphael was a source of data and encouragement. The SSHRC provided funds for two research projects on which this paper is partially based.

References

Allen, M.P. 1992. 'Elite social movement organizations and the state: The rise of the conservative policy-planning network', *Research in Politics and Society* 4: 87–109.

Amick, B.C., III, S. Levine, A.R. Tarlov, and D.C. Walsh, eds. 1995. *Society and Health.* New York: Oxford University Press.

Atkinson, A.B. 1995. *Incomes and the Welfare State: Essays on Britain and Europe.* Cambridge: Cambridge University Press.

Banting, K., ed. 1986. *The State and Economic Interests.* Toronto: University of Toronto Press.

———. 1995. 'Social policy challenges in a global society', in Morales-Gomez and Torres (1995).

Bartley, M., D. Blane, and George Davey Smith. 1998. 'Introduction: Beyond the Black Report', *Sociology of Health and Illness* 20, 5: 563–77.

———, ———, and S. Montgomery. 1997. 'Socioeconomic determinants of health: Health and the life course: why safety nets matter', *British Medical Journal* 314 (19 Apr.): 1194.

Bergthold, L.A. 1990. *Purchasing Power in Health: Business, the State and Health Care Politics.* New Brunswick, NJ: Rutgers University Press.

Berry, A. 1995. 'Social policy reform in Canada under regional economic integration', in Morales-Gomez and Torres (1995).

Brink, S., and A. Zeesman. 1997. 'Measuring social well-being: An index of social health for Canada'. Research Paper Series, Paper R–97–9E. Hull, Que.: Applied Research Branch, Strategic Policy, Human Resources Development Canada.

Brown, L.D. 1993. 'Dogmatic slumbers: American business and health policy', *Journal of Health Politics, Policy and Law* 18, 2: 339–57.

———. 2000. 'Income inequality, social cohesion and the health status of populations: The role of neo-liberalism', *Social Science and Medicine* (May).

——— and M. Fynes. 1995. 'Changing forces in health care in Canada: An exploration of the role of business', paper presented at the Canadian Sociology and Anthropology Association annual meeting, Montreal.

Clarke, T. 1997. *Silent Coup: Confronting the Big Business Takeover of Canada.* Ottawa: Canadian Centre for Policy Alternatives.

Coburn, D. 1992. 'Freidson then and now: An "internalist" critique of Freidson's past and present views of the medical profession', *International Journal of Health Services* 22, 3: 497–512.

———, G. Torrance, and J. Kaufert. 1983. 'Medical dominance in Canada in historical perspective: The rise and fall of medicine', *International Journal of Health Services* 13: 407–32.

———, S. Rappolt, and I. Bourgeault. 1997. 'Decline vs. retention of medical power through restratification: The Ontario case', *Sociology of Health and Illness* 19, 1: 1–22.

———. 1993. 'Professional powers in decline: Medicine in a changing Canada', in F.W. Hafferty and J.B. McKinlay, eds, *The Changing Medical Profession*. Toronto: Oxford University Press.

———. 1999. 'Phases of capitalism, welfare states, medical dominance, and health care in Ontario', *International Journal of Health Services* 29, 4: 833–51.

Coleman, W.D. 1988. *Business and Politics: A Study of Collective Action*. Montreal and Kingston: McGill-Queen's University Press.

Daly, M., G.J. Duncan, G.A. Kaplan, and J.W. Lynch. 1998. 'Macro-to-micro links in the relation between income inequality and mortality', *Milbank Quarterly* 76, 3: 315–402.

Davey Smith, G. 1996. 'Income inequality and mortality—why are they related—income inequality goes hand in hand with underinvestment in human-resources', *British Medical Journal* 312: 987–9.

Esping-Andersen, G. 1990. *The Three Worlds of Welfare Capitalism.* Princeton, NJ: Princeton University Press.

———. 1999. *Social Foundations of Postindustrial Economies.* Oxford: Oxford University Press.

Evans, R.G., M.L. Barer, and T.R. Marmor, eds. 1994. *Why Are Some People Healthy and Others Not? The Determinants of Health of Populations.* New York: Aldine de Gruyter.

——— and G.L. Stoddart. 1990. 'Producing health, consuming health care', *Social Science and Medicine* 31, 12: 1347–63.

Gottschalk, P., and T.M. Smeeding. 1997. 'Cross national comparisons of earnings and income inequality', *Journal of Economic Literature* 35: 633–87.

——— and ———. Forthcoming. 'Empirical evidence on income inequality in industrialized countries', in A.B. Atkinson and Françoise Bourgignon, eds, *The Handbook of Income Distribution*.

Gough, I. 1978. 'Theories of the welfare state: A critique', *International Journal of Health Services* 8: 27–40.

Hirst, P., and G. Thompson. 1996. *Globalization in Question*. Cambridge: Polity Press.

Johnson, A.F., S. McBride, and P.J. Smith, eds. 1994. *Continuities and Discontinuities: The Political Economy of Social Welfare and Labour Market Policy in Canada*. Toronto: University of Toronto Press.

Kaplan, G.A., E.R. Pamuk, J.W. Lynch, R.D. Cohen, and J.L. Balfour. 1996. 'Inequality in income and mortality in the United States: Analysis of mortality and potential pathways', *British Medical Journal* 312: 999–1003.

Kawachi, I., and B.P. Kennedy. 1997. 'Socioeconomic determinants of health', *British Medical Journal* 314: 1037.

Kennedy, B.P., I. Kawachi, and D. Prothrow-Stith. 1996. 'Income distribution and mortality: Cross-sectional ecological study of the Robin Hood index in the United States', *British Medical Journal* 312: 1004–7.

Kenworthy, L. 1998. 'Do social welfare policies reduce poverty? A cross-national assessment', *Social Forces* 77, 3: 1119–39.

Korpi, W. 1989. 'Power politics and state autonomy in the development of social citizenship: Social rights during sickness in eighteen OECD countries since 1930', *American Sociological Review* 54: 309–28.

——— and J. Palme. 1998. 'The paradox of redistribution and strategies of equality: Welfare state institutions, inequality and poverty in the Western countries', LIS, Working Paper No. 174.

Luxembourg Income Studies. Working Paper Series: http://lissy.ceps.lu/wpapers.htm

Lynch, J.W., G. Davey Smith, G.A. Kaplan, and J.S. House. 2000. 'Income inequality and health: A neo-material interpretation', *British Medical Journal* (Mar.).

McQuaig, L. 1992. *Canada's Social Programs: Under Attack*. Toronto: Atkinson Charitable Foundation.

———. 1995. *Shooting the Hippo: Death by Deficit and Other Canadian Myths*. Toronto: Viking.

Manga, P. 1987. 'Equality of access and inequalities in health status: Policy implications of a paradox', in D. Coburn, C. D'Arcy, G. Torrance, and P. New, eds, *Health and Canadian Society*, 2nd edn. Toronto: Fitzhenry & Whiteside.

Martin, C.J. 1993. 'Together again: Business, government, and the quest for cost control', *Journal of Health Politics, Policy and Law* 18, 2: 359–93.

Mishra, R. 1990. *The Welfare State in Capitalist Society*. Toronto: University of Toronto Press.

Morales-Gomez, D., and M.A. Torres, eds. 1995. *Social Policy in a Global Society: Parallels and Lessons from the Canada-Latin America Experience.* Ottawa: International Development and Research Centre.

Moscovitch, A., and G. Drover. 1987. 'Social expenditures and the welfare state: The Canadian experience in historical perspective', in Moscovitch and J. Albert, eds, *The Benevolent State: The Growth of Welfare in Canada.* Toronto: Garamond Press.

Muntaner, C., and J.W. Lynch. 1999. 'Income inequality and social cohesion versus class relations: A critique of Wilkinson's neo-Durkheimian research program', *International Journal of Health Services* 29, 59–81.

Navarro, V. 1988. Professional dominance or proletarianization? Neither', *Milbank Quarterly* 66, Supp. 2: 57–75.

———. 1989. 'Why some countries have national health insurance, others have national health services, and the U.S. has neither', *Social Science and Medicine* 28, 9: 887–98.

———. 1998. 'Neoliberalism, "globalization", unemployment inequalities and the welfare state', *International Journal of Health Services* 28, 4: 607–82.

———. 1999. 'Health and equity in the world in the era of "globalization"', *International Journal of Health Services* 29, 2: 215–26.

Nef, J. 1995. *Human Security and Mutual Vulnerability: An Exploration into the Global Political Economy of Development and Underdevelopment.* Ottawa: International Development and Research Centre.

O'Connor, J., and G.M. Olsen, eds. 1998. *Power Resources Theory and the Welfare State: A Critical Approach.* Toronto: University of Toronto Press.

Popay, J., G. William, C. Thomas, and T. Gatrell. 1998. 'Theorising inequalities in health: The place of lay knowledge', *Sociology of Health and Illness* 20, 5: 619–44.

Quadagno, J. 1987. 'Theories of the welfare state', *Annual Review of Sociology* 13: 109–28.

Raphael, D. 2000. 'Health effects of economic inequality', *Canadian Review of Social Policy.* Forthcoming.

Ross, R.J.S., and K.C. Trachte. 1990. *Global Capitalism: The New Leviathan.* Albany: State University of New York.

Salmon, J.W., ed. 1990. *The Corporate Transformation of Health Care: Part 1.* Amityville, NY: Baywood Publishing.

———, ed. 1994. *The Corporate Transformation of Health Care: Part 2.* Amityville, NY: Baywood Publishing.

Smeeding, T.M. 1997. 'American income inequality in a cross-national perspective: Why are we so different?', LIS, Working Paper No. 157.

Stubbs, R., and G.R.D. Underhill, eds. 1994. *Political Economy and the Changing Global Order.* Toronto: McClelland & Stewart.

——— and ———, eds. 2000. *Political Economy and the Changing Global Order*, 2nd edn. Toronto: Oxford University Press.

Swartz, D. 1977. 'The politics of reform: Conflict and accommodation in Canadian health policy', in L. Panitch, ed., *The Canadian State*. Toronto: University of Toronto Press.

Taylor, M.G. 1978. *Health Insurance and Canadian Public Policy: The Seven Decisions that Created the Canadian Health Insurance System*. Montreal and Kingston: McGill-Queen's University Press.

Teeple, G. 1995. *Globalization and the Decline of Social Reform*. Toronto: Garamond Press.

Useem, M. 1984. *The Inner Circle: Large Corporations and the Rise of Business Political Activity in the United States and the U.K.* New York: Oxford University Press.

Walters, V. 1982. 'State, capital and labour: The introduction of federal-provincial insurance for physician care in Canada', *Canadian Review of Sociology and Anthropology* 19, 2: 157–72.

Wilkinson, R.G. 1996. *Unhealthy Societies: The Afflictions of Inequality*. London: Routledge.

———. 1999. 'Income inequality, social cohesion, and health: Clarifying the theory—a reply to Muntaner and Lynch', *International Journal of Health Services* 29, 3: 525–43.

Wolfe, D.A. 1984. 'The rise and demise of the Keynesian era in Canada: Economic policy, 1930–1982', in M.S. Cross and G.S. Kealey, eds, *Modern Canada, 1930–1980's*. Toronto: McClelland & Stewart.

———. 1989. 'The Canadian state in comparative perspective', *Canadian Review of Sociology and Anthropology* 26, 1: 95–126.

CHAPTER 4

The British National Health Service in the Face of Neo-Liberalism

Colin Leys

Introduction

Since the early 1980s all state-provided health-care systems have been under growing pressures from global financial markets and from an increasingly globalized health-care industry to cut back the scope and accessibility of state provision and make room for private capital. The British National Health Service (NHS), as both the most comprehensive and the most centralized among OECD (Organization for Economic Co-operation and Development) countries, offers a particularly clear example of this process. By the late 1990s its comprehensiveness had been significantly eroded, equality of access was in jeopardy, and the creation of a so-called 'internal market' had opened the NHS to incremental processes of penetration by private capital on a wide variety of fronts. These processes had been retarded by the strength of popular support for the NHS and the resistance of health-care professionals, including doctors. A point could be envisaged, however, when these barriers would also start to collapse and the marketization of health care would accelerate, leaving the state system as a much-reduced provider of last resort for the poor. The similarities and differences between Britain and Canada in this regard are instructive, and suggest the possibility of a general theory of the conditions under which health services are liable to privatization.

The chapter is organized as follows. The first section briefly describes the NHS and its essential logic, drawing attention to some significant differences between it and the Canadian system. The next part describes the main steps in the neo-liberal assault on the NHS. Following this I analyse these changes in terms of the logic of capital accumulation and, in the concluding section, speculate on what governs the relative success or failure of the forces working for or against privatization, once again drawing attention to what seems to be the significance of the British experience for Canada.

The NHS in Britain

Health services are a natural field for collective provision. A relatively predictable minority of us will suffer injuries or acute and chronic illnesses, especially as we get older, but we don't know who. During 1991, in a typical general practice in an English town, 73 per cent of the registered patients required no specialist (hospital-based) care at all; 5 per cent accounted for over two-thirds of the cost of all the required hospital care (Matsaganis and Glennerster, 1994). It is a Rawlsian situation—we are willing to provide for all equally, if we can provide for all adequately, because we can imagine that we may one day be the ones who need it, and even for the relatively well off serious illness can otherwise spell economic disaster. The logic of this, contrasted with the terrible social inequality of health chances before World War II, led to the general development of systems of state-provided medical care after the war, of which the British was the first and for some time probably the best. From 1948 the NHS provided comprehensive medical care (including eye and dental care) for all, based only on need and free at the point of delivery, financed out of general taxation. Hospital doctors were salaried and family doctors, while remaining formally self-employed 'independent contractors' with the NHS, were effectively salaried through a mixture of capitation payments and fees geared to public health needs (such as reaching specified levels of innoculations). Neither had any incentive to over-treat, as in fee-for-service systems like Canada's,[1] and access to specialists could only be had by being referred by a family doctor—i.e., family doctors were gatekeepers for access to more expensive specialist care.

The scheme was enormously successful and popular, and spectacularly economical. Britain's national health statistics are roughly at the OECD average; Britain's life expectancy and infant mortality rates are nearly as good as Canada's and better than those of the US.[2] But Britain only spends two-thirds as much per capita on health services as Canada, and only one-third as much as the United States.[3] To some extent this reflects chronic underspending on the NHS's capital stock and low wages for its huge workforce, especially its nurses and support staff—as we shall see, the NHS has been seriously underfunded.[4] But another significant reason, until the 1990s, was exceptionally low administrative costs—6 per cent of total health-care spending compared with 25 per cent in the US. What could be said of the Canadian system—that it covers all health needs, covers them for everyone, and is far cheaper than the American system—was for a long time even truer of the NHS.

This system of health care, like all state-run systems, presented a major challenge to the neo-liberal project as it developed in the late 1970s and 1980s, led by the new Conservative Party leader, Margaret Thatcher. It was a major sphere of potential capital accumulation from which capital was excluded. It had a built-in tendency to increase state spending when neo-liberal theory called for it to be reduced—spending on the NHS accounted for 11 per cent of government expenditure and was perceived as rising inexorably, when reducing taxes was a top neo-liberal priority. The NHS was easily the largest single employer in the country, with over a million employees out of a total workforce of 27 million;[5] and although the British Medical Association had originally opposed it, by the 1980s a new generation of senior doctors had become solidly identified with it (Webster, 1998: 25–8). Finally it was extremely popular. It represented a popular legacy of socialist ideals, largely identified with the Labour Party, and employed a mass of unionized workers also identified with the Labour Party. Mrs Thatcher famously declared that 'there was no alternative' to market capitalism, but the NHS showed that there was. It was the strongest pillar of the social democratic temple that the neo-liberals wanted to pull down—'a prime test for the assault on collectivism' (ibid., 144).

The Neo-Liberal Assault

In 1982, the third year of Thatcher's first administration, the cabinet began to consider various options for privatizing the NHS. A document proposing this was leaked to the press and there was a huge public outcry. Thatcher was forced to make a famous disclaimer, declaring that 'the NHS is safe with us' (Mohan, 1995: 55–6). Plans for wholesale privatization were abandoned. Instead, the government proceeded piecemeal. Initially there were three main policies. (1) Ancillary hospital services such as cleaning, catering, laundry, pathology laboratories, etc. were increasingly 'contracted out'. (2) From 1984, on the advice of a former managing director of a supermarket chain, Roy Griffiths, a new hierarchy of general managers, backed up by an infusion of businessmen appointed to hospital management boards, was installed in the hospitals to displace the power of senior doctors who had hitherto run them by 'consensus' (Baggott, 1994: 122–32). (3) Spending was cut back below the growth of health needs, forcing the NHS either to deliver the same for less, or to reduce services. Expert opinion thought the NHS needed about a 2 per cent real annual increase in spending just to maintain services, but throughout the 1980s the real annual increase averaged less than half of this (Mohan, 1995: 10–22; Webster, 1998: 151).

These measures, in combination, eventually produced a crisis. From the point of view of the staff, work got harder while conditions got worse. Senior hospital doctors, in particular, found policy increasingly made by general managers on performance-related pay, who were strongly focused on the 'bottom line' and sometimes had little understanding of health-care issues or respect for medical tradition. Nurses no longer had enough time to give patients the care they considered they needed. Support staff found themselves transferred to outside contractors, on lower wages and inferior terms of employment, and typically non-unionized. Patients—unless they were acutely ill, when they almost always continued to praise hospital staff for the care they received—encountered stressed and demoralized staff and longer and longer waiting times to see a specialist or to get surgery when it was needed. By 1994, for example, the average wait just to see an ear, nose, and throat surgeon was three months, and for an orthopaedic surgeon it was six months—sometimes with even longer subsequent waits for the operation itself (Yates, 1995: 128, 133). In some localities and for some specialties, waiting times could be several years. People lived with increasing pain and/or disability and some even died before they could be treated.

Comprehensiveness and equality of access were reduced in other ways as well. Universal access to dental care was removed by the simple expedient of capping the dental budget and freezing dentists' incomes from NHS work. Dentists—who, like GPs, were formally self-employed independent contractors with the NHS—increasingly responded by declining to treat patients 'on the NHS', so that people were obliged to become private patients. By the mid-1990s, while most dentists continued to treat children as NHS patients, fewer and fewer adults could get dental treatment on NHS terms, which in any case now included substantial user co-payments (Webster, 1998: 156–8). Glasses were no longer issued free to children, and charges were introduced for regular eye examinations and were raised for prescription drugs.

Lengthening waiting times, in particular—and occasional well-publicized and not wholly atypical cases of patients with acute conditions waiting on hospital trolleys because of bed shortages—boosted interest in private medical insurance (PMI). A significant difference between Britain and Canada is that, unlike the Canada Health Act, the British legislation never has banned private insurance for medical treatments that the publicly funded hospital system provides. As a result, the NHS's financial squeeze, coupled with a government strongly advocating private-sector provision in all fields, led to a rapid expansion of private medical insurance in the 1980s. Companies now routinely offered senior executives and their families private medical insurance, and the proportion of the population covered by PMI—overwhelmingly through such corporate plans—trebled, from under 4 per cent through the mid-1970s to over 13 per cent by the mid-1990s. The private-sector share of planned (i.e., non-emergency) surgical operations rose from 13 to 20 per cent—in other words, 13 per cent of the population, almost all from the top decile of income earners, were getting a fifth of all planned operations (Yates, 1995: 15). Private hospital facilities expanded from 7,867 beds in 1981 to 11,300 in 1992, and this expansion was encouraged by the government in various other ways (e.g., by removing planning restrictions) (Laing and Buisson, 1996: 103, 125). Most of the increase was in hospitals owned by for-profit companies (Lattimer, 1996: 75). Moreover, virtually all of the treatment provided in this expanding private sector was given by doctors employed, part-time or full-time, by the NHS.[6]

The funding squeeze eventually led to a staff revolt within the NHS. Unprecedented industrial action by the nursing unions, with equally unprecedented support from senior doctors, culminated in December 1987 in a joint open letter to the Prime Minister from the presidents of the three senior royal colleges of medicine, declaring that the NHS was in crisis. Mrs Thatcher's response was to set up a committee, consisting of a handful of ideologically 'sound' ministers and civil servants, meeting in strict secrecy and chaired by herself, to 'review the financing of the NHS'. It rejected the option of moving to either vouchers or an insurance-based scheme but adopted instead the 1985 proposals of an American management consultant, Alain Enthoven, for creating an 'internal market' by the so-called 'purchaser-provider split'.[7] The resulting 'reforms' radically changed the orientation and structure of the NHS.

Hospitals became 'providers'; in due course they all became self-financing 'trusts' that provided services to patients in return for payments by 'purchasers'. There were two kinds of purchasers. The most important were government-appointed Health Authorities or (in Scotland) Boards—eventually about 100 throughout the UK—that were given fixed budgets with which to purchase all hospital-based specialist health care for the patients in their areas. But groups of family doctors could also choose to become purchasers who were given budgets with which they, rather than the local Health Authority, could purchase the bulk of the more routine specialist care required by the patients registered on their 'lists'.[8]

In theory, hospitals were to compete with each other for patients. They could also raise money by selling services to private patients—offering them faster access in more comfortable and better-staffed wards. The argument was that making hospitals depend financially on customer demand would force them to become more efficient and cost-conscious, while the government still controlled total spending.

This so-called internal market was introduced in 1991 without any formal public debate or, indeed, any electoral mandate, and without any prior testing or research. I call it 'so-called' because insofar as it was internal, it was not really a market—the contracts made within it were not legally enforceable, and neither the purchasers nor the providers were actually free to follow market logic (West, 1997). And insofar as it was a market it was not internal—Health Authorities could and did buy services from private hospitals (especially when trying to cut waiting times); NHS hospitals could and did compete for private patients with for-profit hospitals; and senior NHS hospital doctors could and did work in the private sector. Both qualifications are important. The first meant that people were set to behave in a market-oriented way, but not really allowed to, while the second opened up the system, fragmented into over 400 financially autonomous providers (hospital and community care trusts) and over a hundred purchasers (not to mention hundreds of 'fundholding' family doctor practices), to a wide range of external market influences. Such as it was, however, the system was more or less fully operational by the mid-1990s; by 1997, when Labour replaced the Conservatives in office, virtually all NHS hospitals, clinics, and other provider units had become self-governing trusts, and almost 60 per cent of family doctors had become fundholders.

Coupled with these reforms was another change, hardly less significant. Under the NHS and Community Care Act 1990, which established the 'internal market', responsibility for the long-term care of the elderly frail and the mentally handicapped (now called 'people with learning disabilities') was simultaneously transferred from the NHS to local government. Government funding was also transferred from the NHS budget to elected local authorities (county, borough and city councils) to cover this, but with two crucial differences. First, whereas care in the NHS was free to the patient, local authorities could charge people for care and were under strong central government pressure to do so. These patients were now expected not only to use virtually all of their personal incomes but also to dispose of all but a small residue of their savings (including their homes) to pay for their care, before it would be covered by public funds.[9] Second, local authorities were obliged to spend 85 per cent of the new funding for long-term patients, transferred to them from the NHS budget, on residential and nursing home places in privately owned homes.[10] So while NHS long-term beds were rapidly cut back, for-profit nursing and residential homes expanded so that by 1996 these provided 65 per cent of all residential care for the long-term ill and infirm.[11]

This change drove a huge bridgehead into the psychological defences of the NHS by removing equal access to health care from the section of the population most in need of it but least able to fight—the disabled, the chronically sick, and the frail elderly. Support for them was also deflected by shamelessly misrepresenting the change as making their care more humane by moving them out of 'faceless institutions' into 'the community', when in reality it just moved the great majority of them out of one set of institutions (free NHS hospitals) into another (predominantly fee-charging private residential or nursing homes).[12]

The government refused to fund any assessment of the 1990 'reforms'—the idea was to impose them and reduce opposition by minimizing objective discussion. The weight of the evidence collected by experts, however, is that the changes did not achieve any of their proclaimed goals (Robinson and Le Grand, 1993; Radical Statistics Group, 1995; West, 1997). They did not reduce costs significantly except by cutting services, while—ironically enough—they more than doubled administrative costs.[13] They did not make good hospitals better and push bad ones towards improvement or bankruptcy; to have allowed this would have destabilized local health-care provision in a politically impossible way. They did not improve hospital care, because budget pressures took precedence over patient needs. They did not enhance 'patient choice', even when the choice was exercised for them in reality by their family doctors, but reduced it, since their family doctors could now only send patients to the particular provider hospitals with which either they (as fundholders) or the local Health Authority had made contracts.[14] Nor is there any evidence that fundholding made family doctors more efficient or able to provide better care than non-fundholding doctors (Goodwin, 1996: 116-30). The one clear change—the further loss of power by senior hospital doctors to managers and family doctors—was seen by some as a gain, but it is not self-evident that either managers or family doctors (who in effect run their own small businesses) are preferable to specialists when it comes to deciding how best to use health-care resources.

Against all these disappointed promises had to be set some major negative consequences:

- The creation of a 'two-tier' service, if not a three-tier one: immediate deluxe service for private patients in NHS hospitals; fast-track service for patients of fundholding GPs, in cases where the latter bargained for this in making their contracts with hospitals; and consequently longer waiting times and worse service for everyone else—i.e., a further general erosion of the principle of equal access based on health needs alone.

- The impossibility of rational planning for services when hospitals in a given region are competing for the available 'business'.

- Financially driven closures of services, regardless of need, to meet hospital bottom lines, combined with the non-use of existing facilities because contract funds for their use were used up, even though the premises were there and the staff salaries had mostly still to be paid—i.e., a further drop in comprehensiveness and access and a rise in average costs.

- The industrialization of medicine. NHS hospital managers were now supposed to be paid, and hospital budgets allocated, on the basis of performance measured by units of treatment (especially 'finished consultant episodes' or FCEs), not by health outcomes. The problem was no longer, or no longer primarily, the 'medical model' of health care, in which useful care may be displaced by an all-too-often false ideal of 'cure' ('magic bullets aimed at a bestiary of disease'); now 'treatments'—standardized, measurable, and saleable commodities—were being substituted for both care and cure. One effect was that hospital readmissions, due to patients having been discharged too soon (to increase patient 'throughput'), were now counted as new treatment episodes and seen as gains in productivity—even though the patients in question were obviously less well, and cost the system more, than if they had not been discharged too soon in the first place.

The 'New Labour' government of Tony Blair, which took office in May 1997, decided to keep the purchaser-provider split but to end the detailed financial transactions on which it was based. It hoped (though unrealistically, in the view of all experienced observers) to save £1 billion of the annual administrative costs generated by the internal market by shifting from annual contracting, and from billing on a case-by-case basis, to the broad 'commissioning' of specified categories of hospital services for periods of several years. This commissioning would be progressively taken over by new Primary Care Groups, established in 1999, covering populations of around 100,000 each and 'led' by family doctors (but including other local health professionals) in collaboration with the providers rather than in confrontation with them. The greater influence over the speed and quality of hospital-provided services that fundholding had given some family doctors was thus to be retained, but shared among all family doctors (a separate category of fundholders would be phased out). The power of hospital managers vis-à-vis senior hospital doctors (who would continue to have their contracts of employment with individual hospital trusts, not with the NHS) would also remain.

Many other changes were foreshadowed in the new government's 1997 policy document, *The New NHS*, some of which are referred to below; here it is enough to note that the policies just mentioned left the key elements of the Conservatives' 'reforms' intact. To some extent this responded to a widespread feeling within the NHS that it was suffering from an overload of reforms and needed a period of consolidation, if not recuperation, rather than further change. But it also fitted well with Labour's general policy stance to adapt to markets and market-oriented reforms. Mrs Thatcher's NHS 'reforms' did not strike the new Labour leadership as fundamentally anomalous or wrong, and it could be inferred from this that whatever the dynamics of the new structure were, they would largely be left to work themselves out over the coming years.

The Political Economy of the 'Reformed' NHS

Why did the Thatcher government go about 're-forming' the NHS in this particular way? What were the obstacles to outright privatization? Why did the new Labour government so largely accept the Conservatives' reforms? How stable is the resulting structure? The many different processes involved—scientific, technological, demographic, epidemiological, organizational, and social-psychological, as well as economic and political—obviously interact in complex ways. The question is to what extent there is an underlying general logic to which at least many of them conform. This is not the same thing as seeking a super-cause. It is not to deny, for example, that fundamental clashes of professional values (e.g., between medical culture and economic or management cultures) or powerful effects of technology (such as optical fibre and the digital transmission of data) imparted from other spheres play important roles in the evolution of health care. It is simply to raise and explore the explanatory force of hypotheses drawn from an analysis of the socio-economic system in which all these forces operate.

The Conservatives' approach to health care was frankly governed by a wish that it become either more market-based or more market-like. It is therefore natural to begin by asking how the Conservatives' 'reforms', and their retention by Labour, relate to this project. This is approached here by looking at them in the light of four propositions drawn from economic theory.

(1) In order for services to become a sphere of capital accumulation, they must be commodified, i.e., broken down and reconfigured as discrete units of output that can be packaged in such a way that they can be produced in bulk, to some extent interchangeably, and have exchange value independent of use value, so that surplus value can be produced and appropriated by capital.

(2) This requires that people must be persuaded to want these services as commodities, i.e., to think they have use value justifying their price; and they must effectively be denied access to a non-commodified alternative, especially if it is superior or appears to have better value. These two steps complement each other.

(3) The existing labour force of service providers must be redefined and remotivated as wage labourers producing commodities and receiving less in wages than they add in value to the commodities they produce.

(4) Finally, in cases where, as with publicly provided health services, the state's non-commodity production of a good has precluded the development of significant private capital investments, these changes must be accomplished by the state. More-

over, the state must simultaneously foster the development of an industry with the requisite technological and organizational capacity to occupy the sphere of accumulation in question, especially by underwriting risk.

1. *The commodification of health care.* This is probably the most important effect of the internal market. The so-called contracts between the purchasers and the providers (so-called because they were legally unenforceable) were at first rather vague, but over time they became more and more precise and detailed, since money was involved. Some Health Authorities, led by Conservative-appointed businessmen, tried to drive harder and harder bargains, forcing trusts to reduce their prices and seeking to impose penalties for non-performance, to the point where some of them faced effective bankruptcy and had to be rescued by intervention from the centre. By 1998 a third of all NHS hospital trusts had serious financial deficits, as did many Health Authorities (Gaffney et al., 1999a). To survive in this environment, trusts in theory had to try to price each procedure separately, which meant standardizing it and assigning it an appropriate share of fixed costs, which also had to be calculated; and to cut costs procedures had to be still more standardized, if possible, and speeded up, as in any factory. In practice such detailed costing was far beyond the resources of most hospital trusts and contracts were mostly based on existing overall hospital budgets, but detailed costing remained the official goal.[15] The need to cut costs also lay behind the official drive for out-patient surgery (i.e., avoiding the so-called 'hotel costs' involved in keeping patients in hospital beds) and for the adoption of new surgical techniques that promised to permit this, even when these techniques involved higher risks than existing ones, as in crushing kidney stones by endoscopic surgery (Hart, 1994: 76). Clinical directorates (specialist departments) in hospitals were also given internal budgets and required to meet given performance targets, making clinicians more keenly aware of what each procedure cost.

A new culture of cost-consciousness and economy was thus inaugurated, competing with professional-oriented ideals of clinical excellence, and the removal of long-term care from the NHS enhanced it. Care, which is indivisible and is essentially good or not so good, was increasingly replaced by treatments, which could be individuated and standardized. Standard prices can be determined more or less easily for many treatments; for example, hip replacements cost £4,000 each. No price can easily be determined for taking the best possible care, week by week, of an old person with multiple and interacting chronic illnesses.

2. *Creating an effective demand for health service commodities in place of health care.* There are plenty of relevant analogies in the way we have been persuaded to accept automatic tellers in place of bank staff, or fast food in place of more nutritious and aesthetically satisfying meals. On the 'carrot' side, medical science is appealed to in support of the 'magic-bullets' approach, reinforced by TV programs presenting hospital treatment (always surgical) as a set of fast-moving episodes—like the programs themselves—of high-tech care delivered on the run by teams of doctors and nurses whose efforts bear a distinct resemblance to those of the kitchen staff in a McDonald's. Most people's actual experience of non-emergency hospital treatment

increasingly consists of a visit to one or another specialist department with the general characteristics of Midas Muffler, and this gradually becomes the norm. Care becomes less associated with hospitals and more, for most people, only with home, where it is provided by female relatives—if they are lucky enough to have any—and with nursing homes for the very old.[16] As fewer people remember what it used to be like to be cared for in hospital (just as a growing minority no longer remember home cooking),[17] we can expect the concept of commodified health services to be gradually accepted, together with the idea of a range of models, as with cars, the best being only for those who can afford them. And as on Britain's privatized railways the word 'passenger' has been officially replaced by 'customer', so in the NHS 'patient' is beginning to give way to 'service user'—i.e., shifting from words that define people as individuals with particular needs to words that define them abstractly as consumers. The so-called Patients' Charter, introduced in 1992, a list of (admittedly unenforceable) rights patients are supposed to have as individual consumers, such as not to be kept waiting more than 30 minutes after their appointed time in an out-patient clinic, was part of an ideological project to achieve this.

The counterpart of all this—the 'stick'—is, of course, giving people reasons to become disenchanted with the existing free, state-provided service, above all by systematically underfunding it. It is a striking fact that in Canada where, generally speaking, the social democratic tradition is much weaker than in Britain, more people express satisfaction with their publicly provided health service than in Britain. There are no doubt many reasons for this, including the fact that Canadians see the US alternative at close quarters and overwhelmingly reject it (Armstrong and Armstrong, 1998: 1); but the fact that so much more per capita is spent on the Canadian system than is spent in Britain clearly plays a significant part. Down to 1992, for example, Ontario hospitals had come to expect a 'traditional 10 per cent annual increase' in their budgets (McLeod-Dick, 1997). In Britain, by contrast, chronic underfunding pushed the NHS close to the limits of viability. By 1994 Britain had only five hospital beds per 1,000 people, compared with seven in Canada, and only half as many acute-care beds per 1,000. Waiting times for consultations and elective surgery were far longer. The often delapidated premises of the NHS, starved as it was of capital spending by successive governments, contributed to the problem.[18] Why should people step back a generation, in terms of their physical surroundings, at the very moment when they need the best, when they are seriously ill? And the internal market was intended to increase the pressure to cut costs. Often the only practical way to do so was to reduce the service offered by ending comprehensiveness and reducing access. This reality induced many family doctors to become fundholders just to protect their patients from being disadvantaged by others.[19] The resulting two-tier service tended further to weaken public support.

But some seeds of disenchantment go back to the origins of the NHS, in two aspects of the privileges given at the outset to senior hospital doctors to overcome their initial resistance. One was that they got effective control over the hospital service; hospitals were run by committees dominated by them. This meant that the hierarchical and class-conscious culture of the medical profession was entrenched in the NHS. Over time this was modified by fresh generations of doctors influenced by the more democratic—or at least consumerist—culture outside it, but the somewhat hermetic institutional culture of the hospital always tended to lag behind that of the wider world, and patients who were becoming used to a more market-oriented culture and who were no longer grateful for something newly and wondrously available free, as their parents or grandparents were, increasingly found some clinicians' attitudes arrogant and unacceptable. The unhappiness felt in other ranks of the NHS, reinforced by downward pressure on pay and conditions, could also sometimes be expressed in offhand treatment of patients.[20]

A second Achilles' heel of the service was the way senior NHS hospital doctors were allowed to do private practice on so-called 'maximum part-time' contracts. In effect, they could draw about 82 per cent of a full salary (later raised to 91 per cent) for doing half a week's work in the NHS and earn as much more from private practice as they liked (Yates, 1995: 31–3). This led to a good deal of abuse, especially in certain surgical specialties (eye, heart, and orthopaedics); there was a direct relationship between the length of time it took to see a surgeon in any given surgical specialty in any given NHS hospital, the amount of private practice surgery the surgeons in question did, and the number of private hospital beds provided in their district (ibid., 18–22; Audit Commission, 1995). And the main reason for the growth of private medical insurance, and the pre-emption of elective surgery by private patients, was the wish to avoid waiting to see a surgeon and get surgery. Moreover, privately insured patients could always get immediate NHS hospital care if they had an *acute* problem—indeed, even if the problem arose from complications arising from private treatment!

3. *Redefining the labour force as wage workers.* This is first of all a problem of the doctors. In the United States, for-profit Health Maintenance Organizations (HMOs) stepped in and effectively took over the profitable small businesses that self-employed American doctors had built up, and now these HMOs increasingly employ the doctors as salaried employees working to generate profits for the HMOs' shareholders (Hart, 1994: 55–7; Pollock, 1998). This result is much harder to achieve in Britain, where senior specialists have been, in effect, senior partners in a huge monopolistic but not-for-profit guild, deriving satisfaction from a blend of high social status and relatively high salaries (for most of them only modestly supplemented by private practice), almost complete professional autonomy, unchallenged professional authority, and a sense of vocation. By reducing their autonomy, curtailing the time allowed for consultations, limiting the time and funding for research, forbidding them to criticize hospital management in public or to share information with the so-called purchasers (or even their colleagues in other, competing hospitals), and in many other ways, the changes in the system undermined their previous motivation. One NHS trust chairman notoriously said a doctor's duty to the employer came 'before the professional duty to the patient' (Roy Lilley, cited in Health Policy

Network, 1995: 13). Many letters to the *British Medical Journal* and *The Lancet* revealed hospital doctors' frustrations on these points.

Breaking up the doctors' corporate unity and putting them back into competition with each other, as they were before 1948, will become possible if and when this process is more advanced. Some may eventually be lured by high salaries and better working conditions into full-time senior roles in for-profit hospitals, while others continue to double their NHS incomes by part-time private practice. Some Primary Care Trusts will expand into various kinds of for-profit activities in partnership with banks, pharmaceutical companies, and private health-care providers, such as diagnostic laboratories, nursing homes, rehabilitation centres, and private hospitals. Some general practitioners (non-specialist doctors) will take posts in new walk-in clinics, both NHS and private, to be established in railway stations and shopping centres. Gradually, the solidarity of the profession built around the original NHS structure will weaken, and a medical career outside the NHS will then become a relatively normal alternative to one within it, as it has not been for a half-century.

Similar issues arise with nurses. Declining job satisfaction, overwork, and low pay have already raised a serious problem of wastage. The annual rate of turnover among NHS nurses reached 21 per cent in 1997 (Snell, 1998); to reduce stress and get more flexible hours, large numbers have switched to work for nursing agencies, which then 'rent' them back to NHS hospitals to cover shortages, with obvious costs to patients in terms of continuity of care.[21] One agency alone had 150,000 doctors, nurses, and care workers on its books at the end of 1999, most of them working for the NHS.

In the immediate future doctors, nurses, and unionized NHS staff of all kinds will probably continue to resist the transformation of a comprehensive, free, equal-access service into a partial, fee-paid, and unequal one, as attested by successive resolutions by the British Medical Association opposing the Private Finance Initiative (more on this below) and walk-in clinics, and calling for an end to underfunding.[22] Understanding the dynamics of this crucial ideological contest is an important research task, full of fascinating twists and paradoxes. For instance, in NHS hospitals multiple-bed rooms are normal (and relatively large open wards still not uncommon), with the result that they are still places where people of quite different class backgrounds meet and spend time together, and where they are treated more or less equally, something that inevitably has an effect on the staff as well as on patients. Significantly, Laing and Buisson (1995: 116) comment that one of the competitive disadvantages of NHS 'pay bed' units relative to beds in private hospitals 'is believed to be the difficulty of achieving a change in culture among NHS nursing and other staff and altering staff attitudes to reflect the demands of paying customers.' What demands are these, one wonders? For the painstaking, personal approach everyone should get, but which the NHS cuts and market-driven reorganization are making it less and less possible to offer? Or for greater deference to patients who are 'paying customers' (who are in any case mostly not paying, but being paid for by their employers' group insurance schemes)? The general trend, however, both inside and outside the NHS, is towards individual consumerism and away from collective values.

4. *The role of the state in fostering a private health-care industry.* In contrast with some other public services, such as broadcasting, there was no large block of investable capital in Britain ready and able to enter health service provision, partly thanks to the NHS's monopoly but also because the work of commodification had still to be done. Just as health care could only be commodified through the action of the state (often at the expense of the care that people really wanted and that was rationally indicated),[23] the state's intervention was also needed to induce private-sector capital to invest in health care and recruit the requisite workforce.

It did this by a wide variety of means in addition to those already mentioned. For example, companies were given tax breaks for private health insurance premiums for their less highly paid employees; individuals over 60 were allowed to offset individual health insurance premiums against income tax;[24] and private non-profit hospitals registered as charities were exempt from tax, even though they admitted only patients able to pay their very high fees (Lattimer, 1996: 73–89). NHS hospitals were also required to find savings through annual 'efficiency increases' and to pay the Treasury a 6 per cent annual 'capital charge' on the current value of their plant, partly to level the playing field for competition with private-sector hospitals.[25] These requirements were meant to encourage cost consciousness and dynamism. On the other hand, the private sector also put pressure on the government to forbid hospitals to cross-subsidize their various operations by offering any fee-for-service procedures, on the ground that this allowed them to compete unfairly with private-sector providers (even though the latter, not being obliged to offer a full range of services, as NHS hospitals were, were able to 'cherry-pick' the treatments they offered, avoiding the least profitable). The upshot of all these pressures was that a third of all NHS trusts moved into debt.

But two of the Conservative government's measures to boost the private health-care sector were more important than all the rest. One was the diversion of 85 per cent of government funding for long-term care to the private sector via local authorities; by 1995 well over £2 billion of annual tax revenue was being directed into for-profit residential and nursing homes (Walker, 1997: 183). This was important because it showed that the key to privatization was to use public funds to pay for-profit companies to provide services, and that in certain circumstances—in this case, a politically weak group of patients and a divided political opposition in Parliament—it was politically possible to do this.

The second measure was the Private Finance Initiative (PFI), which also diverted large amounts of public funds to the private sector. From 1992 the government required all public-sector organizations, as a condition of being considered for capital funding from government revenues, first to seek private capital funding for all capital projects costing (in the case of the NHS) more than £500,000 (Gaffney et al., 1999a, 1999b, 1999c; Pollock et al., 1999).[26] In the NHS this meant that private consortia of banks, builders, and facilities management companies would build and own hospitals and lease them to NHS hospital trusts. It was apparent, however, that private investors could be attracted only if they were given a significant say in the operation of the services to be provided in the new plant, including the clinical services, whose efficiency would affect the security of their investment, and/or if their risks were effectively underwritten by the government. In the case of a hospital this meant not only that the new building would be owned by a private consortium and leased back to the NHS trust, but also that the private consortium would employ all non-clinical staff, with the possibility (indicated in early government 'guidance' issued to NHS trusts) that 'non-clinical' could eventually be considered as including pathology, physiotherapy, and radiology services, as well as cleaning, catering, and the like.[27] It also meant that the risks involved in the new investment, which were in theory to be borne by the consortium (and were the main reason given for the higher costs involved, compared with using public funds), were in reality minimized.

On entering office in 1997 the Labour Party took over the PFI and immediately passed special legislation, also inherited from the Conservatives, to hasten its implementation. By mid-1999, 31 new privately financed hospitals, costing approximately £3 billion, had been approved, with contracts already signed for 12. These projects had multiple shortcomings, including drastically increased costs relative to publicly funded projects and corresponding cost-driven reductions in bed numbers, well below what needs-based forecasts would call for. But their chief significance is that they portended a radical new shift in the boundary between the public and private sector.

> The consortia running the new hospitals will have no restrictions on their commercial operations: they will be free to sell insurance policies, long-term care and other health service products such as rehabilitation and convalescence. The progressive downsizing of the acute hospital and community health sectors may lead to piecemeal fragmentation of the NHS, reshaping it as an emergency safety-net service. (Pollock et al., 1998)

As Pollock (1998) has also pointed out, there is no legislative ban on the future privatization of clinical services in PFI hospitals; indeed, the hospitals could perfectly well be sold, with their NHS leases, to (for example) American HMOs.

The 2000 NHS Plan: Reversing the Trend?

The overall effect of all these measures was to create the impression of a National Health System that was gradually failing, while resources were being channelled into a gradually strengthening private heath-care sector. In the short run the results were not spectacular, except for long-term residential care. After an initial flurry of investment in private hospitals in the mid-1980s there was a contraction. US health management organizations that had moved aggressively into the British market moved out again to concentrate on defending themselves in a takeover and merger war at home (they were replaced by French and German companies). Private medical insurance premiums rose as more insured people took advantage of their plans and claimed for treatment, just as private-sector health-care prices rose (partly due to the previous over-investment, with an average bed occupancy rate of only 49 per cent) and as higher-risk categories of insured patients had to be competed for. The PMI market stagnated from 1990 to 1996 and grew only slightly thereafter. If the private sector was to be a real alternative for the middle class, public funding would have to be diverted to it, as had been done with long-term care. The PFI pointed one way towards this end, and there would be others.

In 1997, when the newly elected 'New Labour' government took office, the political climate was not propitious for increased privatization. Support for the NHS in opinion polls might have been 'softer', but it had not significantly declined. But the situation was not stable. The degree of exposure of the NHS to market forces and market culture imposed by the Conservatives implied its continued erosion unless countermeasures were taken. *Laing's Review of Private Health Care* for 1995 commented realistically that 'there continues to be a broad trend throughout the entire healthcare sector towards private finance and private supply' (Laing and Buisson, 1995: 93). The Labour government, while proclaiming itself determined to defend and improve the NHS, had done nothing significant to reverse the trend. Pollock and her colleagues concluded their 1999 review of the impact of the PFI as follows:

> The NHS has already undergone major redefinition with the redrawing of boundaries of responsibility for funding and providing long term care, NHS dentistry, optical services and routine elective care. The private finance initiative continues this trend across the NHS and all public services. (Gaffney et al., 1999c).

Eventually a 'tip-over' point seemed bound to be reached, when the forces pressing for privatization would be sufficiently confident and strong and the forces barring the way would have become too weak to resist.

By late 1999, however, after two years in office during which the Labour government had maintained tight controls on all spending and the NHS had become progressively weaker and more demoralized, the party leadership clearly decided that a radical change of course was needed. The NHS had been Labour's creation; Labour's 'modernizers' might be unhappy with its still fundamentally socialist character but opinion polls showed that it was at the top of voters' concerns and the government could not afford to let it drift towards breakdown. So in March 2000, having accumulated a large budget surplus, the Chancellor of the Exchequer announced an unprecedented increase in NHS spending, averaging 6.1 per cent per annum in real terms from 2000 to 2004.

The new largesse came with strings, however: a new plan, worked out by a team of 110 expert advisers drawn largely from outside the NHS, was put in place at the end of July 2000 (Department of Health, 2000). Its key features included:

- an expansion in the number of acute care beds, reversing the excessive reductions of the previous decade;

- a major expansion in the number of both doctors and nurses;
- the elimination of excessive waiting times for consultations and treatments;
- to this end, a new contract for senior NHS doctors (or 'consultants') that would bar them from undertaking private practice for 'perhaps' the first seven years after they were appointed;
- an increased role for nurses and more opportunities for nurses to train with and in some cases qualify as doctors; and
- a new 'concordat' with the private sector under which both intermediate-care beds in private nursing homes and acute-care facilities in private hospitals would be used for NHS patients, relieving so-called 'bed-blocking' in acute hospitals and easing the pressure on NHS facilities in the annual 'winter crisis' period.

The plan also envisaged, among many other changes, a drastic improvement in patients' record-keeping and in the degree of variation in levels of provision and performance standards throughout the country. In conjunction with the National Institute for Clinical Excellence and the Centre for Health Improvement, already inaugurated under the government's 1997 plan (*The New NHS*), the new plan and the resources being devoted to it clearly represented a very determined effort to rehabilitate the service (or 'modernize' it, to use the government's preferred term).

The spending increases were a huge boost to morale in the NHS and the plan had a largely positive reception from commentators, too. How well it would really work, however, and how far it would reverse the trend to commodification and even privatization, were much harder questions to answer. There was to be renewed pressure to identify costs and generalize best practice, in economic as well as clinical terms, across the service. Senior hospital doctors announced their total opposition to a new contract limiting specialists' freedom to do private practice, and resistance from junior doctors to training with nurses, or ceding tasks to them, could also be expected. And while the new sums on offer sounded and indeed were very large, much of the money would go to making up for years of underfunding, including a vast backlog of building and equipment maintenance, leaving relatively little for net improvement in a hugely complex service in which everything ultimately depended on the skill and commitment of a large and diverse workforce.

As for privatization, the new plan included a decision to make all nursing care free, including nursing care provided in private nursing homes, but not the *non*-nursing costs of patients in such homes. This meant that a new category of patients hitherto receiving free care from the NHS would now be liable for non-nursing charges in private nursing homes. These could include patients discharged into intermediate-care beds in such homes—an estimated 300,000 people a year—creating a major new flow of public funds into the private health-care sector. In such cases the NHS's founding principle of providing health care free at the point of delivery would be saved only by a drastic narrowing of the definition of 'nursing' care. And would this then give rise to an argument for also charging NHS hospital patients for the non-clinical aspects of their care—more and more of which would be provided in any case by the privately employed staff of the new privately owned hospitals that were coming on stream, leased from the PFI consortia? Such speculations take us too far from the facts. All that could fairly be said at the time of writing was that it was not clear that the new plan represented the end of the trend to privatization.

The Conditions of Survival of Public-Sector Health Services

Analysing the determinants of this dynamic is a major challenge for political economy, the nature of which can only be indicated here in very general terms. In the first place, the legal boundaries set by the state between the public and private sectors are crucial. The freedom of the private medical insurance industry to compete with the NHS is a critical factor that distinguishes the British case from the Canadian. The PMI industry has been able to build a significant alternative system, which in 1996 accounted for just under 20 per cent of total hospital and nursing home expenditure in the UK, three-quarters of it in for-profit facilities, and employed 22 per cent of the nurses (Laing and Buisson, 1998: 38, 69). This industry now has a very substantial base for further advance. The incoming Labour government also refused to rule out the private provision of clinical services in PFI hospitals in the future (Pollock, 1998), suggesting either that promises had already been made to permit this or that it was seen as a possible price to be paid for raising more private capital in the future. The scope given in practice to the autonomous Primary Care Groups and trusts will likewise be critically important. Several observers have seen the latter as potential HMOs on the American model, which will be able to use their public funding to build a whole range of new alliances with private-sector providers and insurers (e.g., Pollock 1998; see also Glendinning and Bailey, 1998).

The process of commodification, driven by the internal market in the UK, had several Canadian parallels. Canada, too, had a new breed of hospital managers, under pressure from provincial governments to cut costs using most of the means already adopted in Britain, from hospital closures, mergers, and downsizing to contracting out, staff downgrading ('multi-skilling'), and casualizing. Indeed the scale of the assault in Canada, when it came, seemed almost more severe after so many years of generous provision. In Canada, as in Britain, the boundary between the public and private sectors began to be redrawn as hospitals turned to community fund-raising, business sponsorship, and charity to plug the holes in their financing.[28] Canada, on the other hand, did not try to impose an 'internal market', even in name; and it would be useful to know if the internal market had a stronger tendency to commodify services—to 'bundle' and price them in discrete saleable units—than the 'total quality management' (and the associated obsession with quantitative measurement) favoured by the managers of Canada's nominally independent hospitals (Armstrong and Armstrong, 1996: 121–33). Perhaps these distinctions will prove relatively unimportant. Whatever the structure, however, global market forces are driving commodification everywhere and forcing non-commodified health-care providers to defend their systems by showing that they are cheaper, heart for heart and hip for hip.[29]

What determines whether, when, and how far people become ready to accept commodified treatments in place of health care, and to look to the private sector to provide it, is obviously very complex. One good hypothesis might be that a key barrier to this happening is if the public system is sufficiently well funded to avoid significant rationing and to maintain general confidence in the standard of treatment given. As in other spheres, such as pensions, cutting back public provision drives individuals to look for private sector alternatives. It is noteworthy that while cuts have weakened the Canadian health-care system, at the end of the 1990s the main public reaction—fortified perhaps by awareness of the failings of the US model next door—seemed to be to demand that cuts be restored, not to turn against the system (Ekos Research Associates, 1999). In Britain, by contrast, the medical insurance industry was at that time working optimistically on new 'products', such as offering limited private coverage for modest premiums, to attract middle-class families who were losing confidence in the NHS but whose employers did not give them private coverage and who could not, for the moment, afford the cost of full self-paid medical insurance (Baker, 1998).

In general, the ambient consumerist culture probably militates against publicly provided health care. From this point of view the Canadian system, with its fee-for-service payment system and patient freedom to choose doctors, may well be better adapted than the NHS, with its cost-restraining payment system for family doctors, fixed family doctor patient lists, and no direct access by patients to specialists. The role of the media is also likely to be significant, especially if confidence in the public system is shaken by cuts or for other reasons and if the popular media deliberately seek to accentuate this, as is the case with the right-wing tabloid press in Britain.[30]

The forces determining the role of the health-care labour force are once again complex. The general state of the economy affects union strength. Union organization and leadership can be crucial for the possibility of successful resistance to privatization. Member solidarity is affected by the effectiveness of unions, and by the extent to which alternative employment opportunities exist. Public-sector downsizing may generate resistance, but less so if it is accompanied by private-sector expansion. The central role of the medical profession is key. In Britain, successive governments have sought to reduce the power of senior hospital doctors, producing at first a notable solidarity with other NHS staff in its defence, but over time a weakening of will that could make the medical profession relatively open to further measures of privatization. The central role envisaged for the still formally self-employed family doctors in the new primary care-led NHS could, at least on worst-case assumptions, accelerate this tendency.

Finally, the role of health-care market forces must be understood in a global context. The pharmaceutical industry, the medical equipment industry, the information technology industry, the health management industry, the medical insurance industry, and the legal services industry (to mention only a few) operate globally. In their view, the NHS or any other publicly financed and run system is a potential market to be opened up by a variety of means—lobbying, competition, technological penetration (e.g., 'gifts' of equipment with major current spending implications), advertising. The various markets in which they operate have differing characteristics. Some are dominated by players with strong political assets (e.g., the British construction industry, which has historic links to the Conservative Party, played a key role in promoting the PFI); others are dominated by a small number of players with exceptional market strength (e.g., pharmaceuticals); some have particularly effective political lobbies (see White, 1993). An adequate political-economic analysis of what determines the fate of any health-care system must include an analysis of these—an analysis that in many instances leads away from the national to the global plane.

In this way, the story of the attempt to remake the NHS in the image of private business becomes a chapter in a wider story, in which all public health-care systems, including Canada's, figure. This is not to say that all the changes that have occurred have been driven by external market forces or global corporate pressures, although there has been no shortage of lobbying from both British and American interests. The converse is at least equally true: globalization is the result of a state-led project to restore market society, that is, a society subordinated to market forces, and the assault on publicly provided health care is a stage in the implementation of this project.

In relation to health care, resistance to this project has so far been ineffectual in Britain. From 1980 to 2000 the trade union movement was gravely weakened by industrial job losses, public-sector cutbacks, and anti-union legislation. Unison, the main NHS non-clinical employees union, could not prevent almost half of its members from being transferred into the private sector over the course of these two decades, or prevent the closure of smaller hospitals, even when this mobilized intense local opposition; nor did Unison receive consistent support from the nurses' unions, let alone doctors. Public opinion was tempted by the promise that the internal market would make for efficiency and reduce waiting times for treatment, and that the PFI would make possible the much-needed modernization of hospital buildings. It is possible that public opinion will eventually grasp what is at stake and insist on calling a halt to the commodification of health care. There were some signs of this in Britain at the end of 1999, which undoubtedly influenced the government in committing itself, early the following year, to the previously mentioned dramatic increase in public funding for the NHS.

Failing a serious turnaround in public thinking, however, the project to re-establish a 'market society', including the further commodification of health care, will continue. In that case we will eventually have forgotten what health care was and have become used to the idea that health treatments are commodities like car repairs, among which we must choose and for which we are individually responsible. The link between medicine and science, which was briefly glimpsed in the maturity of publicly provided health-care systems and points so clearly in the direction of the equalization of work, status, and income, as well as health care (Wilkinson, 1996), will have been broken, displaced by the link between medicine and profit. Only those applications of science that yield profitable units of treatment will be developed and implemented. Many people, perhaps most, will be less healthy than they could be, and a growing number will be less healthy than they are now; but the global health-care industry will be in good shape.

Notes

Thanks are due to the Killam Program for financial support for the preparation of this chapter.

1. See Hart (1994: 23, 25, 76–7): 'Britain (before NHS "reform") seems to be the only country so far studied where cholcystectomy [surgical removal of gallstones] rates correlate rationally with local prevalence of gallstones' (p. 77). For Canadian evidence, see Armstrong and Armstrong (1996: 168–72).
2. In 1996 infant mortality per 1,000 live births was 6.0 in Canada, 6.1 in the UK, and 7.8 in the US (OECD, 1998).
3. In 1996 health-care expenditure per capita in purchasing power parity dollars was: UK, $1,317; Canada, $2,065; US, $3,898 (OECD, 1998).
4. Britain's gross domestic product per capital being 20 per cent lower than Canada's, this might seem understandable enough, but nurses and non-clinical staff in the NHS are low-paid by British standards.
5. Data for 1979. They do not include 287,000 health workers making home visits, working in residential homes, etc.
6. The biggest opportunities were enjoyed by surgeons. In 1992 four out of five NHS consultants engaged in some private practice. Of these, most made between £10,000 and £100,000 a year on top of their NHS salaries; 1,300 made between £100,000 and £300,000; 90 made more than £300,000 (Laing and Buisson: 1995, 120, citing a study by the Monopolies and Mergers Commission).
7. For a caustic comment on Enthoven's qualifications and logic, see Hart (1994: 56, 58–61). For slightly conflicting accounts of the genesis of the reforms, and Mrs Thatcher's role in them, see Mohan (1994: 65–7); Webster (1998: 182–92); West (1997: 18–22).
8. Most fundholding general practices were only responsible for the cost of secondary care up to a maximum of £5,000 a year per patient. Costs above this figure were met out of the local Health Authority budget. In other words, the risks continued to be effectively pooled for populations of around a half-million. Tertiary care—i.e., highly specialist treatment for the rarest and most complex conditions—was provided by a few hospitals with independent budgets. Thus, these risks were pooled nationally.

9. Initially, long-term patients had to dispose of all assets above £8,000 to pay for their care before the costs would be met by the local authority. The figure was later doubled to £16,000, but since the average value of a home was about five times this figure, patients still had to sell. The average length of stay in long-term care being about three years, the bulk of the resulting cash balance would still be available for their children at their death, but not only could this cause immediate problems for other members of the family, it had the perverse consequence that if a patient recovered enough to leave nursing home care he or she could well no longer have a home to return to.
10. Private-sector residential care had been expanding rapidly since 1981 under a government policy that allowed people in private homes, but not in local authority-run homes, to claim central government-funded social security payments. Cash-strapped local authorities therefore encouraged people to move into private-sector homes and claim social security support. The 1990 Act made local authorities take over these costs and means-test all future admissions as a condition of using central government funds for them.
11. The distribution of the total of 568,000 places for elderly, chronically ill, and physically and mentally disabled people in the UK in 1996 was: for-profit, 370,000; voluntary sector, 72,000; NHS and local authority combined, 126,000 (Laing and Buisson, 1998: 146).
12. The reality was an often abrupt, budget-driven move from fully funded care in a hospital, which was actually not at all 'faceless' and which for many elderly people had long been their real home, to means-tested care in a strange, often less well-staffed private home, not necessarily even in a community with which the patient had any connection at all. In one instance, aged patients were shipped from a London hospital to a private nursing home in Yorkshire. In a number of cases, only some of which were subsequently investigated, the death rate among these old people, abruptly displaced from their familiar surroundings, rose sharply in the immediately following weeks. A legal challenge to these changes was eventually defeated by the government in the Court of Appeal in the *Mardon House* case, in July 1999 (*Guardian*, 17 July 1999).
13. Estimates vary but Webster (1998: 203) accepts that down to the 1980s administrative costs were 5 per cent of total NHS spending and that by 1997 they were 12 per cent, while 'managers talk of 17 per cent as an eventual target'.
14. I ignore for present purposes 'extra-contractual referrals', which provided a limited safety valve for the pressures this created.
15. Prices need not be closely related to costs. In the early days of the internal market, hospital contracting teams (usually led by financial personnel, not clinicians) had to establish prices with virtually no cost information. It would take years of expensive administrative drudgery to arrive at the situation in American hospitals where the precise cost of every element of treatment, down to the toothpaste supplied to each patient, could be built into the price (see Armstrong and Armstrong, 1998: 66) for treatments like hip replacements. NHS trust hospitals could

take the prices charged in the private sector as a guide and just charge 20 per cent less.

16. In Britain in 1992 an estimated 1.3 million people, nearly all women, one-third of whom were themselves ill as well as elderly, devoted 20 hours a week or more to providing unpaid care to others, nearly all relatives, who were unable to look after themselves. The situation had not changed significantly since Hart's summary of the situation in the mid-1980s, which makes painful reading (Hart, 1988: 266–9; see also Walker, 1997).
17. At the last count 40 per cent of all food expenditure in the US was on eating out or takeout meals.
18. The first serious attempt to rebuild Britain's lamentably decrepit stock of hospitals, many of them inherited from the Victorian era, was initiated in a 1962 plan comprising 224 building schemes; but down to 1999 only a third were completed and another third partially completed. 'Between 1980 and 1997, only seven public schemes costing more than £25 million were completed' (Gaffney et al., 1999a).
19. According to K. Milne (cited in Fierlbeck, 1996: 536), a majority of GP fundholders polled in 1995 were actually opposed to the 'reforms'.
20. 'Forty years is a long time to go on feeling grateful for gifts you have already paid for with taxes. People . . . know very well that the charm of shop assistants is superficial, motivated more by bonus payments for sales than by personal concern for the customer, but they prefer being valued only as consumers, to not being valued at all' (Hart, 1994: 32).
21. A minor but significant source of resentment is that nurses are not paid anything extra for working in private patient wards, units, or theatres, while the physicians and surgeons involved charge fees (on top of their salaries) at extraordinarily high rates—higher than in any other major country for which reliable fee data exist, including Canada, the US, Germany, and Australia (Laing, 1992).
22. The BMA originally opposed the introduction of the NHS in 1946 and now opposed its dismantling. At its 1999 annual conference its chairman accused the Prime Minister, Tony Blair, of alienating the entire medical profession. Blair in effect replied that the BMA was unrepresentative of the profession (*Guardian*, 8 July 1999).
23. Hart (1988, 1994) shows very persuasively that the scientific evidence now indicates clearly that the key to real improvements in both the quality and length of life is not the current concentration on high-tech treatments but the careful joint *management* of chronic illness by a new kind of collaboration among patients, doctors, and other health professionals. It is likely to come as something of a surprise to most laymen (and perhaps even some doctors?), for example, to read that there is no evidence that heart attack victims' survival chances are any better in hospitals equipped with high-tech intensive-care units than in those without.
24. This concession, made at the instigation of Mrs Thatcher, proved ineffective and was withdrawn in 1997.

25. For the practical problems involved in this, see Heald and Scott (1996). For the political dimension of the way the NHS hospitals were obliged to amortize their imputed debt on private-sector terms even though their other operations were controlled so as to make them unable to meet those terms, see Shaoul (1996); Gaffney et al. (1999a, 1999b).
26. Virtually all the serious critical research on the PFI in the NHS has been carried out by a small group of scholars led by Professor Allyson Pollock at the School of Public Policy, University College, London. A series of four articles in the *British Medical Journal* in July 1999 (Gaffney et al., 1999a, 1999b, and 1999c; Pollock et al. 1999) summarized much of this work and are the source for the following discussion.
27. For a succinct summary of the PFI controversy, see Kelly (1997). See also Ham (1995: 415-16): 'The private finance initiative is . . . beginning to affect the mainstream of NHS provision . . . as lawyers, financial advisers, and consultants search for creative solutions as they scent the prospect of profits from the increasing commercialisation of health care. Those providing private finance and putting their investment at risk will not expect to play a passive part in the management of services, and they will no doubt take a close interest in the appointment and performance of trust managers.'
28. For the effects on the NHS of dependence on charity, see Lattimer (1996).
29. A health policy consultant in London told me of a meeting with a group of directors from a New York hospital who came to England in search of hip replacement patients to help boost revenue. My informant was happy to be able to tell them that hip replacement in the NHS cost less than the price of the return airfare to New York; this was at least a mild exaggeration, but the fact that there was a quotable price is still significant.
30. In 1998 the Fraser Institute, with press assistance, tried to whip up fears of lengthening waiting times in Canada. The evidence for this, however, was nonexistent (see McDonald et al., 1998).

References

Armstrong, P., and H. Armstrong. 1996. *Wasting Away: The Undermining of Canadian Health Care*. Toronto: Oxford University Press.

——— and ———. 1998. *Universal Health Care*. New York: New Press.

Audit Commission. 1995. *The Doctors' Tale: The Work of Hospital Doctors in England and Wales*. London: HMSO.

Baker, T. 1998. Norwich Union Healthcare, interview, 22 May.

Baggott, R. 1994. *Health and Health Care in Britain*. London: Macmillan.

Department of Health. 2000. *The NHS Plan*. Command 8418–1.

Ekos Research Associates. 1999. 'Rethinking Government IV', National Conference on Home Care.

Fierlbeck, K. 1996. 'Policy and ideology: The politics of post-reform health policy in the United Kingdom', *International Journal of Health Services* 26, 3: 529–46.

Gaffney, D., and A. Pollock. 1997. *Can the NHS Afford the Private Finance Initiative?* London: BMA Health Policy and Economic Research Unit.

———, ———, D. Price, and J. Shaoul. 1999a. 'The private finance initiative: NHS capital expenditure and the private finance initiative—expansion or implosion?', *British Medical Journal* 319: 48–51.

———, ———, ———, and ———. 1999b. 'The private finance initiative: PFI in the NHS—is there an economic case?', *British Medical Journal* 319: 116–19.

———, ———, ———, and ———. 1999d. 'The politics of the private finance initiative and the new NHS', *British Medical Journal* 319: 249–53.

Glendinning, C., and J. Bailey. 1998. 'The private sector and the NHS: The case of capital developments in primary healthcare', *Policy and Politics* 26: 387–99.

Goodwin, N. 1996. 'GP fundholding: A review of the evidence', in *Health Care UK 1995/96*. London: The King's Fund.

Ham, C. 1995. *British Medical Journal* 310 (18 Feb.): 415–16.

Hart, J.T. 1988. *A New Kind of Doctor*. London: Merlin.

———. 1994. *Feasible Socialism: The National Health Service: Past, Present and Future*. London: Socialist Health Association.

Heald, D., and D.A. Scott. 1996. 'NHS capital charging after five years', in *Health Care UK 1995–96*. London: The King's Fund, 131–40.

Health Policy Network. 1995. *In Practice: The NHS Market*. London.

Kelly, J. 1997. 'Private finance guide', *Health Service Journal* (27 Feb.): 16.

Laing, W. 1992. *Healthcare Report: UK Private Specialists' Fees—Is the Price Right?* Eastleigh, Hampshire: Norwich Union Healthcare.

Laing and Buisson. 1995, 1996, 1998. *Laing's Review of Private Health Care*.

Lattimer, M. 1996. *The Gift of Health: The NHS, Charity and the Mixed Economy of Healthcare*. London: Directory of Social Change.

Matsaganis, M., and H. Glennerster. 1994. 'Cream-skimming and fundholding', in W. Bartlett et al., eds, *Quasi-Markets and the Welfare State*. Bristol: School for Advanced Urban Studies.

McDonald, P., et al. 1998. *Waiting Lists and Waiting Times for Health Care in Canada*.

McLeod-Dick, I. 1997. *Health Care Reform in Ontario Hospitals During 1994 to 1996*. Toronto: Schulich School of Business, York University.

Mohan, J. 1995. *A National Health Service? The Restructuring of Health Care in Britain Since 1979*. London, Macmillan.

Organization for Economic Co-operation and Development. 1998. *OECD Health Data 1998*. Paris: OECD.

Pollock, A.M. 1998. 'Primary Care—From Fundholding to Health Maintenance Organisations?', unpublished paper.

———, M. Dunnigan, D. Gaffney, D. Price, and J. Shoul. 1999. 'The private finance initiative: Planning the "new" NHS: downsizing for the 21st century', *British Medical Journal* 319: 179–84.

———, D. Gaffney, and M. Dunnigan. 1998. 'Public health and the private finance initiative', *Journal of Public Health Medicine* 20, 1: 1–2.

Radical Statistics Group. 1995. 'NHS "indicators of success": What do they tell us?', *British Medical Journal* 310 (22 Apr.): 1045–50.

Robinson, R., and J. Le Grand, eds. 1993. *Evaluating the NHS Reforms*. London: The King's Fund.

Shaoul, J. 1996. 'A capital way of accounting', unpublished paper, Department of Accounting and Finance, University of Manchester.

Snell, J. 1998. 'When the going gets tough', *Health Service Journal* (26 Feb.): 28–30.

Walker, D. 1997. 'Community care: Past, present and future', in S. Iliffe and J. Munro, eds. *Healthy Choices: Future Options for the NHS*. London: Lawrence and Wishart.

Webster, C. 1998. *The National Health Service: A Political History*. Oxford: Oxford University Press.

West, P. 1997. *Understanding the National Health Service Reforms: The Creation of Incentives?* Buckingham: Open University Press.

White, G. 1993. 'Towards a political analysis of markets', *IDS Bulletin* 24 3: 4–11.

Wilkinson, R. 1996. *Unhealthy Societies*. London: Routledge.

World Bank. 1993. *Investing in Health: World Development Report*. Washington: World Bank.

Yates, J. 1995. *Private Eye, Heart and Hip: Surgical Consultants, the National Health Service and Private Medicine*. Edinburgh: Churchill Livingstone.

PART TWO

Locating Evidence

Evidence-based everything is the new panacea for the millennium. The National Forum on Health 'believes that one of the key goals of the health sector in the 21st century should be the establishment of a culture of evidence-based decision-making' (National Forum on Health, 1997: ch. 5, 3). Indeed, the adoption of such a culture seems to be well under way. According to the newsletter of the Canadian Health Services Research Foundation (1999: 1), 'Across Canada, interest in indicators that measure the performance of regional health authorities, integrate health systems, physicians' services, and other health care services and systems is mushrooming.'

This move to evidence-based decision-making in all areas of health care is strongly promoted by the huge infusion of federal government money into the Canadian Institute for Health Information, the Canadian Health Services Research Foundation, and the Canadian Institutes for Health Research and by provincial support for various research organizations, such as the Manitoba Centre for Policy and Evaluation and Ontario's Institute for Clinical Evaluative Sciences. Under these umbrellas, what constitutes evidence is often assumed rather than defined and the central notion is that all treatments, as well as the services that deliver them, will be based on 'proven' methods.

It is difficult to oppose a call for the use of evidence in health-care service delivery, especially when it promises to improve quality and accountability, access and choice. The commitment to research funding seems particularly attractive given the new emphasis on integrating social sciences and humanities into traditional biomedical approaches. However, a political economy approach would suggest caution in accepting the claims for evidence-based decision-making. For political economists, the central questions about evidence in health care are similar to those raised about the economy as a whole: Who benefits, who determines what counts as evidence, and how is evidence created, valued, structured, interpreted, and used in this particular time and place? And, within each question, political economists are looking for contradictions, especially those that contribute to and reflect resistance to the dominant forces or directions.

A political economy analysis of the production and use of evidence begins with the social relations and material conditions in which knowledge is defined, created, and employed. O'Connor's *The Fiscal Crisis of the State* drew attention to roles states play in setting the stage. For O'Connor (1973: 6), states in capitalist societies 'fulfill two basic and often contradictory functions—accumulation and legitimation'. States provide the infrastructure that makes stable profits possible. They also help to ensure that the system of production for profit is itself understood as the only way to live, as the common-sense way of organizing societies.

This legitimation function may require limits on capital or even, at times, conflict with the interests of various parts of capital. In Canada, the state infrastructure has included payment for health care and controls on profit-making in the health-care industry. As O'Connor suggests, the effects are contradictory. State support for public care reduces employers' expenditures on health. Indeed, the public health-care system has been identified as a key factor in Canada's international competitiveness. At the same time, however, the largely non-profit, publicly funded system has encouraged notions of shared responsibility and risk while providing an example of how non-market services can work to reduce inequality and increase access. It has also provided many decent, paid jobs, especially for women, as state funding contributed to the commodification of many women's tasks. In other words, public health care not only legitimates existing relations but also provides an example of an alternative to for-profit services and to the individual responsibility at the heart of market economies. In addition, it has contributed to the conditions that made it possible for women successfully to demand improved work relations.

The contradictions that O'Connor identified have, in recent years, disappeared in some areas as states collapse their legitimation and accumulation functions. Increasingly, support for accumulation has become the main legitimate function of the state. The business of the government is business. The public education system provides just one example. In Chapter 5, on the 'not-so-hidden curriculum', Linda Muzzin shows how pharmaceutical sciences in state-funded universities offer students particular ways of seeing that support the drug industries. State-supported partnerships with business, encouraged by cutbacks in state funding, permeate the curriculum and the research that produces the evidence. Yet even here, there are signs of contradiction and resistance. Students complain that their education does not give them 'the space, scope, or opportunity to explore different avenues'.

Strong popular support for health care continues even in the face of growing media talk of crisis, of demographic pressures that will overburden public care, and of the merits in private care. Such popular support helps to ensure that politicians cannot get elected without swearing their commitment to the principles of the Canada Health Act. At the same time, all governments face enormous pressure from international organizations and corporations to allow profit-making in the 'unopened oyster' of Canadian health care. And many public decision-makers share with these organizations and corporations a fundamental belief in market forces.

The new emphasis on evidence-based decision-making may help to reduce this contradiction by transforming many political decisions into technical ones to be made by experts in a manner that makes profit easier to achieve. Population health, report cards, and surveys of patient satisfaction are presented as objective means of deciding about care. But, as Pat Armstrong points out in Chapter 6, context matters in developing and using such evidence, as well as in creating the conditions for health. And this context is not only characterized by inequalities but dominated mainly by white men searching for profit. Under these conditions, the social determinants of health initially identified as created by the organization of political economies are increasingly defined as individual problems of employment, lack of social support, and so on. In their insightful and thorough critique of the population health approach, Blake Poland, David Coburn, Ann Robertson, and Joan Eakin, along with others from the critical social science group (1998: 793), stress the importance of 'joining explanation for the social determinants of health with the explanation of the social determinants of care'. This means starting with the assumption that 'Canada is a capitalist society with a specific history and a particular location in the continental world capitalist economy'. It means a political economy approach, but one, as Eric Mykhalovskiy points out in Chapter 7, that understands the 'organization of knowledge about health care around numericalization and aggregation represents more than technical advancement; it holds implications for how health-care services are understood, organized, and delivered.'

Political economists certainly have asked similar questions of evidence applied to other parts of the economy. In *Labor and Monopoly Capital* (1974), Harry Braverman carefully analysed Frederick Taylor's 'scientific management' in goods production. Like the new evidence-based decision-making in health care, Taylor's approach to organizing work was defined as an objective, technical exercise that promoted efficiency. Such efficiency was presented as benefiting management and workers alike, in much the same way as evidence is now talked about as a necessary good for all. Yet Braverman showed quite clearly that the main purpose of the exercise was to increase managerial control through the separation of conception from execution. Taylor's effort to break down work by precisely measuring and counting each aspect was designed to allow managers to divide jobs into small tasks that could be quickly learned by readily replaceable workers. In the process, workers lost the skills that not only gave them pride and satisfaction in their work but also the power that their skills provided.

Today in health care, more than a half-century after Taylor did his research, the work of care providers is being similarly measured, similarly divided up, and similarly transferred to quickly trained providers. A vast amount of management literature leaves little doubt about the source of such ideas in health reform. For example, in *Leading the Health Care Revolution* (1996: 35), a publication of the American College of Healthcare Executives, Kissler traces the new management to Taylor and sets out what he sees as Taylor's defining contribution: 'His approach, scientific management, had as its basic tenet the idea that, through careful analysis, work could be broken down into essential elements. Moreover, by forcing strict adherence to a prescribed set of efficient steps, productivity could be increased.' What limited Taylor, Kissler (1996: 37) goes on to explain, was the technical capacity to manage data. This has been solved by the new computers, making it possible to apply Taylor's approach quickly and easily throughout health care. Evidence-based decision-making in management often means the Taylorism that Braverman so effectively analysed. However, Mykhalovskiy cautions that what he calls the 'Taylor metaphor' may hide the features of health care that 'have a distinct development and social form'. Health care has different relations and conditions than those in manufacturing industries, and these differences alter significantly the possibilities for scientific management techniques. Mykhalovskiy argues that 'the contemporary evaluation of medical practice is concerned with the construction of the patient as a rational consumer and with furnishing a knowledge for use in government, hospitals, and other sites of professional work to manage new problems of inefficiency'.

There are other limits to Braverman's analysis. His critique of Taylor has been criticized for failing to recognize the contradictory nature of skill development, particularly the emergence of new skills as other skills are reduced and the role employees play in both resisting and constructing work reorganization (Beechey, 1982). Equally important, Braverman, like O'Connor, paid scant attention to the gendered nature of work and even less to the connection between households and formal economies. For Braverman skills were concrete and agreed-upon capacities valued by both workers and employers but used differently by both. The socially constructed and gendered value of skills was not part of his account. As Pat Armstrong makes clear in Chapter 6, these issues are especially relevant in health care, where women constitute 80 per cent of the paid workforce and a similar proportion of those doing the unpaid work in the household. Women also account for the majority of the patients, making up three-quarters of those in long-term care.

Jacqueline Choiniere's (1993) research reveals how many nurses initially supported the attempt to measure their tasks. They did so because they were convinced that such measures would expose their heavy workloads and the skilled nature of their work. The nurses were right about the first run at measurement, at least in terms of the evidence demonstrating how hard they worked. It did indicate that nurses were working '120 per cent' (Armstrong et al., 1994: 81). Similarly, the nurses often supported the off-loading of specific tasks that would allow them more time for complicated care work. In other words, they saw it as a process for allowing them to focus on the most skilled aspects of the work. Nurses also supported the development of critical care pathways setting out in detail what was to be done for patients because many of them saw these pathways as freeing them from the need to obtain the doctor's permission for a range of interventions.

What the nurses failed to recognize until later was that the purpose was not to ensure that there were enough workers to do the work. Rather, the purpose was both to increase productivity through a 'prescribed set of efficiency steps' that limit nurses' control and to deskill aspects of the job in order to assign much of nursing work to what are often called generic workers. Nor was the project simply a matter of objective measurement. What initially appeared as nurses working at 120 per cent became, through a manipulation of the formulas, nurses working at '90 per cent' (ibid.). In addition, the measuring left out the care that is a central integrating component of their work. It disappeared in part because it was difficult to measure and in part because the skills are undervalued and invisible as a result of their link to women in and out of the labour force. Invisibility and undervaluing were not only factors in the measurement and assignment of tasks in the paid workforce. They also influenced strategies designed to shift care to households, a shift often described as community care but in fact home care by women never formally trained in the skills required and seldom paid for the work. Even when care in households is done by paid providers, the tasks for which people are trained have been broken down into their 'efficiency elements' and defined as quickly learned or simply what any woman can do.

Increasingly, these strategies are explicitly defined as derived from Taylor, along with some input from the new managerial strategies such as Total Quality Management. The work of Braverman and his critics provides a way of initiating an analysis of the processes in this kind of evidence-based decision-making. But such an analysis must pay attention to the nature of care for people in this particular time and place, to the gendered nature of power and to the role of the state in mediating relations between households and formal economies, as well as those between the state and capital. It must also recognize the contradictory elements in the application of Taylor-like techniques, as well as the context in which they are employed and the ways they are resisted. Some nurses have acquired more skill and power through patient care pathways, for example, and many women have been willing to take action against employers or the state, not because they seek more benefits for themselves, but rather because they want to defend the right to care. And many groups have used evidence to support their demands for greater equality and a greater share of power. Equally important, such an analysis must recognize the new techniques and constructions that are part of the new evidence-based decision-making, ones that owe little to Taylor's ideas of scientific management.

Dorothy Smith's notion of relations of ruling offers one means of exploring these contradictory and complex developments within the context of specific institutional arrangements (Smith, 1990a, 1990b). This perspective guides Muzzin's examination in Chapter 5 of the everyday practices in pharmacy education and allows her to reveal how 'the topics covered (and the decontextualized way in which they are presented) can be clearly linked to the research and the marketing interests of the pharmaceutical industry, rather than to "neutral" science.' Mykalovskiy also draws on Smith, among others. This approach allows him to explore health services research 'as a practical exercise of power, as an activity that helps order action in health care through the questions it asks and the forms of visibility of health care it offers, all of which are a consequence of a particular configuration of calculative practices, narrative strategies, and forms of expertise.'

One of the difficulties in understanding evidence is that many kinds of evidence are produced and used in health and health-care work. Some, such as the population health data, become the basis for both systemic reform and for changes in individual practices. Some, such as workload measurements, become the basis for defining what work needs to be done by whom and how many need to do it within the institutions, although these data, too, may be used for more system-wide calculations. Some, such as outcomes data, presume to determine what is effective and what is not in providing care. But there are common characteristics. Most of this evidence is eventually presented as numbers, in part because numerical data can be collected and processed readily by the new technologies. In the end, it is decontextualized and simplified. In the process, differences, complexities, and contradictions disappear. It is the job of political economy to locate evidence in all its specificity. It is a job that has barely begun.

References

Armstrong, P., H. Armstrong, J. Choiniere, G. Feldberg, and J. White. 1994. *Take Care: Warning Signals for Canada's Health System*. Toronto: Garamond.

Beechey, V. 1982. 'The sexual division of labour and the labour process: A critical assessment of Braverman', in Stephen Wood, ed., *The Degradation of Work? Skill, Deskilling and the Labour Process*. London: Hutchinson, 54–73.

Braverman, H. 1971. *Labor and Monopoly Capital: The Degradation of Work in the Twentieth Century*. New York: Monthly Review Press.

Canadian Health Services Research Foundation. 1999. *Newsletter* (Winter).

Choiniere, J. 1993. 'A case study examination of nurses and patient information technology', in P. Armstrong, Choiniere, and E. Day, *Vital Signs: Nursing in Transition*. Toronto: Garamond, 59–87.

Kissler, G.D. 1996. *Leading the Health Care Revolution*. Chicago: American College of Healthcare Executives.

National Forum on Health. 1997. *Canada Health Action: Building on the Legacy*, vol. 2. Ottawa: National Forum on Health.

O'Connor, James. 1973. *The Fiscal Crisis of the State*. New York: St Martin's Press.

Poland, B., D. Coburn, A. Robertson, and J. Eakin, and members of the Critical Social Science Group. 1998. 'Wealth, equity and health care: A critique of a "population health" perspective on the determinants of health', *Social Science and Medicine* 46, 7: 785–98.

Smith, D.E. 1990a. *The Conceptual Practices of Power: A Feminist Sociology of Knowledge*. Toronto: University of Toronto Press.

———. 1990b. *Texts, Facts and Femininity: Exploring the Relations of Ruling*. London: Routledge.

CHAPTER 5

Academic Capitalism and the Hidden Curriculum in the Pharmaceutical Sciences

Linda Muzzin

Introduction

In *Ideology and Curriculum*, Michael Apple (1990) suggested that a close examination of the dynamics of education reveals a 'hidden school curriculum' by which children are taught to be compliant and non-critical in their thinking as part of their preparation for the world of waged work. Apple's characterization of educational institutions is that they 'help create people (with the appropriate meanings and values) who see no other serious possibility to the economic and cultural assemblage now extant' (ibid., 6). Similar processes operate in our university-based professional schools. I will use the example of the pharmaceutical sciences because my familiarity with the everyday routine in this field enables me to begin what Smith (1987, 1994) calls an 'institutional ethnography' of the particular program in which I taught for eight years. In advocating such an approach, Smith, like Apple, has argued that it is not acceptable for sociologists to present sociological reasoning as a set of 'mystical connections' without grounding their work in an examination of everyday events and texts, where relations of ruling are manifested. The approach she advocates involves a critical examination of the institutional context, including institutional policies, within which work is accomplished. An understanding of 'how things work' should be informed by an analysis of the 'invisible work' that takes place within such settings.

Apple and Smith question the 'claim to neutrality' represented in the work of economists and other social scientists who do not reflect on and declare their political standpoints. Apple debunks their claims of neutrality and steers us away from an approach of 'standing above' what he calls this 'withered' idea of a society, which 'makes it nearly impossible for educators and others to develop a potent analysis of widespread social and economic justice' (Apple, 1990: 10). Instead, he invites us to examine critically the moment-to-moment knowledge production of educators as well as to declare commitment to a completely different set of values than are implicit in these 'neutral' curricula. He calls for declaration of our commitment to 'a social order that has at its very foundation not the accumulation of goods, profits and credentials, but the maximization of economic, social and educational equality' (ibid., 11).

In the eyes of our students and in the rhetoric of governments, the main function of the modern university is to train young people for work, and, since at least two-thirds of the resources of research-oriented universities in Canada are controlled by professional faculties such as law, engineering, business, medicine, and other health professions, it follows that universities are largely in the business of training young people for the professions. While some have argued that this is an inappropriate role for our universities, I am not one of them. I have a strong commitment to contributing to providing those who serve us as professionals with a broadly based education, including a concentration on professional ethics and the values of an anti-racist society. In this respect, I feel that it is entirely appropriate that future practitioners attend universities where they can learn to think critically about the structures and practices of power in our world. However, students of the professional program in which I participated for eight years—that is, a faculty of pharmacy—protested that the curriculum they encountered attempted to narrow, rather than broaden, their minds and hearts through concentrating almost exclusively on molecules rather than health.

The rationale for the molecular concentration was to provide the basis for understanding the drugs being dispensed by the pharmacist. Who better to teach this science than those professors at the 'cutting edge' of research in the pharmaceutical sciences? But without a context for practice, the students saw themselves required to learn about the research interests of their basic science professors rather than what they needed to know as health professionals. 'Cutting edge' research in the pharmaceutical sciences pursued by faculty operating in a 'publish or perish' scenario to gain tenure/promotion is potentially of great interest to global pharmaceutical firms, even if it does not always interest students in the professions. Thus, the attempt to make the curriculum more relevant to pharmacy practice and to promote 'patient-centred care' that occurred in my school between 1989 and 1994 was, in its challenge to the molecular component of the curriculum, quite a revolutionary movement.

The apparent movement away from molecules in pharmacy education that occurred in the 1990s is, according to pharmacists, the creation of two American educators, Linda Strand and Charles Hepler (Hepler and Strand, 1990). I have suggested elsewhere that this 'pharmaceutical care' movement in pharmacy education is the latest in a series of professional ideologies adopted by pharmacy in response to the appropriation of much of the profession's 'turf' by medicine and the pharmaceutical industry. In other words, each time professional turf has been lost historically (first to medicine, second to the pharmaceutical industry, and most recently to large chains), resulting in a further proletarianization or deskilling of pharmacy work, the profession has responded with a 'reprofessionalization' project. In the 1930s, the 'project' was hospital pharmacy; in the 1960s, it was 'clinical pharmacy'; and in the 1990s, it is 'pharmaceutical care', or what Peter Morley calls 'patient-driven care'.[1]

Despite the appearance of change towards more clinical content in the curriculum, the 'Toronto experiment' was a case of 'dynamics without change' (a model originally proposed by Alford, 1975), in that the renewed clinical emphasis provided little dilution of the molecular concentration in the curriculum. Further, the added emphasis on pharmaceutical care excluded all but the drug-related aspects of the cases being considered by students, stripping away any contextual considerations. Such a decontextualized curriculum, I believe, is part and parcel of how science is taught in capitalist society. The goal is to produce compliant pharmacists who will unproblematically promote drugs rather than health.

My analysis of both old and new curricula in the Toronto pharmacy faculty leads to the conclusion that the 'hidden curriculum' is easy to see when the curriculum is viewed from a critical perspective. The topics covered (and the decontextualized way in which they are presented) can be clearly linked to the research and marketing interests of the pharmaceutical industry, rather than to 'neutral' science or the promotion of health. In fact, an examination of the pharmacy (and medical) curriculum reveals just how much the pharmaceutical industry shapes all of health care through the use of prescription and non-prescription drugs. The addition of a reductionist clinical and pharmaco-economic emphasis to the curriculum, which I will be examining here (with its undeclared commitment to corporate efficiency and a reduced scope of practice concentrating only on *drugs*), can be seen as an appropriation of *social* science by pharmaceutical interests. That is, social science is presented as the promotion of appropriate drug use rather than as social justice, parallel to the appropriation of curiosity-driven science and its reduction of the maintenance of health to the production and use of synthetically produced drugs.

The Many Faces of Academic Capitalism

The topic of academic capitalism in its various forms is not a new one in North American scholarly circles (Brown, 1979; Noble, 1977; Newson and Buchbinder, 1986), although the volume of literature on this trend has increased exponentially in the past decade (Currie and Newson, 1998; Bell and Jones, 1992; Bell and Sadlak, 1992; Peters and Etzkowitz, 1990; Slaughter and Leslie, 1997; Shumar, 1997). It was particularly easy to see some of the ways in which pharmaceutical corporations influenced post-secondary education in the academic unit where I worked. Two of my fellow faculty were executives of drug companies. An entire building was built by Shoppers Drug Mart, a company chiefly owned by the largest tobacco company in the world. Like other pharmacy schools and faculties in Canada, all the doors of this building and even the elevator were adorned with plaques advertising the generosity of transnational corporate funders. Clinical material used in class was, in many cases, written by contract to, and bore the logo of, a drug company. Conferences were little more than trade shows. Whole laboratories of the scientist-professors in the academic unit were renovated by drug companies, and the research that they did, while mostly funded by federal government grants, was also indirectly steered by the pharmaceutical industry. Most of my colleagues and most graduate students in the unit believed that the main purpose of graduate studies was to prepare graduates for work in the pharmaceutical manufacturing industry. The undergraduates, who would mostly become pharmacists, were minor players.

It might be argued that pharmacy represents an anomaly at the university, both in its molecular reductionistic curriculum and in the clear influence of the industry on this curriculum. But pharmaceutical education is very similar to medical education and education for other professions in that their curricula are typically bifurcated. In the health professions, the bifurcation can be seen to reflect a split between 'caring' and 'curing', with the 'curing' portion of the curriculum closely tied to industrial research agendas.[2] This observation that the science conducted at our universities is incongruous with the education of health professionals has been a theme re-emerging periodically in the critical literature on the professions. Samuel Bloom (1988), for example, linked the basic science emphasis in medical education to the need for basic scientists to carry out pharmaceutical research to maintain the research component of university funding, the same dynamic that underlies pharmaceutical education. Researchers in the two areas do the same kind of investigations, which are directly and indirectly funded by transnational corporations (e.g., in pharmacology, toxicology, immunology, etc.). Further, the way in which professors, university administrators, and the governments who fund them approach their work is saturated with 'corporate-think', a way of thinking that links traditional scientific values such as simplicity, efficiency, results, and outcomes with slogans and subservience to the 'reality of capitalist society'. Corporate-think also undergirds the pragmatism of some faculty members in building their international stature on the goals of these transnational corporations, despite the appalling record of these corporations with respect to the environment, our health, and global justice.

Bloom has argued that despite repeated modifications of medical curricula to 'humanize' them in the past 75 years, they remain essentially the same. This point could be generalized because of the global hegemony of scientific medicine. Bloom traces this 'dynamics without change' to 'the concentration of academic medicine on a scientific mission that has crowded out its social responsibility to train physicians for the society's most basic needs in the delivery of health care.' He characterizes medical education as a contradictory mix of reductionist science and what he calls the 'social ecology' challenge to reductionism. Good and Good (1993) also note this dichotomy, in which caring is as important as curing. The dichotomy, Bloom says, reflects the *competition* for resources between scientific research and professional education. In the growing climate of academic retrenchment that accompanies economic globalization, the medical school, along with other professional schools, such as law, engineering, and pharmacy, is forced to depend on and be influenced by external groups. In the health professions, a major source of support for educational development comes from those who fund university scientific research. In the United States, as elsewhere, this has meant the crowding out of the medical school curriculum much of the community-oriented primary-care perspectives that were popular in the 1960s and 1970s.

The emphasis on high-technology specialization is congruent with the direction of pharmaceutical profit-making. In the US, drug companies have even been able to 'create' academic medical departments within hospitals, where research on molecules of interest to them would be conducted. In Toronto, the situation involves setting up research institutes alongside or inside teaching hospitals. The pharmaceutical industry is eager to fund chairs in particular specialties (e.g., cardiology, neurology, and immunology, areas in which many profitable drugs are in use and development). Although not many scientists are happy with the arrangements forged in such medical curricula, Bloom concludes that 'the financial gain for each party has driven the process inexorably forward.' The consequences are that caring becomes what Bloom calls 'window dressing' for molecular research and the *business* of patient care. Not all are compliant in the pharmaceutical world. Resistance to this appropriation comes from the students, the scientists, the professors, health professionals (including pharmacists), the surrounding community, the media, and politicians. After analysing recent changes in the pharmacy curriculum, I will describe some of this largely invisible resistance, not with the goal of creating a heroic counter-discourse, but only to detail the complexity of what takes place daily in these settings.

Since Bloom wrote his article, it can be argued that the influence of both home-grown and transnational drug manufacturing corporations has grown substantially. There are many reasons for this trend. Most importantly, industrial support for basic science research has been pursued with increasing vigour as Medical Research Council (MRC) funding has been curtailed. In 1995, for example, the MRC and the administration of the University of Toronto jointly issued an invitation with the generic drug company, Apotex, to 'celebrate the announcement of the single largest university/industry research grant ever awarded in Canada through the Medical Research Council to the University of Toronto.' The grant was for $5 million. In the same mailout to university faculty, an invitation was extended to attend a presentation by the 1994 Nobel laureate in chemistry in the 'Distinguished Scientist Lecture Series' at the Apotex Training Centre in north Toronto. These announcements were not unusual, but only two of a continuing series of research projects, special events, and publications 'made possible by our sponsors'. And what is wrong with a little sponsorship?[3]

To answer this question, it is worth a brief diversion to illustrate the state of current university-corporate relationships in Canada. Although such arrangements are typically hidden from public view, the ethics of such drug company sponsorship recently came under intense public scrutiny for a two-year period. A well-respected researcher, Nancy Olivieri, for reasons of patient safety, decided to discontinue a drug trial of deferiprone being conducted at the Hospital for Sick Children (HSC) in late 1996, resulting in termination of the research agreement by Apotex and the threat of legal action. Although a 'gag order' prohibiting publication of the results of the trial had been part of the agreement, Olivieri published her results in the *New England Journal of Medicine* in August 1998. As voluminous media coverage emphasized, such gag orders are incompatible with both patient safety in such trials and the process of science, and merely protect the interest of the corporate firms that demand them. Further, the university and its teaching hospital at first did not step in to protect the scientist involved. Thus, Olivieri filed a grievance against the University of Toronto administration in December 1998 for failing to protect the academic freedom of a faculty member. The following month, she was demoted from her position as head of hemoglobinopathy at HSC and finally agreed to move to the Toronto Hospital to run the pediatric and adult hemoglobinopathy programs there. Internal university memos and media coverage suggested that the issues were settled to everyone's satisfaction and that new conflict-of-interest policies at the university would preclude such events from ever happening again. My own prediction, however, is that this is unlikely, given the increasing dependence of the university on corporate funding and the incompatibility of academic and corporate values.

Since 1995, the University of Toronto, foremost among Canadian universities, has been trend-setting in its pursuit of industry support. One national newspaper, the *Globe and Mail*, is typically seen as oriented towards corporate interests, but even one of its reporters has raised questions about the propriety of these arrangements (Cole, 1998), echoing concerns expressed by faculty about academic freedom.[4] Specifically, there are concerns that faculty hired under these agreements might be beholden to the sponsors at the time of tenure review. But even if such direct influence did not exist, one might speculate that anyone hired under such an arrangement would feel some gratitude for his or her position and might pursue interests relevant to the firm's niche rather than interests in other areas. Further, it might be expected that such a faculty member might link his or her research interests with his or her teaching in such a way that students would learn about these new directions being taken in pharmaceutical research. The Olivieri case notwithstanding, it might be asked whether such a professor is in any position to be able to perform the task that I am performing in this chapter: that is, to question the current economic and cultural assemblage.

Constructing a Hidden Curriculum in the Pharmaceutical Sciences

Like research at the university, classroom teaching, graduate supervision, and other instruction are largely hidden from public scrutiny. It might be possible, by recording observations of faculty and their students, to reconstruct how teaching and learning are subtly steered to promote topics of interest to pharmaceutical firms and suppress any critique of them.[5] Such a reconstruction, however, is a laborious task for detailing how pharmaceutical industry interests are daily woven into the teaching of pharmacy students.

How, then, can we do what Apple and Smith encourage us to do more simply? At hand is a starting point publicly available to anyone who wants to examine it. The result of steering effects over decades is evident in the published pharmaceutical sciences curriculum, which changes ever so slowly. In this section, I critically evaluate the curriculum in the largest Canadian school of pharmacy, which resembles very closely the curricula in the eight other schools in the country and the scores of other schools in the world. The subjects taught mainly reflect the expertise of the pharmaceutical scientists who teach them, as well as the interests of the pharmaceutical firms who apply the research of the faculty scientists. Just as important as this molecular hegemony is the rapidly decreasing proportion of the curriculum devoted to community-based health promotion, indigenous healing, illness narratives, or any other non-molecular approach. Even the clinical material in the curriculum focuses only on which drugs are appropriate, not on health or healing. The curricular revision towards presenting more clinical material at this particular school,[6] to the limited extent that it succeeded, only had the overall effect of reinforcing the molecular hegemony introduced in the basic sciences courses in the curriculum. Consistent with the fact that this type of 'pharmaceutical care' also reflects the interests of the industry, some of the faculty involved in teaching it have been able to obtain small amounts of financial support for their 'research'. Unlike the research of the basic scientists, however, the Medical Research Council is not the intermediary. Fledgling research on pharmacy practice is able to seek *direct* funding from the pharmaceutical industry.

Molecular Hegemony in the Pharmacy Curriculum

The undergraduate curriculum in Canadian pharmacy schools, until recently, was 95 per cent basic science in its initial years of study, as presented in courses that focused on the molecular level. Molecular-level courses dominate the curriculum and include organic chemistry, microbiology, biochemistry, medicinal chemistry, and pharmacology. The mechanisms and processes relevant to the synthetic drugs produced by the pharmaceutical industry are featured in depth in medicinal chemistry, which is generally regarded by pharmacists as the 'core' of the pharmacy curriculum. There is no room for discussion about indigenous medicines in medicinal chemistry courses. The human being is presented as the container for sets of receptors, which can be precisely turned on by those drugs synthesized by the industry. Herbal remedies, by way of contrast, are assumed to produce imprecise, generalized effects—and thus their use is not regarded as consistent with scientific practice.

The molecular hegemony of the pharmacy curriculum is obvious in the first-year curriculum in the year 1988–9, when I joined the Toronto faculty and when only students with mathematics and science qualifications were being recruited. The first year after high school (Table 5.1) appeared somewhat balanced, with biology, calculus, and inorganic chemistry set in the context of an introductory pharmacy course and a social science requirement. But by second year, students were experiencing only molecules and body sections in their courses: anatomy, organic chemistry, microbiology, pharmaceutics, and chemistry courses focusing on analysis of chemicals, with one non-molecular course, social issues (assigned to me as a junior professor), counting for just a little over 5 per cent of their grade for the year. In the

Table 5.1: First- and Second-Year Curriculum, University of Toronto Faculty of Pharmacy, 1988–9

Subject	Classroom Hours/ Week (26 weeks)	Course Description	Weight[a]
Year 1			
Biology	5	the nature of living organisms	24
Chemistry	5.25	general chemistry (inorganic)	24
Mathematics	4	calculus for physical and life sciences I	24
Intro. to Pharmacy	3.5	history, ethics, laws/communication	22
Social Science	3	economics, psychology, or sociology	24
Year 2			
Anatomy	2.5	histology, neuroanatomy, and embryology	18
Quantitative Analysis	2.5	gravimetric, volumetric, and electro-chemical techniques of chemical analysis	12
Organic Chemistry	4	structures, reactions of organic compounds	24
Qualitative Organic Analysis	0.75	laboratory analysis of five organic unknowns via wet chemical/spectroscopic methods	3
Microbiology	4	classification, structure of organisms/hosts	24
Intro. to Statistics	1	experimental design/statistical analysis	8
Pharmaceutics I	4	preparation and math of dosage forms	24
Analysis	2	assays of medicinals and pharmaceuticals	12
Social Issues	1	the family, children, aging, death and dying, rural gerontology, social class and compliance, and health	8

[a]Grades achieved in these courses were multiplied by the number shown in this column rather than each course counting as equal weight towards the student's average. In Year 2, for example, the Microbiology course, consisting of four times as much instruction as the Social Issues course, was weighted three times the value of the Social Issues grade in the final average grade calculations.

third year of the 1988–9 curriculum in Toronto (Table 5.2), the molecular hegemony continued, with pathology, medicinal chemistry, more pharmaceutics, more biochemistry, pharmacology, physiology, and a course in jurisprudence (because of the

Table 5.2: Third-Year Curriculum, University of Toronto Faculty of Pharmacy, 1988–9

Subject	Hours/week	Course Description	Weight
Pathology	1	structural changes in important diseases	8
Medicinal Chemistry	3	drugs affecting the central nervous system, autonomic nervous system, cardiovascular system, etc.	24
Pharmaceutics II	4	design and efficacy of pharmaceuticals	24
Biochemistry	2	cellular structures, functions, and drug action	16
Pharmacology	2.5	drug classes and mechanisms of action	22
Physiology	3.5	functions of the blood, nervous system, etc.	22
Jurisprudence	1	federal and provincial acts and regulations	8
OTC Drugs; or Pharmacy Mgmt; or an elective in Arts or Science	1.5	therapeutic advising around OTCs; or, managing a pharmacy, general principles of marketing and how health care is provided to Canadians	12

peculiar weighting system, accounting for only about 6 per cent of students' final grades). Students were also allowed to take an elective, which could, if the student preferred, be taken from among the arts and sciences outside pharmacy. But they were strongly encouraged to learn about the over-the-counter drugs they would be selling. As Hornosty (1989) pointed out after interviewing pharmacy classes in the 1980s, by the end of third year, with such a concentrated molecular curriculum and so little clinical training, students were frightened that they would not be able to practise their profession. This was not just a problem in Toronto, but worldwide. Neither were these complaints restricted to pharmacy, surfacing also in medicine. When I interviewed pharmacy graduates, they pointed out that they were relieved to get exposure to the clinical side of their chosen profession in their final year of study. In addition to clinical biochemistry, more medicinal chemistry, biopharmaceutics, and pharmacokinetics (accounting for a little over a third of their final grade), students also took compounding and dispensing (which allowed them to practise filling prescriptions), therapeutics, clinical pharmacy, three elective courses, and the history of pharmacy.

In summary, at the end of the 1980s, pharmacy students were presented with little contextual information with which to understand the environment in which they would use the extensive knowledge of molecular behaviour they were acquiring. Even training for what they would actually do behind the counter was tucked into non-required courses or delayed until a few months before graduation. They protested this situation, but were not heard, at least until the early 1990s.

Structurally, the emphasis on molecules in the Toronto curriculum reflected the backgrounds and education of the faculty. In 1989, two-thirds of the full-time faculty, mainly male and tenured, had molecular training, including the dean. However, during the curricular revision, clinical teaching increasingly became the responsibility of a new group of faculty, mainly female and with untenured positions. In the next section, I describe how the scenario unfolded in this particular school.

New Kid on the Block: Pharmaceutical Care

Curricula in pharmacy have been revised substantially at approximately 30-year intervals over the past century as part of a reprofessionalization exercise when professional turf has been lost to the pharmaceutical industry, medicine, and most recently, large drug chains. As part of this cycle, the major curriculum redrafting that happened in Toronto in 1994 was almost entirely at the initiative of the dean, who championed pharmaceutical care. (There was a parallel move towards 'problem-based learning' in the University of Toronto medical curriculum at the same time.) Two new initiatives were taken: pharmacy was made what is called a 'second entry-level program', such that students were no longer admitted directly from high school but were selected from among the more successful who had already attended university and, in many cases, who already had undergraduate degrees. Pharmacy came to this practice somewhat late, since it had already been in operation in medicine at the University of Toronto for 50 years.[7] The second initiative was to try to 'balance' the curriculum so that there was more clinical and less basic science emphasis.

The 1994 Toronto curriculum in the pharmaceutical sciences came about after some acrimonious interchanges with basic scientists who resisted the downsizing and de-emphasizing of their courses through the mechanism of a clinical faculty-dominated curriculum committee. In this new curriculum, as shown in Table 5.3, the more sophisticated entering student faces a 'first professional year' featuring the molecular classics of physical and organic chemistry and chemical analysis alongside the traditional anatomy, made more relevant to a molecular focus (i.e., now covering the chemical basis of human anatomy rather than histology, neuroanatomy, and embryology, as in the former curriculum). But the student also takes courses geared to improving his or her 'interface' with the public. These include, if a proficiency test is failed, 'oral communication skills for pharmacy students whose first language is not English', 'written communication skills for pharmacy students whose first language is not English', and a 'writing workshop'. It is worth mentioning at this juncture that this division of the students into ESL and non-ESL students was experienced as discriminatory by many non-white students, despite its apparent 'progressive' nature. Other courses include clinical ones such as 'Communication Skills in Pharmacy Practice', and 'Professional Practice I'. Altogether, again with the peculiar weighting system, the basic science component was reduced (for this equivalent of what formerly had been 'second year') from 95 per cent to 55 per cent.

The apparent reduction in molecular hegemony appeared to carry into the 'second professional year' (or equivalent of the third year of study). However, a closer

Table 5.3: First-Year Curriculum, University of Toronto Faculty of Pharmacy, 1994

Subject	Total Hours	Course Description	Weight
Anatomy	52	chemical, physical basis–human anatomy	16
Physical Chemistry	117	emphasis on biological and life sciences	24
Organic Chemistry	104	structures, reactions of organic compounds	24
Qual. Organic Analysis	20	laboratory anlysis of five organic unknowns	6
Intro. to Pharmacy	54	intro. to health care and role of pharmacist	17
Communication for ESL Students	65	compulsory for ESL students selected by a test of spoken and written English	n/a
Jurisprudence	26	regulations–emphasis on application	8
Intro. to Statistics	26	skills for interpreting the drug literature	8
Professional Practice I	79	drug information, professional ethics, communications, and professional practice	24

examination of the curriculum suggests that this impression is somewhat deceptive. In the new curriculum, the molecular favourites of microbiology, medicinal chemistry, and pharmaceutics persisted. New courses were added, which were called 'Pharmaceutical Care 1a' and 'Professional Practice II'. My old social issues course emerged as 'Health Systems and Society I', still only worth 5 per cent of the final grade. The tally for this year of study, again using the peculiar weighting system, shows that molecular studies were reduced from 91 to 81 per cent in the new curriculum.

The muting of molecular hegemony in the second year of the 1994 program, however, was offset by an *increase* in molecular content in the final year of study. In 1989, 58 per cent of the final year was non-molecular; in the new curriculum this had shrunk to 35 per cent. Thus, the lessening of the molecular stranglehold was less spectacular than the course listings might indicate. True, the placements in clinical settings planned for the new curriculum (partly integrated into the three professional years of the curriculum and in a 'fourth professional year' following the three years) reduce the total *proportion* of molecular-oriented courses. But little had been sacrificed; the clinical emphasis had been *added.*

The Experience of Education by Molecular Researchers

At this point it is germane to say something about those who do basic pharmaceutical research in our universities, how they approach and teach students who will become health practitioners, and the situation they face as scientists. In my experience, even the kind-hearted among these professors who are researchers, who may actually wish to be at a university (rather than in industry or at a research institute) because they enjoy teaching, may be hard-pressed to fulfil their obligations as teachers. This is because many voluntarily work in their laboratories seven days a week at least until evening every day, past what most workers would consider quitting time. Some often go without dinner or just wolf something down to get back to their work. They might get into a discussion with a colleague, only to remember that they have a grant proposal deadline coming up or that they have to produce a result to report in their next publication or to justify their next proposal. That is, my experience of them is that they work with little time to contemplate the context within which they work or to question its legitimacy. Further, unlike those of us who have experienced critical pedagogy, most have been educated in a molecular paradigm themselves, so that they may have difficulty problematizing the context within which they work. Even those who put a great deal of effort into their teaching are acutely conscious that any time taken away from research reduces the likelihood that they can obtain funding. Further, as described above, the students themselves are not necessarily receptive to what they are receiving from these professors. Having sat in on most of my colleagues' lectures, I observed some classroom scenarios involving scores of students, sitting in rows, silently facing a professor who might be so frightened of them or disinterested to the point of complete disconnection—it is sometimes difficult to tell which—that he or she does not make eye contact with students during the whole 50 minutes of the lecture.

The point is that there is a great deal working against the possibility that pharmaceutical researchers will inspire their students, who are not going to be scientists but pharmacists. In some cases, the professors might have been pharmacists, so may have some conception of what practice is like, but they certainly would not have any vision of 'patient-driven care', given the type of training they had in a pharmacy or science faculty. Molecular science has to do with, for example, finding out how the receptor systems work in the body so that chemical entities can be 'plugged in' to be more precise in their turning on and off of the body's functions. The body, according to this approach, is like a machine, a car, in which one plunks a new transmission when the old transmission fails. Neither psychobiological nor social structural aspects of health are considered in this paradigm.

Since these scientists have been trained from the perspective of molecular science rather than the promotion of health—indeed, many of them may feel that it is not possible to have a rational or scientific approach to social phenomena—they may be sceptical of taking a rational approach to the study of health. Worse, they may actively oppose teaching about health and ways of achieving it other than through drugs, out of fear for what they perceive as political interference affecting their ability to do science. Or, they may really believe in what they are doing, unaware of how they are reproducing the relations of corporate ruling in their research. Thus, despite all the rhetoric of curricular reform, a blunt way of characterizing pharmacy education might be that it is education for a degraded practice, conducted by people who are themselves unwitting captives of an industry.

Appropriation of the Social/Holistic by the Scientific in the Pharmacy Curriculum

The molecular hegemony documented above was supplemented by the presentation of the practice of pharmacy in clinical courses with almost no social context, where the pharmacist faces the patient devoid of details about the setting, health policies, and hierarchical environment of practice in which it presumably takes place. This is symbolized on the cover of the 1996–7 calendar, which pictures a dyad: the white woman pharmacist, white-coated, smiling down at a vial of medication also being regarded by a gentle, professorial-looking, bearded, white, older man. This emphasis in clinical pharmacy education on the individualistic 'case study' reduces the potential for clinical studies to help the student grasp the overall context of limited autonomy in which he or she must practice pharmacy. It also fails to encourage students to ask critical questions about pharmaceutical care, such as the extent to which 'research' on 'pharmaceutical care' is in the interests of the pharmaceutical industry. And finally, the pictured white dyad fails to acknowledge the significant non-white minority of pharmacy students, professors, and practitioners.[8]

What happened to the one required course in the curriculum that was 'context-laden'? Over the years, I had placed this course less within a sociological context and more within an ethical context. I was reacting to the difficulties expressed by students who had already, in high school, been reinforced to think in reductionist terms. They generally reacted negatively to the prospect of thinking relatively or contextually. They were confused by my strategy of inviting speakers to present different sides of issues—many wondered, what is the 'right answer' for the exam? If my own opinion is as good as any other, is this a 'science'? In the new curriculum, I was allowed to continue to teach professional ethics, but it was circumscribed to a small part of the first-year introductory pharmacy course, in which I also had to cover the broad area of the nature of a profession, the hierarchy of the health-care professions, the history of pharmaceutical ideologies, client-professional relationships, etc., all in 10 hours of the 52-hour course. In my own course, I was not initially prevented from teaching critical thinking about overprescribing and polypharmacy, pharmaceutical industry marketing and control, corporate control of dispensing, and the degradation of pharmacists' work in business settings, but this was privately criticized by my colleagues, who felt I was presenting an 'unbalanced view'. The number of hours devoted to my 'nonsense' was reduced to make way for several hours of instruction on pharmaco-economics.

Pharmaco-economics, and how it was framed in the new pharmaceutical curriculum, is worth considering for a moment. The title implies that it is a 'social' science. (Isn't economics?) The instructor who taught it as part of the course I co-ordinated emphasized the current 'realities' of the health-care system: cutbacks, efficiency, the need for pharmacists to show that, by their presence, they are 'saving money' for their employers or (if self-employed) themselves, not 'wasting' it. In fact, that is what pharmaco-economic research, according to this instructor, was all about. Its *raison d'être* was not the accumulation of knowledge per se (at least not in the course under consideration) but the justification of drug therapy and the work of clinical pharmacotherapists as *cost-effective*. The important point here is that in my pharmacist colleague's teaching, there *was* a context, which was presented as a 'given'. It is a context in which people's health is a peripheral consideration to the generation of pharmaceutical profit and the 'saving' of public money spent on these products and services. Consistent with my training in medical sociology and health promotion, I had earlier in the course presented a different context: the idea that health was more than just the absence of disease, but was part of a realization of what might be called the 'political freedom' of human beings to exist, with *all* members having their needs for autonomy, subsistence, and creativity honoured within their societies. But in the lectures on pharmaco-economics, ideas of health promotion, which emphasize the seizing of control over one's health by disadvantaged groups, were set aside and replaced with an unproblematized 'cost-conscious' context that is consistent with contemporary economic globalization discourses.

Student Resistance to Appropriation by Corporate Ideology

I will never forget the looks of confusion and disbelief that appeared on the faces of students as they listened to these pharmaco-economics lectures, which followed and clashed with the previous coverage of the concepts of health and health promotion within the context of a just society. One student sitting next to me in one of the classes turned to me with his mouth open, stifling a cry of protest: how did *this* material fit with my course? The students' reactions would probably not have been so intense had the class not changed so much in character from those I had met in my early days at the faculty. In this, the last course I taught there, the more mature students, many of whom had first degrees in the social sciences, found ideas of holism more resonant than did the classes of 1991–6, who had come to my courses just out of a high school program saturated with reductionist mathematics and science. Most of the class of 1998 had at least some exposure to non-molecular-level thinking.

Paolo Freire (1995) has argued that education for consciousness-raising about relations of ruling can be based on what he labelled a dialogic process, in which the educator assists oppressed peoples in becoming conscious of their oppression. Further, if those oppressed in the relations of ruling are able to contextualize themselves as reproducing those relations (or 'housing the oppressor'), there is hope for emancipation. I believe that the conditions described by Freire were partly met in the situation of the class of 1998, because the students experienced the two conflicting approaches of pharmaco-economics embedded within a course based on health promotion and criticism of scientific/capitalist ideology. The juxtaposition of the two contradictory approaches to health helped, I think, to raise the consciousness of these students about how they were being conditioned and co-opted into 'molecular thinking' in the rest of the curriculum. My evidence for saying this is contained in the answers they wrote on the final exam in this course, 'Health Systems and Society'. I set two questions, the answers to which were examined for evidence of holistic/contextual vs molecular/reductionist thinking. Although this analysis is presented in greater detail in a separate paper (Boon and Muzzin, 1996), some excerpts illustrate the awareness of these students of the processes I am describing.

Students could choose questions asking them to explain insights they had achieved by taking the course or inviting them to design an ideal pharmacy curriculum. A content analysis showed that the most frequently cited insights were a realization that this course was 'different' from others in the curriculum; a recognition that molecular 'science' is not the only way of knowing; and articulation of a holistic world view. It is important to emphasize that the attention of the students was never explicitly drawn to the disjunctions referred to in their answers. *The following criticisms are the students' alone, not mine.* In retrospect, I think, I owe part of my own consciousness of their co-optation to what they wrote on the exam. For example, most students recognized that the course was different. In their words:

> Generally speaking, I found that this course was a needed and refreshing change from all the other scientific courses. The most important insight or reinforcement that I obtained was the importance and necessity of keeping an open mind on all issues, and to realize that there is more than one way in thinking about the same issue; in other words, critical thinking is a must!

> This course has provided a unique perspective on pharmacy that is missing in the more scientifically-centred courses in this curriculum. Pharmacists are NOT scientists; we use scientific knowledge to help people better their lives. Our social responsibility is as important as our scientific obligations; my calling is not to be a scientist but to be a health care professional.

> In general, I feel that the Health Systems in Society course is the only one in which we look at anything other than drugs and disease. While I believe that many of the other courses are pertinent to my future career, I feel that we have failed/are failing to move away from the medical model and thus may be slightly out of touch with the needs of our clients that don't involve such specific drugs or diseases.

Students realized that not only was course content different, but its perspective was something other than 'scientific', which they identified as limited for the practice of a profession. The perspective of the course was identified as 'open-minded', 'broad', 'sociological', 'empathetic', and 'critical'. Students were eloquent about how 'science' was not the only epistemological option.

> [T]he pharmacy curriculum, nearly exclusively based on scientific research, is missing out on important aspects of health. . . . I question why we are not taught to critique and question science and how it is performed so that we may read papers and not just analyze the

> statistics (as our wonderful statistics course taught us) but also the validity of the entire process. The fact that my future profession is so heavily based on the scientific model of health leads me to believe that I may feel 'trapped' in this scientific model. Pharmacists treat people with drugs. Drugs are an essential part of the scientific model of health and most allopathic treatments. As a result, I will be forced to mainly deal with patients through the scientific model of allopathic medicine.

> I gained awareness of various models of health and a recognition of the prominence of the medical model in pharmacy. I have realized that I am uncomfortable with the traditional view of the medical model which depicts health as the absence of disease, and disease as an identifiable state which can be cured or controlled with treatment.

> This course has allowed me to think of various issues with a different perspective and it has also taught me to be more critical of what I hear and read. It has provided me with the skills to be more analytical but also more compassionate about the issues surrounding us.

> My insights vary [by] topic, but they all have a common theme—the realization that pharmacy is NOT only based upon drugs, science and medicine, but other social, ethical and political issues.

These comments show that many students were successful in gaining a standpoint other than the 'molecular', from which they could view their feeling of alienation from science and express their emotions about political and personal issues.

Some students strongly identified with a contextualizing epistemology, rather than one based on studying individual components of a system in isolation:

> Almost every other course is directed towards pharmacy (e.g., microbiology for pharmacy) and is taught by a professor in the Faculty. I think maybe we are becoming too specialized. We are losing the broader spectrum of education. We are being trained for only one task.... I feel like we are living and learning in our own little world. We need a broad understanding of the material—in areas of science, philosophy, sociology and more.

> Currently pharmacy does a fine job educating students scientifically [pharmacologically]; it also addresses some economic aspects, but fails miserably to provide the necessary holistic exposure.

> Unfortunately, I feel that my education so far has not given me the space, scope or the opportunity to explore different avenues. I have been trained to be a reductionist—where all the answers can be found under the microscope, where an electron can hold the key to understanding. I find it difficult to open my mind and find answers somewhere other than in the laboratory. I believe that only through courses such as this one, can students learn to see other views and accept other people's opinions. Issues can be dealt with on a more macroscopic level which is beneficial and conducive to learning.

It doesn't really matter whether the students expressed these views because they have more social science preparation, are more mature, or felt more free to be critical than in other courses. The point is that the students were resisting being exposed to only one worldview and were voicing their preference for a broader vision.

Pharmaceutical Appropriation of Science

What some of the students had discovered was that pharmaceutical research is what can be characterized as 'hegemonic' science—a science created and promoted by multinationals for profit, including pharmaceutical manufacturers, who are now in the strategic position to define what scientists do both as instructors and within university medical and pharmaceutical research. Scientists could tell their own stories, which they know better than I. However, busy trying to salvage their careers in the rough-and-tumble hierarchy of academic science, or worse, co-opted by the expectation of profit, not many will have the time or opportunity to do so. One of the parallels between the progressive appropriation of pharmaceutical scientists and of pharmacists themselves is that the younger among the cohorts, and the least advantaged in other ways, are most affected by the process of appropriation.

When I interviewed about 60 of my pharmaceutical colleagues across the country recently, I heard, simply put, that pharmaceutical scientists are increasingly prone to manipulation by the pharmaceutical industry. Pharmaceutical industry 'consultants' show up at meetings of faculty. They encourage scientists to write grant proposals that would be supported by particular pharmaceutical companies. They brag that they can 'get around the funding agencies', although they say that this is easier in the US than in Canada. It is increasingly difficult to achieve funding of scientific research through the Medical Research Council, the main granting agency for this purpose. For example, $16 million was available to scientists for operating grant support for their laboratories and proposed experiments in the January 1997 competition, but only 253 of 1,111 submitted grant proposals were funded (Pennefather, 1997). It is possible that scientist-peers will decide that an applicant's reputation and proposal for research are worthy, but that the MRC will not fund the work. Some 'hit rates' as they are called, are as low as 6 per cent of the total number of proposals submitted in a particular competition.

The consequences of such a situation are easy to imagine. If a professor works on an area of research for about 15 or 20 years, with an established laboratory and technicians with particular expertise, a loss of funding is disastrous. A number of scientists I have interviewed have described how, when scientists at certain large, prestigious American institutes lose their funding, they are locked out the next day. The Canadian situation is less brutal; however, a scientist would be well advised not to lose his or her funding. In order to *get* funding, he or she might be prepared to enter competitions for money with a better hit rate, such as research sponsored by the pharmaceutical industry. In fairness, many scientists would consider taking funding directly from pharmaceutical firms to be 'selling out' because they believe in research for its own sake or 'science with no strings'. But industrial control of medical research is difficult to ignore: industry became the largest funder of medical research in Canada in 1991, as well as providing millions of dollars worth of scholarships (PMAC, 1993).

There is also the matter of what some professors called 'stipends'. Although the science literature suggests that it is commonplace for scientists to receive stipends for consultation to private industry and that there is no problem with this state of affairs, this is not exactly how I experienced the phenomenon. Occasionally, some middleman would call, offering as much as $100,000 of research funding to do a particular 'research project' of interest to a particular pharmaceutical company. Given my background and position within the field, these enticements were easy for me to turn down (but not, I noted, for a few of my colleagues, who did more 'contract' than 'peer-assessed' research and who, unethically, I felt, involved their graduate students in meeting the deadlines of these pharmaceutical firms). When what I am calling the offer of a 'stipend' came to me, it came from outside of pharmacy. A colleague I had known for many years invited me to his office; he had done a little favour for me, and he suggested that I might think about doing a little favour for him. This would involve me making myself available to his favourite drug company for a healthy stipend. All I would have to do was stand by as someone to perhaps give talks, participate on committees, or make recommendations for the company. When I said that I wouldn't do that, because I was critical of these activities, the interview ended quickly. It was a very uncomfortable moment. I knew immediately that if this kind of offer was made to me that it must have been made to other people as well. I knew that more than one colleague went on lecture tours funded in this way, and that *they* didn't see it as an ethical problem. Later, I heard criticism of a speaker at a pharmacy conference who, participants felt, had come out too strongly in favour of the product of a drug company. Apparently, drug companies prefer that you not endorse their wares so strongly that you lose your credibility as an 'unbiased' advocate.

Conclusion: So What? Contextualizing Molecular-Level Professional Education

As many authors have pointed out, we live in a society where *psychologizing* is part and parcel of the construction of social reality. In other words, there is a tendency to generate explanations of social phenomena by focusing on the individual psyche. Professional education writing tends to reproduce this mode of knowledge production, as reflected in journals on education in medicine and other health professions. As far as I am aware, except for the sociological and feminist enclaves within which Apple and Smith teach (and which are threatened in the academy), no critical tradition exists inside professional education. In 'insider' journals devoted to these topics, there is little attempt, as is the case in 'outsider' social sciences, to define a theoretical context. Quantitative analysis often appears alone, decontextualized within these research articles. Such literature is unlikely to present reductionist education as in any way problematical.

Neither are most professionals aware of the various critiques of professional education and practice that have emerged in recent years—from conservative, liberal, and socialist to more radical political positions. For example, Schon (1983, 1987) has characterized the problem in professional education as an overemphasis on technical rationality in the professions and called for a 'reflective contract' between clients and professionals. Freidson (1970a, 1970b) is more sophisticated in his representation of medicine and other professions as engaged in what I would call 'hegemonic' knowledge construction. But he has also called for a 'fix' that would rely unproblematically on citizen participation. Critiques of professions from the left have instead focused on the deskilling and proletarianization of professional workers, supported by the discourse of capitalist efficiency and downsizing, of which there is much evidence, including that presented in this volume. But perhaps the most promising critique of professional work in a global transnational corporate world comes from feminists who have characterized scientifically based professions and professional education as environmentally destructive, racist, sexist, and neo-colonial (Shiva, 1995, 1997; Harding, 1998). Needless to say, none of this radical discourse can be found either in the journals read by professionals or in the curricula of professional programs in the university oriented towards academic capitalism.

What I am suggesting here is that, in the manner of what John Ralston Saul (1995) characterizes as an 'unconscious civilization', it is not just *my* particular little course in the pharmacy curriculum that was faced with appropriation by molecular hegemony, but the whole social science project itself. And it is not just *my* pharmacy students whom the curriculum attempts to narrow into reductionist thinking about their profession, but potentially all students of professions, where the curricula are inherently reductionist. Finally, and this is the concern that I feel most personally, it is not just *my* university that is in the business of selling truth to the highest bidder, which may be, variously, a tycoon, a communications giant, or a pharmaceutical industry. When a corporation controls scientific praxis, I would argue that the possibility of truth itself has been sold. When it controls social scientific praxis, the curriculum is no longer about health and respect for environment and social justice, but instead about unproblematically producing compliance with pharmaceutical industry interests.

Notes

Research on pharmaceutical care and academic pharmacy was made possible by SSHRC grants 816–95–0025 and 410–95–0857. The views expressed here are not necessarily shared by my co-investigators.

1. Peter Morley, personal communication, 1994. This term was suggested in our discussion about the term 'patient-centred care', which is used occasionally in literature promoting pharmaceutical care. Morley, an anthropologist, and the

husband of Linda Strand, pointed out that the concept of 'patient-*driven* care' would emphasize patient decision-making around drug care, while the notion of 'patient-*centred* care', although still paternalistic, could shift the traditional pharmacy emphasis away from products and towards people. A key article written by Strand and the other leader of this movement, Charles Hepler, is referenced below. It is important to note Hepler's funding by the Sandoz drug company (now Novartis). Morley argues that he is conscious of drug company interests and that promotion of pharmaceutical care can be done without compromising the profession. For more analysis of the history of reprofessionalization projects in Canadian pharmacy, see my 'Professional ideology in Canadian pharmacy', Ch. 13 in D. Coburn, C. D'Arcy, and G. Torrance, eds, *Health and Canadian Society: Sociological Perspectives*, 3rd edn (Toronto: University of Toronto Press, 1998), ch. 13. A brief history of pharmacy problematizing and gendering the idea of 'pharmaceutical care' can be found in my 'Pawns among patriarchies: Women in pharmacy', in E. Smythe et al., eds, *Challenging Professions: Historical and Contemporary Perspectives on Women's Professional Work* (Toronto: University of Toronto Press, 1999).

2. In the early years of the curricula in law, architecture, engineering, dentistry, medicine, so-called 'allied' health professions such as medical laboratory technology and even alternative medical curricula such as naturopathy, there is an emphasis on the 'basic theoretical building blocks' that the student of the professions is presumed to require before proceeding to specific training for actual practice in the later part of the curriculum. The irrationality of this bifurcation has often been noted by those studying the professions (e.g., Boon, 1995; Longo, 1999; Schon, 1983, 1987). Professional educators have occasionally attempted to integrate these 'two halves' of the curriculum and, thus, the gaps between theory and practice. The 'problem-based' curriculum designed by McMaster Medical School in Canada, which has been copied by other prestigious institutions, is such an example. More commonly, the theory-practice dichotomy and the justifications for including particular aspects of theory or practicum training are accepted unproblematically. I would argue that this bifurcation and the nature of what is covered in each fraction of these curricula need to be problematized not only in the pharmaceutical sciences but in these other professional curricula where, variously, corporate interests can be articulated via what is covered in both theoretical background and training for practice. In engineering, an extreme case, 'ethics' is crowded into the licensing examination, while 'beam construction' is a prominent aspect of the civil engineering curriculum (Hyde, 1999). In law, on the other hand, there is no theoretical orientation in continuing education in the one law school that has been studied, where corporate interests appear to set the agenda in this post-licensing program (Shanahan, 1999).
3. It is worth noting here that the American Society of Hospital Pharmacists prohibits pharmacist-members from accepting any direct offer from a company to pay costs for 'educational opportunities' (Bayley and Mount, 1996). Not so for

academics, as is documented in the Olivieri scandal described here. My understanding of what transpired in the Olivieri case is partly based on work done by former students who collected and analysed the media coverage on this scandal (Chachra, 1999; Garcia and Raphael, 1999; Yu, 1999). Their work, in addition to my own inside knowledge of the situation, brings me to the conclusion that it was also important that Olivieri was a woman, that is, a member of a marginalized group in science research. We also believe that it was important that she is a physician represented as devoted to her patients, most of whom were children and many of whom, with the disease thalassemia, are not white.

4. For example, Bill Graham, then University of Toronto Faculty Association president, in his review of donor agreements involving funded chairs, emphasized that 'the terms of such agreements must make clear that who is appointed to the chairs, what is taught and researched by the chairs and how they are evaluated, is the responsibility of the academy alone, and not the role of the donor' (Graham, 1998: 1). He pointed out that the University of Toronto had originally drafted such agreements in secrecy, including donations with potential steering effects on the future direction of faculty work, to the Faculty of Management by the Joseph Rotman Charitable Foundation and to the Centre for International Studies by Peter Munk. He concludes with questions about how many such agreements exist in private and to what they commit the university.
5. For example, I could expand on the Toronto faculty's marked negative reaction to teaching about herbal medicines and other such topics, which opened a space for critical thinking about the prime interest of pharmaceutical firms in synthetic molecules and designer drugs. Pharmacognosy, or the study of the considerable legacy of pharmacy knowledge regarding the medicinal use of indigenous plants, had long disappeared from the curriculum; when those of us who wanted to broaden the curriculum reintroduced related topics, the course was marginalized as an elective in 'alternative medicine', scheduled so that few students could take it.
6. 'Pharmaceutical care' is supported in key documents produced by the American Association of Colleges of Pharmacy, the governing co-ordinating organization for US colleges of pharmacy (AACP, 1991). This body also provides guidelines for teaching methods (AACP, 1993). Although occasionally critical of the imbalance between research and teaching in pharmacy schools, annual meetings of this body are liberally sponsored by the drug industry. (One I attended in 1996 was held in a gambling casino in Reno.) Academic awards, fellowships, and grants sponsored by drug companies are worth several million dollars annually and are administered by the AACP. While Canadian pharmacy schools have their own accreditation body, their curricula have been directly influenced by developments in the US.
7. Robert Gidney and Wyn Millar pointed this out in a presentation that they made to the Higher Education Seminar Series in 1994, at the Ontario Institute for Studies in Education in Toronto, in which they were discussing their book,

Professional Gentlemen: The Professions in Nineteenth-Century Ontario (Toronto: University of Toronto Press).

8. The picture could also be seen as symbolic of the North's hegemony in the global licit drug trade. Discussion of this can be found in Ali (1996). A recent discussion of globalization from an African perspective can be found in Amin (1997).

References

Alford, R. 1975. *Health Care Politics: Ideological and Interest Group Barriers to Reform.* Chicago: University of Chicago Press.

Ali, K. 1996. 'Multinational Drug Corporations, Intellectual Property Rights and the Canadian State: A Historical and Critical Analysis', MA thesis, Brock University.

American Association of Colleges of Pharmacy (AACP). 1991. *AACP Commission to Implement Change in Pharmaceutical Education: Special Report.* Alexandria, Va.: AACP.

———. 1993. 'Academic change in instruction delivery: An option', *AACP News* 24, 5: 1–3.

Amin, S. 1997. *Capitalism in the Age of Globalization: The Management of Contemporary Society.* London: Zed Books.

Apple, M. 1990. *Ideology and Curriculum.* New York: Routledge.

Bayley, C., and J.K. Mount. 1996. 'Relationships with the pharmaceutical industry', in B. Weinstein, ed., *Ethical Issues in Pharmacy.* Vancouver, Wash.: Applied Therapeutics.

——— and J. Sadlak. 1992. 'Technology transfer in Canada: Research parks and centres of excellence', *Higher Education Management* 4, 2: 227–44.

Bell, S., and G. Jones. 1992. 'Paid consulting in Ontario colleges of applied arts and technology', *Canadian Journal of Higher Education* 22, 3: 1–13.

Bloom, S.W. 1988. 'Structure and ideology in medical education: An analysis of resistance to change', *Journal of Health and Social Behaviour* 29: 294–306.

Boon, H. 1995. 'The making of a naturopathic practitioner: The education of alternative practitioners in Canada', *Health and Canadian Society* 3, 1–2: 15–41.

——— and L. Muzzin. 1996. 'Holistic and scientific worldviews among pharmacy students', paper presented at the 9th International Social Pharmacy Workshop, Madison, Wis., Aug.

Brown, E.R. 1979. *Rockefeller Medicine Men.* Berkeley: University of California Press.

Chachra, D. 1999. 'Media critique: Nancy Olivieri, the Hospital for Sick Children, and Apotex', unpublished paper.

Coburn, D., C. D'Arcy, and G. Torrance, eds. 1998. *Health and Canadian Society: Sociological Perspectives*, 3rd edn. Toronto: University of Toronto Press.

Cole, T. 1998. 'The ivy-league hustle: The University of Toronto fundraising team is raking in both cash and controversy as they put the touch on corporate Canada', *Globe and Mail Report on Business* (June): 34–44.

Currie, J., and J. Newson, eds. 1998. *Universities and Globalization*. California: Sage.
Freidson, E. 1970a. *Profession of Medicine*. New York: Harper and Row.
———. 1970b. *Professional Dominance*. Chicago: Atherton.
Freire, P. 1995 [1970]. *Pedagogy of the Oppressed*. New York: Continuum.
Garcia, B., and S. Raphael. 1999. 'Media perceptions and gender issues in the Olivieri and Morrison cases', unpublished paper.
Good, B.J., and M.D. Good. 1993. 'Learning medicine: The construction of medical knowledge at Harvard Medical School', in S. Lindebaum and M. Lock, eds, *Knowledge, Power and Practice*. Berkeley: University of California Press.
Graham, B. 1998. 'Corporatism and the university: Part 2', *UTFA Newsletter*, 28 Feb.
Harding, S. 1998. *Is Science Multicultural? Postcolonialisms, Feminisms and Epistemologies*. Bloomington: Indiana University Press.
Hepler, C., and L. Strand. 1990. 'Opportunities and responsibilities in pharmaceutical care', *American Journal of Hospital Pharmacy* 47: 533.
Hornosty, R. 1989. 'The development of idealism in pharmacy school'. *Symbolic Interaction* 12: 121–37.
Hyde, R. 1999. 'Educating Engineers for Environmentally Sensitive Practice', Ph.D. thesis, University of Toronto.
Longo, M. 1999. 'The dual discourses of medical laboratory technology', paper presented at the annual conference of the Canadian Society for the Study of Higher Education, Sherbrooke, Que., 10–12 June.
Newson, J., and H. Buchbinder. 1986. *The University Means Business*. Toronto: Garamond.
Noble, D. 1977. *America by Design: Science, Technology and the Rise of Corporate Capitalism*. Oxford: Oxford University Press.
Pennefather, P. 1997. 'Open letter concerning federal funding of fundamental science', unpublished paper.
Peters, L., and H. Etzkowitz. 1990. 'University-industry connections and academic values', *Technology and Society* 12: 427–40.
Pharmaceutical Manufactureres' Association of Canada (PMAC). 1993. *A Five-Year Report on the Canadian Brand-Name Pharmaceutical Industry*. Ottawa: PMAC.
Saul, J.R. 1995. *The Unconscious Civilization*. Concord, Ont.: Anansi.
Schon, D. 1983. *The Reflective Practitioner: How Professionals Think in Action*. New York: Basic Books.
———. 1987. *Educating the Reflective Practitioner: Toward a New Design for Teaching and Learning in the Professions*. San Francisco: Jossey-Bass.
Shanahan, T. 1999. 'The professional development program at Osgoode Hall Law School: A discussion of corporate influence on the curriculum', essay prepared for course credit for graduate course, 'Academic Capitalism', University of Toronto.
Shiva, V. 1995. *Monocultures of the Mind: Perspectives on Biodiversity and Biotechnology*. London: Zed Books.
———. 1997. *Biopiracy: The Plunder of Nature and Knowledge*. Boston: South End Press.

Shumar, W. 1997. *College for Sale: A Critique of the Commodification of Higher Education.* London: Falmer Press.

Slaughter, S., and L. Leslie. 1997. *Academic Capitalism: Politics, Policies and the Entrepreneurial University.* Baltimore: Johns Hopkins University Press.

Smith, D. 1987. *The Everyday World as Problematic.* Toronto: University of Toronto Press.

———. 1994. *Conceptual Practices of Power.* Toronto: University of Toronto Press.

Smythe, E., et al., eds. 1999. *Challenging Professions: Historical and Contemporary Perspectives on Women's Professional Work.* Toronto: University of Toronto Press.

Yu, E. 1999. 'Conflicts of interest: A lesson from The Hospital for Sick Children', unpublished paper, OISE/UT.

CHAPTER 6

Evidence-Based Health-Care Reform: Women's Issues

Pat Armstrong

Introduction

What is new about health-care reform? And what is in it for women? If you read the flurry of reports released over the last decade or so by the various provinces, health reform is primarily about continuity and integration, about quality and accountability, about disease prevention and health promotion (Mhatre and Deber, 1992). Framed within the determinants of health literature, the reforms promise to deliver better quality and more appropriate, lower-cost care closer to the community, primarily by adopting managerial strategies taken from the business sector and by practising evidence-based decision-making. Indeed, evidence is at the core of the new reforms, which are in turn linked to viewing health care as a business. Decision-making based on evidence promises quality and accountability, equity and appropriateness as a result of the application of value-free technologies and techniques.

Although current reforms share some continuity with past efforts, they represent what Thomas Kuhn would call a paradigm shift (Kuhn, 1970). The new paradigm reflects and reinforces the increasingly explicit dominance of capitalism at the international, national, and provincial levels. It is a business paradigm, with an emphasis on cost, on management, and on evidence of a particular kind. And it is a paradigm that has consequences far more complex than those set out in the provincial reports. Paradigms matter. Paradigms establish the way of seeing, of understanding, of talking about the issues; they provide the basis for policy development and for practical change. Such paradigms simultaneously reinforce and construct relations of ruling, serving as invisible limits on possibilities for alternatives.

Take the rather stark example offered in a recent book on agencies, actors, and policies in health at the international level. In *Making a Healthy World*, the authors document the movement of the World Bank into health policy. According to these authors, the World Bank is committed to act on economic grounds and is staffed primarily by economists who share a paradigm that views strategies in terms of neo-classical economic criteria (Koivusalo and Ollila, 1997: 37). It was this kind of thinking that led the World Bank's chief economist to suggest that the Bank should consider encouraging 'dirty' industries in the developing world. The recommendation was a logical outcome of his paradigm, as his memo setting the three reasons for his conclusions made clear:

> (1) The measurement of the costs of health-impairing pollution depends on the forgone earnings from increased morbidity and mortality. From this point of view a given amount of health-impairing pollution should be done in the country with the lowest cost, which is the country with the lowest wages. (2) The costs of pollution are likely to be non-linear, as the initial increments of pollution probably have very low cost. The underpopulated countries in Africa are vastly underpolluted: their air quality is probably vastly inefficiently low compared to Los Angeles and Mexico City. (3) The demand for a clean environment for aesthetic and health reasons is likely to have very high income elasticity. (Quoted ibid.)

In quoting this memo, I am not suggesting that this is the conclusion all economists would reach, that economists alone are setting health-care policy, or that all policy-makers in the World Bank would take such a view. Rather, I seek to emphasize that paradigms structure our thinking in ways that can serve to exclude alternatives.

Current reforms and the call for evidence-based decision-making, then, cannot be understood in the abstract. They must be located within the context of the powerful forces supporting markets for everything as the only viable option. And they must be located within a paradigm that defines choices mainly in terms of the purchases consumers make, efficiency in terms of competition, accountability in terms of economic pressure, and evidence as objective truth. Equally important, the context is a gendered one, and the primacy of the market leaves many women without the market power to exercise choice and influence evidence. To understand the gendered impact of reforms, the context must be linked to the concrete and specific experiences of individual women in ways that use evidence that goes beyond what is traditionally recognized as scientific.

The provincial reports on health-care reform have said little about women. Yet women provide about 80 per cent of the paid and unpaid care and constitute a majority of those receiving the care. Although women remain a minority of the decision-makers, in the years since these reports they have managed to convince policy-makers that health care is a women's issue. A section on women was included in the report from the National Forum on Health, and Health Canada has taken a range of initiatives designed to address women's health-care concerns. Indeed, gender-based analysis has become increasingly common in health reform not only in Canada but throughout the world. It has even been made a condition of some structural adjustment programs instituted by the World Bank.

The issue in gendered evidence is not simply one of numbers, of collecting data by sex, or of paying attention to reproductive concerns. Gender is not a variable like the rest. Women are everywhere subordinate, even though this subordination takes different forms in different times and different places and for different classes and races. In all societies, domestic work is women's work. In all societies, having babies has profoundly different consequences for women than for men. This understanding of what a difference this difference makes is only slowly making its way into health-care research and reform. And the new paradigm is one that does not necessarily accommodate such a gender-based analysis, even if there are data on women and even if there is an explicit policy concern. The paradigm can preclude alternatives that take women's various concerns and critiques seriously or alternatives that make policies for women effective in ways that make sense to different groups of women. The new paradigm may also exclude the kinds of evidence that women see as relevant and the ways of using evidence that women see as effective.

In this chapter I employ a feminist political economy perspective to explore evidence-based decision-making in order to draw out the implications for women. The reasons for my focus are twofold. First, the business paradigm is both most obscure and most obvious here. And second, evidence-based decision-making has profound consequences for women as patients, providers, and decision-makers, as well as different consequences for women from different groups.

Feminist Political Economy

In traditional social sciences, hospitals, asylums, sickness, and sick roles were understood mainly in their own terms, with little reference to the setting of the setting. The influential Talcott Parsons (Parsons, 1955) did consider the function of health care more broadly. But his approach assumed that it served a society based on shared values and differentiated according to socio-economic status that reflected agreed-upon rewards. Profit did not enter the picture, although this is perhaps not surprising given that even in the United States health care was primarily a non-profit enterprise until the 1980s. Instead, biology and technology, developed through objective investigation and motivated by agreed-upon needs, were assumed to be central to explaining what services were introduced and how they were provided. Change, to the extent it was considered, came primarily from technological innovation and new evidence, themselves driven by scientific concerns, and from progressive adaptation to the new conditions that resulted. Applied by trained professionals, evidence played a central role.

Professions were understood as composed of men devoted to altruistic concerns, guided both by a code of ethics and by scientific knowledge in exercising the power necessary to diagnose, treat, and control patients. Female-dominated occupations, if considered at all in this literature on professions, were defined as semi-professions (Witz, 1992). The 'semi' label indicated they lacked many of the central features that gave professions their authority.

In contrast, political economy begins with the setting of the setting. The relations of production are at the core of traditional theory, with an assumption that the search for profit sets the historically specific conditions under which health care develops and changes. Class, value, and power differences, rather than shared notions of appropriate rewards linked to the functional worth of occupations, are understood as integral to market societies. The search for profit and conflict over the practices that result are keys to explaining changes that are seldom smooth or simple reflections of progress, as they often appear in functionalist social science. Indeed, contradictions are part of both everyday life and historical development. Evidence is understood as contingent, reflecting the context and power relations of the location in which it is produced. And few women are involved in the most powerful forces that establish this context, although traditional political economy did not spend much time thinking about women.

Professions, therefore, are also seen as struggling for power, with considerable scepticism about the claims of altruism, scientific knowledge, and necessary authority (Illich, 1977). Health-care institutions are viewed with equal scepticism, based as they are on medical models that focus on illness, not health, and on doctors' power, not patients' rights. Unlike the functionalists, political economists stress the need to locate health care and health within the context of economies and of relatively autonomous states often equally intent on promoting profits. They also emphasize the need to view health as produced within the broader society in ways that reflect the organization for profit and the efforts to resist the consequences of the unregulated search for profit. It was this kind of thinking that spawned the determinants of health approach, the approach that understands health as structured by unequal economic, social, and cultural forces and not simply by care.

Feminists were attracted to political economy by the notion that change is possible, that people make their own history, albeit not under conditions of their own choosing. The idea that history is actively and socially constructed was far more promising than a functionalist perspective that saw change as an inevitable unfolding of progress. Such functionalist history placed women in complementary but subordinate roles. Feminists, however, were less attracted by political economy's preoccupation with wage labour and with its failure to recognize or integrate the relations of reproduction into the theory. And they were not attracted by the absence of a gendered analysis in the political economy approach to professions and institutions. They were also concerned with how little attention was paid to values, ideas, and discourses that simultaneously reflected and structured our experiences of the world, and did so in ways that were not only different for women and men but also in ways that subordinate women. Feminists became increasingly concerned as well with theory that tended to obscure the differences among women and that too often assumed all women were the same (Doyal, 1995).

Taking up the tools of political economy, feminists have attempted to transform the theory in ways that allow it to fulfil the claim of examining the integrated nature of politics, economy, and society. From this perspective, in order to analyse paid work it is necessary also to analyse unpaid work; to understand the relations of production it is necessary to examine the relations of reproduction. Neither can be understood without reference to the other. They are part of the same whole. And that whole is gendered. It is also divided by class, race, ethnicity, age, region, sexual orientation, and individual differences. States play a critical role in this gendering. They help structure what is done in the formal economy and the private household, what is done by the for-profit sector and the public one, and how much the search for profit and households are regulated.

Health care, therefore, is not only about what happens in the formal system, nor can the formal system be understood without reference to households and communities, to informal care. And it has different consequences for women and men, as well as for women from different groups and with different experiences. Just as political economists were central to the recognition of what determines health, so, too, have feminist political economists been active in the recognition of women's unpaid health-care work and of the integral link between formal and informal care.

Drawing on political economy, Dorothy Smith (1987, 1990) theorized about what she called the relations of ruling. These relations are pervasive and gendered. Connecting our personal worlds to the larger political economy, they are evident in the documents of our daily lives, in the way our experiences are recorded, translated, and managed through texts and numbers. Facts are not simply lying around waiting to be gathered and analysed for our collective benefit. They are, as various feminist critiques of social science explain, embedded in these relations of ruling and therefore need to be analysed for their gendered impact, as well as for the power relations embedded in them.

Institutional practices, such as evidence-based decision-making, are part of these relations and thus require careful analysis to reveal their gender-specific impact. In addition to exposing the power relations embedded in the way data are collected, structured, interpreted, and used, feminists also expressed concern about the exclusive focus on reason and on quantitative analysis. Emotion and intuition had no place in this evidence. Nor did women's experiences. This was particularly the case in women's encounters with health care.

Feminist political economy, then, starts from premises different from those found in traditional social sciences. It is particularly critical of a paradigm that defines evidence as objective truth or gender differences as complementary roles. It also challenges many of the assumptions in political economy, emphasizing the need to recognize the importance of reproduction, of gendered formal economies, and of women's subordination. As in traditional political economy, there is a recognition that contexts, power, and paradigms matter. Using this perspective, I want to raise questions about the new evidence-based decision-making that is central to the new, dominant paradigm in health care.

The New, Dominant Paradigm

The dominant paradigm in health care today is said to have been developed out of a concern with cost, efficiency, and quality. Certainly, health-care expenditures have been rising in Canada. Research has indicated that many tests, such as ultrasounds, and some surgery, such as Caesarean deliveries, are often wastefully or inappropriately performed. The plethora of service agencies frequently meant a lack of continuity among them. Equally important, there was more and more talk about the limits of care. Increasing investment in health care, according to a wide range of theorists, did not necessarily lead to better health (Evans et al., 1994). And feminists have been among the most vocal critics of care quality and institutional services, exposing multiple sources of poor care for women (see, e.g., Bolaria and Bolaria, 1994; Sherwin, 1992, 1998).

Yet the consistency in reform strategies across national borders suggests that deficits, quality, and inefficiency are not the only motivating forces for change. Public care expanded enormously in the postwar period, when the citizenry was demanding a better world in the aftermath of war and economic depression. The war had not only expanded the state but provided lessons on how intervention could control some excesses of capitalism. It had also made it clear that the state could provide, even in the face of huge deficits. Health care in Western countries had been delivered primarily by non-profit concerns and those seeking profits had plenty of other places to invest. Moreover, public care relieved demands on employers faced with strong unions seeking health protection. Consequently, there was only limited resistance to public care from investors. Public care also relieved some of the demands on women to provide care without pay, while creating paid jobs for women in health care. The care was commodified in the sense that it was paid labour but much of the waged work remained outside the profit sphere.

By the early 1970s, however, the conditions had changed. Corporations, running out of places to invest, looked more and more to the public sector. Health care offered an untapped, and highly lucrative, resource. They moved most rapidly and obviously in the United States. 'By 1994, for-profit health maintenance organizations had more enrollees than their not-for-profit counterparts, which had previously dominated the scene' (Wong, 1998). Hospitals, too, increasingly became for-profit concerns, often as part of huge health-maintenance corporations (Fuller, 1998). And these institutions were very sound investments indeed. Between 1988 and 1996, profits rose from $5.6 billion to $21.3 billion in 1996. Hospitals saw their aggregate profits rise by 25 per cent in 1996 (Bellandi, 1998: 68). But by the end of the decade these corporations were looking to health care in Canada as an 'unopened oyster' for investment, demanding greater freedom to enter under free trade (Nelson, 1995: 7). By 1999 they were demanding that the World Trade Organization grant foreign companies the right to deliver health, education, and transportation services.

Those seeking profit have to tread carefully, however, because public care is Canada's best loved social program (Graves, 1996). There have been few frontal attacks. Instead, the corporations have expressed support for the principles of the Canada Health Act and have offered to help cut costs by providing managerial advice and other kinds of support. This fits well with government reforms that support a business approach to what has been defined as government excess and mismanagement (Shields and Evans, 1998).

They also tread carefully in relation to the professions. Convinced by the notion that their power was both necessary to their practices and a reflection of their knowledge, and supported by a public payment system, professions have strongly resisted managerial attempts to limit their authority. Here, too, there has not been an obvious frontal attack. Instead, there has been an appeal to evidence and the scientific basis of reforms. Similarly, evidence-based decision-making has been used to appeal to those defending the public system while remaining critical of it. The result will be a more effective and efficient public system. The promise to feminist critics is a system that cuts back on unnecessary medical intervention, limits physicians' patriarchal power, and responds more to communities while placing more emphasis on the social determinants of health.

The cost-cutting emphasis and the pressure from corporations, combined with a new philosophy that stresses 'getting government right' (Martin, 1995), encouraged policy-makers to focus on 'private sector management techniques' and perspectives taken from economics (Angus, 1992: 58). As is the case in the rest of the broader public sector, reformers look to market competition for efficiencies. Those needing and receiving care are now described as consumers or customers, in spite of the significant limits on choice in care and the differences between health-care and other purchases (Feldberg and Vipond, 1999; Armstrong et al., 1997). Choice, defined in terms of individual consumer preferences, enjoys a new prominence. The discourse in this paradigm is that of the market, with talk of one-stop shopping becoming commonplace in health care. In a recent book subtitled 'A Blueprint for Canadian Health Care Reform', for example, the authors recommend that 'The Physician should shop on behalf of his [*sic*] patient to provide the best possible service at the most effective cost' (Jerome-Forget and Forget, 1998: 15).

In this paradigm, it is assumed both that the private sector is efficient and that lessons learned in that sector are applicable to the provision of care through the public sector. Evidence supporting either of these assumptions is scarce.[1] Yet evidence-based decision-making is 'one of the key goals of the health sector', as the National Forum on Health (1997: 3) made clear. This is the case throughout the OECD countries where there is an increasing emphasis on measurement and accountability defined in terms of numbers. It is not a surprising development, given the notion central to new government that 'if you can't measure it you can't manage it.' In the new paradigm, 'effectiveness means doing the right thing, at the right time and in the right way' (Christie, 1996: 13). Management science is united with medical science, although not everyone sees this as a marriage made in heaven.

This reform paradigm is becoming part of our common-sense way of seeing health care. This perhaps explains why the *Toronto Star* claimed that the Canada Health Act 'requires that health care be accessible, accountable, affordable, portable and universal' (Walker et al., 1999: A7). Yet the Act itself says health care should be universal, accessible, comprehensive, portable, and publicly administered. There is no talk of affordability, and accountability is defined in terms of public administration in the Act.

The new approach to health reform is not simply biased in favour of markets and management. It is also gender-biased, just as economics itself is gender-biased. As Julie Nelson explains in the preface to *Feminism, Objectivity and Science*:

> Economics is gender-biased in its definition, methods and models. The emphasis on questions of choice and markets, on the use of mathematical methods, and on models based on individual, rational action reflect a way of conceptualizing the world which has a distinctly masculine slant. (Nelson, 1996)

The same could be said of health-care reform today. This does not mean that notions of equity are absent from this dominant paradigm or from economics. However, equity tends to be defined in terms of treating everyone the same, regardless of circumstance or gender. There is little recognition in practice of the pervasive, systemic bias against women in the markets that are promoted or of the structural consequences for women of state transformation. Indeed, health determinants such as employment, income, working conditions, and social support are increasingly defined as individual matters, and gender is seen as a variable like the rest.

An Alternative, Gender-Based Paradigm

The assumptions that gave rise to gender-based analysis were quite different, although there are overlaps in terms of both concepts and discourses with the new, dominant paradigm for health reform. In a gender-based paradigm, analysis begins with the socially and materially located whole person, a person who is gendered and who exists in relations of inequality. While many factors may contribute to unequal relations in particular times and places, gender always does. Context matters, and this context is both global capitalism and specific histories. As Dorothy Smith would say, analysis begins from below but necessarily relates to the above, with relations of ruling pervading the whole.

The importance of the global context is evident in the example of reproductive rights. Rosalind Petchesky (1995: 152) argues that the 1994 Program of Action of the Cairo International Conference on Population and Development 'enshrines an almost feminist vision of reproductive rights and gender equality in place of the old population control discourse and retains a mainstream model of development under which that vision cannot possibly be realized.' She goes on to explain that the Program of Action represents the success resulting from years of effort by women's groups around the world to 'gain recognition of women's reproductive and sexual determination as a basic health need and human right' (ibid.). Yet the program not only failed 'to address the real implications of privatization' for women (ibid., 156).

It went even further, making a commitment to 'increasing the involvement of the private sector'. In Petchesky's words:

> the Cairo document promotes the very privatization, commodification and deregulation of reproductive health services that, by its own admission, have led to diminished access and increasing mortality and morbidity for poor women, who constitute 'the most vulnerable groups' in both developing and developed countries. (Ibid., 157)

The Canadian context not only includes a free trade agreement that permits foreign ownership of such services as long-term care and the foreign management of Canadian hospitals (D'Arcy, 1998: 19). It also includes living in poverty on the shores of James Bay, where services are inaccessible in both physical and cultural terms. And it includes the particular experiences and related expertise of women who provide unpaid care in their homes while working for pay in the market.

Relations with others matter, and matter in ways that may contradict, or compensate for, aspects of the context. In a political economy framework, these relations include those in the formal economy as well as those in the household and the community. Equally important, these are relations of power and inequality in which gender plays a major role. It is, to use old feminist terminology, simultaneously capitalist and patriarchal (Hennessey and Ingraham, 1997; Oakley and Mitchell, 1997). Relations and locations are understood to have a profound impact on health in general, and on choice in particular. As a result, there is rarely a single right way, right time, or right thing to be done. And often what is determined to be right has power implications.

For these reasons the theories central to the development of gender-based analysis stressed both sameness and difference (Bacchi, 1990). While women as a group share some important experiences, there are also significant differences not only between women and men but also among women. Specific histories and relations are central to appropriate care. This means that treating people the same is often not good enough. Indeed, it may be quite inappropriate for care. Evidence from population health, then, must be treated with caution because it may conceal more than it reveals, especially given that it usually fails to take location into account. At best, this evidence applies only to the most common, leaving the marginal out. This means there is a need for multiple, rather than single, strategies and for a recognition of the concrete along with the abstract or general (Harding, 1986, 1991).

Similarly, feminist political economists see women both as actors and as a group with few choices to make. Women are in contradictory relations. These relations set conditions that are themselves structured by women, albeit usually under conditions of subordination. In health care, this means they are not simply at the mercy of the medical system, although they have often been victimized by it. They are also active in constructing that system. For example, as Mitchison (1998) makes clear, women have never merely taken doctors' orders. Rather, they have always been active in the construction of the relationship with the doctor and with those in the health-care system as a whole. In a similar manner, women have been active in constructing the documents of their lives at the same time as those documents help structure their lives.

The emphasis for feminists is more on connections than on isolated individuals. It is therefore inadequate simply to treat parts to be fixed or to count the number of tasks performed, as is common in evidence-based decision-making. Numbers cannot readily record or assess the quality and context of these connections that are so central to health. Indeed, gender itself is defined in terms of relationships rather than in terms of fixed categories that can be measured simply as another variable in the statistics so central to what counts as evidence in the dominant paradigm.

The emphasis in the gender-based paradigm is also on emotions as well as on reason, in terms of both relations and what counts as evidence. As Nelson (1996: 17) puts it, emotions 'play an important part in truly rational judgement; in a world in which human life is in fact vulnerable—to mortality, illness, want of all kinds—emotional acknowledgment of need is, though sometimes painful, a requisite for good judgement.' While men, too, have emotions, their association with women has helped to denigrate emotions as evidence and has contributed to feminist fears of supporting such evidence.

Central to this paradigm is a critique of objectivity, both as an ideal and as a practice. As Karen Messing (1998: 55) puts it in *One-Eyed Science*, 'What passes for scientific rigor among researchers may in fact be as much a symptom of racism, sexism, or class bias as a burnt cross or a thrown stone, and may do as much psychological and physical harm.' The truths claimed for numerical data have come under particular scrutiny.

Of course, feminist political economists are not alone or even original in their contention that all evidence is socially constructed by social beings, based on culturally and materially bound notions of value and limited by the particular context in which the evidence is developed, as well as by the power relations embedded within this evidence. What is much less common is the positive value feminists place on recognizing the locations of the researchers, their personal experiences, and the knowledge acquired through experience. So, too, is the emphasis feminists place on allowing women to speak for themselves (Burt and Code, 1995). For feminists, experience is both evidence and expertise.

Nor are feminists original in their suspicions of numbers. Writing in 1956 about an earlier phase of faith in numbers, Pitirim Sorokin (1956: 115) spoke of the cult of numerology that is based on three dogmatic assumptions:

> first, that counting and the manipulation of its results is the only—or the best and the surest—method for discovering uniformities in psychosocial phenomena; second, that the results of the counting can be generalized far beyond the phenomena counted, and can be expressed in quantitative formulae as either universal or significant uniformities; third, that these numerological operations permit one to define precisely and quantitatively many a fundamental category, entity, relationship otherwise not clearly definable.

And he went on to stress the importance of recognizing the complexity of social phenomena and of the context in which data are collected. Feminists move beyond the kind of criticism Sorokin makes, however, when they stress the gender-specific nature of the scientific gaze and the critical aspects of health and care rendered invisible by the emphasis on quantitative methods (Armstrong, 1998: 249–66; Moss, 1996; Stein, 1997). In traditional evidence-gathering, the focus is on eliminating as much complexity as possible in order to get to the smallest unit as uncontaminated as possible by values or other forces and relations. In feminist evidence-gathering, complexity is both the focus and the objective, a complexity understood to be gendered. The relations and values, the discourses and representations are critical evidence rather than noise to be eliminated.

A feminist political economy, then, does not reject evidence. Nor does it restrict concepts and methods for evidence-gathering to those associated with qualitative approaches or to what Nelson (1996: 36) calls 'the socially created cognitive category of "feminine"'. Indeed, calls for gender-based analysis often draw on quantitative sources to demonstrate the need for such analysis. For example, statistics have been used to establish the female domination of care work, the connections between reductions in public services and the expansion of women's unpaid care work, the preponderance of women among patients and those who take family members for care, and the unequal position of women in the health-care field. Statistics have also been used to reveal the systemic discrimination embedded in the market and to show that women enjoy better access in public health systems. However, like the two male authors who have written about mathematics, feminists see 'the pursuit of precision alone, without richness, as a vice' (Davis and Hersh, quoted ibid., 30). Such richness cannot come from simply adding more variables, expanding the sample, or running more statistical tests.

Instead, an alternative approach begins by recognizing the context for data collection. It is a context in which profit, or at least cost defined in for-profit terms, is an increasingly central concern. So is managerial control, and this control is often exercised through the collection and use of data or other research. Data collection itself has become a profit-making venture, as has the sale of the technology used to collect, analyse, and distribute information. An alternative approach means not simply being sceptical about truth claims. It also means seeking a wide variety of sources for information recognized as evidence and always remembering that, while patterns exist, individual differences and judgement based on experience must remain. From this perspective, individual stories are not merely anecdotes but critical evidence, and numerical data are understood as based on more—but less rich—anecdotes.

Evidence-Based Decision-Making: A Gender Issue

There is little debate in Canada about whether evidence-based decision-making should play a major role in health reform. The National Forum on Health, the group appointed by the Prime Minister to advise him on health reform, made evidence-based decision-making a central feature of its recommendations. Similarly, provincial reports on health reform have stressed evidence-based decision-making. And 'report cards', based on evidence of performance, are a critical component in the current federal reform agenda. The term 'report cards' is a short form for what is variously described as an 'accountability system' (Walker, 1999: A7), as providing details on 'how well the health care system is working' (McIlroy, 1999: A4), as responding to a 'need to know more about what we're getting for our money' (*Toronto Star*, 4 Feb. 1999: A6), and as a way to assess quality. A wide range of data would be collected and standardized, with a view to influencing policy development. Such report cards are just one example of the new stress on evidence and a renewed emphasis on measurement defined as objective. For the most part, however, evidence-based decision-making has not been discussed as a gender issue in spite of the evidence indicating that the consequences are different for women and men.

It is important to know what is meant by evidence in the dominant paradigm guiding much of health-care reform, particularly when assessing it for gender bias. Two kinds of evidence are privileged. The first is data of the sort that measure such things as number of beds and nurses per population, such processes as length of stay, required nursing time, and outcomes or number of Caesareans per doctor, and such attitudes as patient satisfaction. But no number is innocent, as Deborah Stone so succinctly put it (Stone, 1988: 130). What is counted, how it is counted, how it is processed, and what is done with what is found are value- and power-laden choices. These choices are frequently biased against women or at least fail to take their interests, locations, and critiques into account. Indeed, the very privileging of quantitative data conflicts with the kind of gender-based analysis discussed here. Equally important, these choices are more likely to reflect the interests of managers and owners, who are focused primarily on issues related to their control over processes and products rather than on the interests of those who directly provide or receive care. This kind of evidence plays a major role in the restructuring of health-care services and is used to suggest that the choices are merely scientific rather than also political and social.

The second kind of evidence is clinical. Here the gold standard is the randomized, clinical trial. But as those who argued for a feminist analysis have demonstrated, the standard has too often been established from trials usually conducted with 70-kilogram adult males (Laurence and Weinhouse, 1997: 5). The elimination of variability, often used to justify this standard, also eliminates validity. Women's hormone levels may make them more variable as subjects, but it also makes them more variable as patients, if the assumption is correct. More attention has been paid to this bias than to the bias in the numerical data, perhaps because it is so obvious. However, efforts to address the problems have too often been restricted to including women in trials, and the bias that arises from problem selection, methodologies, the categories used for analysis, and the uses to which the data are put have been a much less frequent concern (Oakley, 1990: 167–94).

The role corporations play in determining the issues and methodologies has received some attention, demonstrating a wide range of biases created by a focus on profit. In spite of this evidence, however, governments are granting such corporations decision-making powers by making partnerships with funders a condition of research support. Even when partnership is not required for research support, by not forbidding such partnerships on the grounds that they constitute a conflict of interest, governments are at least providing implicit support for them. Similarly, such corporations are being invited to be members of the decision-making bodies determining what evidence should be collected and distributed.

The kind of evidence used in restructuring health-care services, then, raises a whole range of questions for women. The issue is not whether or not such data could be useful for decision-making in health care. Indeed, much has already been collected, and some has been used, to promote women's health issues. However, from the perspective I have been describing, at least four questions must be addressed if a feminist analysis is to be about taking women into account, not simply about counting women, and if choices are to be expanded rather than further constrained. And in asking these questions, it is important to remember that the dominant paradigm and power relations shape how the questions are asked and how the answers are used. As Gary Belkin (1997: 510) puts it, 'we need to examine the important connection between being convincingly scientific and being successfully powerful in health policy.' And we need to remember that power is gendered.

What Data Are Collected and How Are They Classified?

The data on health-care delivery provide a useful example. The Advisory Council on Health Infostructure recommended to the Health Minister that the standards for information systems be set by the Canadian Institute for Health Information (Advisory Council on Health Infostructure, 1999). Bringing together tasks previously assigned to Statistics Canada and Health Canada, CIHI already exists as an independent agency intended to 'define and adopt emerging standards for health care informatics' (CIHI, n.d.).

In its membership form, CIHI promises members 'influence on the direction of national health care standards' and is described as having 'substantial representation from the private sector' on its board (*Toronto Star*, 4 Feb. 1999: A6). This statement alone demonstrates the Institute recognizes that facts do not collect or speak for themselves. Important choices are being made that will have a significant impact on health-care services and our choices about these services.

It is perhaps not surprising that private-sector firms involved in the health-care or health information business would be interested in membership, given this promise of influence and the potential for profit growth in the information industry. It is more surprising that they are invited, given the potential for a conflict of interest. Their presence reflects and reinforces the business paradigm, a paradigm that can have a profound impact on what information is available to whom. The representation from women's organizations or from the women who provide care in and out of the home may well be limited by the fact that voting memberships require contributions beginning at $1,000 for one member and vote.

Membership is important because the decisions made by this agency are not simply technical, although they are often presented as if they were. How categories are created, catalogued, processed, and published can have a fundamental impact on care. So if we are to reach the objective of 'public accountability and transparency', as *A Framework to Improve the Social Union for Canadians* (Canada, 1999a: 2) claims, then membership and transparency in the organization that sets the standards for the accounts are critical. It is also critical that this organization take women's critique and concerns into account.

Let's take the decision about the definition of acute care. A recent Manitoba study (DeCoster et al., 1996: 1) began by asking the question: 'Were there patients in the hospital whose health care needs could be more appropriately met in an alternative setting—such as long term care, home care, outpatient?' To answer the question the study began with criteria—developed for hospital utilization review in the United States—described as 'objective, measurable', and relevant 'for all acute hospital care, regardless of location or size of hospital' (ibid., 2). There is, it should be noted, no indication that these criteria have been assessed for their gender-sensitivity or developed with women in mind. Nor is there any evidence that the particular Canadian context has been considered.

Yet location matters. Criteria developed for American purposes are not automatically transferable to Canada or from men to women. In the US, for example, many jurisdictions have sub-acute care, a classification not found in Canada and not directly comparable to long-term care because it provides more complex care services and more highly qualified staff. The definition of 'acute' may well reflect the availability of this alternative level of care. Equally important, there is no universal care system in the US and therefore the pressures contributing to the definition may well be quite different. And rural areas may well have quite different demands from those in major urban areas, in the US as well as in Canada. Perhaps most importantly, Canada has a much different cultural and social population mix, as well as a different social security system that is very important to women in particular. Same treatment does not mean equity for women or for different groups of women, and definitions developed for for-profit care are not necessarily those that Canadians would support if they were fully informed about the implications for care.

In Canada, the adoption of a definition of 'acute care' that includes only the most severely ill, and among those, considers only the ones who can receive immediate treatment, has profound consequences especially for the women who form the majority of those likely to be defined out of acute care. It means an increasing emphasis on the medical model that feminists, among others, have so strongly criticized for treating people as body parts to be fixed as quickly as possible, rather than as whole individuals needing social, psychological, and physical support (Armstrong and Armstrong, 1996). It contributes to what the nurses we interviewed in California for our study of management in health-care reform described as 'drive-by surgery', resulting in enormous pressures on both staff and patients as the primary criterion becomes how fast you can be made to leave (Armstrong et al., 1998).

The nurses, most of whom are women, say they have no time to treat patients as individuals or to feel the sense of satisfaction of helping people get better. This satisfaction once made up for other inadequacies in their conditions of work, and it also helped patients get better. Perhaps surprisingly, given the stated commitment to evidence, the definition of 'acute' ignores the literature on the determinants of health, a literature that stresses the importance of environments and social support to health. As became clear in our interviews with British Columbia nurses who were part of our study of health-care management, women feel responsible—and are held responsible—for the caring work. More and more are sacrificing their own health to make up for the gaps in care left by reforms based on a new definition of 'acute' (Armstrong et al., 1999).

In Canada, this new definition of acute care can also mean that patients, the majority of whom are women, are defined as outside the protection of the Canada Health Act. And many are defined into care by unpaid female caregivers in the home. Or they are defined into care for which they must pay, care that is increasingly provided by for-profit firms. Those few who remain in hospital are now defined as bed-blockers, abusers of the system who are responsible for the long lineups and even deaths in emergency wards (Boyle, 1999a: B1). Most of these bed-blockers, too, are women. Moreover, as a result of this new definition of 'acute', the care work of those in home care and long-term care has intensified, often without additional support or training. Most of this care is also provided by women for women.

In sum, the standards and categories established by organizations such as the CIHI have implications not only for women but also for the health system as a whole. They are about the relations of ruling. That is precisely why the private corporations want to be at the table. Their presence demonstrates both the political nature of these decisions and the extent to which such decisions are being made within a new business paradigm and within new power relations.

How Well Do the Data Reflect the Experiences and Choices of Women in Their Daily Lives?

In their comparative study of health systems, Raisa Deber and Bill Swan (1998: 318) maintain that 'existing ways of measuring health outcomes miss most of the picture, and policy made on this basis may similarly miss significant improvements (or harms) in the health of the population.' The same could be said of other performance measures and of those that calculate workload as well.

There are really three issues within this question about the quality of data. The first is about how accurately the tools measure what they are supposed to measure. The second is what is left out of these measures. And the third is what cannot and should not be measured by quantitative means.

All three problems can be illustrated by the measurements used to calculate how many nurses are required on each shift. According to one group of nurses we interviewed, they were told during the work sampling study not to record what happened at three o'clock in the afternoon because the work was too irregular then. Yet, as one nurse put it, 'That's what health care is about, irregularity'. The same kind of focus on regularity has been used to argue that women's hormonal cycles make them unsuitable subjects for clinical trials (Laurence and Weinhouse, 1997: ch. 3). The search for averages, means, and regularities denies the variation that is central to the kind of care nurses have learned to provide and that patients both demand and require, especially now that only the most complex cases are admitted. It is the kind of regularity that car manufacturers search for in their attempt to separate conception from execution and in their effort not only to deskill but also to control workers.

The measurements of nursing work focus on individual, countable tasks, often missing the richness referenced earlier. A bath is reduced to a quick application of water to skin, and the way nurses use the bath to comfort, support, educate, and assess disappear, as do the varied skills involved in getting the patients to co-operate and in lifting them without injury. Any time not spent directly on tasks is defined as wasted, not productive in terms of the illness line. While some of this variation and the missing skills could be made visible with improved measurement tools, some are not possible to assess by quantitative means.

Caring is one aspect of the job that has been repeatedly identified by nurses as impossible to measure this way. So are the satisfaction they feel when they help someone become well and the responsibility they feel when they fail. There are other, more tangible aspects that could be far better captured by qualitative means, such as the complexity of communication with a person who does not share the nurse's language and culture. And some aspects of caring cannot be captured at all by our measurement tools but may nonetheless be critical to care and to health. As Patricia Benner and Suzanne Gordon (1996: 46) point out, 'When the craft is practiced in relationships with people, the identity of those involved in that relationship . . . become determinants of the outcome of each encounter.'

The issue is not only that inadequate data are collected. Also, the evidence collected may deny women's own experiences as either patients or providers. It challenges our ways of knowing, with significant consequences for women's power.

How Is Evidence Used?

The National Forum on Health (1997: 6) maintains that evidence-based decision-making is not

> tyranny over providers; it is not value free; it is not a suggestion that evidence is not being used now; it is not a methodological straitjacket and it is not an excuse for inaction. Nor is evidence-based decision-making based solely on evidence. It is influenced by values, interests and judgements as well as external pressures and conditions. It is simply getting the best information in place so that people can make the best decision which is consistent with their values and circumstances.

The Forum would have been better to say that this should not be what evidence-based decision-making is, because there is increasing evidence to suggest that in various places throughout the US, the evidence is used to develop rigid formulas for care (Kassler, 1994; Woolhandler and Himmelstein, 1997: 271–6). Within the context of the new managerial paradigm in health reform and with practices imported from the US, there is some evidence to suggest this is beginning to happen in Canada as well.

A recent interview I read suggested that care pathways are being used to provide a form of straitjacket and an excuse for inaction. The person interviewed explained that the data collected by Ontario's Institute for Clinical Evaluative Sciences indicated that the appropriate length of stay for a hip replacement was five days.[2] Nurses had been told to develop a plan that would ensure patients leave in five days. Initially, the nurses had patients staying six or seven days. The interviewee explained that the nurses had clearly not understood that the answer was five, and that another training session was required to fit patient care into the five days determined by the evidence. Asked if any accommodation was made for patients who could not fit, the interviewee explained that the evidence showed 20 per cent would not fit, so it was only necessary to guarantee that 80 per cent left in five days. In the process, the standards came to structure the very procedures they were supposed to reflect and left the female providers with little choice about how to care.

Another example comes from Ontario home-care services. New government directives set out a maximum of 2.6 hours of home care a day for those discharged from hospital, without regard for their illness or conditions at home. After 30 days, the maximum drops to two hours, again without regard to the progress of the illness or conditions at home (Boyle, 1999b: A8). What is taken into account is women's support in the household. For someone to be eligible for even this limited care, the support from family friends and community must be exhausted. One set of guidelines says, 'Individuals who have a capable caregiver are not eligible for home support services. This includes caregivers who work outside the home' (cited in Ontario Health Coalition, 1999: 2).

Such definitive formulas leave limited room for nurses' professional judgements, for patient differences, or for patients' and unpaid providers' preferences. The knowledge patients and providers gain from experience no longer counts. And these formulas fail to recognize how such data are constructed or the choices and power relations embedded in such constructions. 'Equity' is defined in terms of sameness, with treatment or choices based on differences not allowed. Moreover, because the main purpose of these formulas is to reduce costs and increase managerial control, the result is a race to the bottom with each counting exercise intent on providing less. Tomorrow the magic number for hip replacement will be 4.5 days and for home care 1.75 hours.

A second example of evidenced-based decision-making that contradicts the dictum from the National Forum can be found in the use of data developed through work-sampling. As one Ontario RNA we interviewed explained, the work sampling showed that:

> We're working at 120 per cent, which is saying that maybe we need a little more staff to cover this workload. And suddenly, we're going to be on [another study] and they change all the numbers again. So even though last week we were working at 120 per cent . . . in two

> weeks time that's going to be down to 90 per cent [while we are still doing the same work]. (Armstrong et al., 1994: 81)

In other words, the data are manipulated to reduce the number of nurses required on a shift, even though the original evidence demonstrated more, rather than less, nursing staff was required. The nurses who remain feel they are no longer trusted to use their judgement and are so rushed they cannot maintain their own health, let alone provide support for their patients (Armstrong et al., 2000). At the same time, the patient satisfaction surveys that are supposed to ensure accountability indicate 'The nurse couldn't come often enough' (ibid., 54), a fact interpreted too often as the nurse's fault. These uses of evidence may help to explain why we are now experiencing a nursing shortage in Canada—many nurses have left the profession because of job pressures, lack of positive feedback, and personal health concerns.

The new merger and integration plans for hospitals provide a third example of evidence being used to implement reforms inconsistent with values and circumstances, again in contradiction to what the National Forum on Health sets out. Planning for the mergers has been primarily based on population data, on definitions of acute care, on evidence that major teaching hospitals produce better outcomes when it comes to extremely high-tech treatments, on notions of equality rather than of equity, and on data from the US indicating minimally acceptable bed ratios.

The adoption of merger strategies, however, is not based on research investigating the efficacy for care or even the consequences for long-term costs. Indeed, Markham and Lomas (1995) argue that there is no empirical evidence to demonstrate economic, quality, or human-resource gains with multi-hospital arrangements, and some evidence suggests that costs may increase, flexibility and responsiveness to individual patients' needs decline, and relationships with employees deteriorate. Some mergers may be appropriate, given that many hospitals were established long before public payment or current methods were introduced and that many facilities are quite old. The nurses we interviewed in Victoria, BC, did see quite positive benefits coming from the concentration of specialized heart surgery, for example, in one hospital. The mergers reduced expenses for high-tech equipment and brought together highly skilled teams who then had the opportunity to gain frequent experience, thus further developing their skills. Moreover, such surgery was often scheduled to allow families to plan for support. However, applying the same strategy to all acute care, the nurses said, meant not only shipping people around the city, depending on their diagnosis, but also removing them from the community and family supports that have been identified as critical to health. Community hospitals were closed in the name of community care, leaving women scrambling to follow family members around the city and travelling long distances to provide care (Armstrong et al., 1999).

Within a paradigm that adopts practices developed for the production of goods, formulas for care are more likely and room for choice, judgement, recognition of differences, and values more limited. Indeed, this is the purpose of the evidence-based strategy from the perspective of those managing for profit or the bottom line, and it is a purpose that has been imposed first on the female-dominated care providers in health. For patients there is one-stop shopping, but one-stop shopping can mean one size fits all or that there are no services that fit your size. Instead of integrated care, it can mean integrated denial, as the California nurses made clear to us. The elimination of what is called duplication is also the elimination of choice. Ironically, the elimination of duplication is done in the name of the same paradigm that relies on competition, in spite of the fact that competition requires duplication. Such practices directly contradict the feminist emphasis on recognizing differences among patients and the skills of providers.

In stating what evidence-based decision-making is not, the National Forum on Health ignored the context, the setting of the setting for the use of evidence. In the context of a business paradigm, cost and control are central. Tyranny over providers may well be the result, the values and relations of ruling embedded in the evidence hidden by the presentation of evidence as objective—the whole truth and nothing but. The Forum also missed the gender consequences of this context and evidence.

How Is the Evidence Made Available?

Although health data are presented as a means of making more informed choices, there is little discussion of how data are to be made available so that citizens can hold the government, and the services they pay for in our names, accountable. This, in turn, raises at least four issues. How much do they cost? How accessible are they? What about privacy? And how are they constructed for use?

Currently, much of the evidence is not readily accessible to the public, both because it is sold at a high price and because it is made difficult to read or to find. Thus, the women who make up the majority of the poor will find little in the evidence to improve their choices. For evidence to be useful, it must be varied and have varied sources. It must also be transparent in terms of the sources and construction of categories. Only then can women assess the information in light of what we know about the relations of ruling and their gender implications.

At the same time as women find good information hard to locate, they may well find their private records available to a broad spectrum of people involved in the care system. This could include the corporations selling services or employing providers. Consequently, women testing positive on a test, for example, could find themselves inundated with sales promotions or denied insurance and employment. There are safeguards recommended in the report from the Advisory Council on Health Infostructure (1999), although it seems appropriate to remain cautious about the strength of such safeguards given that recently confidential information on 'air miles' became publicly available due to a technical error.

The report from the Advisory Council does recommend that patients have access to their own files. This is critical for everyone, but women have a particular concern. They are much more likely than men to have their symptoms defined as psychological and to be prescribed medication for psychiatric disorders, for example (Harding,

1994: 157–80). Such misinformation could contribute to future problems with treatment and, in an increasingly privatized system, to a denial of coverage for care. It is therefore important that women not only have access to their files, but also have the right to challenge their content. This would mean the additional requirement of keeping records in ways that women could understand.

Perhaps most importantly, the availability of data should not be taken to mean accountability.[3] Accountability cannot be equated with counting, because numbers have all the limitations I have just described. They can be used more as propaganda than as a means to ensure accountability and they can serve that purpose even if that is not the intent. One simple, but obvious, example is the counting of nurses. Published data indicated that the total number of employed nurses has increased in British Columbia over the last three years. However, more detailed analysis revealed that the numbers were based on a body count, and the actual number of nursing hours had declined (British Columbia Nurses' Union, 1997: 2). Moreover, women need tools with which to assess the available data. Comparators matter. If the comparator offered is the equivalent of measuring pollution against the standard of Los Angeles or Mexico City, then women will not be justly served. Finally, even if information is made readily available, it may not only hide as much as it reveals but also reflect and reinforce relations of ruling that leave women subordinate.

Conclusion

A feminist political economy approach does not mean an opposition to any health reform. Indeed, women have long called for reforms in health care, especially for ones that move away from a medical model and current forms of institutional care. And women have benefited from some aspects of health reform. Nor does a political economy approach mean a rejection of evidence-based decision-making or even of quantitative data. In fact, women have often used quantitative data to argue for reform and for an analysis that is sensitive to women's concerns.

A feminist political economy approach, however, does involve much more than including women in the data collection, the clinical trials, and the membership of organizations such as the CIHI. The question is not only whether they are included, but how they are included, and both context and power always matter. It means assessing 'quality of care in terms of its relevance to women in the context of their everyday lives, rather than in terms of service delivery indicators' (Muecke, 1996: 389). That context is global and capitalist, as well as local and familial. It means assessing care work on the basis of women's experience in and out of the formal economy, recognizing the relationships among home, community, and work along with relationships among people. It means highlighting difference and context, while avoiding single solutions and simple, dichotomous choices such as community vs institution, current reform vs no reform, current evidence vs no evidence, ration vs emotion. It thus means focusing on both equity and equality while recognizing that evidence is only part of the issue. The strategies must be democratic and social rather than simply technical and individual.

Under the dominant reform paradigm, however, the cult of numerology is a real risk, especially when managerial practices assume that 'if you can't measure it you can't manage it' and that short-term cost, for profit or not, is the central concern (Newcomer, 1994: 16). It could mean a race to the bottom, with decisions presented as an inevitable result of the evidence. Single solutions are becoming the practice, with little attention paid to context, location, culture, ethnicity, or resources. And the market is offered as a means to efficiency even though, as the business columnist in the *Globe and Mail* put it, 'Critics of government-run health care are either rich hypochondriacs who want to buy more medical services than the state will allow them or lousy economists' (Reguly, 1999: B2). Women are not numerous in either group, but they are among those most likely to suffer from privatized care and from a reliance on current evidence alone. At the same time, women could benefit from the 'race to the top' promised by the new social union (Canada, 1999b: 2), if a gender-based analysis is part of the race and if we recognize that fundamental political and social choices that cannot be reduced to issues of evidence—and that the evidence itself is suspect.

Notes

1. See Deber and Swan (1998: 329). According to these authors, 'cost control has been best in precisely those sectors where there is significant public funding (e.g., hospitals), and most problematic where the private role is greatest (e.g., pharmaceuticals).'
2. It should be noted that the ICES cautions against such rigid formulas in its report (ICES, 1994).
3. Gary Belkin (1997) refers to the stress on scientific objectivity as an attempt 'to resolve contentious issues and/or clothe their resolution as scientifically logical and natural' as 'the technocratic wish'.

References

Advisory Council on Health Infostructure. 1999. *Canada Health Infoway Paths to Better Health*. Final Report. Ottawa: Minister of Public Works and Government Services.

Angus, D.E. 1992. 'A great canadian prescription: Take two commissioned studies and call me in the morning', in R.B. Deber and G.G. Thomson, eds, *Restructuring*

Canada's Health Services System: How Do We Get There From Here? Toronto: University of Toronto Press, 49–62.

Armstrong, P. 1998. 'Women and health: Challenges and changes', in Nancy Mandell, *Feminist Issues: Race, Class and Sexuality*. Scarborough, Ont.: Prentice-Hall, 249–66.

——— and H. Armstrong. 1996. *Wasting Away: The Undermining of Canadian Health Care*. Toronto: Oxford University Press.

——— et al. 1994. *Take Care: Warning Signals for Canadian Health Care*. Toronto: Garamond.

——— et al. 1997. *Medical Alert: New Work Organizations in Health Care*. Toronto: Garamond.

———, principal investigator, et al. 1998. Preliminary Report, 'Promoting profit, preventing health: California nurses experience managed care'. Interviews conducted for research project on Managed Care vs Managing Care, mimeo.

———, principal investigator, et al. 2000. *Heal Thyself: Managing Health Care Reform*. Toronto: Garamond.

Baachi, C. 1990. *Same/Difference*. Sydney: Allen and Unwin.

Belkin, G. 1997. 'The technocratic wish: Making sense and finding power in the "managed" medical market', *Journal of Health Politics, Policy and the Law* 22, 2 (Apr.): 509–32.

Bolaria, B.S., and R. Bolaria, eds. 1994. *Women, Medicine and Health*. Halifax: Fernwood.

Boyle, T. 1999a. 'Hospitals turn away patients at 12 ERs', *Toronto Star*, 5 Feb.

Boyle, T. 1996b. 'Province limiting home care to 2 hours a day: Hampton', *Toronto Star*, 23 July.

Benner, P., and S. Gordon. 1996. 'Caring practice', in Gordon, Benner, and N. Noddings, *Caregiving*. Philadelphia: University of Pennsylvania Press.

British Columbia Nurses' Union. 1997. 'BCNU researcher unearths real story about LPN/RN skills mix ratio', *Bulletin*, 3 Apr.

Burt, S., and L. Code, eds. 1995. *Changing Methods: Feminists Transforming Practice*. Peterborough, Ont.: Broadview Press.

Canada. 1999a. *A Framework to Improve the Social Union for Canadians: An Agreement Between the Government of Canada and Governments of the Provinces and Territories*. 4 Feb.

———. 1999b. *Collaborative Use of the Spending Power for Intergovernmental Transfers: The Race to the Top*. 5 Feb.

Canadian Institute for Health Information (CIHI). n.d. *A Partnership Invitation*. Ottawa.

Christie, W. 1996. 'Keynote Address', in *Health Reform: The Will to Change*, OECD Policy Studies No. 8. Paris: OECD.

Darcey, J. 1998. 'A futuristic nightmare', *Health Sharing* (Fall): 18–21.

DeCoster, C., S. Peterson, and P. Kasian. 1996. *Alternatives to Acute Care*. Winnipeg: Manitoba Centre for Health Policy and Evaluation, July.

Deber, R., and B. Swan. 1998. 'Puzzling issues in health care financing', in National Forum on Health, *Health Care Systems in Canada and Elsewhere*, vol. 4. Ottawa: National Forum on Health.

Doyal, L. 1995. *What Makes Women Sick: Gender and the Political Economy of Health*. New Brunswick, NJ: Rutgers University Press.

Evans, R., M. Barer, and T. Marmor. 1994. *Why Are Some People Sick and Others Not? The Determinants of Health of Populations*. New York: Aldine de Gruyter.

Feldberg, G., and R. Vipond. 1999. 'The virus of consumerism', in D. Drache and T. Sullivan, eds, *Health Reform: Public Success, Private Failure*. New York: Routledge.

Fuller, D. 1998. *Caring for Profit*. Ottawa: Canadian Centre for Policy Alternatives.

Graves, F. 1996. 'Canadian health care—What are the facts? An overview of public opinion in Canada', in *Access to Quality Care for All Canadians*. Ottawa: Canadian Medical Association.

Harding, J. 1994. 'Social basis of the overprescribing of mood-modifying pharmaceutics to women', in Bolaria and Bolaria (1994: 157–80).

Harding, S. 1986. *The Science Question in Feminism*. Ithaca, NY: Cornell University Press.

———. 1991. *Whose Science? Whose Knowledge? Thinking from Women's Lives*. Ithaca, NY: Cornell University Press.

Hennessey, R., and C. Ingraham. 1997. *Materialist Feminism*. London: Routledge.

Illich, I. 1977. *Limits to Medicine: Medical Nemesis*. Harmondsworth: Penguin.

Institute for Clinical Evaluative Sciences (ICES). 1994. *Patterns of Health Care in Ontario*. Ottawa: Canadian Medical Association.

Jerome-Forget, M., and C.E. Forget. 1998. *Who Is The Master? A Blueprint for Canadian Health Care Reform*. Montreal: Institute for Research on Public Policy.

Kassler, J. 1994. *Bitter Medicine*. New York: Birch Lane Press.

Koivusalo, M., and E. Ollila. 1997. *Making a Healthy World: Agencies, Actors and Policies in International Health*. London: Zed Books.

Kuhn, Thomas. 1970. *The Structure of Scientific Revolutions*. Chicago: University of Chicago Press.

Laurence, L., and B. Weinhouse. 1997. *Outrageous Practices: How Gender Bias Threatens Women's Health*. New Brunswick, NJ: Rutgers University Press.

McIlroy, A. 1999. 'Canadians' medical data should be on computer, panel says', *Globe and Mail*. 4 Feb.

Markham, B., and J. Lomas. 1995. 'Review of the multi-hospital arrangements literature: Benefits, disadvantages and lessons for implementation', *Health Care Management Forum* 8, 3 (Fall): 24–35.

Martin, P. 1995. *1995 Budget Speech*. 27 Feb.

Messing, K. 1998. *One-Eyed Science*. Philadelphia: Temple University Press.

Mhatre, S.L., and R.B. Deber. 1992. 'From equal access to health care to equitable access to health: A review of Canadian provincial health commissions and reports', *International Journal of Health Services* 22, 4: 645–68.

Mitchison, W. 1998. 'Agency, diversity, and constraints: Women and their physicians, 1850–1950', in Sherwin (1998).

Moss, K.L. 1996. *Man-Made Medicine: Women's Health, Public Policy and Reform.* Durham, NC: Duke University Press.

Muecke, M. 1996. 'The gender analysis imperative: introduction to the special issue', *Health Care for Women International* 17, 5 (Sept.-Oct.): 1–17.

National Forum on Health. 1997. 'Creating a culture of evidence-based decision-making in health', in *Canadian Health Action: Building on the Legacy*, vol. 2. Ottawa: National Forum on Health.

Nelson, J. 1995. 'Dr. Rockefeller will see you now: The hidden players privatizing Canada's health care system', *Canadian Forum* (Jan.-Feb.): 7–11.

Nelson, J.A. 1996. *Feminism, Objectivity and Economics.* Routledge.

Newcomer, L.N., MD. 1994. Quoted by Working Group on Health Services Utilization, 'When Less is Better: Using Canada's Hospitals Efficiently', paper written for Conference of Federal/Provincial/Territorial Deputy Ministers of Health, June.

Oakley, A. 1990. 'Who's afraid of the randomized controlled trial? Some dilemmas of the scientific method and "good" research practice', in H. Roberts, ed., *Women's Health Counts.* London: Routledge, 167–94.

——— and J. Mitchell, eds. 1997. *Who's Afraid of Feminism?* New York: New Press.

Ontario Health Coalition. 1999. *Fact Sheet #8.* Toronto, Jan.

Parsons, T. 1955. *Essays in Sociological Theory, Pure and Applied*, 2nd edn. Glencoe, Ill.: Free Press, 1995.

Petchesky, R. 1995. 'From population control to reproductive rights: feminist fault lines', *Reproductive Health Matters* (6 Nov.): 152–61.

Reguly, E. 1999. 'Market forces won't cure health care', *Globe and Mail*, 6 Feb.

Sherwin, S. 1992. *No Longer Patient.* Philadelphia: Temple University Press.

———, ed. 1998. *The Politics of Women's Health.* Philadelphia: Temple University Press.

Shields, J., and B.M. Evans. 1998. *Shrinking the State.* Toronto: Garamond.

Smith, D. 1987. *The Everyday World as Problematic: A Feminist Sociology.* Toronto: University of Toronto Press.

———. 1990. *The Conceptual Practices of Power: A Feminist Sociology of Knowledge.* Toronto: University of Toronto Press.

Sorokin, P. 1956. *Fads and Foibles in Modern Sociology.* Chicago: Henry Regnery.

Stein, J. 1997. *Empowerment and Women's Health Theory, Methods and Practice.* London: Zed Books.

Stone, D. 1988. *Policy Paradox and Political Reason.* New York: HarperCollins.

Toronto Star. 1999. 'Report cards proposed for health care services', 4 Feb.

Walker, W. 1999. 'PM forging ahead on health accord', *Toronto Star*, 27 Jan.

———, E. Stewart, and T. Harper. 1999. 'Ottawa offers premiers $5 billion', *Toronto Star*, 4 Feb.

Witz, A. 1992. *Professions and Patriarchy.* London: Routledge.

Wong, K. 1998. *Medicine and the Marketplace*. Notre Dame, Ind.: University of Notre Dame Press.

Woolhandler, S., and D. Himmelstein. 1997. 'Extreme risk—The new corporate proposition for physicians', in C. Harrington and C.L. Estes, eds, *Health Policy and Nursing Crisis and Reform in the U.S. Health System*, 2nd edn. Boston: Jones and Bartlett, 271–6.

CHAPTER 7

Towards a Sociology of Knowledge in Health Care: Exploring Health Services Research as Active Discourse

Eric Mykhalovskiy

Introduction

How might one research formal discourses of health knowledge as social? How does one get at the ways in which health sciences enter into and help to shape the restructuring of the health-care system? How can one go about researching health-related knowledges in ways that foreground social relations and that attend to the organization of power in contemporary society? This chapter comments on the possibilities of a sociology of knowledge in health care. Rather than focusing on the above questions by providing conclusive answers, it suggests them as the conceptual ground for an inquiry of health-care restructuring that takes seriously the operation of new modes of knowledge.

Political economy is the dominant research tradition in North America offering a critique of contemporary health-care restructuring. Political economists have presented the most important scholarly countervoice to recent preoccupations with business practices as solutions for health-care problems and, in Canada, are the leading source of intellectual defence of medicare.

The specific research problems addressed by political economy approaches to health-care reform are numerous and wide-ranging. One form of research draws on state theory and other conceptual resources to critique the quality and accessibility of restructured health care programs (Burke and Stevenson, 1993; Glennerster and Le Grand, 1995; Terris, 1992; Reinhardt, 1992). In both the United States and Canada, a tradition of inquiry explores changes in state/corporate/medical relations and their consequences for the power of the medical profession (McKinlay and Arches, 1985; Navarro, 1988; Coburn, 1993; Coburn et al., 1997). Among other research, work has been done on the relationship between the pharmaceutical industry and government regulators (Lexchin, 1984), on transformations in the organization of nursing (Campbell, 1994; Beardwood et al., 1999), on the restructuring of the labour process in hospitals (Armstrong et al., 1997), and on the reorganization of long-term care services and the individualization of responsibility for health and health care (Aronson and Neysmith, 1997; Aronson, 1990).

While research approaches vary, political economy generally explores the restructuring of health care in terms that focus on the shifting and contested boundaries between the state and the market (Armstrong and Armstrong, 1996; Drache and Sullivan, 1999). Political economy investigations are based in conceptual strategies that examine changes in state/market relations and the implications of cost-containment and privatization initiatives that introduce market principles into the organization of a public welfare service (Armstrong et al., 1997; Appleton, 1999; Stewart, 1999; Sonnen and McCracken, 1999). From such a perspective, the reform of health care is understood as a substantiation of neo-liberal ideology, as a form of corporatization, and/or as part of a more general retrenchment from the welfare state.

Important as these critiques have been, they have only partly illuminated the power relations that operate in contemporary health-care reform. While their analytic frameworks are well-suited to describe state/capital/professional relations, they are less able to shed light on the circuitry of knowledge relations that suffuse contemporary programs of health-care restructuring. Whether articulated as projects for making health-care practitioners more focused on quantifiable outcomes (Evidence-Based Medicine Working Group, 1992; Sackett et al., 1991; Rosenberg and Donald, 1995) or as initiatives for restructuring health-care services as integrated delivery systems or as managed care (Shortell et al., 1996; Marriott and Mable, 1998), contemporary programs for governing health care rely on new forms of population-based information about health-care practices.

The organization of knowledge about health care around numericalization and aggregation represents more than technical advancement; it holds implications for how health-care services are understood, organized, and delivered. If the critique of health-care restructuring is to be concerned with the social organization of reform, then inquiry must attend to the play of knowledge forms in health care. Political economy has begun to take steps in this direction, for example, in the important ideology critiques of population health offered by Poland et al. (1998) and Robertson (1998). However, in addition to formal critiques of the content of health knowledge, analyses need to explore knowledge at the level of social practice (Hopwood and Miller, 1994). We need to put into view the social processes through which formal discourses of knowledge operate as active constituents of heath-care reform.

This chapter offers an invitation to political economy to take up the challenge of such an inquiry. It provides an example of what that inquiry might look like. It also suggests directions for research that would develop a more extended project of explicating the social relations of formal knowledges in health-care reform.

The particular health science that grounds my discussion in this chapter is health services research (HSR), a highly applied, often numerically based form of knowledge that contributes and responds to the treatment of health care as a managerial problem in need of 'fixing'. HSR is extremely popular in health policy circles, where it is widely promoted as a remedy for current health-care cost problems (Eisenberg, 1998; Ginzberg, 1991a; National Forum on Health, 1997; Goel et al., 1996; Naylor et al., 1994). HSR is a ruling discourse. Increasingly, it operates as the standard intellectual paradigm for thinking about health care in Canada and its problems. As discourse, HSR provides an intellectual technology that privileges questions of efficiency and effectiveness and that informs and realizes current neo-liberal policy objectives.

In writing about HSR, my interest is to explore how it operates as a social practice. This involves foregrounding social organization (Smith, 1987) and the relation of discourse and action. Put simply, my broad aim is to show how HSR is part of the way things get done in health care. The particular empirical site of discussion in this chapter is policy-based social science research on health-care reform. My main objective is to display some of the conceptual mechanics through which HSR colonizes social science research and thinking about health care. As knowledge workers, social scientists are deeply implicated in the forms of expertise and professional discourse through which health care is governed. Drawing attention to how HSR enters into and shapes academic health-care research opens up for scrutiny an important dimension of the relations of knowledge in health care. It puts into view how forms of scholarly knowledge are hooked into ruling relations[1] and points to ways of producing research that are positioned otherwise.

The chapter offers a close reading of two important articles on health-care restructuring in Canada (Chappell, 1993; Evans, 1992), in which I suggest how discourse objects constituted by health services research co-ordinate academic analysis of health care. The analytic strategy treats academic writing as data for an examination of HSR as active discourse. Rather than focusing on what is said about HSR in academic prose, analysis is aimed at displaying HSR at work, actively organizing the site of academic knowing about health care as a site of health-care management.[2] While focused on HSR as conceptual co-ordinator of academic analysis of health care, my discussion also considers the entry of HSR into the management of health care in other institutional settings.

Health services research is a relatively new form of expert knowledge, not well known outside of health sciences circles. Some brief remarks on the nature of HSR and on its commentary within the relevant literature are first in order.

What Is Health Services Research?

Getting a conceptual hold on health services research is no simple matter. Disputes about its nature have been a recurring feature of practitioners' self-justifications since the term first became widely used in the US in the 1960s. Most efforts to define it emphasize that HSR is not a formal discipline but a field of research or program of inquiry (Flook and Sanazaro, 1973; Institute of Medicine, 1979; DeFriese, 1989; White et al., 1992). HSR is applied and multidisciplinary, and draws on the conceptual and methodological resources of epidemiology, biostatistics, economics, and other disciplines to create knowledge about the delivery of health-care services (Frankford, 1994; Shortell, 1997; Pittman, 1995). The topics it addresses are wide-ranging and include, for example, the structure, processes, and organization of health-care services, their use, quality, and relationship to health status, access to services, the efficiency and effectiveness of services, and the uses of medical knowledge (Crombie, 1996; Institute of Medicine, 1995).

The field's applied character is related to its development in relation to state concerns about health and health care. HSR has been generally understood as a response to state demands for a better understanding of how health-care services are 'organized, financed, and delivered and with what consequences' (Institute of Medicine, 1995: 25). As health-care services expanded and became more complex, HSR emerged as a site for systematic inquiry about health-care systems and practices, how they contribute to health, and what makes them costly. In both Canada and the US, the concerns of governments about increasing health-care costs are offered as the primary impetus behind the emergence of HSR as a coherent field of research (Rappolt, 1996; Ginzberg, 1991b; Institute of Medicine, 1979).

While HSR embraces a range of research activities, much of the contemporary work is population-based, addressing questions about medical service delivery through the use of statistical methods. HSR traffics in aggregate data sets made available by the installation of large-scale administrative databases and computing facilities in the health-care sector in the 1960s (Anderson and Mooney, 1990). It has a strong numerical base. Among the most popular forms of current HSR are studies of geographic and temporal variations in such health services as surgical practices (Wennberg and Gittelsohn, 1982; Wennberg, 1984; Vayda et al., 1984; Roos, 1989; Naylor et al., 1994) and studies of the cost-effectiveness and outcomes of medical interventions (Ellwood, 1988; Young and Cohen, 1992; Ganz and Litwin, 1996; Goodwin and Llewellyn-Thomas, 1994).

Health services research is further distinguished by its treatment of health-care systems and/or their constituent parts (however understood) as an object of managerial reflection. The accounts of health-care practices it produces are not made for purposes of philosophical or theoretical reflection, but for the pragmatic work of 'improving' health care. Within the contemporary context of concern for costs, HSR further operates as a problematizing knowledge, responding to 'unwieldy', 'costly' health-care systems by seeking to make the actions of health-care providers administratively knowable.

Through various calculative practices, forms of numerical representation, and narrative commentary, HSR gives shape to health-care activities as a patterned universe of increases, decreases, and dispersions, known as such through comparison of surgical utilization rates, average lengths of hospital stay, rates of hospital readmission, and other statistically derived objects of discourse. The patterns made visible by HSR present new objects of attention for health-care policy. Such is the case, for example, in the suggestion of wasteful or unnecessary care by research that points to wide variations in the rates of surgical procedures (Goel et al., 1996). At the same time, HSR proposes solutions to such problems, for example, in calls to decrease expenditures and rationalize health care by realigning wayward hospital-specific surgical rates with provincial or regional averages.

Through such means, HSR operates as a technology of visibility and judgement in health care. While many distinguish health services research from other forms of health research, such as clinical trials, by virtue of a realm of actual medical practice that it observes and represents (Naylor, 1994; Frankford, 1994; Tanenbaum, 1994), HSR is better understood in terms of its constitution of health care as a particular kind of object to be known. What is important about HSR is how it grounds a particular medico-administrative rationality, a particular way of understanding what the substance of health care is, what its problems are, and how they should be ameliorated.

Since its consolidation in the 1960s, HSR has enjoyed considerable institutional success. Professional health services research associations, journals, and granting bodies have been established. In university settings, the field is now routinely taught in graduate programs in health policy, administration, clinical epidemiology, and public health (Institute of Medicine, 1995). Under the aegis of the concern for health-care costs and their containment, HSR has been installed as the primary intellectual and justificatory base of contemporary health-care policy. In Canada, HSR institutes funded largely by provincial governments and committed to producing knowledge about the effectiveness, efficiency, and appropriateness of health-care services abound.[3] HSR institutes and health services researchers are linked with one another and with the public and private sectors through the Health Evidence Application and Linkage Network, established in 1995 as one of Canada's Networks of Centres of Excellence (NCE).[4] Most recently, in 1997, the federal government committed $65 million to help establish the Health Services Research Fund, administered by the Canadian Health Services Research Foundation.

Health Services Research—How Has It Been Thought About?

Given its considerable popularity and institutional success, one might expect an established scholarly inquiry of the relation of expertise, knowledge, discourse, and restructuring processes to have formed around health services research. Unfortunately, this has not been the case. The applied character of much social research on health care is such that the most common textual presence of HSR within social science literature on health-care reform is as a conceptual resource rather than as an explicit object of analysis. Rather than posing questions of health services research, such forms of inquiry draw on its named or unnamed premises to formulate policy-oriented assessments of health-care reform (see Chappell, 1993; Evans, 1992). In so doing, they give shape to a technical narrative of HSR, one that understands its positioning in relations of health-care restructuring in terms of a putative capacity to remedy problems of cost escalation.

Fortunately, policy-based narratives that constitute HSR as little more than a technical fix for current woes do not exhaust the available frameworks for understanding its political significance. While far from well developed, a scholarly discussion that treats HSR as a central object of analysis has begun to appear in the critical social science literature on health-care restructuring. This discussion departs from the scientistic claims of health services researchers and the relevances of policy-based narratives. It begins to pose questions about HSR and generally avoids seeing HSR as a neutral technique for guiding health-care reform.

Much of this discussion has taken place in the United States, where health services research is well developed and closely tied to the development of managed care (Belkin, 1997). Political economists and others working in the US have begun to write in ways that treat seriously the character of HSR as a knowledge form. The primary analytic framework organizing their consideration of HSR is the critique of professional power. Tanenbaum (1994, 1996), for example, examines claims made about the relevance of outcomes research for clinical and policy decision-making.[5] While arguing that clinical decision-making is fundamentally interpretive and therefore irreducible to research findings, she suggests that the political significance of outcomes research rests in the relations through which it is epistemologically privileged over what practising physicians know.

Concerns about how HSR can overrun the judgement of individual practising physicians are also raised by Belkin (1994, 1997). For Belkin, the ascendancy of HSR is but one expression of a 'technocratic wish'. Belkin describes this wish as a 'history of how democratic societies rely on an objectivity of standardized measures to broker disagreement, rather than rely on individual expert judgment' (1997: 511). Drawing on the history of science and medicine, he raises questions about how authority over physicians is justified by processes through which knowledges that rely on 'objective' measures come to be authorized and considered 'truthful'.

Political economy perspectives have also been employed in work that treats HSR as a knowledge form deserving of explicit critique. Like the analyses of Tanenbaum and Belkin, work on HSR informed by political economy is framed by questions about medical autonomy (see Rappolt, 1997). One of its more distinctive features, however, is its emphasis on HSR as an objectifying discourse. Here, the tendency is towards analyses of HSR that rely on a negative theory of power (Foucault, 1979, 1980b). By negative theory of power, following Foucault's critique of it, is meant ways of conceptualizing power as a repressive, constraining, and limiting quantity. The recent work of Navarro (1993) and Frankford (1994) suggests some of the possibilities and limitations of this form of critique of HSR.

Navarro offers an analysis of the nature of health services research based on his response to an important anthology (White et al., 1992) that draws together previously published HSR dating from 1913 to 1991. Navarro's critique of the text and of HSR more broadly is framed within a perspective that focuses on the social determinants of health. He notes that the relatively exclusive focus of HSR on clinical medicine prevents an examination of the broader social, political, and economic relations that shape the delivery of health-care services and the nature of health problems faced by most individuals. He further argues that its emphasis on 'conjunctural details', to the exclusion of the structural determinants of health and health care, serves to reflect and reinforce the interests of the 'health policy establishment' (1993: 1).

In a more complex argument, Frankford (1994: 784) likens HSR to a 'new form of Taylorism in which data collection and analysis will supposedly lead to optimal processes of diagnosis and treatment'. Drawing on Habermas (1971), he critiques HSR as a form of scientism and economism. For Frankford, HSR enters into contemporary relations of health-care reform as an objectifying discourse. In his view, by representing reality as consisting only of 'phenomena that can be quantified and measured', HSR operates in ways that obscure the fullness of human activity in relation to health and the body (Frankford, 1994: 774).

The analyses offered by Navarro and Frankford are instructive in a number of ways. Their respective remarks about health policy establishments and Taylorism help to locate HSR within a broader social, political, and economic context of health-care restructuring. They also help to distinguish HSR as an organization of assessment by suggesting its association with related forms of measurement and calculation and with a set of political uses. More broadly, both authors shed light on an important property of discourses of knowledge—how they constrain or limit possibilities of thought. Their discussions are suggestive of how HSR negates the complexity of people's interactions with health-care providers by textually transforming them into a set of standardized and objectified rates and averages of medical events.[6]

At the same time, there are problems with how Navarro and Frankford treat HSR as a knowledge form implicated in health-care restructuring. The use of Taylorist metaphors to describe health services research is at risk of projecting a history and set of social relations unique to industrial capitalism onto contemporary health-care developments that have a distinct development and social form. In the American political economy literature, Taylorism appears as a common rhetorical device in discussions linking population-based medico-administrative data and control of the medical profession (Salmon et al., 1994; Feinglass and Salmon, 1994).

However, the social relations through which contemporary medical practice has become an object of investigation and has been constructed as a site of inefficiency and ineffectiveness, and the work practices that organize its assessment, are different from those that shaped Taylorist scientific examination and management of industrial labour processes. While both forms of assessment share the use of statistical and calculative techniques, the contemporary evaluation of medical practice constructed the patient as a rational consumer and furnished a kind of knowledge for use in government, hospitals, and other sites of professional work to manage new problems of inefficiency. This is not the same process that appeared as the monitoring of labour during the heyday of industrial capital.

Inscribing the social character of HSR in terms of its support of 'interested positions', as Navarro does, also has analytic shortcomings. Health services research is not part of a master plan of rule. Its support of political interests cannot be read off the surface of its texts. Feminists and midwives, for example, have used data on regional variations in hysterectomy rates as part of a challenge to the organization of health-care services that is not part of the emphasis on cost-reduction.

In addition to missing the contradictory uses of HSR, the perspectival approach to knowledge that claims HSR supports this or that interest also limits the terrain of the analytic category 'the social'. Understanding HSR only as reinforcing the interests of a 'health-care policy establishment' treats it in a derivative fashion. This approach, in other words, presents a new way of knowing in ways that merely extend an established scholarly discussion about the relative power of physicians, the state, and capital. The risk of such an analytic strategy is that HSR appears as significant for health-care reform only as a resource or tool in a contest for power, which is the main object of analysis. Within this analytic framework, the burden of exploring HSR as a practical exercise of power does not present itself. HSR, after all, helps to order activity in health care through the questions it asks and the forms of visibility of health care it offers, all of which are a consequence of a particular configuration of calculative practices, narrative strategies, and forms of expertise.

Lastly, the analyses of HSR put forward by Frankford and Navarro are limited by their failure to consider the productive character of discourses of knowledge.[7] While health services research negates, it also enables. Even as it sullies the ground of experience and prevents an understanding of the broader social determinants of health, it provides positive ways of thinking about the substance and problems of health care.

Representing health care as a patterned universe of numerically based rates and averages of medical events is not simply a move of negation; it also produces a form of intelligibility of health care that shapes thought and action directed at it. As such, the critique of HSR should not focus exclusively, or perhaps even primarily, on what it prevents or represses. If the play of HSR within contemporary relations of health-care restructuring is of concern, then analyses of how it enables forms of health-care management are required. Theoretical approaches to power that emphasize its relationship to knowledge through a negative mechanics are not an appropriate resource for such an undertaking.

Reading through Technical Narratives to an Active Conception of Health Services Research

The remainder of this chapter examines some of the ways that health services research operates as a productive exercise of power. The main point of the analysis is to explore the discursive mechanics through which HSR provides for the terms of understanding within which questions and answers about health-care reform are made in policy-based academic discussions. The main empirical site of the analysis is the technical narratives of HSR mentioned above, particularly as they are expressed in work by Chappell (1993) and Evans (1992). These two articles are important expressions of applied academic work on health-care reform in Canada and have often been cited in the literature.

My discussion is not meant as a critique of the specific arguments made by the two authors, nor have I selected these two texts as representational devices, that is, as sources of HSR information. Instead, I treat them as data for an analysis of HSR as active discourse. My interest is to think through the texts in order to suggest the discursive resources that enable them. Based on a close reading of their arguments I suggest that a technocratic notion of appropriateness, in Chappell's case, and the problem of efficiency, in Evans's case, represent points at which HSR as discourse is activated and constructed as part of the work of managing health-care problems. While the two texts are not 'about' HSR, their manner of argumentation exposes a productive exercise of power on the part of HSR, one that organizes the doing of social science as a managerial effort. Drawing from my analysis, I conclude with suggestions for examining health services research in ways that would begin to display how it enters into other sites where the management of health care goes on.

The two articles under examination are examples of applied social science that engage technical, policy-based narratives. Following contemporary health-care policy, they are preoccupied with the problem of 'excessive' health-care expenditures.[8] In both cases this involves an assessment of current efforts to reduce health-care costs and the promotion of a preferred alternative.

Chappell's discussion is shaped by a critique of medically organized care from the perspective of health promotion and a concern for structuring health care so that it meets the needs of an aging society. Chappell reviews federal and provincial strategies for containing health-care costs and argues against their focus on reducing medical and institutional spending. In her view, regulating the supply of physicians or reducing hospital costs should give way to an emphasis on redistributing expenditures to community care, understood as a more appropriate and cost-efficient form of care for societies with aging populations.

Evans, on the other hand, reviews Canada's health-care policy agenda within a framework that compares American and Canadian forms of organizing the financing of health care. Evans supports Canadian medicare and examines measures such as the regulation of the health-care labour force supply, control over the extension of technology, medical fee schedule negotiation, and control over the costs of administering health-care financing. Evans is distinguished by his recommendation of aggregate medico-administrative information as a preferred strategy for attending to the problem of health-care costs. More specifically, he argues that the costliness of the health-care system is best addressed through the increased use of management information systems to determine what forms of care should be delivered under what circumstances (Evans, 1992: 754).

Having summarized the content of the two articles, let me now consider the play of health services research within each of them. I begin with Chappell. HSR can be seen to co-ordinate Chappell's analysis by providing a set of structuring concepts. This is most apparent in how her call for community care, as a preferred form of organizing health care in Canada, is established negatively through a critique of medicine that centres on a technocratic notion of appropriateness. Early in her discussion, Chappell argues for the appropriateness of community care in relation to its presumed capacity to respond to the needs of an aging population. However, her arguments about appropriateness are also structured in relation to the preoccupations of health services research. This is apparent in her focus on the cost-effectiveness of forms of community care and in a shift in her discussion through which appropriateness comes to be argued for in terms of an HSR critique of medical care.

Early in Chappell's argument the appropriateness of a form of care is located in its putative correspondence with an aggregate need of society, but later it becomes an effect of HSR. Chappell's critique of medicine takes aim at medicine's failure to demonstrate, through research, the effectiveness of its practices:

> There is disagreement on precise rates but there is no longer a question that some portion of medical intervention is unnecessary, inefficient, or produces small returns. Further, the principal role of most physicians is to restore functioning, but there are no measures of their ability to fulfill this task. (1993: 495)

As such, medicine, at least in certain of its manifestations, is inappropriate for Chappell because it has been so deemed by the current organizing framework of HSR. The shift from a needs-based argument to one that reproduces an evidence-based critique of medicine is important, for it serves to demonstrate the anchoring of Chappell's discussion about the appropriateness of community care within the distinctive calculative logic of HSR.

What we have in Chappell's work, then, is an example of the use of HSR to support a policy-oriented argument about the direction that health care reform should take. In tying her arguments about the value of community care to a technocratic notion of appropriateness, she organizes her analysis in relation to a field of discourse created in part by HSR. Appropriateness infers a whole series of related objects—outcomes, practice variations, cost-effectiveness, efficiency—whose detection and remedying follow from calculative technologies of health services research.

Chappell's work thus relies on and, in fact, calls for more HSR. Organized within the terms of its visibility, the immediately available relation of her work to health services research suggests itself as a reproduction of the central claims of health services research. Reading her article, one would easily understand HSR to be an objective knowledge that operates within health care by detecting and remedying health-care problems. More interesting than this reproduction of a technical narrative of HSR is the more implicit relationship of HSR to relations of power suggested by her analysis. When read as data, Chappell's discussion displays HSR at work, conceptually coordinating academic analysis of health care as a managerial effort. This is not meant to suggest that health services research somehow determines the shape of analytic work. Rather, it underscores how HSR operates as a discursive practice, generously offering up categories of discourse that enable a way of speaking and acting on health care.[9] This way of speaking and acting, what I call a medico-administrative rationality, can be expressed only on the basis of the constitution of health care as a numerically based patterned set of medical events. Chappell's work suggests one form of its articulation.

While in Chappell's work a technocratic notion of appropriateness acts as a point of entry into the relevances of health services research, in Evans's article, analysis is structured by the concept of efficiency. Like Chappell, Evans displays HSR in action, in this instance by offering an example of how social science analyses of health-care reform come to be organized as calls for the efficient restructuring of health-care services. Evans's explicit remarks about management information systems position HSR within a technical narrative of power. At the same time, the manner of his argumentation suggests that HSR is implicated in relations of reform through processes that make it possible to speak and act about health care in a medico-administrative way.

Efficiency enters into Evans's assessment of health-care reform strategies as a longed-for end of health-care services. In his analysis, Evans positions the state as a purchaser of care for its population and argues that its primary responsibility in this role is to achieve 'value for money'. In Evans's view, value for money can only be realized by the state on the basis of a new kind of information, namely, a scientific knowledge that demonstrates the effectiveness of various forms of medical intervention. In his analysis, knowledge of effectiveness is linked with efficiency through its promise to reduce costs by eliminating wasteful practices, including those that are minimally effective or of no proven benefit.

At the level of textual surface, Evans's analysis inscribes HSR within a technical narrative of power. Indeed, his explicit recommendation of population-based forms of information as a strategy for reform suggests HSR as a practical remedy for contemporary health-care problems. When his article is read for the discursive resources that enable its form of argumentation, however, HSR appears as politically significant for how it gives shape to a medico-administrative rationality of health.

Evans's problematization of efficiency, for example, takes his work into contemporary forms of managing health-care problems as a result of health services research. His positioning of the value and cost of health care within an input/output equation infers the various forms of calculating and measuring health care accomplished by HSR. Much of the knowledge produced by HSR is designed to improve 'value for money', that is, to contribute to the organization of a cost-efficient health-care system so that health outcomes are improved or at least maintained while inputs or expenditures decline. Evans's discussion of efficiency thus depends on HSR's organization of a stance towards health care as object, which makes measurement possible and also makes it possible to speak and know of its performance.

Evans's work further suggests certain of the discursive mechanics through which health services research co-ordinates the site of academic inquiry. One of these involves a colonization of questioning, such that the problems posed by HSR come to be those posed by social science more generally. Evans's assessment of health-care reform efforts continually refers back to the question of which practices might best promote cost-efficiency. His repeated valorization of efficiency as a policy and program goal positions the social scientist as seeker of efficiencies. Overall, the effect is a fashioning of social science *for* HSR, as social science comes to ask the same questions raised by HSR, in this case how best to realize an efficient health-care system.

A second aspect of discourse made visible in Evans's work involves a certain circularity of reasoning whereby health services research is positioned as a solution to problems that it constitutes. As I have already suggested, Evans's remarks on efficiency represent a way of speaking about health care made possible by HSR. When Evans attends to what is problematic about the contemporary organization of health care, he does so in terms of an analytic gaze that mirrors the forms of understanding health care produced by HSR. Thus, what concerns him is hospital care of questionable benefit, medical interventions of unknown effectiveness, and uncertain health outcomes. These problems rely on HSR for the conditions of their expression—they are known and detected on the basis of its calculative practices. Evans's work thus suggests part of how a medico-administrative rationality of health operates. It displays a way of knowing and acting on health care in which a particular organization of knowledge production is taken up as a solution for problems that it originates.

Conclusion

In my commentary on articles by Chappell and Evans I have offered a reflexive discussion of health services research as social practice. My discussion focuses on a site where I and many others who will read this article are located—the academy—and explores how HSR gives shape to particular forms of applied inquiry about health-care reform made within the academic community. The point of the discussion is to suggest new ways of understanding how HSR is implicated in contemporary relations of health-care reform. Technical, policy-based narratives suggest that HSR enters health-care reform as a resource for ameliorating the escalation of costs. Drawing on a negative theory of power, political economy perspectives emphasize that HSR works as an obfuscating discourse that negates more politicized or embodied ways of understanding the organization of health care.

The alternative offered by my discussion treats policy-based narratives as data for an analysis of HSR that emphasizes its enabling rather than disabling character. Applied academic work on health-care restructuring can be read not simply as a source of information about HSR but as a site that displays its organizing capacities. The articles by Chappell and Evans express a way of understanding the substance and problems of health care that, in many ways, is supplied by health services research. In my remarks I have underscored both how the articles rely on and call for the forms of intelligibility of health care produced by the knowledge-making practices of HSR and how their analyses are organized around discourse objects—accountability and efficiency—that HSR produces and generously promotes. In an important way, the articles provide a window into the mechanics of HSR as active discourse, showing how the conceptual ordering of academic work by HSR places such work into the relations through which health care is managed.

My remarks are intended as part of an analytic move that foregrounds the significance of contemporary forms of health science for the restructuring of health care. It builds on work that treats HSR as a central and sufficient object of analysis by inverting the gaze of technical, policy-based narratives of heath-care reform. Rather than formulating an analytic project in the service of HSR, one that treats the questions posed by health services researchers as its own, it begins to pose questions about HSR and how it works as a social practice. While focused on the site of academic knowledge and its making, my discussion suggests directions for exploring the play of HSR within other sites where health care is managed, a move required for developing a broader project of sociological inquiry of HSR and its implications for health-care reform.

As I have suggested, the analyses of health-care reform offered by Chappell and Evans authorize the project of assessment put forward by health services research. Formulated as contributions to a social science *for* HSR, they endorse its forms of understanding health care. A social science inquiry *of* HSR, rather than one made in its service, would do otherwise. Rather than underwriting the verity and objectivity of HSR and its discourse objects, such an inquiry would explore the social organization of its calculative practices as constituting of new forms of governing health care.

Health services research is but one of a variety of numerically based forms of expertise that increasingly are being drawn upon in the administration and management of contemporary social life (Rose, 1991; Rose, 1994; Miller and Rose, 1990; Porter, 1995). Understanding how health and health care are now governed requires forms of analysis that will aid an understanding of the social character and operation of discourses of knowledge present in the sphere of health care. As I have suggested, HSR makes up versions of what health care is. It renders health care intelligible in a medico-administrative form—as sequences of patterned, numerically based aggregate medical events, such as variations in rates of surgical practices or cost-(in)effective outcomes of medical interventions.

These forms of intelligibility render health care amenable to certain forms of managerial practice. Among the most important of these are ways of acting on health care across place and time. On the basis of the translation of local events into a standardized, aggregate, numerically based form, utilization managers in one hospital site can now compare 'their' rates of surgical practice with those of other institutions as part of identifying 'opportunities' for decreasing lengths of stay. Provincial governments can fine-tune funding priorities by comparing standardized data on the cost-effectiveness of alternative methods of treatment. Patients can enter into new relations of accountability by using performance indicators of one sort or another to make judgements about health-care providers and institutions, and so on.

Clearly, the contemporary relations through which health care is managed involve the workings of knowledge forms in ways that are about much more than negation or the support of a given interest. Theoretical and empirical work in the social organization of knowledge (Smith, 1998; McCoy, 1998; Campbell and Manicom, 1995), in social studies of science and technology (Latour, 1987; Callon, 1986), and in recent studies of governmentality (Barry et al., 1996; Chua, 1995; Preston et al., 1997) all provide conceptual resources for making sense of co-ordinated forms of governing health that rely on standardization and involve new relations of competition and accountability. Political economists interested in the operation of health services research and other health sciences can play an important role in an interdisciplinary project of opening up such relations to scrutiny.

At the risk of sounding trite, there is much work to be done. We need to understand better the complex of inscriptive, calculative, and other practices through which health services research and related forms of knowledge are produced. We need to better understand who is involved in promoting HSR and how they go about promoting it. Most importantly, we need careful empirical analyses to help us to understand better how, and with what consequences, HSR and related discourses of knowledge are used in the work of formal governments, in the work of managing and delivering hospital care, in community and public health work, in primary medical care, and in private industry and in other sites where health and health care are produced and managed.

Notes

An earlier version of this chapter was presented as a paper at the International Conference on Knowledge, Economy and Society, Université de Montréal, July 1997. In addition to the editors and anonymous reviewers, I thank Michael Bresalier, Liza McCoy, and Lorna Weir for their comments on earlier drafts of the chapter.

1. The term 'ruling relations' is Smith's. She uses it to refer to a complex of activities in the spheres of management, the professions, government, and the academy through which contemporary capitalist societies are organized, regulated, and administered (Smith, 1990a: 14; 1990b: 2).
2. This approach draws on Smith's work on textually mediated social relations and, in particular, on her discussion of the 'active text' (Smith, 1990b: 120–58).
3. These include the Institute for Clinical and Evaluative Sciences in Ontario; the Centre for Health Services and Policy Research, University of British Columbia; the Manitoba Centre for Health Policy and Evaluation; Saskatchewan's Health Services Utilization and Research Commission; the Centre for Health Economics and Policy Analysis, McMaster University; the Population Health Research Unit, Dalhousie University; the Institute for Health and Outcomes Research, University of Saskatchewan; and the Centre for Health Evaluation and Outcomes Sciences, St Paul's Hospital, Vancouver. '

4. The NCE program is a Federal Initiative linking research and development across the public, private, and academic sectors for the purpose of stimulating the economy and improving the 'quality of life' of Canadians.
5. Outcomes research is a variant of HSR that draws on aggregate statistics to define probabilistic relationships between medical interventions and desired health-care effects (see Tanenbaum, 1996: 519; Lohr, 1988).
6. For a discussion of the textual practices that give shape to objectified knowledge forms, see Smith (1990a, 1998).
7. The conception of expert knowledges as positive or productive derives from Foucault's later work on power/knowledge (Foucault, 1980a, 1982, 1991). Examples of analyses of expertise as a productive exercise of power can be found in the governmentality literature. See especially Miller and Rose (1990) and Rose (1994).
8. For a discussion of the organization of contemporary health-care policy around the issue of cost and its containment, see Hurst (1991) and Chernichovsky (1995).
9. Nikolas Rose suggests that contemporary relations of expertise should be understood not as a monopolization or shoring up of knowledge, but as involving an outward spread or proliferation of expert vocabularies and conceptual resources. For his discussion of the 'generosity of expertise', see Rose (1994).

References

Appleton, B. 1999. 'International Agreement and National Health Plans: NAFTA', in Drache and Sullivan (1999).

Anderson, T.F., and G. Mooney. 1990. 'Medical practice variations: Where are we?', in Anderson and Mooney, eds, *The Challenge of Medical Practice Variations*. London: Macmillan.

Armstrong, P., and H. Armstrong. 1996. *Wasting Away: The Undermining of Canadian Health Care*. Toronto: Oxford University Press.

———, ———, J. Choiniere, E. Mykhalovskiy, and J. White. 1997. *Medical Alert: New Work Organizations in Health Care*. Toronto: Garamond.

Aronson, J. 1990. 'Women's perspectives on informal care of the elderly: public ideology and personal experience of giving and receiving care', *Ageing and Society* 10: 61–84.

——— and S. Neysmith. 1997. 'The retreat of the state and long-term care provision: implications for frail elderly people, unpaid family careers and paid home care workers', *Studies in Political Economy* 53: 37–66.

Barry, A., T. Osborne, and N. Rose, eds. 1996. *Foucault and Political Reason*. Chicago: University of Chicago Press.

Beardwood, B., V. Walters, J. Eyles, and S. French. 1999. 'Complaints against nurses: a reflection of the "new managerialism" and consumerism in health care?', *Social Science and Medicine* 48: 363–74.

Belkin, G. 1994. 'The new science of medicine', *Journal of Health Politics, Policy and Law* 19, 4: 801–8.

———. 1997. 'The technocratic wish: making sense and finding power in the "managed" medical marketplace', *Journal of Health Politics, Policy and Law* 22, 2: 509–32.

Burke, M., and M. Stevenson. 1993. 'Fiscal crisis and restructuring in Medicare: the politics and political science of health in Canada', *Health and Canadian Society* 1, 1: 51–80.

Callon, M. 1986. 'Some elements of a sociology of translation: domestication of the scallops and fishermen', in J. Law, ed., *Power, Action and Belief: A New Sociology of Knowledge?* London: Routledge & Kegan Paul.

Campbell, M. 1994. 'The structure of stress in nurses' work', in B.S. Bolaria and H.D. Dickinson, eds, *Health, Illness and Health Care in Canada.* Toronto: Harcourt Brace.

——— and A. Manicom, eds. 1995. *Experience, Knowledge and Ruling Relations: Explorations in the Social Organization of Knowledge.* Toronto: University of Toronto Press.

Chappell, N.L. 1993. 'The future of health care in Canada', *Journal of Social Policy* 22, 4: 487–505.

Chernichovsky, D. 1995. 'Health system reforms in industrialized democracies: an emerging paradigm', *Milbank Quarterly* 73, 3: 339–72.

Chua, W.F. 1995. 'Experts, networks and inscriptions in the fabrication of accounting images: a story of the representation of three public hospitals', *Accounting, Organizations and Society* 20, 2–3: 111–45.

Coburn, D. 1993. 'Professional powers in decline: Medicine in a changing Canada', in F.W. Hafferty and J.B. McKinlay, eds, *The Changing Medical Profession.* New York: Oxford University Press.

———, S. Rappolt, and I. Bourgeault. 1997. 'Decline vs. retention of medical power through restratification: an examination of the Ontario case', *Sociology of Health and Illness* 19, 1: 1–22.

Crombie, I.K. 1996. *Research in Health Care: A Practical Approach to the Design, Conduct and Interpretation of Health Services Research.* New York: John Wiley & Sons.

DeFriese, G., T.C. Ricketts and J.S. Stein, eds. 1989. *Methodological Advances in Health Services Research.* Ann Arbor: Health Administration Press.

Drache, D., and T. Sullivan, eds. 1999. *Health Reform: Public Success, Private Failure.* London and New York: Routledge.

Eisenberg, J. 1998. 'Health services research in a market-oriented health care system', *Health Affairs* 17, 1: 98–109.

Ellwood, P.M. 1988. 'Shattuck lecture—outcomes management: A technology of patient experience', *New England Journal of Medicine* 318, 23: 1549–56.

Evans, R.G. 1992. 'Canada: the real issues', *Journal of Health Politics, Policy and Law* 17, 4: 739–62.

Evidence-Based Medicine Working Group. 1992. 'Evidence-based medicine: A new approach to teaching the practice of medicine', *Journal of the American Medical Association* 268, 17: 2420–5.

Feinglass, J., and J.W. Salmon. 1994. 'The use of medical management information systems to increase the clinical productivity of physicians', in Salmon (1994).

Flook, E.E., and P.J. Sanazaro, eds. 1973. *Health Services Research and R&D in Perspective.* Ann Arbor: Health Administration Press.

Foucault, M. 1979. *Discipline and Punish.* New York: Vintage Books.

———. 1980a. *The History of Sexuality. Vol. 1: An Introduction.* New York: Vintage Books.

———. 1980b. 'Two Lectures', in C. Gordon, ed., *Power/Knowledge: Selected Interviews and Other Writings, 1972–1977.* Brighton: Harvester.

———. 1982. 'The Subject and Power', *Critical Inquiry* 8: 777–95.

———. 1991. 'Governmentality', in G. Burchell, C. Gordon, and P. Miller, eds, *The Foucault Effect: Studies in Governmentality.* Chicago: University of Chicago Press.

Frankford, D.M. 1994. 'Scientism and economism in the regulation of health care', *Journal of Health Politics, Policy and Law* 19, 4: 773–99.

Ganz, P.A., and M.S. Litwin. 1996. 'Measuring outcomes and health-related quality of life', in R.M. Andersen, T.H. Rice, and G.F. Kominski, eds, *Changing the U.S. Health Care System: Key Issues in Health Services, Policy and Management.* San Francisco: Jossey-Bass.

Ginzberg, E., ed. 1991a. *Health Services Research: Key to Health Policy.* Cambridge, Mass.: Harvard University Press.

———. 1991b. 'Health services research and health policy', in Ginzberg (1991a).

Glennerster, H., and J. Le Grand. 1995. 'The development of quasi-markets in welfare provision in the United Kingdom', *International Journal of Health Services* 25, 2: 203–18.

Goel, V., J. Williams, G. Anderson, P. Blackstien-Hirsch, C. Fooks, and C.D. Naylor, eds. 1996. *Patterns of Health Care in Ontario*, vol. 2. Ottawa: Canadian Medical Association.

Goodwin, P.J., and H.A. Llewellyn-Thomas. 1994. 'Outcome measurement in oncology', *Annals of the Royal College of Physicians and Surgeons of Canada* 27, 3: 175–8.

Habermas, J. 1971. *Knowledge and Human Interests,* trans. J.J. Shapiro. Boston: Beacon Press.

Hopwood, A.G., and P. Miller, eds. 1994. *Accounting as Social and Institutional Practice.* New York: Cambridge University Press.

Hurst, J.W. 1991. 'Reforming health care in seven European nations', *Health Affairs* (Fall): 7–21.

Institute of Medicine. 1979. *Health Services Research: Report of a Study.* Washington: National Academy of Sciences.

———. 1995. *Health Services Research: Work Force and Educational Issues.* Washington: National Academy Press.

Klein, R. 1995. 'Big bang health care reform—does it work?: the case of Britain's 1991 National Health Service reforms', *Milbank Quarterly* 7, 3: 299–337.

Latour, B. 1987. *Science in Action: How to Follow Scientists and Engineers through Society*. Cambridge, Mass.: Harvard University Press.

Lexchin, J. 1984. *The Real Pushers: A Critical Analysis of the Canadian Drug Industry.* Vancouver: New Star Books.

Lohr, K.H. 1988. 'Outcome measurement: concepts and questions', *Inquiry* 25, 1: 37–50.

McCoy, L. 1998. 'Producing "what the Deans know": textual practices of cost accounting and the restructuring of post-secondary education', *Human Studies* 21: 395–418.

McKinlay, J.B., and J. Arches. 1985. 'Towards the proletarianization of physicians', *International Journal of Health Services* 15: 161–95.

Marriott, J., and A. Mable. 1998. 'Integrated Models: International Trends and Implications for Canada', in National Forum on Health, *Canada Health Action: Building on the Legacy. Papers Commissioned by the National Forum on Health: Striking a Balance: Health Care Systems in Canada and Elsewhere.* Ottawa: Édition Multi-Mondes.

Miller, P., and N. Rose. 1990. 'Governing economic life', *Economy and Society* 19, 1: 1–31.

National Forum on Health. 1997. *Canada Health Action: Building on the Legacy. Synthesis Reports and Issues Papers.* Ottawa: National Forum on Health.

Navarro, V. 1988. 'Professional dominance or proletarianization? Neither', *Milbank Quarterly* 66, Supp. 2: 57–75.

———. 1993. 'Health services research: What is it?' *International Journal of Health Services* 23, 1: 1–13.

Naylor, C.D. 1994. 'Introduction', in Naylor et al. (1994).

———, G. Anderson, and V. Goel, eds. 1994. *Patterns of Health Care in Ontario*, vol. 1. Ottawa: Canadian Medical Association.

Pittman, M. 1995. 'HSR: past, present and future', *Health Services Research* 30, 1: 3–5.

Poland, B., D. Coburn, A. Robertson, J. Eakin, and members of the Critical Social Science Group. 1998. 'Wealth, equity and health care: a critique of a "population health" perspective on the determinants of health', *Social Science and Medicine* 46, 7: 785–98.

Porter, T. 1995. *Trust in Numbers: The Pursuit of Objectivity in Science and Public Life.* Princeton, NJ: Princeton University Press.

Preston, A.M., W. Chua, and D. Neu. 1997. 'The diagnosis-related group-prospective payment system and the problem of the government of rationing health care to the elderly', *Accounting, Organizations and Society* 22, 2: 147–64.

Rappolt, S. 1996. 'In the Name of Science: The Effects of the Clinical Guidelines Movement on the Autonomy of the Medical Profession', Ph.D. thesis, University of Toronto.

———. 1997. 'Clinical guidelines and the fate of medical autonomy in Ontario', *Social Science and Medicine* 44, 7: 977–87.

Reinhardt, U. 1992. 'The United States: Breakthroughs and waste', *Journal of Health Politics, Policy and Law* 17, 4: 637–66.

Robertson, A. 1998. 'Shifting discourses on health in Canada: From health promotion to population health', *Health Promotion International* 13, 2: 155–65.

Roos, N. 1989. 'Using administrative data from Manitoba, Canada to study treatment outcomes: Developing control groups and adjusting for case severity', *Social Science and Medicine* 28: 109–13.

Rose, N. 1991. 'Governing by numbers: Figuring out democracy', *Accounting, Organizations and Society* 16, 7: 673–92.

———. 1994. 'Expertise and the government of conduct', *Studies in Law, Politics and Society* 14: 359–97.

Rosenberg, W., and A. Donald. 1995. 'Evidence-based medicine: An approach to clinical problem-solving', *British Medical Journal* 310: 1122–6.

Sackett, D.L., R.B. Haynes, G.H. Guyatt, and P. Tugwell. 1991. *Clinical Epidemiology: A Basic Science for Clinical Medicine*, 2nd edn. Boston: Little, Brown.

Salmon, J.W., ed. 1994. *The Corporate Transformation of Health Care, Part II: Perspectives and Implications*. Amityville, NY: Baywood.

———, W.D. White, and J. Feinglass. 1994. 'The futures of physicians: Agency and autonomy reconsidered', in Salmon (1994).

Shortell, S. 1997. 'Shaping the future', *Health Services Research* 31, 6: 655–8.

———, R.R. Gillies, D.A. Anderson, K.M. Erickson, and J.B. Mitchell. 1996. *Remaking Health Care in America: Building Organized Delivery Systems*. San Fransisco: Jossey-Bass.

Smith, D.E. 1987. *The Everyday World as Problematic: A Feminist Sociology*. Toronto: University of Toronto Press.

———. 1990a. *The Conceptual Practices of Power: A Feminist Sociology of Knowledge*. Toronto: University of Toronto Press.

———. 1990b. *Texts, Facts and Femininity: Exploring the Relations of Ruling*. London: Routledge.

———. 1998. *Writing the Social: Critique, Theory and Investigations*. Toronto: University of Toronto Press.

Sonnen, C., and M. McCracken. 1999. 'Downsizing, passive privatization and fiscal arrangements', in Drache and Sullivan (1999).

Stewart, A. 1999. 'Cost-containment and Privatization: An International Analysis', in Drache and Sullivan (1999).

Tanenbaum, S. 1994. 'Knowing and acting in medical practice: The epistemological politics of outcomes research', *Journal of Health Politics, Policy and Law* 19, 1: 647–62.

———. 1996. '"Medical effectiveness" in Canadian and U.S. health policy: The comparative politics of inferential ambiguity', *Health Services Research* 31, 5: 517–32.

Terris, M. 1992. 'Budget cutting and privatization: The threat to health', *Journal of Public Health Policy* 13, 1: 27–41.

Vayda, E., J. Barnsley, W. Mindell, and B. Cardillo. 1984. 'Five-year study of surgical rates in Ontario's counties', *Canadian Medical Association Journal* 131: 111–15.

Wennberg, J.E. 1984. 'Dealing with medical practice variations: A proposal for action', *Health Affairs* 4: 6–32.

——— and A. Gittelsohn. 1982. 'Variations in medical care among small areas', *Scientific American* 246: 120–34.

White, K.L., J. Frenk, C. Ordonez, J. Maria Paganini, and B. and B. Starfield, eds. 1992. *Health Services Research: An Anthology.* Washington: Pan American Health Organization.

Young, G.J., and B.B. Cohen. 1992. 'The process and outcome of hospital care for Medicaid versus privately insured hospital patients', *Inquiry* 29, 3 (Fall): 366–71.

PART THREE

Locating Risk

It is indisputable that the pace of change is accelerating. The term 'globalization' has entered everyday language to capture the realities—and the threats—posed by the increased and faster movements across national borders of capital (especially speculative capital), information, popular culture, and trade, if not people. A 'new economy' of Internet-related companies is fast overtaking 'old economy' firms, at least in terms of volatile stock market values. National governments, including many with social democratic parties in office, shrink from the challenge of balancing accumulation and legitimation goals, declaring that the pursuit of accumulation is the preeminently legitimate goal of state activity as they cede transnational rights to corporations through so-called free trade agreements. Paid work is increasingly casualized, as workers are enjoined to be 'flexible' in taking part-time, part-year, and temporary jobs, and to switch careers, such as they are, five or more times during their working lives. Governments are reinvented, corporations re-engineered, and social services restructured, all in ways that undermine the various degrees of social and employment security achieved in the industrialized countries after World War II. Household structures are transformed, as marriages more frequently dissolve, as birth rates decline, as women take on more labour force work to add to the domestic responsibilities they disproportionately bear, and as the care of the elderly and those with disabilities is increasingly located in the household. Finally, and perhaps most ominously, there is the annual introduction of hundreds, if not thousands, of new chemical compounds to the estimated four million already in existence on planet earth.

If the accelerated pace of change is indisputable, it is also disputed. Not infrequently, it is judged to be unhealthy, for individuals and for communities. A striking recent site for contestation was the 1999 'battle in Seattle', where activists demonstrated, especially on environmental and labour grounds, against the closed-door World Trade Organization negotiations designed to further globalization. Although the WTO negotiations were stalled, as had been the related negotiations to establish a Multilateral Agreement on Investment for the industrialized world, powerful economic and political forces can be relied upon to renew their efforts to make the world safer for corporations through international trade and investment agreements, including the General Agreement on Trade in Services. It can also be confidently assumed that opposition movements will renew their efforts to resist these agreements.

Nowhere is the clash between those promoting and resisting changes that favour corporate capital more pronounced than in the related fields of health and health care. In Canada, public opinion polls consistently rate health as a central, if not the central, concern of the electorate. Canadians rate our universal, publicly funded health-care system more highly than any other government program. Indeed, as the threat of health-care privatization is perceived to grow, so, too, does the support for the public system. The effect of the Alberta government's introduction of a bill to allow for-profit firms to perform surgical operations requiring overnight stays has been to make health care a major concern for 72 per cent of that province's population, up from 47 per cent before the bill was announced (Mahoney, 2000, reporting on an Angus Reid poll).

Other health-related examples of resistance to changes enhancing corporate power include the growing opposition to genetically modified organisms entering the food supply, the controversies that swirl around the federal Health Protection Branch and its large contingent of dissatisfied and occasionally whistle-blowing scientists, and the mounting legal actions taken—and won—against tobacco companies for allegedly denying that their product is unhealthy and addictive when they know it to be both, for allegedly spiking their product to make it even more addictive, and for allegedly targeting children under 16 in their promotions. Union consciousness and union militancy are growing among health-sector workers, notably among nurses whose provincial organizations are joining the Canadian Labour Congress and its provincial affiliates and are threatening and leading strikes, even when strikes are considered illegal. And women increasingly resist being 'conscripted' (National Forum on Health, 1996: 19) into providing more home care for family members.

The concept of 'risk' helps us to understand better the impetus for changes as they affect health and health care, and the sources of resistance to these changes. Leonard Marsh (1975: 10), an architect of the Canadian welfare state, deemed it 'impossible to establish a wage that will allow every worker and his family to meet the heavy disabilities of serious illness, prolonged unemployment, accident and premature death'. Hence the development, in the quarter-century after World War II, of universal programs like medicare, unemployment insurance, and old age income security on the basis of a 'collective pooling of risks' (ibid., 9).

Now, however, a revised notion of risk predominates, in health and more generally. Replacing the *pooling* of risks through universal public programs is the *assessment* of risks based on the sorts of calculation undertaken by private insurance companies. Instead of social solidarity to cope with risks, there is social differentiation in the distribution of risks. For Ulrich Beck, industrial society, with its spectacular if unequal production of goods, is being replaced by risk society with its increasingly complex production of 'bads' or dangers. On the one hand, the production of risks threatens us all—'Poverty is hierarchical, smog is democratic', as Beck (1992: 36) puts it—but the risks are often imperceptible and long-term. On the other hand, the risks create 'market opportunities' (ibid., 46) in which there are profits to be made from the uneven perceptions of risk, realities of risk, and resources with which to buy protection from risk. New drugs, new forms of insurance, new therapies, new security services are brought to market, as the health of individuals and of communities is increasingly threatened.

One manifestation of this revised perspective on risk is the concerted effort by the companies that produce risk and the governments that 'partner' with them to overthrow the precautionary principle (First: do no harm), replacing it with complicated risk assessments. Consider, for example, Bill C-80, the Canada Food Safety and Inspection Act introduced in Parliament by the government of Canada in early 1999. One effect of this legislation would be to shift the burden of proof. Instead of banning foods that might be injurious, it would ban them only if demonstrated to be so. Instead of 'hazard' being the sole criterion, it would make 'risk' the criterion, opening the way for a broadened concept of risk to include loss of market share, liability, political risks, etc. Instead of the goal of the legislation being to protect the public, it would be to contribute to food safety.

Later that year, and after a considerable public outcry, the government announced that it was delaying passage of Bill C-80 pending more public consultation and possible amendments. This was a victory for the Council of Canadians, the Canadian Health Coalition, the National Farmers' Union, and other organizations and individuals determined to contain and turn back the health risks that the proposed legislation represented. The victory may turn out to be temporary. Or, heartened by their success, the opposition to this kind of legislation may strengthen sufficiently to make it permanent. The point to be made here is that political economy helps us to understand the structures and agents that both promote and resist initiatives like Bill C-80.

In this section of *Unhealthy Times*, three fundamental sources of health risk are addressed. John Eyles considers some complex questions of environmental contamination in Chapter 8. Peggy McDonough, in Chapter 9, explores the world of paid work in terms of the health risks at particular work sites and those risks associated with the overall organization of labour force work. And finally, in Chapter 10, Dennis Raphael assembles and assesses a wealth of research findings on the impacts of economic inequalities on the health of individuals and communities. Like the other contributions to this volume, these three chapters raise almost as many issues as they resolve. Readers may be particularly surprised by the sceptical stance adopted by Eyles in his consideration of claims concerning health risks in the environment. The chapters all demonstrate, however, the diversity and utility of political economy approaches to health and to health care.

References

Beck, U. 1992. *Risk Society: Towards a New Modernity*, trans. by Mark Ritter. London: Sage.

Mahoney, J. 2000. 'Klein's support sinks in polls over private clinics', *Globe and Mail*, A6.

Marsh, L. 1975 [1943]. *Report on Social Security for Canada*. Toronto: University of Toronto Press.

National Forum on Health. 1996. 'Values Working Group Synthesis Report', *Canada Health Action: Building on the Legacy*. Vol. 2, Synthesis Reports and Working Papers. Ottawa: Minister of Public Works and Government Services.

CHAPTER 8

A Political Ecology of Environmental Contamination?

John Eyles

Introduction

This chapter will examine the political economy of contamination using Canadian examples. It will argue that the complexity of measuring exposure to contaminated soil, water, air, and food and of relating these exposures to specific health outcomes means that this arena is ripe for contested claims-making on what constitutes a hazard or risk to health. Further, the difficulties of measurement mean that the problems of contamination are universalized so all the population is seen to be harmed to equivalent degrees. This harm occurs in a sensitized environment in that the notions of 'pollution' and 'contamination' are significant cultural referents for uncertainty and danger. Yet, there is a significant political economy of contamination—in other words, the specific production and distribution of the phenomena that expose individuals and groups to the potential of contaminated sites and events are not socially neutral but are produced disproportionately by corporations and affluent social groups with their effects distributed in socially unjust ways. Further, a political ecology of contamination will also be addressed. We begin, however, by defining our terms and pointing to their roles as cultural referents.

Pollution and Contamination

Last (1995: 36) defines contamination as 'the presence of an infectious agent on a body surface; also on or in clothes, bedding, toys, surgical instruments or dressings, or other inanimate articles or substances including water, milk and food. Pollution is distinct from contamination and implies the presence of offensive but not necessarily infectious matter in the environment.' Yet his definition of pollution elides the distinction somewhat, it being 'any undesirable modification of air, water, or food by substance(s) that are toxic or may have adverse effects on health or that are offensive though not necessarily harmful to health' (ibid., 125). The distinction becomes even more blurred when we turn to a standard dictionary, with the *Oxford English Dictionary* defining 'contaminated' as 'defiled', a cross-reference to 'contagion', and a full definition of 'contaminate' as 'render impure by contact or mixture; to corrupt, defile, pollute, sully, taint, infect'. 'Pollute' means to 'render ceremonially or morally impure; to profane, desecrate, sully, corrupt'. 'Pollution' is the state of defilement, uncleanness, or impurity. In this essay, 'pollution' and 'contamination' will be used interchangeably and seen as some modification of physical substances—air, water, soil, food—to an adulterated state such that more often than not human and/or ecosystem health is threatened.

As we see in the definitions, 'contamination' and 'pollution' are saturated with social meaning and cultural significance. They have metaphoric significance, as was noted by Douglas (1966: 12) in her work on pollution and danger: 'Dirt is essentially disorder. . . . In chasing dirt . . . we are not so much governed by anxiety to escape disease, but are possibly reordering our environment, making it conform to an idea.' She goes on, however, to point to the correspondence between the avoidance of contagious disease and ritual avoidance, with washings and separations serving both practical and religious or cultural purposes. These ideas are strongly entrenched in our culture (see Meigs, 1978). Clark and Davis (1989) argue that the clean or the pure (and the unclean and impure) become vital parts of identity construction and maintenance. While Corbin (1986) has argued that defilement and impurity can be used by the relatively powerless to challenge dominant ways of thinking and acting, most try to avoid the impure, the defiled, the contaminated. This may be seen in the struggles over unwanted land uses, such as waste and waste disposal sites (see Eyles et al., 1996). It is also expressed in the powerful imagery of contagion and infection that still dominates many lay accounts of contamination (see Tesh, 1987; Edelstein, 1988) despite present-day scientific knowledge that points to the biophysical (and biobehavioural) pathways for many diseases.

The cultural significance of 'contamination' provides a basis for the disjuncture between lay and scientific accounts of environmental pollution and its associated health impacts. Scientists may point to the insignificance of a particular exposure, detected at so many parts per million or billion. Yet the public's reaction is often one of great anxiety and concern. While much work in the perception of environmental risk has highlighted such factors as lack of personal control, involuntary exposure, lack of personal experience with the hazard, concern over delayed impacts, and anxiety over complex technological systems (see Otway and von Winterfeldt, 1982; Cutter, 1993), the different frames or value-sets of the public and the experts are also key. The cultural saturation of the terms 'pollution' and 'contamination' means that many individuals and groups are predisposed to see polluted environments as defiled and impure, and therefore dangerous and to be avoided. Further, if such events occur, which are then perceived as defilements of nature as well as threats to health and well-being, someone must be responsible, blamed, or charged with the task of righting the wrong. These perceptions make environmental pollution situations fertile arenas for claims-making.

This approach to looking at the struggle over ideas, definitions, and courses of action was first developed in the social problems literature (see Best, 1987; Spector and Kitsuse, 1977) to analyse how a problem is typified and presented to others. It has been applied to science itself (see Aronson, 1984), which helps point up the problematic nature of science and its potential to be used, manipulated, and presented for specific purposes. Such a perspective allows for a problematization not only of scientific evidence but also of science itself, for it recognizes that the normal practices of science are accumulated and evaluated in society (Kuhn, 1970; Woolgar, 1988; Mulkay, 1979). Science, then, is not fixed but historically and institutionally situated (see Barnes et al., 1996), as evidenced by the nature of intelligence and intelligence testing (Gould, 1973) and the development of numerical accounting for mercantile purposes (Poovey, 1998). Given its power, claims-making has been extended to the environmental arena (Harrigan, 1995; McMullan and Eyles, 1999). Thus, stakeholder groups such as Greenpeace use these cultural referents in their claims-making. Not only, as Eyerman and Jamison (1989) point out, do they choose topics that lend themselves to the widest public resonance, but they also choose cases where nature has been altered—i.e., 'defiled'—with an apparent disregard for the ecosystem or human health, for example, the Greenpeace campaigns pointing to an association between chlorination and breast cancer and that which focused on vinyls, dioxin, and cancer end-points, which was used to telling effect in the plastics fire aftermath in Hamilton, Ontario. Claims-making can occur in powerful ways in arenas of uncertainty. Further, in such circumstances the cultural models held by individuals become the basis of responding to those conditions. Human beings are cognitive misers (Fiske and Kinder, 1981)—we fit new data into existing interpretive schemes if we can or if we have choice, or if the data are difficult to understand. This is often the case with environmental pollution and its associated health effects.

The Power of Numbers

> The appeal of numbers is especially compelling to bureaucratic officials who lack the mandate of a popular election, or divine right. . . . A decision made by numbers (or by explicit rules of some other sort) has at least the appearance of being fair and impersonal. Scientific objectivity thus provides an answer to the moral demand for impartiality and fairness. (Porter, 1995: 8)

The development of scientific communities to enshrine such objectivity is beyond the scope of this essay (see Harre, 1986; Kuhn, 1970; Fish, 1980; Aronson, 1984). But it should be noted that while we must be sceptical about the role of science—as its function in claims-making attests—it remains possible to grant some authority to science in its systematic and replicable applications of tools to produce evidence. Scientific authority is not rejected by the inclusion of a social dimension. Nor does recognition of social context make science necessarily illegitimate. It is necessary to apply the rigour of scientific questioning to the claims of science itself (see, in particular, Haack, 1995; Golinski, 1998). But the effects of objectivity are central.

Objectivity demands measurement and the absence of bias, an approach effectively pioneered by Hill (1962) in the context of medicine with tremendous impact on all health-related issues (see also Porter, 1995).

Measurement, in our scientific culture, becomes an effective way of describing an issue. Stone (1997: 167–8) succinctly links measurement and numbers to their role in civil society when she comments that 'measures imply a need for action, because we do not measure things except when we want to change them or change our behaviour in response to them.' Anything measured is thus deemed important, although there may well be problems with the measurements in terms of assumptions, standardization, and synergistic effects. Indeed, as Allen and Hoekstra (1992) put it, we can only observe and measure what our instruments allow us to measure. This in itself may intensify public concern in arenas of uncertainty such as environmental contamination. In her discussion around public anxiety over contaminated milk, Adam argues that despite showing incidence of contamination, the measurements gave no insight into the scale of the problem. Adam (1998: 207) notes that 'the same conclusion applies to the contamination of land and water, animals and people.' As we cannot measure every possible event at every spatial or temporal scale that may be relevant:

> science has no means of establishing with certainty the extent of the problem. Citizens cannot even be sure that all the worst contaminated areas and beings have yet been identified. With complete cover of measurement an impossibility, scientists rely on mathematics, models and theory to establish 'truth' and 'proof' whilst expediency plays a substantial role in defining the boundaries of 'safety'. (Ibid.)

There is indeed a questioning of the utility of employing standard toxicological and epidemiological ways of assessing risk (see Schettler et al., 2000). With the mistrust of expertise by many publics, an arena exists for greater uncertainty about effects, divergent claims-making, and anxiety over what the numbers mean. It may be difficult, then, to gauge the extent of despoliation, but its measurement at some time or place means it exists. And this existence—reinforced by the cultural saturation of the concept of contamination—will shape the politics of pollution, especially as a universalizing theme. But as we shall see there is an unequal social and geographical distribution of the adverse effects of contamination.

Contaminating the Environment

Conventional wisdom has it that some 200–300 years of European settlement and activity in Canada have resulted in the pollution of the physical environment (Colburn et al., 1996). The Federal government (Canada, 1991) reviewed the various impacts on different features of the environment. For example, in agriculture organic matter content of soil has fallen 30–40 per cent since the 1960s and as much as 40–50 per cent from presettlement levels in the Prairies. This loss has led to an increase in fertilizer use to meet the nutrient demands of high-yielding crops. In addition, an increase in pesticide use has led in some instances to the contamination of aquatic ecosystems. Pesticide use has also increased significantly in forested areas (Ecobichon, 1990).

The sum of human activities is seen to have put certain Canadian regions at risk. The government report, *The State of Canada's Environment* (Canada, 1991), emphasized six case studies—the Arctic, the lower Fraser River basin, the Prairie grasslands, the Great Lakes basin, the St Lawrence River, and the Bay of Fundy. For example, the Arctic has significant localized environmental problems associated with mining, oil and gas extraction, and community waste. Further, the trends of long-range contaminant deposition in the Arctic are worrisome. There is evidence of chlorinated organic compounds from industry (PCBs, HCB) and agricultural sources (HCH, DDT), and by-products of human activities (dioxin, furans) and heavy metals (mercury, cadmium, lead, arsenic) are also present in the Arctic environment. Further, a winter pollution phenomenon—arctic haze—first observed in the 1950s is composed of sulphates, soot, and hydrocarbons. Through such measurable evidence the Arctic is seen as an indicator of the rate and extent to which pollutants are entering the global environment.

The Great Lakes have played a pivotal role in the rise of industrial society in North America, particularly Canada. They have suffered profound environmental degradation, with ecosystem damage stemming from industrial and agricultural chemicals, municipal sewage, and overfishing. Urban and industrial developments have taken over some two-thirds of the basin's wetlands and have contributed to the accumulating load of toxic contaminants. The flow of nutrients from fertilizers and municipal wastes into the lakes led to eutrophic conditions, with the addition of phosphates, nitrogen, and potassium increasing biomass and algae growth so much so that Lake Erie was perceived as 'dying'. The continental natural system is demonstrated by the fact that in the 1970s the insecticide toxaphene, largely used to control insects on cotton crops in the southern US, was found in dangerously high levels in Great Lakes fish. The Great Lakes present a veritable chemical soup—the International Joint Commission, the binational advisory body on water quality has identified some 362 chemicals in the waters of the basin. Of these, 11 critical pollutants were deemed capable of producing adverse and often irreversible effects in mammalian and aquatic species (Table 8.1 identifies the chemicals and their sources). By being passed up the food chain, pollutants can biomagnify. For example, DDT has been shown to cause egg-shell thinning and birth deformities among cormorants (Bishop and Weseloh, 1990; Noble, 1990). These and other findings have acted as sentinels and over the past 25 years have galvanized action around persistent toxins. Water and sediment samples, as well as indicator species of algae, fish, and other wildlife, have shown general reductions in contaminant levels since the 1970s. A joint US and Canada report (1995) points to the improving or restored state of many aquatic communities and to a reduction in nutrient and contaminant stresses. Yet contaminant levels may have stabilized at high levels, especially in identified hot spots like Hamilton harbour and the St Clair River, and great uncertainty remains about the effects of their exposures on human health and well-being.

Table 8.1: The 11 'Critical Pollutants' on the International Joint Commission's 'Primary Track'

Chemical	Production and Release	Source
TCDD TCDF	Unintentional Unintentional	Created in the manufacture of herbicides used in agriculture and range and forest management. Also produced as by-products of combustion of chlorinated additives in fossil fuels and chlorine-containing wastes, through production of pentachlorophenol (PCP), and in pulp and paper production processes that use chlorine bleach. TCDD is the most toxic of 75 congeners (forms) of polychlorinated dibenzodioxins, and TCDF is the most toxic of 135 congeners of polychlorinated dibenzofurans.
Benzo(a)pyrene	Unintentional	Product of incomplete combustion of fossil fuels and wood, including forest fires, grills (charcoal broiling), auto exhausts, and waste incineration. One of a large family of polycyclic aromatic hydrocarbons (PAHs).
DDT and its break-down products, including DDE	Intentional	Insecticide used heavily for mosquito control in tropical areas.
Dieldrin[a]	Intentional	Insecticide used extensively at one time, especially on fruit.
HCB	Unintentional	By-product of combustion of fuels that contain chlorinated additives, of incineration of wastes that contain chlorinated substances, and of manufacturing processes using chlorine. Found as a contaminant in chlorinated pesticides.
Alkylated lead	Intentional	Used as a fuel additive and in solder, pipes, and paint.
	Unintentional	Released through combustion of leaded fuel, waste, and cigarettes, and from pipes, cans, and paint chips.

Table 8.1 continued

Chemical	Production and Release	Source
Mirex[b]	Intentional	Fire retardant and pesticide used to control fire ants. Breaks down to more toxic form, photomirex, in presence of sunlight. Present sources are residuals from manufacturing sites, spills, and disposal in landfills.
Mercury	Intentional	Used in metallurgy.
	Unintentional	By-product of chlor-alkali, paint, and electrical equipment manufacturing processes. Also occurs naturally in soils and sediments. Releases into the aquatic environment may be accelerated by sulphate deposition (i.e., acidic deposition).
PCBs[c]	Intentional	Insulating fluids used in electrical capacitors and transformers and in the production of hydraulic fluids, lubricants, and inks. Was previously used as a vehicle for pesticide dispersal. PCBs comprise a family of 209 forms of varying toxicity.
	Unintentional	Primarily released to the environment through leakage, spills, and waste storage and disposal.
Toxaphene[a]	Intentional	Insecticide used on cotton. Substitute for DDT.

[a]Use restricted in the United States and Canada.
[b]Banned for use in the United States and Canada.
[c]Manufacture and new uses prohibited in the United States and Canada.
Sources: Colborn et al. (1990); Canada (1991).

Assessing Human Health

What have the contaminated environments got to do with human health? It is not possible to give a definitive answer, but it is certainly true to say that most individuals in North America are engaged by environmental issues only insofar as they may adversely affect human concerns, such as security, health, and well-being (see World

Wildlife Fund, 1996). In fact, Burger (1990: 133) argues that 'threats' to human health have been used to 'sell' environmental legislation and regulation, 'often in ways or to a degree that contradicts scientific evidence'. Health is used as a surrogate for the environment or as a hook for political action. Burger's argument is very much in keeping with a thesis of this chapter: that the uncertainty around the science and the numbers in the exposure assessments and the cultural saturation of 'contamination' make the arena fertile for claims-making. The ubiquity of public anxiety and its formulation as metaphor (e.g., contaminated site or ozone hole) are important ingredients in creating and assuring a political following in which simple solutions may be advanced despite the complexity of a situation (see Edelman, 1971). In this, the most powerful number becomes zero, as in zero tolerance, zero discharge—an impossibility given existing contaminant loads, naturally occurring sources, and prohibitive cost. Further, it is not possible for science ever to prove that something will not occur—there is no such thing as zero risk—and the conditions are ripe to maintain and reinforce public anxiety over environmental contamination and on a range of issues, such as PCB-contaminated soil, electrico-magnetic fields, low-dose ionizing radiation, dioxin release from incineration, and chemical leaching from waste facilities.

So is it possible to assess health risk from exposure to contaminated environment? There is, in fact, a sophisticated procedure of health-risk assessment. Health Canada (1993) points out that risk analysis begins with the identification of health hazards through case reports, epidemiological investigations, toxicological studies, or chemical analysis. It is then necessary to estimate the risk to human health by assessing the levels at which the hazard is a risk, who is exposed, and the probability of exposure. Exposure itself depends on the contaminant source, the media through which the hazard travels (air, water, soil, food), the route of exposure (ingestion, inhalation, dermal contact), and the receptor person or population and their relative immunity (Health Canada and Ontario Ministry of Health, 1997). Given the complexity of the assessment, it is not surprising that assumptions have to be made that may limit the general applicability of an assessment based on a particular set of data and that few full assessments have been carried out. This means that assessing health impacts is usually based on the few primary studies that have been carried out. In many instances, given the difficulties of measuring exposure and outcome, the results of primary studies can vary. And given the real-time, real-place nature of scientific research in the arena of environmental contamination, it is difficult to meet the strength-of-evidence criteria for epidemiologic studies (see Frank et al., 1988; Hill, 1965). Table 8.2 outlines the criteria accepted by most researchers in the field. Further, many studies point to relatively low levels of additional risk, but the impact of chronic exposure to low levels of contaminants is not known. In such cases, lay publics are often forced to use their own cognitive and cultural models to make sense of the evidence. These often take the form that no dose is safe. To provide more assurance, some attempts are being made to link the assessments from different agencies (TERA, 1998).

Table 8.2: Criteria for the Evaluation of Epidemiological Studies Linking Environmental Toxicant Exposures and Health Effects

1. Basic design of study
   (a) What type of study was used (cohort, case-control, ecologic)?
      - strengths
      - weaknesses
2. Exposure assessment
   (a) Is the nature of the suspected exposure known?
   (b) Is the overall dose known?
      - timing and duration of exposure
      - route of exposure
      - body burden
   (c) Is a dose gradient known? How accurate is (are) the exposure category(ies)?
   (d) Were controls used? How accurate is the non-exposed or (non-diseased) classification?
3. Outcome assessment (measurement of health effect)
   (a) How appropriate to the particular exposure in question is the outcome being studied?
      - Does other human or animal evidence relate the health effect to suspected exposure? How strong is it?
      - Is the outcome assessment appropriately timed? (latency period considered)?
      - Is the health effect which was examined validated as adversely affecting human health?
   (b) How accurate is the outcome assessment?
      - completeness (few false negatives)
      - correctness (few false positives)
   (c) Is there possible bias in the ascertainment of the health outcome for the various exposure category(ies) and controls?
4. Control for other factors influencing outcome
   (a) Are the exposed category(ies)—or cases, in a case control study—and controls comparable (except for exposure)?
      - nature of underlying populations
      - sampling bias
   (b) How great is the problem of confounders likely to be?
      - specificity of health outcome studied for the particular exposure
   (c) How successfully were possible confounders controlled for?
      - adequacy of matching or adjustment of all possible confounders (age, sex, socio-economic status, ethnicity, other exposures to toxicants, access to medical care, secular time trends)
5. Strength of association between exposure and outcome (relative risk)
   (a) Does the relative risk have clinical or practical significance?
   (b) Does the relative risk have statistical significance?

Table 8.2 continued'

   (c) Was a clear-cut dose-response gradient demonstrated?
   (d) If no statistically significant relative risk with exposure was found, was the statistical power of the study adequate to find a risk of practical importance if it existed?
6. Evaluation of final conclusion
   (a) If the result is positive, could it be a false positive association?
   (b) If the result is negative, could it be a false negative association?
   (c) Is the result consistent with other well-conducted studies of the same association and/or related epidemiological knowledge on the distribution and dynamics of the health outcome or condition in question?

Source: Frank et al. (1988: 138).

So caution must be exercised in commenting on the relationship between environmental contamination and human health. Much depends on whether the focus is on the environmental exposure or the health outcome. There has, for example, been much recent interest in the quality of environmental media. With respect to drinking water, bacterial contamination is no longer a major problem in municipal water systems, although some protozoan parasites (giardia and cryptosporidium) seem resistant to chlorination and have resulted in outbreaks of gastrointestinal illness in British Columbia and Ontario during the 1990s. There are, however, contaminant concerns related to water treatment. Alum, used to remove pathogenic micro-organisms and organic particulate matter, is weakly associated (as measured by its concentration in drinking water) with dementia. But the etiology of Alzheimer's disease indicates that alum or aluminum is very unlikely to be responsible for a major burden of illness. Some studies have shown an association between chlorinated drinking water and cancers of the bladder, colon, and rectum (Wigle et al., 1986; Morris et al., 1992). A recent study in Ontario points to the fact that chlorination by-products, such as trihalomethanes, can be an important risk factor for bladder cancer in particular (King and Marrett, 1996). Of course, diet and smoking are significant risk factors, too.

Air pollution has arguably become the major environmental health issue in Canada, linked as it is so closely to our current social and economic practices. Although Canadians enjoy very good air quality, many recent studies have been sought to improve our knowledge of the relationship between air quality and human health. In fact, as Table 8.3 shows, in the mid-1990s US standards existed for only seven air pollutants. Canada has air quality objectives and guidelines. Table 8.3 also indicates that the main sources of outdoor air pollution are energy production, vehicle use, and some industrial processes. Health effects vary from difficulty in breathing to the aggravation of existing respiratory and cardiac conditions. In recent years, Burnett et al. (1995) have shown a significant association between ambient

Table 8.3. The Seven Air Pollutants for which US Standards Exist, Their Main Sources, and Their Health Effects

Pollutant	Description	Main Sources	Health Effects
Ozone	Main component of smog, formed in air when sunlight 'cooks' hydrocarbons (like gasoline vapours) and nitrogen oxides from automobiles	Not directly emitted but formed from emissions of automobiles, etc.	Irritation of eyes, nose, throat; impairment of normal lung function
Carbon monoxide	By-product of combustion	Cars and trucks	Weakens heart contractions; reduces oxygen available to body; affects mental function, visual acuity, and alertness
Particles	Soot, dust, smoke, fumes, ash, mists, sprays, aerosols, etc.	Power plants, factories, inciner-ators, open burning, construction, road dust	Respiratory and lung damage, in some cases cancer; hastens death
Sulphur dioxide	By-product of burning coal and oil, and of some industrial processes; reacts in air to form sulphuric acid, which can return to earth as 'acid rain'	Power plants, factories, space-heating boilers	Increases acute and chronic respiratory disease; hastens death
Nitrogen dioxide	By-product of combustion; is 'cooked' in the air with hydrocarbons to form ozone (smog); on its own, gives smog its yellow-brown colour	Cars, trucks, power plants, factories	Pulmonary swelling; may aggravate chronic bronchitis and emphysema

Table 8.3. continued

Pollutant	Description	Main Sources	Health Effects
Hydrocarbons	Incompletely burned and evaporated petroleum products; are 'cooked' with nitrogen dioxide to form ozone (smog)	Cars, trucks, power plants, space-heating boilers, vapours from gasoline stations	Negligible
Lead	A chemical element	Leaded gasoline	Brain and kidney damage; emotional disorders; death

Sources: Adapted from the US Environmental Protection Agency; Green and Ottoson (1994: 514).

particulate sulphate and cardiac respiratory admissions to Ontario hospitals. There has been much local interest in air quality, especially in the Great Lakes basin (see, e.g., Szakolcai and Weiler, 1994; Pengelly et al., 1997). In a Hamilton study conducted by Pengelly et al., particulate matter resulted in around 90 cases of premature mortality per year and 180 additional hospital admissions per year. Nationally, in a later study of Canadian cities, Burnett et al. (1998) attribute 8 per cent of non-accidental deaths to ambient air pollution. The Suzuki Foundation (1998) points to vulnerability of those with existing heart and lung conditions, the elderly, and children as being particularly at risk, these potential risk factors being compounded by low income, poor nutritional status, higher exposure to cigarette smoke, poorly designed and maintained buildings, and the general environment for children in poverty. This theme of relative disadvantage is taken up later in the essay.

Perhaps the two health outcomes of greatest concern associated with environmental contamination are cancer and reproductive and developmental effects (see Table 8.4). Cancer remains a dreaded disease. It expresses fantasies about contamination. As Sontag (1978) puts it, it is a scourge, the ultimate insult to natural order. With pollution, it conjures up terrible images of the despoliation of the land being visited upon the flesh. We have already noted the association between chlorinated drinking water and certain cancers, and ecological studies have shown the strong relationship between socio-economic variables (low income, population density) and cancer incidence (Health Canada, 1997). Of specific concern in recent years is breast cancer, the incidence of which has continued to rise. Several risk factors have been identified: family history and genetic predisposition, reproductive history, hormonal factors such as estrogen, diet, and socio-demographic factors. Yet these account for perhaps 30 per cent of cases. Environmental contaminants have been invoked as a possible additional risk factor. However, little evidence supports the link

Table 8.4: Current Human Health Concerns Relating to Environmental Contaminants

Health Concern	Description
Cancer	There are over a hundred different types of cancer, but the incidence of potentially hormone-stimulated cancers, such as breast, testicular, and prostate cancers, has increased in the last few decades.
Inheritable damage	Exposure can result in changes in the inheritable genetic material (i.e., DNA).
Birth defects	Physical defects or malformations that occur during embryo development resulting in deformed offspring. Certain chemicals can also affect the growth and development of the children of the person who has been exposed.
Reproductive damage	Reduced fertility is the reduced ability of a couple to produce a live offspring, possibly due to reduced quality and/or quantity of eggs and/or sperm.
	Prenatal exposures can affect reproductive organ development and sexual development, which appear during childhood or post-adolescence, and can cause reproductive tract disorders.
	Hormone-disrupting organochlorines possibly play a role in causing reproductive damage.
Developmental and behavioural effects	Contaminants affect the development and function of the central nervous system, leading to developmental and behavioural problems (e.g., lead adversely affects childhood learning).
Damage to the immune system	Exposure can reduce the body's ability to protect against and fight disease.
Effects on the respiratory and circulatory systems	There are direct effects on the lung, heart and blood vessels, lung volume, and airways (e.g., asthma).
Viral and bacterial infections	The effects of microbial contaminants are well known and can range from mild (e.g., skin rashes) to severe (e.g., death).

Source: Health Canada and Ontario Ministry of Health (1997).

between organochlorines and an increased incidence of breast cancer. Some studies show non-significant associations (Krieger et al., 1994; Wolff et al., 1993; Falck et al., 1992) and others a possible association between hormone disruption and the onset of estrogen-dependent breast cancer (Dewailly et al., 1994). But many of these studies have been challenged because they do not adequately address possible effect modifiers, such as smoking and diet.

The state of knowledge concerning reproductive and development effects is also limited. Adverse effects on the fetus and newborn have been documented following high-level accidental or occupational exposures to PCBs, lead, methylmercury, TCDD, and some organochlorine pesticides. At present, there is little evidence from human studies that present low-level exposures to hormone-disrupting contaminants are causing adverse effects. PCBs, DDT, and DDE have little apparent biological effect at current levels in human tissues (Health Canada, 1997). While European studies have shown variations in sperm count and quality (Pajarinein et al., 1997; Auger et al., 1995; Bujan et al., 1996), there is little clarity yet on the role of genetic, natural, and temporal variation and how these changes may be associated with fertility (see Fisch et al., 1997). Environmental factors may be implicated in that the highest sperm counts in Finnish studies came from rural areas (Suominen and Vierula, 1993; Vierula et al., 1996).

If it is difficult enough to take into consideration the confounders or effect modifiers for breast cancer, it is more so for reproductive dysfunction. We are left with a mass of evidence but no clear conclusions on the health effects of environmental contamination. Table 8.4 highlights the main areas of concern. Given the paucity of decisive conclusions, it may be best to concentrate on at-risk groups such as infants and those who regularly eat Great Lakes fish to see if there are stronger relationships. The evidence, in fact, suggests that while the need for vigilance and surveillance remains, things on the whole seem reasonably stable. For example, samples of breast milk show a decline over time of concentration of PCBs, DDT and metabolites, and HCB (Newsome et al., 1995), but the concentrations were higher in women who ate more than 100 grams of fish a week. Yet the body burdens of organochlorines in fish-eaters in general in the Great Lakes-St Lawrence region have declined over the last 25 years (Health Canada, 1997). Body burdens of mercury and PCBs were higher in Aboriginal communities with greater fish consumption (Health Canada, 1997). More worrying are the US longitudinal studies of Jacobson and Jacobson (1996) that show developmental delay in infants and children born to mothers who consumed Great Lakes fish during pregnancy. Yet not all such children are at risk, nor are all Aboriginal communities. Nevertheless, we should caution against any overwhelming optimism, as damage to the reproductive system (or with the developmental one) is likely a non-threshold event, with any exposure possibly resulting in damage (see Schettler et al., 2000). Before we deal with the issues of the distribution among populations of these contamination events and adverse health effects, there remains a further element to consider—psychosocial health.

All in the Mind

Given the cultural saturation of 'contamination' and the anxiety that environmental risks and hazards engender, it is not surprising that much stress and adverse psychosocial health effects have been documented. Often such effects are discussed as bias in that respondents will 'overreport' adverse effects, especially if they think remedial action will result. There has been a significant debate on whether psychosocial effects are real or simply reporting bias (see Neutra et al., 1991). It is a battle of ideas between epidemiologists and social scientists. For this discussion, if the perceived effects have consequences (i.e., health impact) then they are real in themselves.

Early work in this area is from the US. Edelstein (1988) documented the stigma and stress in being associated with a contaminated community, while at Love Canal in Niagara Falls, New York, there were psychosocial as well as physical effects (Levine, 1982). The association of physical health impacts and the environmental exposure at Love Canal was not demonstrated scientifically (see Frank et al., 1988), nor was it in Woburn, Saskatchewan, for the link between leukemia and contaminated water (Harr, 1996). The rigorous risk assessments usually demonstrate that there is no 'real' or 'objective' danger or hazard. This is also the case with numerous disease clusters brought to political and scientific attention by lay publics and concerned residents. With careful scientific inspection, the clusters may disappear (Last, 1995). The power of numbers becomes partial and is then further set against the psychosocial impacts experienced by the residents. Their fears are downgraded as the risk assessments do not support them, and their anxieties are seen as groundless as they seldom have been (or can be) quantified. It is sometimes argued that the hazard is all in the mind, that if logic and reason are applied and the risk assessment is accepted, those fears will dissolve. This trivialization of psychosocial health stems from the scientific experts seeing the public as irrational (Schrader-Frechette, 1991) and failing to recognize that they are grounded by different values and interests, ones that see lifestyle and cultural mores as important as scientific evidence. The trivialization is also strengthened by many of the psychosocial concerns emphasizing environmental annoyances—noise, odour, unwanted land uses—rather than 'real' hazards such as chemical and physical danger. Yet after a careful epidemiologic study of the Upper Ottawa Street landfill in Hamilton, Hertzman et al. (1987) concluded that the psychosocial was as likely a source of illness as the biophysical.

Research, both qualitative and quantitative, has begun to explore these issues. In a path-breaking book, Vyner (1988) examined the traumatizing effects of invisible hazards, such as radiation and those with long latency periods. Taylor et al. (1991) developed a model to investigate psychosocial impacts in populations living close to solid waste facilities. Impact was seen as a function of contaminant type and source, individual characteristics, family and household, and the wider community and social network. In a series of studies, they demonstrated the importance of contaminant type and history as well as distance from the pollution source in understanding psychosocial health response and coping (Elliott et al., 1993). Longitudinal investigation of the population close to the Milton, Ontario, landfill has shown that most (but not all) individuals over time reappraise the threat and their coping strategies, which appears to enhance their psychosocial health (Elliott et al., 1997).

One of the reasons for such enhancement is the human desire to get life 'back to normal' after an unanticipated event or a fractious situation that impinges on the conduct of everyday life. Certainly the qualitative component of the psychosocial impacts research has emphasized disruption not only to family life but also to 'lifescape', the foundational assumptions and interests that chart our lives (family, property, environmental safety, and so on) (see Eyles et al., 1993a; Baxter and Eyles, 1999). These similar concerns and anxieties (adverse psychosocial health) are found in communities that have experienced an environmental accident. Thus, in Hagersville, Ontario, in the aftermath of the tire fire in 1990, stress, frustration, anger, and anxiety were all present and linked to threats to everyday life and the values that underpin it (Eyles et al., 1993b). Similar, as yet unresolved tensions and stresses exist in the north Hamilton community close to the plastics fire of summer 1997.

This research, by emphasizing the psychological consequences for health of environmental contamination, highlights the social actions and interactions of an event, does not denigrate numerical estimates of risk, and provides the context (and effects) of the hazards that science is assessing. Indeed, the very act of assessing risk can be deleterious to health in that it can bring to the surface previously unconsidered phenomena and label them as risky. The act of labelling (and communicating) may thus amplify risk (see Kasperson et al., 1988), as may be also evidenced by the furore caused by poor and inadequate communication over BSE and mixed public messages in the uncertain scientific environment of electrico-magnetic fields (see Leiss and Chociolko, 1994; Powell and Leiss, 1997). Further, by examining context, the psychosocial health research emphasizes the community and population and not merely the individual and her/his relation to environmental contamination, as is the case in most physical health effects research.

Political Economy of Environmental Contamination

Despite emphasizing the community, the examination of the relationship between human health and environmental contamination remains largely asocial insofar as it seldom looks at the social distribution or production of contamination effects and events. This is in part due to the sheer difficulty of understanding and charting all the factors (and interactions between the factors) that shape the relationships between environmental exposure and health outcome. Thus, few studies take into account what epidemiologists call 'confounders' or 'effect modifiers'. These social scientists see various factors as key to understanding any social setting—social position, income, income inequality, education, family size and status, ethnicity, social support, and so on. The centrality of these factors in differentiating health status is well understood (Amick et al., 1995; Wilkinson, 1996; Evans et al., 1994). Yet, few Canadian studies have marshalled environmental exposure evidence for the analysis. The US is a different story. Initiated by a civil rights protest against a hazardous waste disposal facility in North Carolina, environmental exposures have been seen as costs that have been distributed inequitably along racial and economic lines (see Bullard, 1990; Goldman, 1991). An early investigation by the US General Accounting Office (1983) found above-average proportions of poor people and African-Americans living near three out of the four hazardous waste sites it investigated. Other work seemed to support this conclusion but more recent analyses at the census tract and county levels have challenged these findings. In a study of Ohio only minorities in the population remain positively associated with pollution emissions (see Anderson et al., 1994; Bowen et al., 1995) and this may simply be an effect of the nature of urban areas.

In Canada, Goldman (1994) could not assess the distribution of environmental burdens among social groups in studying the impacts of uranium mining. Jerrett et al. (1997), using data from the National Pollutant Release Inventory, examined the spatial distribution of pollution in Ontario at the county level. Urbanization was strongly associated with pollution emissions. Above-average manufacturing employment and the presence of primary industry were also associated with pollution 'hot spots'. In examining the income distribution of pollution in Ontario, Jerrett et al. found a positive relationship between pollution emissions and household income, manufacturing employment, and population size. Dwelling value is negatively related to the emissions. The relationship between income and emissions seems to argue against the environmental inequity perspective. The authors thus suggests a temporal model in that polluting industries may initially locate in areas of low income and low dwelling value to reduce compensation claims and opposition (Hamilton, 1995), but once there, workers might demand higher wages to compensate for lower environmental quality, greater health risk, and lower quality of life in general.

This work has been extended to examine the socio-economic and environmental covariates of premature mortality (death among those 64 years of age and younger) at the county level in Ontario (Jerrett et al., 1998). For female premature mortality, education, smoking status, the proximity of primary industry, and the supply of primary-care physicians exert considerable effects. For male premature mortality, income, education, municipal expenditure on environmental protection, smoking, primary industry, manufacturing, and Aboriginal nativity are significantly associated. It is interesting to note the relevance of environmental variables in the associations. There were important differences between the male and female models in the analysis, with income, environmental protective expenditures, and manufacturing employment exerting no effect on female premature mortality.

But to demonstrate what many feel are obvious associations requires different research designs. It is possible to state that environmental exposures are socially differentiated. We certainly know from studies of US cities (see Mielke, 1999, and

Mielke and Reagan, 1998, for the concentration of lead exposure in inner cities) and investigations of social well-being in a variety of contexts (Herbert and Smith, 1989; Smith, 1994) that a coincidence of deprivation exists (Eyles, 1987). Only recently have the health impacts of these environmental deprivations been investigated (Pampalon et al., 1990; Ellaway et al., 1997).

The production of and the response to environmental exposures are also socially differentiated. Community response to environmental contamination is reasonably well documented for specific cases (see Chociolko, 1995; Richardson et al., 1993; Renn et al., 1991). Those who participate and mobilize tend to be overrepresented by white, middle-aged, middle-class individuals, although people with such characteristics may act as advocates for more disadvantaged communities. Yet in Canada, the state has played a catalytic role in mobilizing communities around the remediation of environmental contamination, as Harrison and Hoberg (1993) show with respect to regulating dioxin discharge in the Great Lakes and Gould (1993, 1994) indicates for remediation of areas of concern in the basin. But a full social analysis of patterns of social mobilization around contamination remains to be undertaken. Work also remains to be done analysing the patterns of contaminant production. Inventories of pollutant releases are being published by the US Environmental Protection Agency, Environment Canada, the Commission for Environmental Co-operation (CEC), and the NAFTA environment office in Montreal. In the two reports released by the NAFTA office, Ontario has been shown to be the third worst jurisdiction on the continent for pollutant releases (CEC, 1997). In 1994 the largest pollutant releases in Ontario were recorded for the following corporations: Kronos Canada Inc., Samuel Bingham Co., Sherritt Inc., Methanex Corporation, and Shell Canada. The CEC's 1997 report is an important source, which if used in conjunction with census material and health effects knowledge will provide a localized picture of the distribution of pollution and potential adverse health outcomes. A complete picture, however, awaits further research, as does a politics of pollution production and waste management (but see Macdonald, 1991; Gourlay, 1992). It is a complex issue with many different and interacting production points and flows, made more complex by the contribution of individual practices, such as car use, home energy consumption, garden herbicide and pesticide use.

Conclusion: A Political Ecology of Environmental Contamination?

Much work remains to be done to understand the political economy—the social conditions and differentiation of existence—of environmental contamination, of which differential adverse health effects are a key sentinel condition. Yet does a political economy go far enough? Some 15 years ago, Turshen (1984: xi) argued that 'most analyses separate ecological change from malnutrition, political struggle from epidemics, and social upheaval from health and healing. None consider the relation of ecological, political, and social aspects of disease to the economic change wrought by colonialism and capitalism.' Recently, Mayer (1996) has advocated a political ecology of disease to assist in understanding large-scale social, economic, and political influences on the structure and events of local areas. Bond and Vincent (1991) suggest that to understand the impact of HIV/AIDS it is necessary to examine the macro-dimensions of political economy and the micro-conditions of specific contexts. Such broad-based approaches are necessary for investigating transboundary issues that encompass interregional and potentially intergenerational equity, for example, the fragility of the Arctic ecosystem and the impacts on indigenous health (Doubleday, 1995). An ecologic-political-social-clinical approach is necessary to understand the newly emerging and resurging infectious diseases, such as dengue fever, the Ebola virus, and hemorrhagic fever. Such an approach requires investigation of microbes; migration, population mix, and altered immunities; human behaviour; economic development and land use; and public health practices (see Institute of Medicine, 1992; Garrett, 1994). The impact of climate change on human health is a further topic that could usefully employ a political ecological framework. Many adverse outcomes are indirectly related to climate change through habitat change and population growth and migration (see McMichael, 1993; Epstein, 1997).

Many of the exposures and health effects discussed earlier in this chapter could also benefit from a political ecological approach. It contextualizes the issues and in so doing may allow some comment to be made about air pollution in the environmental (and overall) burden of illness in the Great Lakes. Gutenshwager (1991) provides a useful model to think through these relationships, though it is unlikely to be complete. Further, as we adopt a political ecological perspective, we cannot forget the importance of evidence—numerical or otherwise—in persuading others that political action is needed to protect and promote human health. Nor must we forget that what is deemed important to protect and promote is passed through a filter of values and interests that frame 'contamination', 'exposure', and 'health' in particular ways. Our first step must be to understand this complex reality. Without that, it cannot be changed.

References

Adam, B. 1998. *Timescapes of Modernity*. London: Routledge.

Allen, T.F.H., and T.W. Hoekstra. 1992. *Toward a Unified Ecology*. New York: Columbia University Press.

Amick, B., et al. 1995. *Society and Health*. New York: Oxford University Press.

Anderson, D.L., et al. 1994. 'Environmental equity', *Demography* 31: 229–48.

Aronson, N. 1984. 'Science as a claim-making activity', in J. Schneider and J.I. Kitsuse, eds, *Studies in the Sociology of Social Problems*. Norwood, NJ: Ablex.

Auger, J., et al. 1995. 'Decline in semen quality among fertile men in Paris during the last 20 years', *British Medical Journal* 312: 471–2.

Barnes, B., D. Bloor, and J. Henry. 1996. *Scientific Knowledge*. London: Athlone.

Baxter, J., and J. Eyles. 1999. 'The utility of in-depth interviews for studying environmental risk', *Professional Geographer.*

Best, J. 1987. 'Rhetoric in claims-making', *Social Problems* 34: 101-21.

Bishop, C., and D.V. Weseloh. 1990. 'Contaminants in herring gull eggs from the Great Lakes', SOE Fact Sheet 90–2. Burlington, Ont.: Canadian Wildlife Service.

Bond, G.C. and J. Vincent. 1991. 'Living on the edge: Changing social structure in the context of AIDS', in H.B. Hansen and M. Twaddle, eds, *Changing Uganda.* London: James Currey.

Bowen et al. 1995. 'Toward environmental justice', *Annal AAG* 85: 641–63.

Bujan, L., et al. 1996. 'Time series analysis of sperm concentration in fertile men in Toulouse, France between 1977 and 1992', *British Medical Journal* 312: 471–2.

Bullard, R.D. 1990. *Dumping in Dixie.* Boulder, Colo.: Westview Press.

Burger, E.S. 1990. 'Health as a surrogate for the environment', *Daedalus* 119, 4: 133–53.

Burnett, R., et al. 1995. 'Association between ambient particulate sulphate and admissions to Ontario hospitals for cardiac and respiratory diseases', *American Journal of Epidemiology* 142: 15–22.

Burnett, R., S. Cakmak, and J.R. Brook. 1998. 'The effect of the urban ambient air pollution mix on daily mortality rates in 11 Canadian cities', *Canadian Journal of Public Health* 89: 152–6.

Canada. 1991. *The State of Canada's Environment.* Ottawa: Ministry of Supply and Services.

Chociolko, C. 1995. 'The experts disagree', *Alternatives* 21, 3: 19–25.

Clark, P., and A. Davis. 1989. 'The power of dirt', *Canadian Review of Sociology and Anthropology* 26: 650–73.

Colburn. T.E., A. Davidson, S.N. Green, et al. 1996. *Great Lakes, Great Legacy?* Ottawa: Institute for Research on Public Policy.

Commission for Environmental Co-operation (CEC). 1997. *Taking Stock: North America Pollutant Releases and Transfers.* Montreal: CEC.

Corbin, A. 1986. *The Foul and the Fragrant.* Cambridge, Mass.: Harvard University Press.

Cutter, S. 1993. *Living with Risk.* London: Arnold.

Dewailly, E., et al. 1994. 'High organochlorine body burden in women with estrogen receptor-positive breast cancer', *Journal of the National Cancer Institute* 86: 232–4.

Doubleday, N.C. 1995. 'Arctic contaminants and the environment', in T. Fleming, ed., *The Environment and Canadian Society.* Toronto: Nelson.

Douglas, M. 1966. *Purity and Danger.* London: Routledge.

Ecobichon, D. 1990. 'Chemical management of forest pest epidemics', *Biomedical and Environmental Sciences* 3: 217–39.

Edelman, M. 1971. *Politics of Symbolic Action.* Chicago: University of Chicago Press.

Edelstein, M. 1988. *Contaminated Communities.* Boulder, Colo.: Westview Press.

Ellaway, A. 1997. 'Does area of residence affect body size and shape?', *International Journal of Obesity* 21: 304–14.

Elliott. S.J., et al. 1993. 'Modelling psychosocial effects of exposure to solid waste facilities', *Social Science and Medicine* 37: 791–804.

———. 1997. 'It's not because you like it any better . . . Residents' reappraisal of a landfill site', *Journal of Environmental Psychology* 17: 229–41.

Epstein, P.K. 1997. 'Climate, ecology and human health'. www.gcrio.org/CONSEQUENCES/vol3no2/climhealth.html

Evans, R.G., et al. 1994. *Why Are Some People Healthy and Others Not?* New York: Aldine de Gruyter.

Eyerman, R., and A. Jamison. 1989. 'Environmental knowledge as an organizational weapon', *Social Science Information* 28: 99–119.

Eyles, J. 1987. 'Poverty, deprivation and social planning', in M. Pacione, ed., *Social Geography: Problems and Prospects*. London: Croom Helm.

——— et al. 1993a. 'Worrying about waste', *Social Science and Medicine* 37: 805–12.

——— et al. 1993b. 'The social construction of risk in a rural community', *Risk Analysis* 13: 281–90.

———, D. Cole, and B. Gibson. 1996. *Human Health in Ecosystem Health*. Windsor: IJC.

Falck, F., A. Ricci, M.S. Wolff, J. Godbold, and P. Deckers. 1992. 'Pesticides and polychlorinated biphenyl residues in human breast lipids and their relation to breast cancer', *Archives of Environmental Health* 47: 143–6.

Fisch, H., et al. 1997. 'The relationship of sperm counts to birth rates', *Journal of Urology* 157: 840–3.

Fish, S. 1980. *Is There a Text in This Class?* Cambridge, Mass.: Harvard University Press.

Fiske, S.T., and D.R. Kinder. 1981. 'Involvement, expertise and schema use', in N. Cantor and J.K. Kohlstrom, eds, *Personality, Cognition and Social Interaction*. Hillsdale, NJ: Erlbaum.

Frank, J.W., B. Gibson, and M. Macpherson. 1988. 'Information needs in epidemiology', in C. Fowle, ed., *Information Needs for Risk Management*. Toronto: Institute of Environmental Studies.

Garrett, L. 1994. *The Coming Plague*. New York: Farrar, Straus and Giroux.

Goldman, B.A. 1991. *The Truth about Where You Live*. New York: Random House.

———. 1994. *Discounting Human Lives*. Aldershot: Gower.

Golinski, J. 1998. *Making Natural Knowledge*. Cambridge: Cambridge University Press.

Gould, K.A. 1993. 'Pollution and perception', *Qualitative Sociology* 16: 157–78.

———. 1994. 'Legitimacy and growth in the balance', *Industrial and Environmental Crisis Quarterly* 8: 237–56.

Gould, S.J. 1973. *The Mismeasurement of Man*. New York: Norton.

Gourlay, K.A. 1992. *World of Waste*. London: Zed Books.

Green, L., and Ottoson. 1994. *Community Health*. St Louis: Mosley.

Greenpeace. 1993. *Organochlorines, Breast Cancer and the Environment*. Chicago: Greenpeace.

———. 1996. *Vinyls and Health*. London: Greenpeace.

Gutenschwager, G. 1991. 'Why disease risk?', in C.E. Marske, ed., *Communities of Fate*. Lanham, Md: University Press of America.

Haack, S. 1995. 'Puzzling out science', *Academic Questions* 8, 2: 20–31.

Hamilton, J.T. 1995. 'Testing for environmental racism?', *Journal of Policy Analysis and Management* 14: 107–32.

Hannigan, J. 1995. *Environmental Sociology*. London: Routledge.

Harr, J. 1996. *A Civil Action*. New York: Harper.

Harre, R. 1986. *Varieties of Realism*. New York: Blackwell.

Harrison, K., and G. Hoberg. 1993. 'Setting the environmental agenda', *Canadian Journal of Political Science* 24: 3–27.

Health Canada. 1993. *Health Risk Determination*. Ottawa: Health Canada.

———. 1997. *State of Knowledge Report on Environmental Contaminants and Human Health in the Great Lakes Basin*. Ottawa: Health Canada.

——— and Ontario Ministry of Health. 1997. *The Health and Environment Handbook for Health Professionals*. Ottawa: Health Canada.

Herbert, D.T., and D.M. Smith, eds. 1989. *Social Problems and the City*. Oxford: Oxford University Press.

Hertzman, C., et al. 1987. 'Upper Ottawa Street landfill site health study', *Environmental Health Perspectives* 75: 173–95.

Hill, A.B. 1962. *Statistical Methods in Clinical and Preventive Medicine*. Edinburgh: Livingstone.

———. 1965. 'The environment and disease', *Proceedings of the Royal Association of Medicine* 58: 295–300.

Institute of Medicine. 1992. *Emerging Infections*. Washington: National Academy Press.

Jacobson, J.L., and S.W. Jacobson. 1996. 'Intellectual impairment in children exposed to polychlorinated lifestyles in utero', *New England Journal of Medicine* 335: 783–9.

Jerrett, M., J. Eyles, D. Cole, and S. Reader. 1997. 'Environmental equity in Canada', *Environment and Planning A* 29: 1777–800.

———, ———, and ———. 1998. 'Socioeconomic and environmental covariates of premature mortality in Ontario', *Social Science and Medicine* 47: 33–49.

Kasperson, R.E., et al. 1988. 'The social amplification of risk', *Risk Analysis* 8: 177–87.

King, W., and L. Marrett. 1996. 'Case-control study of bladder cancer and chlorination by-products in treated water (Ontario, Canada)', *Cancer Causes and Control* 7: 596–604.

Krieger, N., et al. 1994. 'Breast cancer and serum organochlorines', *Journal of the National Cancer Institute* 86: 589–99.

Kuhn, T. 1970. *The Structure of Scientific Revolutions*. Chicago: University of Chicago Press.

Last, J. 1995. *A Dictionary of Epidemiology*. New York: Oxford University Press.

Leiss, W., and C. Chociolko. 1994. *Risk and Responsibility*. Montreal and Kingston: McGill-Queen's University Press.

Levine, A. 1982. *Love Canal*. Lexington, Mass.: Lexington Books.

Macdonald, D. 1991. *The Politics of Pollution*. Toronto: McClelland & Stewart.

McMichael, A.J. 1993. 'Global environmental change and human population health', *International Journal of Epidemiology* 22: 1–8.

McMullan, C.A., and J. Eyles. 1999. 'Risky business: An analysis of claims-making in the development of an Ontario drinking water objective for tritium', *Social Problems* 46: 294–311.

Mayer, J.D. 1996. 'The political ecology of disease as one new focus for medical geography', *Progress in Human Geography* 20: 441–56.

Meigs, A.S. 1978. 'A Papuan perspective on pollution', *Man* 13: 304–18.

Mielke, H.W. 1999. 'Lead in the inner cities', *American Scientist* 87, 1: www.sigmax.org/amsci/articles/99articles/Mielke.html

Mielke, H.W., and P.L. Reagan. 1998. 'Soil as an important pathway of human lead exposure', *Environmental Health Perspectives* 106 (Supp 1): 217–29.

Morris. R., et al. 1992. 'Chlorination, chlorination by-products and cancer', *American Journal of Public Health* 82: 955–63.

Mulkay, M. 1979. *Science and the Sociology of Knowledge*. Boston: Allen and Unwin.

Neutra, R., et al. 1991. 'Hypotheses to explain the higher symptom rates observed around hazardous waste sites', *Environmental Health Perspectives* 94: 31–8.

Newsome, W.H., D. Davies, and D. Doucet. 1995. 'PCB and organochlorine pesticides in Canadian human milk', *Chemosphere* 30: 2143–53.

Noble, D. 1990. 'Contaminants in Canadian seabirds'. SOE Report 90–2. Ottawa: Environment Canada.

Otway, H., and D. von Winterfeldt. 1982. 'Beyond acceptable risk', *Policy Sciences* 14: 247–56.

Ozonoff, D. 1994. 'Conceptions and misconceptions about human health impact analysis', *Environmental Impact Assessment Review* 14: 499–515.

Pajarinen, J., et al. 1997. 'Incidence of disorders of spermatogenesis in middle-aged Finnish men 1981–91', *British Medical Journal* 314: 13–18.

Pampalon, R., D. Gauthier, G. Raymond, and D. Beaudry. 1990. *La Santé à la carte*. Quebec: Quebec Ministry of Health.

Pengelly, L.D., A. Szakolcai, B. Birmingham, et al. 1997. 'Hamilton-Wentworth air quality initiative: Human health risk assessment for priority air pollutants', Hamilton: HAQI.

Poovey, M. 1998. *The History of the Modern Fact*. Chicago: University of Chicago Press.

Porter, T.M. 1995. *Trust in Numbers*. Princeton, NJ: Princeton University Press.

Powell, D., and W. Leiss. 1997. *Mad Cows and Mother's Milk*. Montreal and Kingston: McGill-Queen's University Press.

Renn, O., T. Webber, and B.B. Johnson. 1991. 'Public participation in hazard management', *Risk* 2: 197–226.

Richardson, M., et al. 1993. *Winning Back the Words*. Toronto: Garamond.

Schettler, T., G. Solomon, M. Valenti, and H. Huddle. 2000. *Generations at Risk: Reproductive Health and the Environment*. Cambridge, Mass.: MIT Press.

Schrader-Frechette, K.S. 1991. *Risk and Rationality*. Berkeley: University of California Press.

Smith, D.M. 1994. *Geography and Social Justice*. London: Arnold.

Sontag, S. 1978. *Illness as Metaphor*. New York: Farrar, Straus and Giroux.

Spector, M., and J.I. Kitsuse. 1977. *Constructing Social Problems*. Menlo Park, Calif.: Cummings.

Stone, D. 1997. *Policy Paradox*. New York: Norton.

Suominen, J., and M. Vierula. 1993. 'Semen quality of Finnish men', *British Medical Journal* 306: 1579.

Suzuki Foundation. 1998. *Taking our Breath Away*. Vancouver: Suzuki Foundation.

Szakolcai, A., and R. Weiler. 1994. *Windsor Air Quality Study: Health Effects Assessment*. Toronto: Queen's Printer.

Taylor, S.M., et al. 1991. 'Psychosocial impacts in populations exposed to solid waste facilities', *Social Science and Medicine* 33: 441–7.

TERA (Toxicology Excellence for Risk Assessment). 1998. International Toxicology Assessment for Risk. www.tera.org

Tesh, M. 1987. *Hidden Arguments*. New York: Basic Books.

Turshen, M. 1984. *The Political Ecology of Disease in Tanzania*. New Brunswick, NJ: Rutgers University Press.

United States and Canada. 1995. *State of the Great Lakes*. Burlington, Ont. and Chicago: Environment Canada and Environmental Protection Agency.

United States General Accounting Office. 1983. *Siting of Hazardous Waste Landfills and Their Correlation with Social and Economic Status of Surrounding Communities*. Washington: GAO.

Vierula, M., et al. 1996. 'High and unchanged sperm counts of Finnish men', *International Journal of Andrology* 19: 11–17.

Vyner, H.M. 1988. *Invisible Trauma*. Lexington, Mass.: D.C. Heath.

Wigle, D.T., Y. Mao, R. Semenciw, M.H. Smith, and P. Toft. 1986. 'Contaminants in drinking water and cancer risks in Canadian cities', *Canadian Journal of Public Health* 77: 335–42.

Wilkinson, R.G. 1996. *Unhealthy Societies*. London: Routledge.

Wolff, M.S., et al. 1993. 'Blood levels of organochlorine residues and risk of breast cancer', *Journal of the National Cancer Institute* 85: 648–52.

Woolgar, S. 1988. *Science: The Very Idea*. New York: Tavistock.

World Wildlife Fund. 1996. *Biodiversity Project*. Washington: WWF.

CHAPTER 9

Work and Health in the Global Economy

Peggy McDonough

Introduction

Work[1] has fascinated sociologists for many years. Reflecting humans' relations with the material world and with one another, work reveals the essential features and consequences of the dominant mode of production as it exists in historically specific periods. Presently, capitalism is undergoing profound change as it expands the focus of its accumulation activities from national to global sites. The consequences of these developments for the social organization of work are profound in that the spatial mobility of capital is altering 'the structure of business enterprise, the organization of labour and the quality of life on and off the job' (Leach and Winson, 1995: 341).

Despite their relevance, little research examines the implications of these trends for what is, arguably, one of the most central dimensions of quality of life—health. Considerable research documents the health-damaging effects of work, but such research concerns itself mainly with the specific features of the immediate job. In fact, the burgeoning literature on the political economy of work is seldom used to situate studies of work and health through linking the broader matrix of macroeconomic social relations to their microeconomic consequences. Efforts aimed at mitigating the features of work that harm health need to be shaped by an understanding of the links among globalizing economic forces, work structures and processes, and health.

This chapter begins by outlining what we do know about the social organization of work and health, especially in relation to the physical and psychosocial conditions of jobs. It then steps beyond this immediate substantive concern to consider the key features of global capitalism, including the internationalization of both production and the division of labour, and the facilitative role of the state. The third section examines selected strategies used by employers in response to global competitive pressures. Transformations in production and in the structure of labour markets are discussed as they relate to flexible production, downsizing, and the casualization of the labour force. The final section outlines the few studies that consider the health implications of these social structures and processes, and suggests a number of important areas of focus for future research on the social organization of work and health in the global economy.

Work and Health

On average, work is better for one's health than not working. Considerable research demonstrates that those not in the labour force, including housewives, live sicker, shorter lives (Repetti et al., 1989; Walters et al., 1995; Rogot et al., 1992). At a most basic level, work provides income that purchases goods and services essential to survival. But work also has latent consequences that enhance health, including the structuring of time, the conferring of status and identity, and the provision of opportunities for social interaction and contributing to collective goals (Jahoda, 1982).

Despite these positive associations, work can also damage health. The physical and chemical hazards of work have been documented for many years, particularly those stemming from resource extraction industries. For example, silicosis killed scores of men in the small Newfoundland communities of St Lawrence and Lawn before wet drilling techniques and ventilation were introduced to fluorspar mining operations there. Dry drilling spews dust into miners' faces, causing free particles of silica to lodge in their lungs. The lungs' reaction to this invasion is to build up scar tissue that spreads over the surface of the lungs, obstructing breathing and eventually leading to heart failure. Official claims that 'no one knew' are dubious, according to Elliott Leyton, who documented miners' experiences in the mid-1970s. He noted that Hippocrates spoke of metal diggers breathing with difficulty, others wrote of a connection between corrosive dust from mining and lung ulceration and consumption as early as 1557, and South Africa passed its first Compensation Act for silicosis in 1911. Despite this knowledge, the carnage continued because 'politico-economic forces dictate that resources be exploited and goods produced at minimum expense and without serious regard for the hazards encountered by labour' (Leyton, 1987: 209).

More recently, Barbara Neis outlined the social and organizational aspects of snow crab processing in Newfoundland and Labrador that contribute to occupational asthma among the mostly female plant workers. Exposure to steam laced with ammonia, methylamine, and other substances, as well as warm, cooked crab containing allergens, induces a respiratory allergic response in some workers that endures long after exposure ceases. Primary prevention practices that would reduce levels of exposure are technically feasible, but employers have been slow to introduce them and no state regulations force them to do so. Neis is not optimistic for change in the near future: 'it is arguable that the current fisheries crisis, in combination with already existing limits on employment opportunities for women . . ., have created a context within which protests from workers will be muted and women (and men) will strive to continue working despite significant risks to their long-term health' (Neis, 1995: 24).

National data confirm these local experiences of hazardous work. Figure 9.1 illustrates fatality rates[2] for the five most dangerous industries in Canada. Even though a slight decline in death rates is evident between 1976 and 1993, those for resource extraction, manufacturing, and construction remained considerably higher than the industrial average. For example, from 1988 to 1993, fatality rates ranged from 23 deaths per 100,000 workers for those in construction to 113 deaths per 100,000 workers for those engaged in fishing and trapping activities. The average fatality rate across all industries during the period was 7 per 100,000 paid workers.

Workers in particular occupations within certain industries were at an even greater risk of death (Table 9.1). Among the 10 most dangerous jobs between 1988 and 1993, the fatality rate for those who performed cutting, handling, and loading duties in mining and quarrying was 281 deaths per 100,000 paid workers, while that for insulators in construction was 246 (Marshall, 1996). These rates are a staggering 35–40 times higher than the industrial average.

When sickness absence rates are considered, a slightly different pattern emerges (Figure 9.2). Compared with the all-industry average, days of work lost per worker for reasons of illness or disability in 1997 were *fewer* among workers in primary industries (e.g., fishing and trapping, logging and forestry, and mining, quarrying, and oil wells), while professional and service workers took more time off for health reasons. Although these patterns may reflect any number of underlying conditions of employment, including company sick-leave and compensation policies, they suggest that physical and chemical hazards are not the only aspects of work that affect

Table 9.1: The 10 Most Dangerous Jobs, Canada, 1988–1993

	Fatality Rates (Deaths/100,000 Paid Workers)
All occupations	7
Mining and quarrying: cutting, handling, loading	281
Construction: insulating	246
Mining and quarrying: labouring	139
Air pilots, navigators, and flight engineers	137
Timber cutting	123
Log hoisting, sorting, and moving	116
Net, trap, and line fishing	110
Truck drivers	38
Construction: labouring	35
Construction: pipefitting and plumbing	31

Source: Marshall (1996).

Figure 9.1: Fatality Rates by Industry, 1976–1993

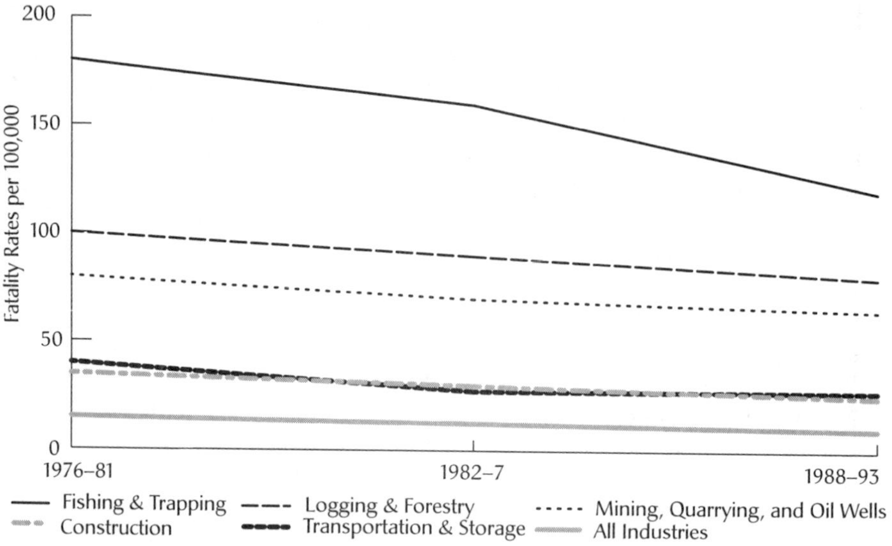

Source: Marshall (1996).

Figure 9.2: Days Lost per Full-time Worker in 1997 for Reasons of Illness or Disability

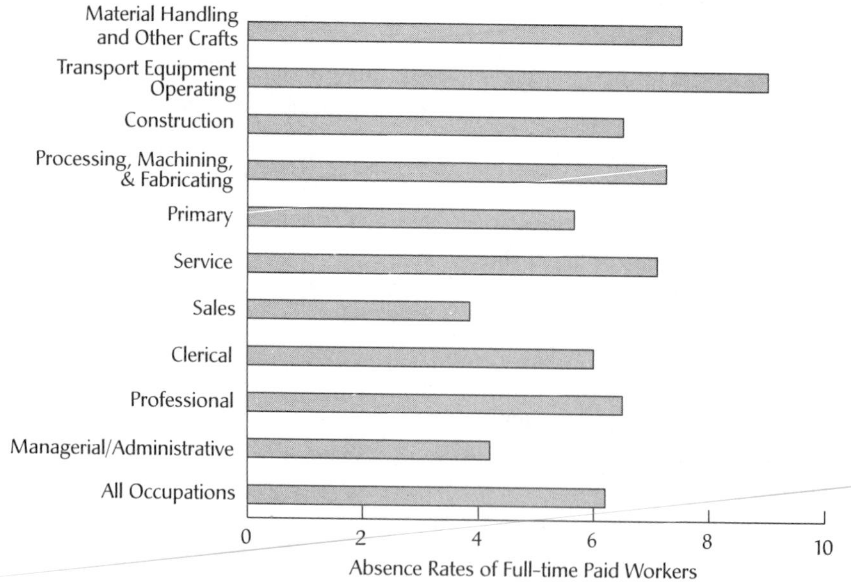

Source: Akyeampong and Usalcas (1998).

health. Less evident than these 'material' conditions, but also significant in health terms, are the psychosocial features of the labour process, such as the pace and intensity of work, opportunities to use and develop skills, and autonomy and social interaction at work. Indeed, as the economy shifts from one driven by manufacturing industries to one dominated by service, psychologically demanding jobs have overtaken those involving physically demanding and 'dirty' work.

Karasek's (1979) demand-control model is probably the best known among conceptions of psychosocial work conditions. His basic premise is that non-challenging jobs that provide little opportunity to control productive activities damage health. The effect of low control is exacerbated when a job is psychologically demanding (e.g., workload is excessive, job is hectic, a large proportion of the work is performed under time pressure, a great deal of concentration is required, etc.). Karasek used the dimensions of control and demand to construct four job profiles that he later matched with actual jobs. *Active jobs* are those with high job control and high psychological demands. They include mainly professional and management occupations with a large proportion of male incumbents. In contrast, *high-strain jobs*, or those with low job control and high demands, are exemplified by assembly-line and low-status service work and represent mainly 'female' occupations. *Passive jobs*, those with low job control and low demands, include occupations such as sales clerk, security guard, janitor, and billing clerk. Finally *low-strain jobs* are those with high control and low psychological demands, best characterized by self-paced occupations such as repairman and lineman.

Despite the commonly held view that those in high-status jobs suffer from the heavy demands of their work, high-strain jobs are the most damaging to health. Compared with other job types, those working under conditions of low control and high demands experience more cardiovascular morbidity and early mortality (Johnson and Johansson, 1991; Karasek et al., 1988; Albright et al., 1992), sickness absence from work (North et al., 1993, 1996), depression (Landsbergis et al., 1992), chronic conditions (Rasanen et al., 1997) and musculoskeletal pain (Ahlberg-Hulten et al., 1995; Hemingway et al., 1997; Krause et al., 1997), and reduced physical functioning and mental health (Lerner et al., 1994). Individuals with low-strain jobs report the best health, while those with active or passive jobs lie somewhere in between.

Data from Statistics Canada's 1994 National Population Health Survey (NPHS) confirm the association between job strain and health. The relationships are illustrated in Table 9.2 for respondents aged 20–64 and working for pay. Those in high-strain jobs were more likely to report poor or fair health than their counterparts in low-strain jobs (8.4 per cent compared with 5 per cent). They were also more likely to say that they experienced pain or discomfort: 17 per cent of those in high-strain jobs reported pain as opposed to 12 per cent of workers in low-strain jobs. Job strain appears to affect mental as well as physical health. Respondents in high-strain jobs were only half as likely as those in low-strain jobs to report being happy and interested in life.

Table 9.2: Job Strain by Self-Rated Health, Pain, and Unhappiness, National Population Health Survey, Canada, 1994

	Job Strain[a]	
Health	No	Yes
Self-rated Health		
Poor/Fair	5.0	8.4
Good	23.5	35.0
Very Good	41.9	34.5
Excellent	29.6	22.1
Total	100.0	100.0
N=7,718		
Pain[b]		
Yes	11.8	17.2
No	88.2	82.8
Total	100.0	100.0
N=7,703		
Unhappy[c]		
Yes	22.8	41.7
No	77.2	58.3
Total	100.0	100.0
N=7,701		

[a]Job strain = high psychological demands at work and low control over work tasks.
[b]Usually free of pain or discomfort.
[c]Describes self as usually unhappy and disinterested in life.

The health-damaging dimensions of work emerge largely because work under capitalism is a relationship of power; that is, it is a political process that produces structures of domination and subordination, mechanisms of social control, and forms of exploitation (Johnson, 1980). Over a century ago, Marx made direct reference to the problems of the capitalist mode of production for worker well-being. He argued that the worker 'does not affirm himself but denies himself, does not feel content but unhappy, does not develop freely his physical and mental energy but mortifies his body and ruins his mind' (Marx, 1964 [1844]: 110). For Marx, this state of affairs arises because, under capitalism, work is externally controlled to serve employers' prerogatives, regardless of the needs and interests of the workers (Garfield, 1980). Marx used the term 'alienation' to refer to workers' loss of control over the labour process and products of their labour, and their subsequent estrangement from their labour and, ultimately, from themselves. Accordingly, alienation is not just an existential experience, but an objective circumstance emerging from the separation of the worker from his or her productive activities (Navarro, 1982). Under these conditions, the job becomes a means to satisfy consumption 'needs' outside of work rather than an end of intrinsic interest. Even in this, however, workers are short-changed. The employment 'contract' guarantees employers legitimate access to the goods and services produced by their employees as long as they agree to pay them a wage. Importantly, this exchange is exploitative in ways that favour the employer because workers produce more than they receive in wages.

Early in the twentieth century, Frederick Taylor (1911) was well aware of the need to control workers in order to exploit them fully. In this regard, he was primarily interested in 'enabling' workers to produce more under conditions of work that stifle their motivation to produce to their maximum potential, and believed that external constraints were necessary to do so. His realization of such constraints in the fragmentation of production processes revolutionized the social division of labour. He used detailed time and motion studies of individuals at work to break jobs down into their constituent components and assigned these smaller pieces to workers who specialized in carrying out only a fraction of what had been a more integrated production process. Taylor's work, combined with advances in technology, formed the basis of mass production that has dominated production practices in industrial societies for almost a century.

Although mass production techniques continue to shape the nature of work processes, the forces of contemporary capitalism are creating new conditions for controlling labour. The Canadian economy, like those of other developed nations, is undergoing major transformations as corporations restructure their operations to adapt to a new global economic environment. In some instances, this means increased investment in more efficient technology to boost productivity; in other instances, firms abandon various sectors of the domestic economy, reduce their investment in them, or focus on lowering labour costs and gaining tax and regulatory concessions from government (Bluestone and Harrison, 1982). The internationalization of financial markets provides corporations with additional options by facilitating the movement of production facilities to nations with lower costs. Regardless of the particular strategy that employers use in response to its competitive pressures, the globalization of the economy is having a profound effect on the production process and the division of labour.

The Globalization of the Economy

> In the late twentieth century a powerful globalizing economic trend thrusts towards the achievement of a market utopia on the world scale. At present, no counter-tendency effectively challenges the globalization thrust. The market appears to be bursting free from the bonds of national societies, subjecting a global society to its laws. (Cox, 1991: 335)

Globalization of the economy is marked by the internationalization of both production and the division of labour. No longer content to focus on domestic sites, capital sets up production facilities in areas of the world that maximize comparative cost advantage, especially as it relates to the availability of abundant and cheap labour (ibid.). Some have suggested that economic globalization represents a new stage in capitalist development, one in which monopoly capitalism is giving way to global capitalism through the process of reorganizing the economic geography of the world (Ross and Trachte, 1990).

Global capitalism is promoted by a number of technological innovations. For example, advances in ocean transport and air freight have dramatically reduced shipping costs, and developments in information technology have spawned world financial markets and facilitated production and distribution on a worldwide scale. However, the key element permitting international capital mobility is the liberalization of nation-states' trade and other regulatory policies that permits the relatively unfettered movement of capital and goods across borders. By shifting production to geographic areas with low labour costs that are often, but not exclusively, in developing countries, global restructuring effectively weakens labour in developed regions, where '[t]he threat of capital mobility becomes a potent weapon in the old contest between labor and capital' (ibid., 7).

Although capital has always been expansionary in its aspirations, the unique features of contemporary economic restructuring on a global scale can be traced to the 1970s. At that time, North American firms, especially those in manufacturing, were facing falling profits. In large part, the profit squeeze arose from growing international competition that affected one mass-production industry after another, including footwear, textiles, apparel, autos, steel, machine tools, consumer electronics, and computers. The production and trade among industrialized and newly industrializing countries of what were essentially the same products led to a chronic excess capacity that found many domestic plants operating well below full capacity. This reduced productivity and raised the unit cost of production (Harrison and Bluestone, 1988). From the point of view of capital, the 'unreasonable demands' of workers for a higher and more equitable standard of living through the expansion of the welfare state also contributed to the profit squeeze. Post-World War II concessions to labour, such as unemployment insurance and enhanced wage and benefit packages, were seen as limiting management's flexibility to regulate its workforce in order to maintain accustomed profit levels (ibid.; Bluestone and Harrison, 1982).

Capital responded to the accumulation crisis by attempting to increase productivity through technological innovation, expanding world markets, and other forms of comparative advantage, such as those linked to reducing labour costs. Domestically, employers have sought 'flexible' arrangements with employees through wage freezes, rollbacks, and other concessions, and have increased their reliance on contingent or casual labour (Harrison and Bluestone, 1988). They are also relocating their production facilities to international sites offering cheap, compliant labour.

While capital mobility has not completely decimated manufacturing in the developed world, its mere existence works effectively to discipline labour.

The decline in labour costs has also been facilitated indirectly by a state increasingly committed to deregulation. The labour movement's post-World War II strength forced the state to develop policies curbing the excesses of crude, competitive capitalism through various regulatory and social welfare programs. At the same time, domestic markets expanded. However, with growing pressure to respond to the new reality of capital mobility, the state is now more interested in directing its efforts towards adapting the domestic economy to participate in the world economy (Cox, 1991). Importantly, the state is reducing barriers to investment and minimizing regulations in order to create a favourable environment for world commerce (Drache and Gertler, 1991b). The North American Free Trade Agreement is one such response on the part of the state, along with a myriad of deregulation policies that degrade minimum wage and working conditions (Glenday, 1997). The irony of these developments is not lost on some commentators: 'Competitiveness becomes defined narrowly on the terrain staked by private sector actors, who want a state strong enough to discipline the workforce and constrain wage movements but one which is increasingly liberal in providing industrial subsidies, tax concessions, and tax expenditures' (Drache and Gertler, 1991b: 9).

In sum, economic globalization creates competitive pressures that force employers to restructure to maintain accustomed levels of accumulation. Their efforts are directed at their productive activities and the labour they hire to undertake them. The next section briefly examines three restructuring strategies—flexible production, downsizing, and casualization of the labour force—that set the stage for a final discussion of the changing nature of the social organization of work and its implications for health.

The Globalization of the Economy and the Social Organization of Work

Economic globalization has profound effects on domestic production processes and the division of labour as firms enact a wide variety of strategies to respond to new competitive pressures. They all reflect the goals of increasing productivity and lowering labour costs, and ultimately result in greater control of labour. Flexible production is one such response that is fast becoming the new paradigm of workplace organization. Pioneered by Japanese auto makers, it implies flexibility in the quantity and type of product and in the human resources needed to meet fluctuating production demands (Rinehart et al., 1997). It purports to use educated, self-motivated, and highly skilled workers who actively participate in the production process, but critics charge that flexible production processes are simply the latest means of controlling labour (Drache, 1991).

The essential features of production necessary to meet flexibility requirements are illustrated by the organization of work in the CAMI auto plant in Chatham, Ontario, where a type of flexible production—lean production—is practised (Rinehart et al., 1997). Lean production is characterized by maximum workloads and minimum staffing. Maximum workloads emerge from just-in-time production practices, highly standardized work, and continuous cost reduction efforts to eliminate 'wasted' labour time. Only what is needed at any given time is made and a continuous production flow is achieved by co-ordinating sub-assembly production and delivery with the needs of the main line. It means that parts are delivered just in time to produce sub-assemblies that are attached just in time to the vehicle as it moves through the shop. This tightly integrated system relies heavily on the rigid standardization of work; it only works when employees do the same tasks in exactly the same way in the same length of time. Such practices severely restrict workers' ability to regulate the pace of their work.

Lean staffing intensifies the labour process. For example, teamwork and rotation of jobs within teams gives the employer flexibility to adapt to the changing demands of production. This provides the opportunity to replace absent workers, not by relief workers, but with other team members who must add the work of their missing colleague to the burden of their own. Such practices lead critics to charge that 'lean production means lean staffing, a penchant to load more and more work onto jobs, and an unquenchable thirst for overtime' (ibid., 25).

Its proponents call lean production 'post-Fordist', claiming that the rigidly fragmented, semi-skilled mass production techniques of Fordist methods have been replaced by flexible automation. Team workers are trained to be multi-skilled, not only familiar with all aspects of the production process but also regularly rotating jobs. Moreover, workers are strongly encouraged to participate actively in modifying production processes by continuously eliminating non-value-added labour. In short, lean production promises job enrichment and greater worker control. However, its detractors argue that, despite such claims, production is not much different from that practised in the 1950s. Most jobs are fragmented, short-cycled, and repetitive. Although workers perform many different tasks, most of them are low-skilled so that 'multi-tasking', rather than 'multi-skilling', more adequately describes the work (ibid.).

Through its diffusion into the service sector, the flexible production paradigm is influencing the organization of the labour process beyond that linked to mass production industries. For example, total quality management (TQM) has been widely introduced into Canadian hospitals (Armstrong and Armstrong, 1996). Outwardly, management claims to be committed to continuous quality improvement and 'customer' satisfaction through work processes that foster active involvement among employees and build their commitment to the organization's main goal of caring for ill people. TQM stresses teamwork, innovation in work practices, and improving care by eliminating variability in service provision. Workers are trained to do a variety of tasks, ostensibly because doing so increases job satisfaction and encourages innovation among workers who now have an overview of the work process.

Although the rhetoric of TQM is compelling, critics argue that, in practice, it is replete with contradictions (ibid.). It promises workers autonomy but gives them increased managerial control. Employee 'accountability' means that workers now spend more time documenting their adherence to standardized practice protocols as demanded by a management increasingly committed to surveillance. Standardizing care has also meant disregarding the unique needs of patients and laying off workers because the streamlined, more 'efficient' work processes supposedly require less labour time. In this context, multi-skilling translates into dumping even more work onto already overburdened employees, who say they have less time than ever to devote to patient care. As in the CAMI factory, TQM renders continuous quality improvement elusive: 'The whole process is aimed at lowering the costs of value added labour activity, reducing the time available for non-value added procedures, obtaining greater flexibility in labour utilization to reduce the idle time, replacing labour by the more extensive use of equipment and new technology, and ultimately reducing hospital labour requirements' (White, 1997: 126).

Along with increasing productivity and cutting costs through the use of new production techniques, the employment relationship is being radically transformed to meet similar ends. Doing more with fewer workers has become almost mantra-like in its appeal to both public and private organizations. This has resulted in massive layoffs that kept unemployment throughout the 1990s at rates second only to those of the Great Depression of the 1930s, leading Osberg et al. (1995: 180) to note that 'having a job in today's labour market is like having a seat in a lifeboat.'

The data presented in Figure 9.3 illustrate the rapid increase in Canadian unemployment rates during the 1990s. After beginning the decade near 8 per cent, the

Figure 9.3: Unemployment Rate, Canada, 1989–1998

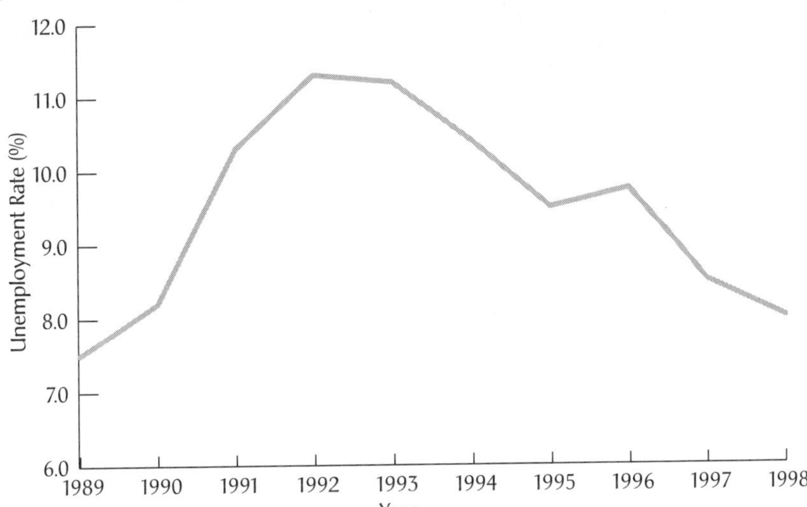

Source: Statistics Canada (1996, 1997, 1998, 1999).

unemployment rate rose to just over 11 per cent by 1992, largely as a result of a global recession in the early 1990s. More recently, economic growth has reduced unemployment, but the persistence of rates that are higher than the 1989 level is a stark illustration of the 'jobless recovery'.

The unskilled and least educated remain the most vulnerable to layoffs, but middle management has not escaped unscathed as corporations merge and 'de-layer' their administrative structures (Burman, 1997). Ide and Cordell (1994) estimate that about two million middle managers have been permanently laid off in the industrial world since the mid-1980s. Many of their responsibilities have devolved downward without the financial and other rewards that formerly accompanied them. In fact, CAMI lauds its relatively flat job classification hierarchy as an example of workplace democracy (Rinehart et al., 1997). A less sanguine interpretation is that the company is benefiting financially from classifying workers as 'low' in skill while loading them 'high' in responsibility.

The experience of unemployment has become all the more difficult as ongoing efforts to dismantle the welfare state erode the little support that was available to unemployed workers. Notably, Brian Mulroney's Conservative government began an attack on unemployment insurance in 1990 with the passage of a bill that reduced the number of unemployed people who could qualify for benefits by increasing the minimum number of weeks for insurable employment. As part of its deficit-reduction program, the Liberal government has carried on this 'slash and burn' strategy through extensive changes to the benefit structure (Canadian Labour Congress, 1999). The data presented in Figure 9.4 illustrate the stark results of their policies. From a high of 74 per cent in 1989, the proportion of unemployed people who

Figure 9.4: Percentage of Unemployed Receiving Unemployment Insurance Benefits in Canada, 1989–1997

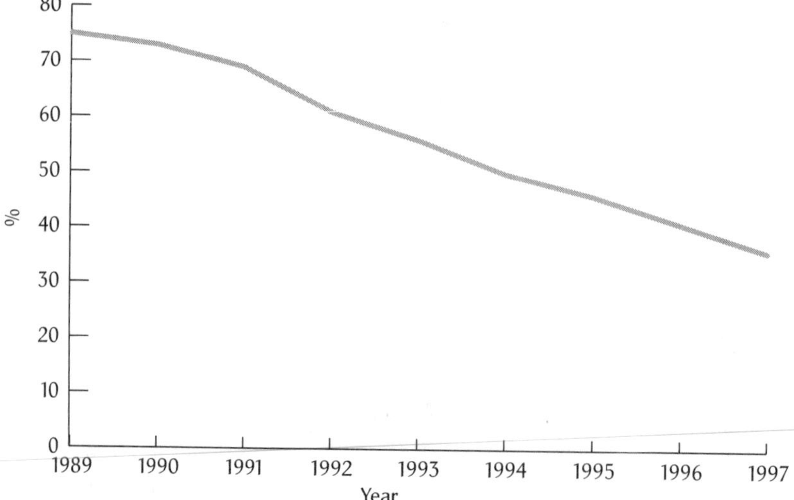

Source: Canadian Labour Congress (1999).

received unemployment insurance benefits dropped to 36 per cent in 1997. Young workers have been affected even more by the changes—55 per cent of unemployed individuals between the ages of 15 and 24 received benefits in 1989, compared with only 15 per cent in 1997. This dramatic decline is partly the result of an increase in the total hours of work (from 300 hours to 910 hours) required of new labour force entrants in order to qualify for benefits (ibid.; Lin, 1998).

The erosion of this social safety net, especially during a decade of high unemployment, has not gone unnoticed by the public. In 1998, the Canadian Council on Social Development (1999) asked Canadians how confident they were that, in the event of job loss, government support programs would adequately sustain them while they looked for a job. Almost two-thirds of respondents were not confident at all, while only 24 per cent reported confidence in such programs.

In addition to downsizing through layoffs, employers are relying increasingly on casual labour to meet production needs. This entails hiring part-time and temporary labour or contracting out work to other employers, many of which are small businesses that pay low wages and poor or no benefits (Glenday, 1997). In fact, firms of less than 50 employees provide roughly one-third of all employment opportunities in Canada (Eakin, 1995) and, in recent years, account for a disproportionate share of net increases in employment (Picot, 1994). The marginalized or 'just-in-time' workforce that emerges from these practices is used to accommodate both short-term instability of firms and long-term fluctuations in demand (Osberg, 1997).

Figure 9.5 charts recent trends in non-standard employment. In contrast to the slight decline of full-time workers as a percentage of all workers, those working part-time grew from just under 17 per cent of the total workforce in 1989 to 19 per cent

Figure 9.5: Full-time, Part-time, Public Sector, Private Sector, and Self-employed as a Percentage of the Total Labour Force, Canada, 1989 and 1998

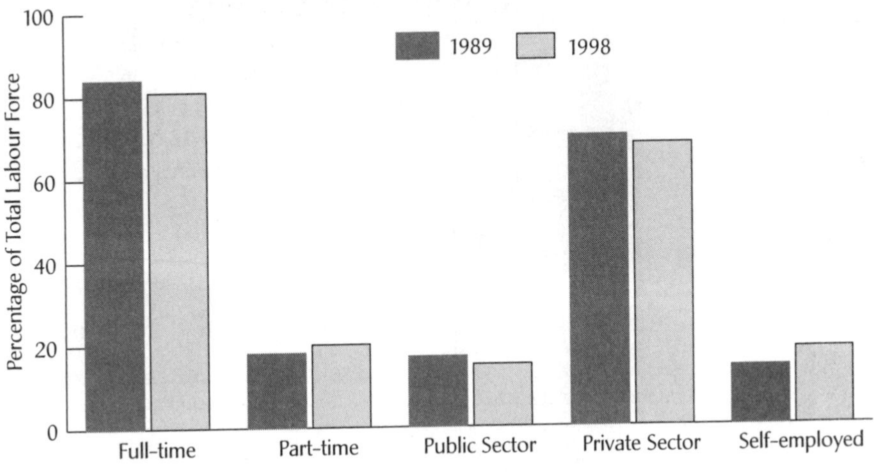

Source: Statistics Canada (1999b).

in 1998. This seemingly small change in the proportion of part-time workers masks a net expansion within this group. Compared with the 1989 total of those employed part-time, the 1998 total rose by 24 per cent, while full-time employment grew by only 8 per cent over the same period. Growth in the numbers of self-employed was even greater. In 1989, 14 per cent of all workers were self-employed; this figure rose to 17.5 per cent by 1998. However, this represents a 42.5 per cent increase in self-employment over 10 years, compared with an increase of only 7 per cent for employees in the private sector and an actual decline of 1 per cent in the public sector. All indications are that non-permanent employment, including temporary, contract, and casual arrangements, is also on the rise (Grenon and Chun, 1997).

Contingent employment arrangements do more than provide employers with greater flexibility to respond to uneven demand for goods and services. They also enhance profit margins by reducing labour costs (Krahn and Lowe, 1998). Figure 9.6 compares employer-sponsored benefits packages received by permanent and non-permanent employees in 1994. While just over half of permanent workers have pension, health, and dental plans and receive paid sick leave, only one-fifth of those in non-permanent employment can expect these benefits. Seventy-eight per cent of permanent employees enjoy paid vacation, compared with only 28 per cent of their non-permanent counterparts. Not surprisingly, the average income of the latter group is also lower. In 1995, non-permanent employees earned only 65 per cent of the weekly wages received by permanent employees (Grenon and Chun, 1997).

Figure 9.6: Employer-Sponsored Benefits by Permanent/ Non-permanent Work, Paid Employees Aged 15–69 Years, Canada, 1995

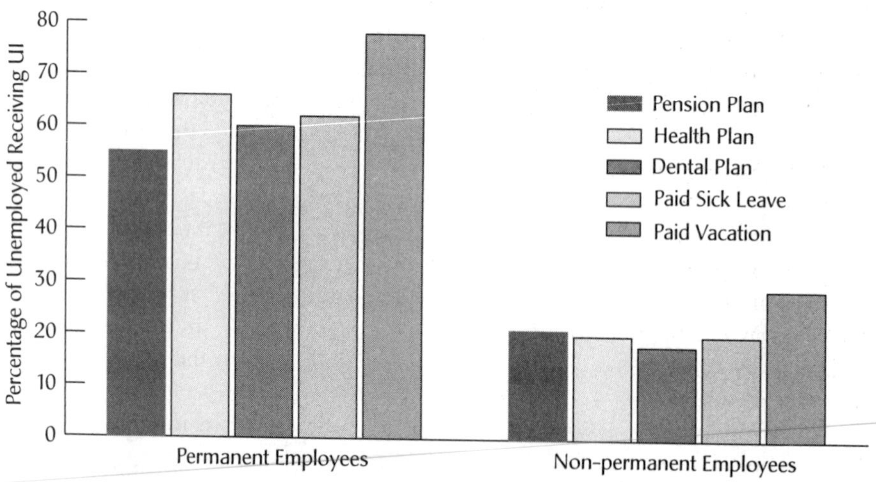

Source: Krahn and Lowe (1998).

This 'occupational skidding' (Leach and Winson, 1995), where 'good' jobs with above-average wages, reasonable security, benefits packages, and advancement potential are being replaced by 'bad' jobs with none of these amenities, is also promoted by the fastest growing area of the Canadian economy, the service sector. Community, business, and personal services comprised only 19.5 per cent of the total employed in 1961. By 1998, this had grown to 38.7 per cent. During the same period, the employment share of manufacturing fell from 24 to 15.4 per cent (Glenday, 1997; Statistics Canada, 1999a). This development, along with increases in the number of small firms with similarly characterized jobs, suggests that the trend to casual or non-standard work will continue.

The use of casual labour is not a new phenomenon. Marx noted that the presence of a reserve army of labour increased employers' control over labour, enabling them to keep wages low and instilling discipline through the threat of unemployment. However, what is new about the contemporary casualization of labour is the growth in the number of individuals reporting that they are involuntarily working part-time (Rothman, 1998; Broad, 1997). Using Canadian census data from 1970 through to 1990, Nakamura et al. (1997) charted this trend, along with an increase in part-time full-year employment for both men and women.[3] Part-time full-year employment increased by 79 per cent for women, and 74 per cent for men, between 1970 and 1990. In 1975, 9.4 per cent of women working part-time who were 25 years and older stated that they would prefer a full-time job. Almost four times as many women in that age group (37.1 per cent) involuntarily worked part-time in 1993. The comparable figures for men are 16.4 and 54.8 per cent.

Finally, changes in the internal organizational structure of firms that lead to sharper distinctions between core and peripheral workers have been accompanied by changes in institutional structures of labour markets. Included here are collective bargaining legislation, the role of unions, work standards legislation, and health and safety regulations. Increasingly, governments are disentangling themselves from policies that protect workers and unions, so much so that collective bargaining is currently under tremendous pressure to accommodate employers' imperatives (Osberg, 1997). This situation is exacerbated by free trade policies that prohibit sanctions against companies that leave the country to avoid 'troublesome' worker demands. Some commentators would argue that worker rights codified by various institutional structures have always been weak since 'management rights under common law explicitly vest the employer with sole control over the business and management of its affairs' (Sass, 1989: 163). Nevertheless, to the extent that regulatory policies may temper some of the excesses of worker exploitation, the deregulating trends evident at all levels of government do not bode well for the social organization of work and the health of workers.

In sum, the transformation of production and labour markets in response to the globalization of capital has led to dramatic changes in work and employment relations in Canada (Drache, 1991). Flexible production techniques increase the pace and intensity of work, while downsizing and casualization of the labour force add job insecurity to the health-noxious mix. The implications of these developments for the relationship between work and health are significant.

The Social Organization of Work and Health in the Global Economy

Although not exhaustive, at least three areas of inquiry concerning the social organization of work and health emerge from contemporary changes in work structures and processes in an era of economic globalization. First, it is important to situate examinations of workplace health in the broader political economy that influences the social organization of work at particular sites. Second, employers' strategies to increase productivity and reduce labour costs may have specific consequences for health. Finally, it is important to consider how worker resistance to these arrangements may prevent the degradations of the workplace from bleeding into the larger fabric of workers' lives (Erikson, 1990: 31).

Most investigations of work and health focus on the immediate task environment, to the relative exclusion of the context of the firm and its relationship to the broader political economy. An exception to this is an investigation of the Canadian meat-packing industry, which documented an increase in repetitive strain injury as the industry restructured after global competition and a drop in the demand for meat products led to falling profits (Novek et al., 1990). One management strategy was to increase productivity through technical innovation. The labour process was altered dramatically by converting older, multi-story production facilities to single-level operations where product flow-through could be greatly speeded up. The altered technical aspects of production were accompanied by changes in the internal labour market. Following restructuring practices in the American meat-packing industry that concentrated on avoiding the high costs of unionized labour (Broadway, 1990), uniform master agreements that set national standards for wages and working conditions in the industry were dissolved. This paved the way for wage rollbacks and markedly lowered starting wages for new employees. With actual or threatened plant closures as added incentive, employees had little choice but to accept lower pay rates. However, poor working conditions and labour relations have led to considerable employee turnover and increasing reliance on unskilled workers who are never adequately trained.

The intensification of the pace of work and involvement of untrained workers resulted in injury rates well above the average for other Canadian manufacturing industries and rising at a faster rate. Especially notable are upper limb repetitive strain injuries which increased by 58 per cent during the study period (1982–5), compared with a 17 per cent increase in all injuries in the industry. Increases in the number of days lost to injury suggested, further, that injuries were becoming more severe. Similar observations were made at CAMI, where the maximum workloads and minimum staffing characteristics of lean production speed up the pace of the line without adding workers. This high-intensity work may have led to an increase in repetitive strain injuries that occurred in the plant. In 1992, 11.7 per cent of all injuries were repetitive strain injuries, compared with 32.7 per cent of all injuries a mere three years later (Rinehart et al., 1997).

Armstrong and Armstrong's (1996) extensive discussion of changes in the provision of services and in the labour market in Canadian health care also highlights several key problems with flexible production. This management tool from the goods-producing sector is being applied to the organization of patient care, but the computer algorithms that use average treatment protocols and patient profiles to determine staffing needs are woefully inadequate for meeting the divergent needs of patients. Lean staffing and a growing reliance on part-time and casual workers, who may require considerable assistance from core staff, have increased the intensity of work. This contributes to higher injury and illness rates. In fact, days lost per nurse because of illness and disability have not only increased since 1986, they are more than double the average for all full-time workers (Figure 9.7). The gap between the two groups has also widened over time and is especially evident for 1997, when an average of 15.4 days was lost because of illness or disability among nurses, compared with only 6.2 days for all workers.

Inasmuch as employers' attempts to increase productivity through technological innovation have increased the intensity of work, contemporary transformations of labour markets may also be consequential for health. The ongoing replacement of workers by technology, deindustrialization, mergers, downsizing, and corporate flight to international sites of cheap labour have sustained unemployment rates at postwar highs for several years. Restructuring in the context of high unemployment leaves growing numbers of workers fearful for their jobs. In fact, job security was the

Figure 9.7: Days Lost per Worker for Nurses and All Full-time Workers Because of Own Illness or Disability, Canada, 1986–1997

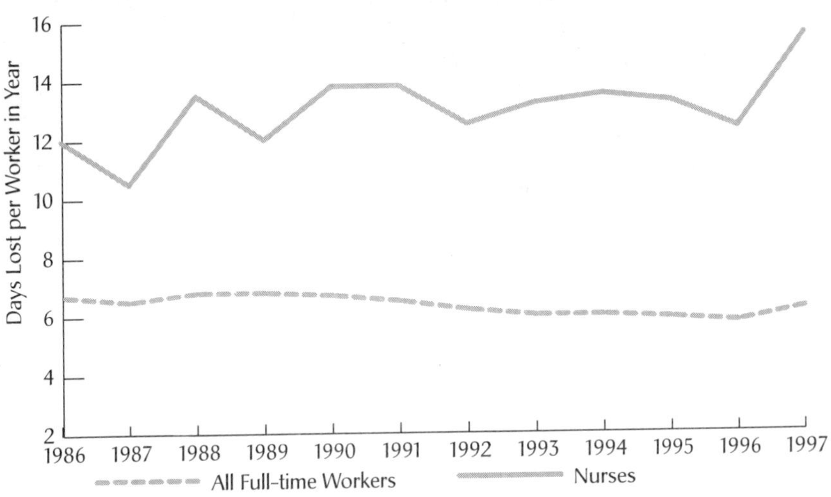

Source: Akyeampong and Usalcas (1998).

number-one issue for the majority of those polled in the Canadian Council on Social Development's (1999) project on well-being. One-third of employed Canadians believed that they could lose their jobs over the next two years, and 37 per cent were not confident that they could find an equivalent job within six months if job loss were to become a reality.

To date, there has been little research on job insecurity. Cross-sectional studies find associations between perceived threats of job loss and psychological symptomatology (Dooley et al., 1987), heavy drinking (Steffy and Laker, 1991), and heart disease (Siegrist et al., 1986), and longitudinal work suggests that the health-damaging effects of job insecurity only worsen. For example, Arnetz et al. (1991) found that after a year of living under the constant threat of unemployment, the mental well-being of blue-collar men and women deteriorated. Their initial health scores, higher than those of the unemployed, resembled those of individuals securely employed. After 18 months, however, the scores of those who were chronically insecure about their jobs converged with those of the unemployed, as the mental health of the former deteriorated and that of the latter improved. Both groups reported poorer mental health than the securely employed. These results are similar to the finding of Heaney et al. (1994) that job insecurity that endured for just over 14 months had a bigger effect on physical symptomatology than insecurity measured at only one point in time at either the beginning or end of this period. They concluded that chronic job insecurity is a potent stressor that should be included in examinations of work and health.

Data from the 1994 National Population Health Survey illustrate an inverse association between job insecurity and some health outcomes (Table 9.3). For example, as levels of agreement waned for the statement, 'Your job security is good', respondents were less likely to report excellent health and somewhat more likely to report fair or poor health. Those with the highest levels of job insecurity were also slightly more likely to report pain and discomfort than other groups, and almost twice as likely to deny being 'usually happy and interested in life', compared to those with the lowest levels of job insecurity (31 per cent as opposed to 17 per cent). The associations among job insecurity and health behaviours, however, were more mixed. Job insecurity was positively related to increased medication use over the past month, with almost 10 per cent of those with strong perceptions of job insecurity reporting use, compared with just under 7 per cent for those with the lowest levels job insecurity. Respondents with high job insecurity were also slightly more likely to smoke. Interestingly, those from the group with the lowest job insecurity were slightly more likely to drink at least 14 or more drinks a week than their counterparts reporting higher job insecurity. This latter observation may reflect a tendency to be more economically frugal in the face of potential job loss, but questions can also be raised about the ability of this measure to capture 'problem' drinking (Greenberg and Grunberg, 1995).

The data presented in Table 9.4 suggest that not all social groups feel equally vulnerable to job loss. Professionals and those in high-level management fared the best

Table 9.3: Job Insecurity by Self-Rated Health, Pain, Unhappiness, Medication Use, Daily Smoking and Drinking, National Population Health Survey, Canada, 1994

Health	Job Insecurity[a]		
	Bottom Third[b]	Middle Third	Top Third
Self-rated health			
Poor/fair	4.9	4.6	6.0
Good	20.1	23.4	27.2
Very good	37.1	44.1	41.4
Excellent	37.9	27.9	25.4
Total	100.0	100.0	100.0
N=7,718			
Pain[c]			
Yes	11.5	9.8	15.4
No	88.5	90.2	84.5
Total	100.0	100.0	100.0
N=7,703			
Unhappy[d]			
Yes	16.9	21.8	30.5
No	83.1	78.2	69.5
Total	100.0	100.0	100.0
N=7,701			
Medication use in past month[e]			
Yes	6.5	7.9	9.8
No	93.5	93.1	90.2
Total	100.0	100.0	100.0
N=7,701			
Daily Smoker			
Yes	30.9	31.2	33.2
No	69.1	68.8	66.8
Total	100.0	100.0	100.0
N=7,718			
>14 Alcoholic drinks/week			
Yes	8.1	7.6	6.3
No	91.9	92.4	93.7
Total	100.0	100.0	100.0
N=6,610			

[a]Grouping into thirds constructed from responses to the following item: 'Your job security is good.' Fixed responses included: strongly agree; agree; neither agree nor disagree; disagree; and strongly disagree.
[b]Bottom third = low job insecurity.
[c]Usually free of pain or discomfort.
[d]Describes self as usually unhappy and disinterested in life.
[e]Reports use of tranquilizers, amphetamines, anti-depressants, prescription pain relievers, or sleeping pills in past month.

Table 9.4: Job Insecurity by Occupational Group, Education, Age, Gender, and Work Hours, National Population Health Survey, Canada, 1994

Social Group	Job Insecurity Bottom Third[a]	Middle Third	Top Third	Total
Occupation				(N=7,460)
Agricultural workers	26.2	48.8	25.0	100.0
Unskilled workers	18.2	48.3	33.6	100.0
Semi-skilled workers	26.6	43.1	30.3	100.0
Mid-management/ semi-professional	23.3	40.6	36.1	100.0
High-management/ professional	30.6	43.3	26.1	100.0
Education				(N=7,712)
Primary school only	27.3	45.6	27.1	100.0
Some secondary	22.3	48.2	29.4	100.0
High school diploma	20.2	48.4	31.4	100.0
Some post-secondary schooling	21.6	45.6	32.8	100.0
Post-secondary diploma	21.5	44.8	33.8	100.0
Post-secondary degree	28.8	38.5	32.7	100.0
Age				(N=7,712)
20–9	19.5	47.1	33.4	100.0
30–9	21.4	44.6	34.0	100.0
40–54	24.8	43.8	31.5	100.0
55–64	30.2	45.1	24.7	100.0
Gender				(N=7,712)
Female	21.2	45.8	33.0	100.0
Male	24.5	44.1	31.4	100.0
Work hours				(N=7,711)
Part-time	19.1	40.4	40.5	100.0
Full-time	23.7	45.8	30.6	100.0

[a]Bottom third = low job insecurity.

among occupational groups, with 31 per cent reporting low levels of job insecurity as opposed to only 18 per cent among unskilled workers. Middle-level managers and semi-professionals, the occupational groups that have sustained considerable job loss under restructuring, reported the highest levels of job insecurity. Surprisingly, those with only primary education joined individuals with post-secondary degrees as most likely to report low levels of job insecurity. The former pattern may reflect the older age of individuals with little formal education whose job seniority may protect them, to some extent, from insecure employment. In fact, Table 9.4 shows that only 20 per cent of workers aged 20-9 reported low levels of job insecurity, compared with 30 per cent among the oldest age group. There were no gender differences in perceptions of job insecurity, but 41 per cent of part-time workers reported high levels of job insecurity, as opposed to 31 per cent of those working full-time.

Restructuring in the context of high unemployment renders job insecurity a vital topic for health research. While 'bad' jobs with little security have always characterized work in smaller firms, restructuring among 'core' firms and government has left formerly secure employees wondering how long they can hang onto their jobs. This suggests the need to target for research those who are exposed to the vagaries of a work environment undergoing restructuring, in addition to those who are historically disproportionately disadvantaged in the labour market, including women, youth, and the unskilled. Moreover, the shift in employment opportunities towards the small business sector and the increasing use of casual labour leave those working under these conditions vulnerable to job insecurity.

Small firms not only offer jobs with low wages and benefits, they also increase the likelihood of being laid off permanently since the companies themselves are at greater risk of folding (Picot, 1994). In fact, job insecurity is a 'stable' feature of employment in these companies. To date, little empirical research examines the links between job insecurity and health in small businesses. In addition, commenting on the general lack of health research on small firms, Eakin (1992: 689) warned that they 'present particular challenges for the promotion of health and safety', largely because of their failure, and that of the regulatory authorities, to implement and enforce practices that minimize health dangers. This observation suggests that job insecurity among those working in small businesses, as well as the work structures and processes of such firms, are worthy topics for workplace health research.

Increasingly, employers are casualizing their workforces to save labour costs. This enhances employers' flexibility because it divests them of any responsibility for long-term employment or systematically scheduling a minimum number of work hours (Polivka and Nardone, 1989). However, we know very little about the health effects of part-time, contract, and temporary work. While some evidence suggests that part-time work may not be universally health-damaging (Macran et al., 1996), the increasingly involuntary nature of non-standard work may, indeed, be harmful to people's health.

Finally, lest the reader be left with the impression that labour is being flattened by the steamroller of global capitalism, worker resistance may mitigate its most grievous work-related consequences. There is a considerable literature on the labour movement's response to globalization and restructuring (Dagg, 1993; Panitch, 1987; Moody, 1997; Cavanagh, 1997), but with few exceptions (Novek et al., 1990) researchers have not examined the interplay of these events and health. Some literature relevant to the issue of resistance considers the health effects of social support in the workplace. The finding that social support from co-workers may buffer or reduce health-damaging effects of job strain (Johnson and Hall, 1988; Johnson et al., 1989) implies that the integrative features of work can minimize its alienating dimensions, even though they may not completely expunge them.

The work of Rinehart and colleagues (Rinehart et al., 1997) at the Ontario CAMI factory suggests that worker resistance to restructuring efforts may also have health consequences. The lean staffing practices of the plant encourage divisiveness within work teams because of workers' reliance on one another to carry out their roles in the production process. With no replacement of workers who are temporarily absent and the company expectation that all workers will maintain a pace that is continuously increasing, workers are hard-pressed to keep up. Although reports of feeling pressured by co-workers emerged, what also became evident were workers' collective acts to decrease workloads. Contrary to management's expectation that work teams foster adherence to company goals and objectives, evidence indicates that they may be a resource to challenge management authority. Workers expressed this team cohesion in various battles with management, including overtime: 'In our group . . . everyone sticks together . . . If we decide we're not working overtime, then no one works overtime' (ibid., 101). Such resistance may minimize the deleterious physical and mental health consequences of work organized in this manner by reducing the speed at which workers are compelled to work and fostering social solidarity. Hence, while flexible production, downsizing, casualization of the labour market are examples of the changing nature of social relations of work in a global economy that may damage health, worker resistance to these structures and processes must not be neglected.

Conclusion

This chapter examined the links between work and health in the context of global capitalism. The impact on health of social organization of work has long been of interest to sociologists. Considerable evidence suggests that, on average, work enhances health, but it can also damage health because of the way it is socially organized. Health can be harmed by the physical and chemical hazards to which individuals are exposed at work, but its psychosocial dimensions are also problematic. In regard to the latter, jobs with high psychological demands and low levels of control over job tasks can lead to physical and mental health problems and even early death.

In spite of the attention focused on work and health, few studies examine this relationship explicitly as it is shaped by the contemporary forces of capitalism. Economic globalization is creating new opportunities for capital accumulation by expanding investor choice in the location of business activity. This has given capital 'an immense increment of bargaining power, directly in its relations with employees and indirectly in matters of state policy' (Ross and Trachte, 1990: 69). Governments have responded by reducing their regulatory activities and social welfare programs to create a climate more favourable to business interests.

At the micro level, the internationalization of capital has spawned restructuring activities that create new conditions for the control of labour. For example, flexible production is being introduced into the production of goods and services as a means of increasing productivity and reducing labour costs. Designed as a highly integrated system that continuously 'improves' the production process by minimizing wasted labour time, it combines rigid standardization of work activities with lean staffing to increase dramatically the pace and workload of those involved. Although prior research has examined the effects of mass production on the health of workers, few studies focus on the health implications of 'neo-Fordist' practices. Their expansion to a wide range of organizations beyond the goods-producing sector underscores the need to document the health effects of what is fast becoming the dominant production paradigm.

As private and public institutions restructure, downsizing and the casualization of the labour force are also employed to maximize profit and reduce costs. These activities have led to unprecedented levels of job insecurity, but relatively little is known about the health effects of this condition. Workers who are particularly vulnerable, although not exclusively so, include middle management and those working in small businesses and the service sector. Relatedly, we know almost nothing about the health effects of involuntary employment in non-standard work forms. The growing numbers of those employed on a part-time, temporary, or contractual basis because of shrinking full-time, long-term employment opportunities present further challenges for health researchers.

While various restructuring activities create new conditions for controlling labour, they also foster worker resistance. Social support at work has received some attention in the health literature, but we know very little about the specific nature of its integrative features or other ways in which collective action may counter the health-destructive elements of work under global capitalism. This knowledge, along with efforts to understand how contemporary globalization forces shape the structures and relationships of the labour process, are essential ingredients of social change that seeks to prevent work from 'mortifying the body and ruining the mind'.

Notes

1. For the purposes of this chapter, 'work' refers to paid work.
2. Work-related deaths per 100,000 paid workers that may be instantaneous or may happen much later.

3. In contrast, part-time part-year and full-time part-year employment opportunities declined, as did full-time full-year work for men. Full-time full-year employment increased for women (Nakamura et al., 1997).

References

Ahlberg-Hulten, G., T. Theorell, and F. Sigala. 1995. 'Social support, job strain and musculoskeletal pain among female health care personnel', *Scandinavian Journal of Work Environment and Health* 21, 6: 435–9.

Akyeampong, E.B., and J. Usalcas. 1998. *Work Absence Rates, 1980–1997*. Ottawa: Statistics Canada, Labour and Household Surveys Analysis Division.

Albright, C.L., M.A. Winkleby, D.R. Ragland, J. Fisher, and S.L. Syme. 1992. 'Job strain and prevalence of hypertension in a biracial population of urban bus drivers', *American Journal of Public Health* 82, 7: 984–9.

Armstrong, P., and H. Armstrong. 1996. *Wasting Away: The Undermining of Canadian Health Care*. Toronto: Oxford University Press.

Arnetz, B.B., S.O. Brenner, L. Levi, R. Hjelm, I.L. Petterson, J. Wasserman, B. Petrini, P. Eneroth, A. Kallner, R. Kvetnansky, and M. Vigas. 1991. 'Neuroendocrine and immunologic effects of unemployment and job insecurity', *Psychotherapy and Psychosomatics* 55, 2–4: 76–80.

Bluestone, V., and B. Harrison. 1982. *The Deindustrialization of America: Plant Closings, Community Abandonment, and the Dismantling of Basic Industry*. New York: Basic Books.

Broad, D. 1997. 'The casualization of the labour force', in Duffy et al. (1997: 53–73).

Broadway, M. 1990. 'Meatpacking and its social and economic consequences for Garden City, Kansas in the 1980s', *Urban Anthropology* 19, 4: 321–44.

Burman, P. 1997. 'Changes in the patterns of unemployment: The new realities of joblessness', in Duffy et al. (1997: 190–216).

Canadian Council on Social Development. 1999. *Personal Security Index 1999*. Ottawa: Canadian Council on Social Development.

Canadian Labour Congress. 1999. *Left Out in the Cold: The End of UI for Canadian Workers*. Ottawa: Canadian Labour Congress.

Cavanagh, J. 1997. 'The global resistance to sweatshops', in A. Ross, ed., *No Sweat: Fashion, Free Trade, and the Rights of Garment Workers*. New York: Verso.

Cox, R.W. 1991. 'The global political economy and social choice', in Drache and Gertler (1991a: 335–50).

Dagg, A. 1993. *Trade Union Response to Global Restructuring: The Case of the International Ladies' Garment Workers Union*. Toronto: Centre for Research on Work and Society, York University.

Dooley, D., K. Rook, and R. Catalano. 1987. 'Job and non-job stressors and their moderators', *Journal of Occupational Psychology* 60, 2: 115–32.

Drache, D. 1991. 'The systematic search for flexibility: National competitiveness and new work relations', in Drache and Gertler (1991a: 249–69).

——— and M.S. Gertler. 1991a. *The New Era of Global Competition: State Policy and Market Power*. Montreal and Kingston: McGill-Queen's University Press.

——— and ———. 1991b. 'The world economy and the nation-state: The new international order', in Drache and Gertler (1991a: 3–25).

Duffy, A., D. Glenday, and N. Pupo, eds. 1997. *Good Jobs, Bad Jobs, No Jobs: The Transformation of Work in the 21st Century*. Toronto: Harcourt Brace.

Eakin, J.M. 1992. 'Leaving it up to the workers: Sociological perspective on the management of health and safety in small workplaces', *International Journal of Health Services* 22, 4: 689–704.

———. 1995. 'Canadian approaches to the promotion of health in small workplaces', *Canadian Journal of Public Health* 86, 2: 109–13.

Erikson, K. 1990. In K. Erikson and S. P. Vallas, eds, *The Nature of Work: Sociological Perspectives*. New Haven: Yale University Press.

Garfield, J. 1980. 'Alienated labor, stress, and coronary disease', *International Journal of Health Services* 10, 4: 551–61.

Glenday, D. 1997. 'Lost horizons, leisure shock: Good jobs, bad jobs, uncertain future', in Duffy et al. (1997: 8–34).

Greenberg, E.S., and L. Grunberg. 1995. 'Work alienation and problem alcohol behavior', *Journal of Health and Social Behavior* 36, 1: 83–102.

Grenon, L., and B. Chun. 1997. 'Non-permanent paid work', *Perspectives on Labour and Income* 9, 3: 21–31.

Harrison, B., and B. Bluestone. 1988. *The Great U-Turn: Corporate Restructuring and the Polarizing of America*. New York: Basic Books.

Heaney, C.A., B.A. Israel, and J.S. House. 1994. 'Chronic job insecurity among automobile workers: Effects on job satisfaction and health', *Social Science and Medicine* 38, 10: 1431–7.

Hemingway, H., M.J. Shipley, S. Stansfeld, and M. Marmot. 1997. 'Sickness absence from back pain, psychosocial work characteristics and employment grade among office workers', *Scandinavian Journal of Work Environment and Health* 23, 2: 121–9.

Ide, T.R., and A.J. Cordell. 1994. 'The new tools: Implications for the future of work', in A. Yalnizyan, Ide, and Cordell, eds, *Shifting Time: Social Policy and the Future of Work*. Toronto: Between the Lines, 73–133.

Jahoda, M. 1982. *Employment and Unemployment*. Cambridge: Cambridge University Press.

Johnson, J.V., and E.M. Hall. 1988. 'Job strain, work place social support, and cardiovascular disease: A cross-sectional study of a random sample of the Swedish working population', *American Journal of Public Health* 78, 10: 1336–42.

———, ———, and T. Theorell. 1989. 'Combined effects of job strain and social isolation on cardiovascular disease morbidity and mortality in a random sample of the Swedish male working population', *Scandinavian Journal of Work Environment and Health* 15: 271–9.

——— and G. Johansson. 1991. *The Psychosocial Work Environment: Work Organization, Democratization and Health*. Amityville, NY: Baywood.

Johnson, T. 1980. 'Work and power', in G. Esland and G. Salaman, eds, *The Politics of Work and Occupations*. Toronto: University of Toronto Press, 335–71.

Karasek, R. 1979. 'Job demands, job decision latitude, and mental strain: Implications for job redesign', *Administrative Science Quarterly* 24, 2: 285–307.

———, T. Theorell, J.E. Schwartz, P.L. Schnall, C.R. Pieper, and J.L. Michela. 1988. 'Job characteristics in relation to the prevalence of myocardial infarction in the US Health Examination Survey (HES) and the Health and Nutrition Examination Survey (HANES)', *American Journal of Public Health* 78, 8: 910–16.

Krahn, H.J., and G.S. Lowe. 1998. *Work, Industry, and Canadian Society*, 3rd edn. Toronto: Nelson.

Krause, N., D.R. Ragland, B.A. Greiner, S.L. Syme, and J.M. Fisher. 1997. 'Psychosocial job factors associated with back and neck pain in public transit operators', *Scandinavian Journal of Work Environment and Health* 23, 3: 179–86.

Landsbergis, P.A., P.L. Schnall, D. Deitz, R. Friedman, and T. Pickering. 1992. 'The patterning of psychological attributes and distress by "job strain" and social support in a sample of working men', *Journal of Behavioral Medicine* 15, 4: 379–405.

Leach, B., and A. Winson. 1995. 'Bringing "globalization" down to earth: Restructuring and labour in rural communities', *Canadian Review of Sociology and Anthropology* 32, 3: 341–64.

Lerner, D.J., S. Levine, S. Malspeis, and R.B. D'Agostino. 1994. 'Job strain and health-related quality of life in a national sample', *American Journal of Public Health* 84, 10: 1580–5.

Leyton, E. 1987. 'Dying hard: Industrial carnage and social responsibility', in D. Coburn, C. D'Arcy, G.M. Torrance, and P. New, eds, *Health and Canadian Society: Sociological Perspectives*, 2nd edn. Markham, Ont.: Fitzhenry & Whiteside, 199–215.

Lin, Z. 1998. 'Employment insurance in Canada: Policy changes', *Perspectives on Labour and Income* 10, 2: 42–7.

Macran, S., L. Clarke, and H. Joshi. 1996. 'Women's health: Dimensions and differentials', *Social Science and Medicine* 42, 9: 1203–16.

Marshall, K. 1996. 'A job to die for', *Perspectives on Labour and Income* 8, 2: 26–31.

Marx, K. 1964 [1844]. *Economic and Philosophic Manuscripts of 1844*. New York: International Publishers.

Moody, K. 1997. *Labor in a Lean World: Unions in the International Economy*. New York: Verso.

Nakamura, A., D. Cullen, and J. Cragg. 1997. 'Trends in part-time and part-year employment, and in earnings', in M.G. Abbot, C.M. Beach, and R.P. Chaykowski, eds, *Transition and Structural Change in the North American Labour Market*.

Kingston, Ont.: IRC Press and John Deutsch Institute for the Study of Economic Policy, Queen's University, 111–25.

Navarro, V. 1982. 'The labor process and health: A historical materialist interpretation', *International Journal of Health Services* 12, 1: 5–29.

Neis, B. 1995. 'Can't get my breath: Snow crab workers' occupational asthma', in K. Messing, Neis, and L. Dumais, eds, *Invisible: Issues in Women's Occupational Health*. Charlottetown, PEI: gynergy books, 3–28.

North, F., S.L. Syme, A. Feeney, J. Heath, M. Shipley, and M. Marmot. 1993. 'Explaining socioeconomic differences in sickness absence: The Whitehall II Study', *British Medical Journal* 306, 6874: 361–6.

———, ———, ———, M. Shipley, and M. Marmot. 1996. 'Psychosocial work environment and sickness absence among British civil servants: The Whitehall II Study', *American Journal of Public Health* 86, 3: 332–40.

Novek, J., A. Yassi, and J. Spiegel. 1990. 'Mechanization, the labor process, and injury risks in the Canadian meat packing industry', *International Journal of Health Services* 20, 2: 281–96.

Osberg, L. 1997. 'Structural change in North American labour markets', in M.G. Abbot, C.M. Beach, and R.P. Chaykowski, eds, *Transition and Structural Change in the North American Labour Market*. Kingston, Ont.: IRC Press and John Deutsch Institute for the Study of Economic Policy, Queen's University, 350–6.

———, F. Wien, and J. Grude. 1995. *Vanishing Jobs: Canada's Changing Workplaces*. Toronto: James Lorimer.

Panitch, L. 1987. 'Capitalist restructuring and labour strategies', *Studies in Political Economy* 24: 131–49.

Picot, G. 1994. *Have Small Firms Created a Disproportionate Share of New Jobs in Canada? A Reassessment of the Facts*. Research Paper No. 71. Ottawa: Statistics Canada.

Polivka, A.E., and T. Nardone. 1989. 'On the definition of contingent work', *Monthly Labor Review* 112, 12: 9–16.

Rasanen, K., V. Notkola, and K. Husman. 1997. 'Perceived work conditions and work-related symptoms among employed Finns', *Social Science and Medicine* 45, 7: 1099–110.

Repetti, R.L., K.A. Matthews, and I. Waldron. 1989. 'Effects of paid employment on women's mental and physical health', *American Psychologist* 44, 10: 1394–401.

Rinehart, J., C. Huxley, and D. Robertson. 1997. *Just Another Car Factory? Lean Production and Its Discontents*. Ithaca, NY: Cornell University Press.

Rogot, E., P.D. Sorlie, and N.J. Johnson. 1992. 'Life expectancy by employment status, income, and education in the National Longitudinal Mortality Study', *Public Health Reports* 107, 4: 457–61.

Ross, R.J.S., and K.C. Trachte. 1990. *Global Capitalism: The New Leviathan*. Albany, NY: State University of New York Press.

Rothman, R. 1998. *Working: Sociological Perspectives*, 2nd edn. Toronto: Prentice-Hall.

Sass, R. 1989. 'The implications of work organization for occupational health policy: The case of Canada', *International Journal of Health Services* 19, 1: 157–73.

Siegrist, J., K. Siegrist, and I. Weber. 1986. 'Sociological concepts in the etiology of chronic disease: The case of ischemic heart disease', *Social Science and Medicine* 22 (Special Issue): 247–53.

Steffy, B.D., and D.R. Laker. 1991. 'Workplace and personal stresses antecedent to employees' alcohol use', *Journal of Social Behavior and Personality* 6 (Special Issue): 115–26.

Statistics Canada. 1996. *Labour Force Annual Averages 1995*. Ottawa: Statistics Canada, Household Surveys Division.

———. 1997. *Labour Force Annual Averages 1996*. Ottawa: Statistics Canada, Household Surveys Division.

———. 1998. *Labour Force Information* (for the week ended December 13, 1997). Ottawa: Statistics Canada.

———. 1999a. 'An Overview of the 1998 Labour Market', *Labour Force Update* 3, 1.

———. 1999b. *Labour Force Information* (for the week ended December 12, 1998). Ottawa: Statistics Canada.

Taylor, F. 1911. *The Principles of Scientific Management*. New York: Harper and Brothers.

Walters, V., R. Lenton, and M. McKeary. 1995. *Women's Health in the Context of Women's Lives*. Ottawa: Minister of Supply and Services Canada.

White, J. 1997. 'Health care, hospitals, and reengineering: The Nightingales sing the blues', in Duffy et al. (1997: 117–42).

CHAPTER 10

From Increasing Poverty to Societal Disintegration: How Economic Inequality Affects the Health of Individuals and Communities

Dennis Raphael

Introduction

The purpose of this chapter is to explore the issue of economic inequality in Canada and how it affects the health of Canadians. *Economic inequality* refers to the differences that exist among Canadians in economic resources. For example, as of 1991 the top 20 per cent of the Canadian population earned 43.8 per cent of total income. In contrast, the bottom 20 per cent of the population earned 4.7 per cent (Ross et al., 1994). These differences are nothing new in Canadian society, but what is new is the sudden increase in economic inequality among Canadians within the past decade. During that time, the after-tax income gap between the top 10 per cent and bottom 10 per cent of families showed unprecedented growth (Yalnizyan,1998). One important by-product of increasing economic inequality in Canada has been increasing poverty, since in Western industrialized societies greater inequality is strongly associated with a greater incidence of poverty (Gottschalk and Smeeding, 1998; Rainwater and Smeeding, 1995).

Health in this chapter refers both to the health status of individuals and to the health of communities. In regard to individuals, 'health' refers to the incidence of illness and premature death, as well as to the presence of physical, social, and personal resources that allow the achievement of personal goals (WHO, 1986). In regard to communities, 'health' refers to the presence of economic, social, and environmental structures that support the physical, psychological, and social well-being of community members (Ashton, 1992; Davies and Kelly, 1993). The health of individuals is related to the health of communities and both of these are related to degree of economic inequality. This chapter also considers, but cannot explore in detail, the reasons for the increases in economic inequality in Canada. Canadian analyses of the factors responsible for increasing economic inequality have been carried out by Coburn (2000), McBride and Shields, (1997) and Yalnizyan (1998, 2000). Work in the US related to increasing economic inequality has been done by Auerbach and Belous (1998), Collins, Hartman, and Sklar (1999), Collins, Leondar-Wright, and Sklar (1999), Galbraith (1998), and Wolff (1995). Comprehensive collections and summaries of the US and British income and health literatures are available (Daniels et al., 2000; Gordon et al., 1999; Kawachi et al., 1999). An overview of issues related to poverty and health in Canada has also been published (Townson, 1998).

Making Explicit the Various Discourses on Health, Poverty, and Economic Inequality

A discourse is the manner or form of conversation by which individuals within a society consider an issue. The form that the analysis of the relationship between economic inequality and health can take is influenced by the world view or frame of reference chosen (Tesh, 1990). Much of the traditional public health concern about economic inequality reflects an adherence to the ideology of individualism in which health problems are considered at the micro level of the person. In Canada and the United States this adherence usually manifests itself as a focus on the percentage of the population living in poverty and the effects of poverty on their health status. This is an important concern, as poverty has strong direct effects on individual health. A poverty focus does not necessarily limit itself to an individual-level analysis since economic, social, and environmental structures support or limit the health status of those living in poverty. A concern with community structures can also lead to an analysis of how poverty levels and the presence of health-supporting community structures are related to the degree of societal economic inequality. This extension of analysis from a focus on individuals living in poverty to the presence of community structures and degree of economic inequality, however, is uncommon in Canadian public health practice (Raphael, 1998; Raphael, 2000).

Nevertheless, a poverty focus ignores the question of why there are health differences among individuals across the socio-economic range. That is, it has been found that even groups relatively high in socio-economic status are less healthy that those with even higher socio-economic status. In addition, a perspective limited only to poverty can direct attention away from potential health effects of economic inequality upon the well-off, an issue that has become increasingly topical as a result of the publication of Wilkinson's (1996) *Unhealthy Societies: The Afflictions of Inequality.*

There are, then, three ways in which economic inequality can be seen as affecting the health of populations. The first is a poverty focus whereby the material and psychosocial deprivations experienced by the poor are considered. In this chapter, evidence concerning the health difficulties resulting from poverty are examined. The second concerns what has been termed the socio-economic and health gradient. This refers to the pervasive differences in health and well-being that exist between individuals at differing levels of social class, income, or education. In this analysis, the issue considered is not only differences between the poor and not poor, but the existence of graded health differences that correspond to individuals' socio-economic life circumstances across the socio-economic spectrum.

The third way of considering the relationship between economic inequality and health is focused on how economic inequality, in addition to creating health problems for the poor and spreading the distribution of health unequally across the population, can have broad detrimental effects on the health of individuals and communities. In this latter analysis, economic inequality is seen as leading to societal effects that potentially injure health (Wilkinson, 1996) through a process that creates decreased social cohesion. Wilkinson's hypothesis, though focused on the individual, also directs attention to how societies allocate economic resources across the population. The means by which societal-level economic inequality affects individual well-being appears to be mediated in part by the presence of community structures that affect the health status of individuals across the socio-economic range. Such ameliorative community structures have the greatest effects on the least well-off. This third focus is broader, emphasizing the general health effects of economic inequality on societal structures as well as on individuals.

In this chapter, the increasing incidence of poverty in Canada is reviewed and the health status of those living in poverty considered. The mechanisms by which poverty directly affects the health of the poor are explored. The socio-economic health gradient is then considered, with documentation of the pervasive differences that exist among income groups. On the broader level of analysis, recent research indicates that not only the poor but all members of a society begin to show health effects within unequal societies. The role of community structures in mediating both poverty and inequality health effects and the means by which economic inequality weakens these structures are considered. The mechanisms by which economic inequality is related to health are varied and include biological pathways within the individual, shifts in service provision that affect the social cohesion of communities, and changing tax structures that shape and, some argue, distort government policy. The chapter concludes by considering the political and economic forces that influence the degree of economic inequality experienced by a society.

Poverty and Health

The health effects of inequality are most apparent among those living in poverty. Levels of Canadian poverty are defined here as those living with pre-tax incomes below the low-income cut-offs established by Statistics Canada (National Council of Welfare, 1998). These cut-offs are based on family and community size and identify individuals living in 'straitened circumstances'. For international comparisons, the criterion of the Luxembourg Income Study, which defines poverty as living with an income of less than 50 per cent of median adjusted disposable income for all persons, is used (Rainwater and Smeeding, 1995).

Poverty Is Increasing in Canada

By 1996, the poverty rate in Canada had risen to 18 per cent from 16.6 per cent in 1986 (Centre for International Statistics, 1998), and child poverty reached a 17-year peak of 21 per cent. Child poverty has become a policy focus in Canada; by 1996, 1.5 million Canadian children lived in poverty, up from 934,000 in 1989 (Campaign 2000, 1998; Statistics Canada, 1998b; 1999). The most recent statistics from the 1996 census indicate that provincial child poverty averages ranged from a low of 18.5 per cent in Prince Edward Island to a high of 26.2 per cent in Manitoba. Ontario, the wealthiest Canadian province in terms of income per capita, experienced an increase in child poverty from 11 per cent in 1989 to 20.3 per cent in 1996. These increasing poverty levels are well publicized, with widely distributed newspapers such as the *Globe and Mail* carrying numerous reports documenting its increase (Gadd, 1997; Little, 1996; Mitchell, 1997).

The effects of poverty on health have been known since the nineteenth century (Sram and Ashton, 1998). More recently, interest in the issue was spurred by the publication in the United Kingdom of *The Black Report* (Black and Smith, 1982) and *The Health Divide* (Townsend et al., 1992). These reports documented how those classified in the lowest employment groups were more likely to suffer from a wide range of diseases and to die from illness or injury at every stage of the life cycle. But these differences were also seen across the socio-economic range, from professional through middle class to the poor. After decades of official neglect of the economic inequality and health issue in the US, documentation is now available of the higher incidence of a range of illnesses among lower-income Americans (US Department of Health and Human Services, 1998). Here as well, health differences are seen across the socio-economic range, with decreasing income associated with greater evidence of poor health.

Within Canada, Wilkins et. al. (1989) found individuals living within the poorest 20 per cent of neighbourhoods to be more likely than the more well-off to die of just about every disease. Data on individuals' social status is not routinely collected at death in Canada, so Wilkins and his colleagues used residence census tracts to estimate socio-economic income level. Even with the inevitable slippage that occurs since some poor people live in more affluent neighbourhoods and vice versa, it was conservatively estimated that 22 per cent of premature years of life lost to Canada could be attributed to income differences. This health cost is close to the total impact of either heart disease or cancer.

The most cogent Canadian presentation of the association between poor health and poverty is the report on *The Health of Canada's Children* (Canadian Institute on Children's Health, 1994), which documents the variation in health and wellbeing between poor and not-poor children. Some of the studies summarized defined being poor as receiving social assistance, while in others it was income below the Statistics Canada low-income cut-off. Health differences were seen in the incidence of illness and death, hospital stays, accidental injuries, mental health and wellbeing, school achievement and dropout rates, and family violence and child abuse, among others.

In fact, poor children showed higher incidences of just about any health-related problem, however defined. As will be seen, expanding the focus to health differences across the socio-economic range shows that these differences exist across the entire range of income differences.

The Effects of Poverty on the Health of Adults and Children

In recent British studies (Townsend et al., 1992) health differences were considered in four ways: artifactual, lifestyle, materialist, and psychosocial. Artifactual arguments saw the income level and health status relationship as either reflecting faulty data definition and collection or due to people in poor health having lower incomes, rather than the reverse. Artifactual arguments have been dismissed because many studies have found that poverty usually does not result from poor health but is usually a precursor to it (Wilkinson, 1996). Lifestyle arguments suggested that poor individuals engaged in behaviours, such as smoking, drinking to excess, and poor nutritional habits, that essentially brought illness upon themselves. These arguments, however, are not supported by studies showing that health differences remain even after these lifestyle factors are considered (Marmot, 1986). In addition, a lifestyle focus does not consider the societal conditions under which lifestyle differences occur (Travers, 1996).

Materialist arguments appear especially relevant to understanding the health effects of poverty. Clearly, poor diet, housing, and sanitary conditions resulting from lack of income can contribute to poor health. The recent *Taking Responsibility for Homelessness* report (Golden, 1999) highlights some health issues related to the most extreme indicator of low income among Canadians, homelessness, and for those not yet homeless, grossly inadequate housing. Canadian studies have also documented the health-related impacts, including lack of control and feelings of hopelessness, that result from hunger and lack of food (Tarasuk, 1996; Tarasuk and Woolcott, 1994).

Health Differences Across the Socio-economic Range

These Canadian studies provide illustrations of the psychosocial argument presented in the British reports. Poverty is described as being associated with feelings of helplessness, lack of control, and uncertainty, all of which are strong predictors of health and well-being (Wallerstein, 1992). As recently stated in the *British Medical Journal*, 'Inequality may make people miserable long before it kills them' (Smith, 1996). These arguments suggest that poverty can affect health through both physical and psychological pathways.

It is common to limit the focus of income and health investigations to the poor, yet careful examination of income and health data reveals that there is more to the relationship than simply poor people becoming ill at a greater rate than those who are not poor. Differences in health and illness exist across the socio-economic gradient.

The Socio-economic Gradient of Health in the United Kingdom

The greatest amount of evidence concerning the socio-economic level and health relationship comes from the UK. Acheson (1998) provides the most recent summaries of some of the differences in death rates among those with differing occupations. Table 10.1 shows the occupational classification scheme in common usage in the UK.

Table 10.1: Occupations within Social Class Groupings in the UK

Social Class	Occupations	
I	Professional	accountants, engineers, doctors
II	Managerial and Technical/ Intermediate	marketing and sales managers, teachers, journalists, nurses
IIIN	Non-manual Skilled	clerks, shop assistants, cashiers
IIIM	Manual Skilled	carpenters, goods drivers, joiners, cooks
IV	Partly Skilled	security guards, machine tool operators, farm workers
V	Unskilled	building and civil engineering labourers, other labourers, cleaners

Source: Drever and Whitehead (1997).

Reliable differences in age-standardized death rates between social classes in England and Wales are pervasive. Among men aged 20–64 overall death rates (per 100,000) for 1991–3 were as follows: Level I: 280; Level II: 300; Level IIIN: 426; Level IIIM: 493; Level IV: 492; and Level V: 806. These differences are seen across a range of diseases (Table 10.2).

Table 10.2: Standardized Mortality Rates per 100,000 Men, Aged 20–64, in England and Wales, 1991–1993

Cause of Death	Class					
	I	II	IIIN	IIIM	IV	V
Lung cancer	17	24	34	54	52	82
Coronary heart disease	81	92	136	159	156	235
Stroke	14	13	19	24	25	45
Accidents, poisoning, violence	13	13	17	24	24	52
Suicide and undetermined injury	13	14	20	21	23	47

Source: Adapted from Acheson (1998).

The ratio of overall death rates between those in Levels IV/V and in Levels I/II for all causes from 1986 to 1992 in England and Wales was 1.68 for men and 1.55 for women. For coronary heart disease, however, this ratio increased to 2.69 for women and was 1.66 for men. Breast cancer, similar to findings in Canada (below), does not show a class effect; the IV/V to I/II ratio is 1.04.

Similar income-related findings are seen for the incidence of illness or morbidity. In 1996 among 45–64-year-old men, only 17 per cent of professional men reported a limiting illness as compared to 48 per cent of unskilled men. Among women, the comparable figures were 25 and 45 per cent. Similar differences are seen for mental health indicators, with women in classes IV/V having an incidence of 24 per cent for neurotic disorders as compared to 15 per cent of women in classes I/II. Among men, 10 per cent of those in classes IV/V were dependent on alcohol compared to 5 per cent in classes I/II.

In an analysis of infant mortality rates by father's social class in England and Wales from 1975 to 1996, Whitehead and Drever (1999) found consistent excess mortality rates of classes IV/V over I/II. In the years 1975–7 the excess rates were as follows: perinatal mortality, 50 per cent; neonatal mortality, 48 per cent; postneonatal mortality, 105 per cent; and overall infant mortality, 64 per cent. The authors report that while the overall rate of infant mortality had declined in England and Wales by 1994–6, the excess mortality rates of classes IV/V over I/II showed 'little narrowing', with rates of 41 per cent for perinatal, 42 per cent for neonatal, and 78 per cent for postneonatal death. Overall infant mortality excess in 1994–6 was 52 per cent. Sram and Ashton (1998) estimate there would be 42,000 fewer annual deaths in England and Wales for people aged 16–74 if death rates were the same for people with manual jobs as for those with non-manual jobs.

American Studies

After a period of not collecting such data, the US Department of Health began to report health-related data in relation to reported income in the 1990s (US Department of Health and Human Services, 1998). One reported study categorized families as being either poor, near poor, middle income, or high income. Poor persons had family incomes below the federal poverty level. For a family of four, the federal poverty level was $15,569 in 1995. Near-poor persons had family incomes between 100 and 199 per cent of the federal poverty level. Middle-income persons had family income at least 200 per cent of the federal poverty level but less than $50,000. High-income persons had family incomes at least 200 per cent of the federal poverty level and over $50,000.

Similar to the British findings, health-related differences were seen consistently across the socio-economic range. Among 1–5-year-olds, 12.3 per cent of poor children had elevated blood lead levels as compared to 4.7 per cent for the near-poor, 3.6 per cent for those from middle-income families, and 1.7 per cent for those whose families were in the high-income category. Among adults, for self-reported health status, 31.1 per cent of poor individuals had fair or poor health as compared to 21.1

per cent of the near-poor, 9.8 per cent of those of middle income, and 4.3 per cent of high-income respondents. Similar findings were seen for activity limitation among children and adults, cigarette smoking, and being overweight—in each of these instances, lower income was associated with greater incidence. A particularly striking finding is that 22 per cent of poor, 22.8 per cent of near-poor, and 8.6 per cent of middle-income children had no health insurance as compared to only 4.2 per cent of children living in high-income families.

The report also provides data on how maternal education is related to low birth-weight live births. Those mothers with less than 12 years of education had a rate of 8.4 per cent, while those with 16 or more years had a rate of 5.7 per cent. Finally, heart disease death rates were reported as a function of family income. The mortality rate for those ages 25–64 earning less than $10,000 was 318/100,000; for those earning $10,000–$14,999, 251; for those earning $15,000–$24,900,142, and for those earning $25,000 or more, 126. Similar findings were obtained for death from lung cancer and diabetes.

Canadian Studies

There is no routine collection of data in Canada that links class with illness and death. One of the few studies to link income with death rates identified a proxy measure of income level of deceased individuals by the income level of their 1986 census tract (Wilkins et al., 1992). For example, the highest-income quintile (the top 20 per cent) tracts (I) had 7 per cent of households with low incomes, the lowest-quintile tracts (V) had low-income household rates of 33 per cent. Remarkably consistent differences in death rates were seen between those living within each census tract so identified.

The average life expectancy in the quintile tracts for 1986 were as follows: I: 78.5 years; II: 78.1; III: 77.5; IV: 76.9; and V: 74.8. The results were more apparent for men (quintile I = 76.1 years as compared to 70.4 years for quintile V) than for women (quintile I = 80.9 as compared to quintile V = 79.1). Infant mortality differences were also seen across the quintile distribution (I: 5.8 deaths/1,000; II: 5.7; II: 7.7; IV: 8.0; V: 10.5).These income-related mortality differences were seen for virtually every disease that one can die from, including infectious diseases, diabetes, uterine cancer, lung cancer, and suicide.

The authors estimated that 22 per cent of total potential years of life lost (PYLL) prior to age 75 among Canadians could be attributed to income differences. Income differences in death rates were associated with deaths due to circulatory disease (25 per cent of PYLL); accidents (17.2 per cent); neoplasms (14.7 per cent); respiratory illness (7.6 per cent); poorly defined illness (7.2 per cent); metabolic disease (6.8 per cent); perinatal deaths (6.0 per cent); and others (15.5 per cent). The authors stated that the potential years of life lost related to income differences were almost as great as those due to accidents (23 per cent of PYLL) alone.

A recent study by Ross and Roberts (1999) provides evidence concerning health problems among children across the socio-economic range. Using a series of aggregated measures, they report that children in low-income families (annual income less than $20,000) were twice as likely (25 per cent compared to 12 per cent) to be living in poorly functioning families as children in high-income families (annual income of more than $80,000). The percentage of children identified as living in poorly functioning families also differed across the socio-economic range. These differences were also seen for measures of chronic stress among parents, living in substandard housing, living within problem neighbourhoods, having less friendly neighbourhoods, and a very large number of other indicators of health and well-being. Finally, 50 per cent of parents earning less than $20,000 rated their children as not being in excellent health; the corresponding figures for those earning over $80,000 was 32 per cent. In virtually every case, the incidence of difficulty was related to income across the total socio-economic range.

The consistency of these findings across the entire socio-economic range and not just between the poor and not-poor, suggests common processes that affect the health of individuals. One hypothesis for these effects concerns issues of personal control and uncertainty associated with social status and income (Wilkinson, 1996). These effects are most pronounced among the poor but have the capacity to affect the health of those across the socio-economic status range. Both the health effects of poverty and the health differences across the socio-economic range can be seen as resulting from economic inequality, an issue discussed in the next section.

An alternative view is that differences in income represent differential exposures to a wide range of material conditions that affect health. British workers explain socio-economic differences in health in terms of how 'the social structure is characterized by a finely graded scale of advantage and disadvantage, with individuals differing in terms of the length and level of their exposure to a particular factor and in terms of the number of factors to which they are exposed' (Shaw et al., 1999: 102). The British workers emphasize 13 critical periods of the life course during which people are especially vulnerable to social disadvantage. These include fetal development, nutritional growth and health in childhood, entering the labour market, job loss or insecurity, and episodes of illness, among others. Material disadvantage and the absence of societal supports during these key periods work against health.

Making the Links of Poverty with Economic Inequality

Poverty increases as economic inequality increases. A reanalysis of the data from the Luxembourg Income Study (Rainwater and Smeeding, 1995; Gottschalk and Smeeding, 1998) shows that the relationship between degree of economic inequality within a nation as measured by the Gini index and child poverty for 16 industrialized Western nations was strong, positive, and reliable ($r = .77$). (The Gini index is a measure of economic inequality. If all the wealth within an area was owned by one person, the index would be 1.00. If there was complete equality the index would be .00.)

The *Growing Gap* report (Yalnizyan, 1998) points out that, within Canada, the 21:1 ratio of pre-tax income between the richest 10 per cent and the poorest 10 per cent of families in 1973 had increased, by 1996, to 314:1. In Canada, the potential health-related effects of economic inequality had been kept in check by the presence of strong social programs (Townson, 1998), but since 1993 social programs have been weakened and the after-tax income gap has begun to grow.

Statistics Canada reports that during the 1980s the real income of most Canadians had decreased. In 1995, men reported average earnings of $31,917, down 5 per cent from a high of $33,458 in 1980. Average income between 1990 and 1995 declined by 4 per cent among two-parent families but by 8 per cent among lone-parent families, and child poverty has increased, yet the well-off in Canada became wealthier (Statistics Canada, 1998b).

There are many reasons, ethical as well as practical, why Canadians should be concerned about economic inequality and its companion, poverty. First, the presence of poverty violates international rights covenants that Canada has signed (Philp, 1998). Samuel Johnson stated over 200 years ago: 'Where a great proportion of the people are suffered to languish in helpless misery, that country must be ill-policed and wretchedly governed: a decent provision for the poor is the true test of civilization' (Smallwood and Biron, 1989). Second, along practical lines, Canadians should be concerned that increasing poverty, a precursor to increasing illness, may begin to strain the health care and other systems that Canadians rely on. Finally, increasing economic inequality can be a threat to the health of all Canadians, an argument developed in the following sections.

Economic Inequality Affects the Health of All Canadians

Wilkinson (1996) brought together much of the research showing that nations as well as communities with greater economic inequality have higher mortality rates than those with less economic inequality. Wilkinson provides a number of international and national analyses of health status with a primary focus on mortality. Among countries that have crossed the epidemiological transition—that point in development where there has been a shift in priority of health concern from infectious to chronic diseases—those with less economic inequality show higher levels of life expectancy and lower mortality rates. For example, in countries such as Norway and Sweden, where the least well-off 70 per cent of the population control almost 50 per cent of the wealth, the average life expectancy is 76 years. In the UK and the US, where the least affluent 70 per cent control 46 per cent of the wealth, the life expectancy is two years less.

These differences among nations are more clearly related to level of inequality rather than to absolute wealth as defined by GDP. Wilkinson showed that life expectancy increased as the distribution of income in counties became more egalitarian, whereas it was unrelated to average income. There was a correlation of $r = -.81$ between the proportion of the total income and benefits received by the least well-off 70 per cent of the population and life expectancy. The correlation with gross domestic product was $r = -.38$.

These findings could simply reflect the relationship between poverty and poor health described above. Societies or communities with more poverty would have a higher incidence of illness and disease. Yet, if economic inequality produces health effects primarily through the inequality > poverty > poor health relationship, it would not be expected that the well-off in economically unequal societies and communities would also show evidence of deteriorating health. But this is happening in some countries.

For example, after decades of rapidly increasing economic inequality, the most affluent in Britain now have higher death rates among adult males and infants than the least well-off in Sweden, despite the British having higher absolute incomes (Leon et al., 1992; Vagero and Lundberg, 1989). Three recent studies bear directly on this inequality hypothesis. The first was a study of population health status within the 50 American states. Kaplan et al. (1996) studied death rates of US residents for 1980, 1990, and 1989–91 as a function of the total household income received by the bottom 50 per cent of households. Controlling for age, they found a correlation of $r = .62$ between state death rates and degree of economic inequality.

These relationships between state economic inequality and health status were pervasive and consistent. Even after controlling for median state income, the association (Pearson correlation coefficient) of inequality with death was seen for those less than one year of age ($r = .54$); 1–24 years of age ($r = .53$); 25-64 years ($r = .76$) and over 65 years of age ($r = .42$). Similarly, inequality was related to death resulting from stillbirths ($r = .65$), homicides ($r = .74$), violent crimes ($r = .70$), disability ($r = .38$), per capita expenditure on protection ($r = .38$), total medical care expenditure ($r = .67$), proportion of the population sedentary ($r = .34$), and proportion of the population current smokers ($r = -.35$). Mortality rates and association with inequality were seen for both the white ($r = .51$) and African-American populations ($r = .52$). These results were considered in terms of the increasing inequality in the US: between 1981 and 1989, 66 per cent of the total gain in net financial wealth was received by the top 1 per cent of the population, and 37 per cent by the next 19 per cent of the population. The bottom 80 per cent of the population lost 3 per cent.

Kennedy et al. (1998) studied income distribution, socio-economic status, and self-rated health differences among residents of the 50 US states. The authors categorized US states as being of low, moderate, or high inequality based on the Gini index. To illustrate, low-inequality states (Gini index <.32) are Connecticut, Delaware, Hawaii, Iowa, North Dakota, South Dakota, Utah, Vermont, and Wisconsin. High-inequality states (Gini index >.35) are Alabama, California, Florida, Georgia, Illinois, Kentucky, Louisiana, Mississippi, New York, and Texas.

With the self-report measure, the percentage of individuals within a state reporting poor to fair health was correlated with mortality ($r = .58$). Annual income was a strong predictor of fair or poor self-reported health status, replicating findings concerning the socio-economic gradient of health: 32 per cent of those in the lowest income category (<\$10,000) reported poor or fair health status compared to 6.3 per cent in the highest category (>\$35,000).

In regard to the overall inequality hypothesis, those living within the most unequal states had a 25 per cent greater chance of reporting poor or fair health even after controls for household income, sex, race, education level, body mass, and smoking status. The investigators also found that the effects of income distribution on self-rated health were not limited to the lowest-income groups; those in the middle-income groups in states with the greatest inequalities in income rated themselves as having poorer health than those in middle income groups in states with the smallest inequalities.

Another study looked at degree of economic inequality and well-being within American metropolitan areas and found that the well-off in economically unequal American communities were showing health problems at greater rates than the well-off in relatively equal communities (Lynch et al., 1998). These findings have led the *British Medical Journal* to editorialize: 'What matters in determining mortality and health in a society is less the overall wealth of that society and more how evenly wealth is distributed. The more equally wealth is distributed the better the health of that society' (*British Medical Journal*, 1996). Why would this be so?

In *Unhealthy Societies: The Afflictions of Inequality*, Richard Wilkinson (1996) argued that societies with greater economic inequality begin to 'disintegrate', showing evidence of decreased social cohesion and increased individual malaise. These are all precursors of increased illness and death. Kawachi and Kennedy (1997) made the case that economic inequality contributes to the deterioration of what has been termed 'social capital', or the degree of social cohesion or citizen commitment to society. Putnam (1993) reported that economic inequality within regions of Italy correlated reliably with evidence of less social capital ($r = .81$).

In the UK, which experienced tremendous increases in economic inequality during the Thatcher years, total reported crime increased by almost 80 per cent and violent crime by 90 per cent during the 1981-91 period. In addition, the number of drug offenders between the ages of 17 and 29 doubled between 1979 and 1989 and the suicide rate among young men ages 15–24 had increased by 1983, to reach a peak in 1990 (Roberts, 1997).

In the US, evidence that the presence of inequality among residents of the 50 states involves a package of indicators of disintegration was provided by findings that the degree of equality was related to levels of unemployment ($r = .48$); proportion of the population incarcerated ($r = .44$); use of income vouchers ($r = .69$); need for food stamps ($r = .72$); and proportion of population with no health insurance ($r = .45$). Similar findings were reported for having no high school education ($r = .71$); high school leaving ($r = .50$); reading proficiency ($r = -.58$); math proficiency ($r = -.64$); education spending ($r = -.32$); and library books per capita ($r = .-42$) (Kaplan et al., 1996).

The specific mechanisms by which social cohesion comes to be important and why its presence or absence should be related to health are unclear. Wilkinson (1996) has drawn on animal models of hierarchy to consider health-related inequality effects. These models suggest that hierarchy and the lack of control associated with such hierarchy is predictive of the development of ischemic heart disease. He also summarized studies showing that lack of personal control is associated with indicators of stress that lead to biological breakdown (Sapolsky, 1991, 1992).

Researchers at the Centre for Health Promotion of the University of Toronto have developed a theory of quality of life that suggests means by which the by-products of economic inequality can produce health effects (Raphael et al., 1997). This model defines quality of life as *the degree to which a person enjoys the important possibilities of his/her life* in three broad domains: *being, belonging, and becoming.* The *being* domain includes the basic aspects of who one is and has three subdomains: *physical being, psychological being,* and *spiritual being. Becoming* refers to the purposeful activities carried out to achieve personal goals, hopes, and wishes and includes *practical, leisure,* and *growth* activities.

Of more direct relevance is the model's axiom that central to human well-being is *belonging,* or the person's fit with his/her environments. *Physical belonging* is defined as the connections the person has with his/her physical environments, such as home, workplace, neighbourhood, school, and community. *Social belonging* includes links with social environments and the sense of acceptance by intimate others, family, friends, co-workers, and neighbourhood and community. *Community belonging* represents access to resources normally available to community members, such as adequate income, health and social services, employment, educational and recreational programs, and community events and activities. This model has been used to consider how community changes, such as the presence or absence of community structures associated with increasing economic inequality, come to affect health and well-being (Raphael et al., 2000). This model can serve as a heuristic for considering micro-level effects that result from increases in economic inequality.

When the level of analysis is shifted to the societal level from the individual, the relationship between economic inequality and health can be considered in terms of societal structures and public policy rather than as a problem of individual health status and coping. Such analyses can provide further insights into how economic inequality affects citizens in general, but poor people in particular.

Economic Inequality Creates Especially Disadvantageous Conditions for Poor People

As we shift the level of analysis from the individual to the society, we can see that economic inequality directly affects poor people as more of a society's resources get shifted to the well-off. Some of this occurs through the reorganization of the tax system, as tax rates for the well-off are decreased and benefits to the poor are reduced. The most obvious recent example is the reduction in welfare benefits in Ontario to people who were already living in poverty, combined with the decreases in income taxes that primarily benefited the wealthy (Raphael, 1998, 1999). Recent income tax reductions in Ontario have allowed the richest top half of 1 per cent of families to benefit by $15,586. Among the poorest 10 per cent of Ontario families the benefit was $150 (Yalnizyan, 1998). However, to pay for these tax cuts, the services being reduced are the ones most likely to be needed by those receiving the least tax relief. Another Canadian example is the federal government's reducing benefits for the unemployed by limiting eligibility for insurance even as poverty levels increased (Raphael, 1999).

Another way economic inequality affects the poor is through reduction of services. Poor people are more likely to become ill and cutbacks in health services affect them the most. Similarly, the community infrastructures that help support people in poverty, such as community and local health programs and centres, see their budgets reduced. In two community studies recently carried out in Toronto, the profound importance of community agencies and resources for low income people was apparent (Raphael et al., 2000; Raphael et al., 1999; Raphael et al., 1998a, 1998b). Yet these are the very institutions under threat as economic inequality increases. Poverty is increasing while supports for those living in poverty are diminished (Raphael, 1999).

Societies with greater economic inequality have weaker social safety nets (Kawachi et al., 1994), an important determinant of health for all individuals, but especially for the poor (Bartley et al., 1997). Coburn (2000) sees this as reflecting the potent influence of neo-liberalism and the retreat of the welfare state. Glyn and Millibrandt (1994) document the economic costs of economic inequality in areas of crime, education, productivity, and health.

Economic Inequality and the Health of Communities

Earlier it was suggested that the health of communities can be seen as reflecting the presence of economic, social, and environmental structures that support health. The World Health Organization's Healthy Cities European Office (1995) argues that municipal housing, environmental, education, social service, and other programs are essential elements that contribute to community health. Economic inequality seems to determine whether these supports are provided within societies. Their presence or absence have the potential to affect the health of all community members.

As noted, societies with higher levels of economic inequality tend to provide fewer health and social services. These societies also tend to produce lower life expectancies and weaker indicators of health and well-being (Kawachi et al., 1994). The means by which this relationship comes about appear to involve the presence of smaller tax bases for the provision of health and social services. European societies tend to have higher tax rates than the US and Canada and also provide more services and have lower levels of poverty (Hurtig, 2000; McQuaig, 1993). Canadian tax revenues have decreased relative to Organization for Economic Co-operation and Development nations over the past 20 years (Luxemburg Income Study, 1995). Had this decrease not occurred Canada would not only have had no deficits in the past decade but also would have virtually no accumulated debt (Brooks, 1998). As a further illustration of the potential effects of national policy differences on health, as of 1991 Canadian provinces and cities had remarkably lower rates of both economic inequality and mortality as compared to American states and cities (Ross et al., 2000).

Societies with high levels of economic inequality begin to show symptoms of societal disintegration. The form that societal disintegration takes in each society may be unique. In Britain these effects have included increased alcoholism, crime rates, deaths by road accidents and infectious diseases, and drug offences, lowered reading scores, poorer family functioning, and decreased voter turnout (Wilkinson, 1996). In the United States economic inequality among the states and between communities is related to levels of unemployment, incarceration, homicide, low birth weight, smoking, need for income assistance, use of food stamps, less spending on education, and disability (Kaplan et al., 1996). Glyn and Millibrandt (1994) have examined the issue of economic inequality in terms of the social as well as economic costs to British society. In Canada, relatively little attention has been paid to considering the economic inequality and health relationship beyond documenting the lower health status of those living in poverty. But there is some evidence that health has been declining in Canada as economic inequality has increased.

Scores on a Social Health Index developed by the Canadian government have been declining since the mid-1980s even as gross domestic product has increased during that same period (Brink and Zeesman, 1997). This index of social health was developed based on the Fordham Index of Social Health. The 15 Canadian measures include infant mortality, child abuse, child poverty, teen suicides, drug abuse, high school dropout, unemployment, average weekly earnings, persons 65 or over in poverty, out-of-pocket health expenses, homicides, alcohol-related fatalities, being on social assistance, access to affordable housing, and the gap between rich and poor.

While the GDP has been consistently growing in Canada, from $112 billion in 1970 to $275 billion in 1995, the Social Health Index in Canada has been declining since 1979—by 1995 the index was at 1972 levels. Brink and Zeesman note that the recovery in the GDP since 1982 has not been reflected in an increase in the Social Health Index. In the US the Social Health Index began to decline in 1977 and bottomed out in 1982 at a level below that of Canada. 'This raises speculation whether the social programs in Canada supported the growth [in the Social Health Index] in the seventies and whether they had a moderating effect, as the two countries have very similar contexts, except for these programs' (ibid., 15).

Similarly, Stanford (1999) documents the increases in economic inequality and decreases in equity and security that are common to Canada and the provinces. His index is based on measures of employment, earnings, equality, and security. Since 1990 scores have declined in all provinces except for Manitoba, Quebec, and British Columbia.

Even without the other careful studies that are needed, in Canada there are signs of civil decay, with record levels of poverty and homelessness. Indeed, 37 per cent of Toronto children now live in poverty, an increase of 66 per cent since 1989 (Campaign 2000, 1998). Decreasing percentages of Canadians are voting in federal elections (Elections Canada, 1998). Percentage turnout in federal elections decreased from 75.3 per cent in 1984 to 67 per cent in 1997; in Ontario the figures were 76 per cent and 66 per cent. An interesting anomaly to the disintegration hypothesis has been the apparently decreasing crime rate in Canada over the past five years (Statistics Canada, 1999).

How Economic Inequality Leads to Poor Health in Individuals and Communities

The mechanisms by which economic inequality leads to poor health are still unclear, but some hypotheses can be advanced. At the individual level, poverty breeds a lack of control and feelings of hopelessness. Wilkinson (1996) reviews how such feelings operate through biological pathways to produce illness and death. High levels of stress produce behaviours aimed at ameliorating tension, such as eating sweets and smoking. Clearly, many individuals engage in high-risk behaviours such as use of alcohol and drugs to try to satisfy needs that are not fulfilled by society. Studies by animal researchers (Shivey et al., 1997; Sapolsky and Share, 1994) have identified the mechanisms by which chronic stress and hierarchical relations create illness and eventually death. Such stress models may go a long way to explaining the socio-economic status/illness relationship documented earlier.

At the community level, economic inequality is associated with provision of fewer services. For those who are not well-off, the lack of such services is a clear threat to health and well-being. Studies have explored how the lack of social supports and services contributes to the incidence of illness and death within societies (Bartley et al., 1997; Montgomery et al., 1996).

Regarding social cohesion, Kawachi and Kennedy (1997) provide illustrations of how increasing economic inequality leads many Americans to opt out of the public discourse by sending their children to private schools, to segregate their neighbourhoods economically, and to hire security guards to protect themselves and their property. As the World Bank argues, social capital 'refers to the institutions, relationships, and norms that shape the quality and quantity of a society's social interactions. . . . Social capital is not just the sum of the institutions which underpin a society—it is the glue that holds them together' (World Bank, 1998). If this is a reasonable assertion, then it becomes apparent how economic inequality may be loosening the glue of Canadian society.

An exaggerated emphasis on reducing taxes directly translates into both increasing economic inequality and reductions in the institutions that support citizens. Societies with high levels of economic inequality are those with lower tax bases, higher incidences of poverty, and, as noted, lower levels of health. These aspects are related, but tax structure may be an important theme that runs through all of it. When a society emphasizes tax decreases, economic inequality increases and community supports deteriorate. Government interest in and ability to maintain traditional entitlements decrease. Social cohesion is at risk.

Why Is This Happening?

Bertolt Brecht (Millet, 1990) asks in 'The Good Person of Szechwan': 'So why can't the gods share out what they've created, come down and distribute the bounties of nature and allow us, once hunger and thirst has been sated, to mix with each other in friendship and pleasure?' There are at least three ways of considering the increases in economic inequality in Canada. I have termed these the *public health view*, the *critical or historical view*, and *neo-Marxist views.*

The public health approach is illustrated by Wilkinson's *Unhealthy Societies: The Afflictions of Inequality* (1996). Wilkinson suggests that once the health effects of economic inequality are understood, responses can be made. He is optimistic that once people realize how inequality 'affects the quality of life for all of us' there will be concerted action on the part of citizens and governments to address such inequality. While there is increased awareness of the presence of economic inequality in Canada, to date there is little evidence of a willingness to address this issue.

Wilkinson's book has been critiqued by Muntaner and Lynch (1999), who point out that the research on the economic inequality and health relationship has been pursued primarily within social epidemiological frameworks. The emphasis to date has been on the health effects of economic inequality rather than on how economic inequality is created in the first place. Nonetheless, the social epidemiological literature is important because it has raised the economic inequality and health relationship discourse from that of individuals' health status and behaviours to those of societal structures and public policy. The question remains as to how economic inequalities come about and what forces maintain and increase the inequalities.

Muntaner and Lynch argue for moving beyond 'neo-Durkheimian' theories of social cohesion towards analyses that draw on a neo-Marxist perspective, that is, a focus on who controls productive assets (Roemer, 1994; Wright, 1997), and a neo-Weberian or labour market perspective (Botwinick, 1993; Morris et al., 1994). This approach urges us to look beyond ameliorative public health measures to identify (and seek to change) the processes that lead to the health problems associated with economic inequality. As Coburn (2000) argues, ideological roots to government policies foster economic inequality, and these need to be considered by those concerned with public health.

The critical view considers the role of ideology and power in promoting economic inequality. The present neo-liberal Ontario government, for example, has supervised a tremendous shift of resources from the poor to the rich through welfare reductions and income tax breaks for the well-off. It has removed rent controls, ended social housing, reduced social and hospital spending, removed free prescriptions for the elderly, removed local control over the six municipalities of Toronto, cut back spending for public transportation, reduced environmental control, downloaded public health services, and reduced pregnancy benefits for those on welfare (Raphael, 1999).

John Ralston Saul (1995) discusses the current state of Canadian society in terms of the rise of corporatism and the grasping for power by economic élites. Saul argues that corporatism is nothing new in this century and suggests that its influence can be resisted through a variety of citizen movements. James Laxer (1998: 163) argues that 'Everywhere in the world, multinational business has launched a frontal assault on the state.' He sees two potential visions of society emerging. The first is the unbridled market economy associated with big business. The other is a society 'made up of communities based in every region of the country that have formed around churches, trade unions, cultural bodies, associations of various kinds and sporting and recreational societies'(ibid., 48). Linda McQuaig (1998) demonstrates how the acceptance of the monetarist economic vision of the American economist Milton Friedman of reducing inflation at the cost of reduced economic growth led to the systematic weakening of the Canadian economy. At the same time, economic élites have benefited from this acceptance. In these analyses, the postwar consensus between labour and business is seen as having broken down, resulting in the concentration of wealth among the élite. McQuaig also discusses the issue of the loss of national control over economic policy due to the growing influence of international trade tribunals such as the World Trade Organization.

Coburn (2000) has analysed how neo-liberalism—the emphasis on the market as the arbiter of societal values and resource allocations—breeds social disintegration and alienation, in addition to economic inequality. Raphael (1999) has considered how the exaggerated emphasis on reducing taxes directly benefits the wealthy and powerful and translates into both increasing economic inequality and a retrenchment for the institutions that help promote civil society. The presence of greater economic inequality is associated with lower tax bases, higher levels of poverty, and lower levels of health. When a society emphasizes tax cuts, inequality becomes rampant and social and civil structures deteriorate.

The neo-Marxist view emphasizes the role and power of capital. Laxer (1998: 1) argues that globalization has led to increasing economic inequality and is moving societies towards open, internal conflict: 'Wars are no less vicious for being undeclared. Such is the case with the conflict that now rages between the social classes. This is a civil war, and by definition, civil wars are not declared.' For Laxer, this is occurring due to the breakdown of the postwar consensus between labour and business and is reflected in part by the decline of any obvious alternative to capitalism. McBride and Shields (1997: 13) write:

> The process of the internationalization of capitalism has fostered 'deep-seated economic and social changes' that have helped to erode 'the social contract—the predominant understandings about core economic and social relationships—that was built during the postwar era' (Banting et al., 1994: 4). The power of capital has been strengthened by threats to relocate if its demands for enhanced flexibility with regard to taxes, state regulation, and labour market policies are not met by policy-makers. The neo-liberal political agenda has both shaped and been advanced by globalization.

Public Policy Implications

Nonetheless, the effects of economic globalization have not been identical across nations. Some nations have resisted efforts to weaken social services and heighten economic inequality (Coburn, 2000; Mishra, 1990). These differences among nations clearly highlight the importance of public policy decisions, since ultimately 'The growing gap between rich and poor has not been ordained by extraterrestrial beings. It has been created by the policies of governments' (Montague, 1996). The time appears ripe for the Canadian public policy community to consider seriously the causes and impacts of increasing economic inequality.

At a policy level, the report on *The Growing Gap* (Yalnizyan, 1998) outlines many ideas by which Canadians can work to decrease the income gap. These range from increasing the minimum wage and improving pay equity to strengthening services and providing affordable housing. In the United Kingdom, the *Independent Inquiry into Inequalities in Health* (Acheson, 1998) provides many recommendations, including improving benefits, investment in training and education, and providing quality day care and early childhood education. Raphael (forthcoming) summarizes a wide range of policy options that could address the increasing income and health gaps.

Alternative voices within Canada to the neo-liberal agenda are rarely heard within the mainstream media. The Canadian Centre for Policy Alternatives (http://www.policyalternatives.ca/) is an important source of ideas and publishes a wide range of publications and newsletters. Montague (1996, 1998) provides concise popular summaries of recent work on the economic inequality and health relationship. The health and income equity Web site at the University of Washington brings together the related academic literature (International Health Program, 2000).

Conclusion

Are increased economic inequality and its partners, increasing poverty, alienation, and poor health, inevitable? Is it possible to reverse these trends? A first step to addressing this issue is to recognize that economic inequality has direct effects on the health and well-being of individuals and communities. The next step is to consider means of reducing economic inequality. The alternative is to head on the same path as the United States:

> In the U.S., government policies of the past 20 years have promoted, encouraged and celebrated inequality. These are choices that we, as a society, have made. Now one half of our society is afraid of the other half, and the gap between us is expanding. Our health is not the only thing in danger. They that sow the wind shall reap the whirlwind. (Montague, 1996: 1)

References

Acheson, D. 1998. *Independent Inquiry into Inequalities in Health*. London: Stationery Office. On-line at http://www.official-documents.co.uk/document/doh/ih/contents.htm

Auerbach, J., and R. Belous. 1998. *The Inequality Paradox: Growth of Income Disparity.* Washington: National Policy Association.

Ashton, J. 1992. *Healthy Cities*. Philadelphia: Open University Press.

Banting, K., G. Hoberg, and R. Simeon, eds. 1997. *Degrees of Freedom: Canada and the United States in a Changing World.* Montreal and Kingston: McGill-Queen's University Press.

Bartley, M., D. Blane, and S. Montgomery. 1997. 'Health and the life course: Why safety nets matter', *British Medical Journal* 314: 1194–6.

Black, D., and C. Smith. 1982. *The Black Report*, in Townsend et al. (1992).

Botwinick, H. 1993. *Persistent Inequalities: Wage Disparity under Capitalist Competition*. Princeton, NJ: Princeton University Press.

Brink, S., and A. Zeesman. 1997. *Measuring Social Well-being: An Index of Social Health for Canada*. Report R979E, Ottawa: Applied Research Branch, Human Resources Development Canada. On-line at http://www.hrdc-drhc.gc.ca/stratpol/arb/publications/research/abr-97-9e.shtml

British Medical Journal. 1996. 'The big idea', *British Medical Journal* 312 (20 Apr.): 985.

Brooks, N. 1998. 'Economic inequality in Canada', presentation to the Progressive Activist Academic Coalition, Toronto, 20 Nov.

Campaign 2000. 1998. 'More poor children today than at any time in Canada's history—Campaign 2000 insists on a commitment in each of the next three years', press release, Toronto.

Canadian Institute on Children's Health. 1994. *The Health of Canada's Children: A CICH Profile*. Ottawa.

Centre for International Statistics, Canadian Centre on Social Development. 1998. 'Incidence of child poverty by province, Canada, 1990–1996', Ottawa. On-line at http://www.ccsd.ca/factsheets/fscphis2.htm

Coburn, D. 2000. 'Income inequality, lowered social cohesion, and the poorer health status of populations: the role of neo-liberalism', *Social Science and Medicine* 51: 135–46.

Collins, C., C. Hartman, and H. Sklar. 1999. *Divided Decade: Economic Disparity at the Century's Turn*. Boston: United for a Fair Economy. On-line at http://www.stw.org

———, B. Leondar-Wright, and H. Sklar. 1999. *Shifting Fortunes: The Perils of the Growing American Wealth Gap*. Boston: United for a Fair Economy.

Daniels, N., B. Kennedy, and I. Kawachi. 2000. 'Justice is good for our health: How greater economic equality would promote public health', *Boston Review* 25, 1: 4–21. On-line at http://bostonreview.mit.edu/BR25.1/daniels.html

Davies, J.K. and M.P. Kelly. 1993. *Healthy Cities: Research and Practice.* New York: Routledge.

Drever, F., and M. Whitehead. 1997. *Health Inequalities: Decennial Supplement.* DS Series no. 15. London: Stationery Office.

Elections Canada. 1998. *Voter Turnout for the 1997, 1993, 1988, and 1984 General Elections.* On-line at http://www.elections.ca/election/results/res_table04_e.html

Gadd, J. 1997. 'People on assistance fall deeper into poverty', *Globe and Mail,* 8 Feb.

Galbraith, J. 1998. *Created Unequal: The Crisis in American Pay.* New York: Free Press.

Glyn, A., and D. Millibrant. 1994. *Paying for Inequality: The Economic Cost of Social Injustice.* London: IPPR/Rivers Press.

Golden, A. 1999. *Taking Responsibility for Homelessness: An Action Plan for Toronto.* Toronto: City of Toronto.

Gordon, D., M. Shaw, D. Dorling, and G. Davey Smith, eds. 1999. *Inequalities in Health: The Evidence Presented to the Independent Inquiry into Inequalities.* Bristol, UK: Polity Press.

Gottschalk, P., and T.M. Smeeding. 1998. *Empirical Evidence on Income Inequality in Industrialized Countries.* Working Paper 154, Luxembourg Income Study. On-line at http://lissy.ceps.lu/wpapersentire.htm; then ftp://lissy.ceps.lu/154.pdf

Hurtig, M. 1999. *Pay the Rent or Feed the Kids: The Tragedy and Disgrace of Poverty in Canada.* Toronto: McClelland & Stewart.

International Health Program. 2000. *Health and Income Equity Web Site.* University of Washington and Health Alliance International. Online at http://depts.washington.edu/eqhlth

Kaplan, J.R., E. Pamuk, J.W. Lynch, J.W. Cohen, and J.L. Balfour. 1996. 'Income inequality and mortality in the United States', *British Medical Journal* 312: 999–1003.

Kawachi, I., and B.P. Kennedy. 1997. 'Socioeconomic determinants of health: Health and social cohesion, why care about income inequality', *British Medical Journal* 314: 1037–45.

———, ———, and R.G. Wilkinson, eds. 1999. *Income Inequality and Health.* New York: New Press.

———, S. Levine, S.M. Miller, K. Lasch, and B. Amick. 1994. *Income Inequality and Life Expectancy: Theory, Research, and Policy.* Boston: Health Institute, New England Medical Center.

Kennedy, B.P., I. Kawachi, R. Glass, and D. Prothrow-Stith. 1998. 'Income distribution, socieconomic status, and self-rated health in the United States: Multi-level analysis', *British Medical Journal* 317: 917–21.

Laxer, J. 1998. *The Undeclared War: Class Conflict in the Age of Cyber-Capitalism.* Toronto: Viking.

Leon, D.A., D. Vagero, and O. Otterblad. 1992. 'Social class differences in infant mortality in Sweden: A comparison with England and Wales', *British Medical Journal* 305: 687–91.

Little, B. 1996. 'How the earnings of the poor have collapsed', *Globe and Mail,* 12 Feb.

Luxembourg Income Study. 1995. *Working Paper No. 127.* Syracuse, NY: Syracuse University, Aug.

Lynch, J.W., G.A. Kaplan, E.R. Pamuk, R. Cohen, C. Heck, J. Balfour, and I. Yen. 1998. 'Income inequality and mortality in metropolitan areas of the United States', *American Journal of Public Health* 88: 1074–80.

Marmot, M.G. 1986. 'Social inequalities in mortality: The social environment', in R.G. Wilkinson, ed., *Class and Health: Research and Longitudinal Data.* London: Tavistock.

McBride, S., and J. Shields. 1997. *Dismantling a Nation: The Transition to Corporate Rule in Canada.* Halifax: Fernwood.

McQuaig, L. 1993. *The Wealthy Banker's Wife: The Assault on Equality in Canada.* Toronto: Penguin.

———. 1998. *The Cult of Impotence: Selling the Myth of Powerlessness in the Global Economy.* Toronto: Viking.

Millet, J., ed. 1990. *Bertolt Brecht: Poems and Songs from the Plays.* Methuen.

Mishra, R. 1990. *The Welfare State in Capitalist Society.* Toronto: University of Toronto Press.

Mitchell, A. 1997. 'Rich, poor wage gap widening', *Globe and Mail*, 13 May.

Montague, P. 1996. 'Economic inequality and health', *Rachel's Environment & Health Weekly #497.* Annapolis, Md: Environmental Research Foundation. On-line at http://www.rachel.org/bulletin/index.cfm?St=3

———.1998. 'Major causes of ill health', *Rachel's Environment & Health Weekly #584.* On-line at http://www.rachel.org/bulletin/index.cfm?St=3

Montgomery, S., M. Bartley, D. Cook, and M. Wadsworth. 1996. 'Health and social precursors of unemployment in young men in Great Britain', *Journal of Epidemiology and Community Health* 50: 415–22.

Morris, M., A. Berhardt, and M.S. Hancock. 1994. 'Economic inequality: New methods for new trends', *American Sociological Review* 59: 205–19.

Muntaner, C., and J. Lynch. 1999. 'Income inequality, social cohesion, and class relations: a critique of Wilkinson's neo-Durkheimian research program', *International Journal of Health Services* 29: 59–81.

National Council of Welfare. 1998. *Welfare Incomes 1996.* Ottawa.

Philp, M. 1998. 'UN committee lambastes Canada on human rights', *Globe and Mail*, 5 Dec.

Putnam, R. 1993. *Making Democracy Work: Civic Traditions in Modern Italy.* Princeton, NJ: Princeton University Press.

Rainwater, L., and T. Smeeding. 1995. *Doing Poorly: The Real Income of American Children in a Comparative Perspective.* Working Paper 127, Luxembourg Income Study. On-line at http://lissy.ceps.lu/wpapersentire.htm; then ftp://lissy.ceps.lu/127.pdf

Raphael, D. 1998. 'Public health responses to health inequalities', *Canadian Journal of Public Health* 89: 380–1.

———. 1999. 'Health effects of inequality', *Canadian Review of Social Policy* 44: 25–40.

———. 2000. 'Health inequalities in Canada: Current discourses and implications for public health action', *Critical Public Health* 10: 193–216.

———. Forthcoming. 'Health inequities in the United States: Prospects and solutions', *Journal of Public Health Policy.*

———, I. Brown, R. Renwick, and I. Rootman. 1997. 'Quality of life: What are the implications for health promotion?', *American Journal of Health Behaviour* 21: 118–28.

———, S. Phillips, R. Renwick, and H. Sehdev. 2000. 'Government policies as a threat to public health: Findings from two community quality of life studies in Toronto', *Canadian Journal of Public Health* 91: 181–7.

Roberts, H. 1997. 'Socioeconomic determinants of health: Children, inequalities, and health', *British Medical Journal* 314: 1122–6.

Roemer, J.E. 1994. *Egalitarian Perspectives.* New York: Cambridge University Press.

Ross, D.P., and P. Roberts. 1999. *Income and Child Well-being: A New Perspective on the Poverty Debate.* Ottawa: Canadian Council on Social Development. On-line at http://www.ccsd.ca/pubs/inckids/es.htm

———, E.R. Shillington, and C. Lochhead. 1994. *The Canadian Fact Book on Poverty.* Ottawa: Canadian Council on Social Development.

Ross, N., M.C. Wolfson, J.R. Dunn, J.M. Berthelot, G.A. Kaplan, and J.W. Lynch. 2000. 'Income inequality and mortality in Canada and the United States', *British Medical Journal* 320: 898–902.

Sapolsky, R.M. 1991. 'Poverty's remains', *The Sciences* 31: 8–10.

———. 1992. *Stress, the Aging Brain, and Mechanisms of Neuron Death.* Cambridge, Mass.: MIT Press.

——— and L.J. Share. 1994. 'Rank-related differences in cardiovascular function among wild baboons: Role of sensitivity to glucocorticoids', *American Journal of Primatology* 32: 261–75.

Saul, J.R. 1995. *The Unconscious Civilization.* Toronto: Anansi.

Shaw, M., D. Dorling, D. Gordon, and G. Davey Smith. 1999. *The Widening Gap: Health Inequalities and Policy in Britain.* Bristol, UK: Polity Press.

Shivey, C.A., K.L. Laird, and R.F. Anton. 1997. 'The behavior and physiology of social stress and depression in female cynomolgus monkeys', *Biological Psychiatry* 41: 871–2.

Smallwood, P., and C. Biron. 1989. *The Johnson Quotation Book.* London: International Specialized Book Services.

Smith, G.D. 1996. 'Income inequality and mortality: Why are they related?', *British Medical Journal* 312: 987–8.

Sram, I., and J. Ashton. 1998. 'Millennium Report to Sir Edwin Chadwick', *British Medical Journal* 317: 592–6.

Stanford, J. 1999. *Economic freedom (for the rest of us).* On-line at http://www.policyalternatives.ca

Statistics Canada. 1998. *Income Distributions by Family Size in Canada, 1996.* Ottawa. On-line at http://www.ccsd.ca/98/fs_pov96.htm

———. 1999. *Crimes by Type of Offence.* On-line at http://www.statcan.ca/english/Pgdb/State/Justice/legal02.htm

Tarasuk, V. 1996. 'Responses to food insecurity in the changing Canadian welfare-state', *Journal of Nutrition Education* 28: 71–5.

——— and L. Woolcott. 1994. 'Food acquisition practices of homeless adults: Insights from a health promotion project', *Journal of the Canadian Dietetic Association* 55: 5–19.

Tesh, S. 1990. *Hidden Arguments: Political Ideology and Disease Prevention Policy.* New Brunswick, NJ: Rutgers University Press.

Townson, M. 1998. *Health and Wealth.* Ottawa: Canadian Centre for Policy Alternatives.

Townsend, P., N. Davidson, and M. Whitehead, eds. 1992. *Inequalities in Health: the Black Report and the Health Divide.* New York: Penguin.

Travers, K.D. 1996. 'The social organization of nutritional inequities', *Social Science and Medicine* 43: 543–53.

US Department of Health and Human Services. 1998. *Health, United States, 1998: Socioeconomic Status and Health Chartbook.* On-line at http://www.cdc.gov/nchs/products/pubs/pubd/hus/2010/98chtbk.htm

Vagero, D., and O. Lundberg. 1989. 'Health inequalities in Britain and Sweden', *Lancet* 2: 35–6.

Wallerstein, N. 1992. 'Powerlessness, empowerment, and health: Implications for health promotion programs', *American Journal of Health Promotion* 6, 3: 197–205.

Whitehead, M., and F. Drever. 1999. 'Narrowing social inequalities in health? Analysis of trends in mortality among babies of lone mothers', *British Medical Journal* 318: 1–5.

Wilkins, R., O. Adams, and A. Brancker. 1989. 'Changes in mortality by income in urban Canada from 1971 to 1986', *Health Reports* 1, 2: 137–74.

Wilkinson, R.G. 1996. *Unhealthy Societies: The Afflictions of Inequality.* New York: Routledge.

Wolff, E.N. 1995. *Top Heavy: The Increasing Inequality of Wealth in America and What Can Be Done About It.* New York: New Press.

World Bank. 1998. Poverty net: Social capital for development. On-line at http://www.worldbank.org/poverty/scapital

World Health Organization (WHO). 1986. *Ottawa Charter for Health Promotion.* Geneva: WHO.

———. 1995. *Twenty Steps for Developing a Healthy Cities Project.* Copenhagen: WHO Regional Office. On-line at http://www.who.dk/tech/hcp/hcppub.htm

Wright, E.O. 1997. *Class Counts: Comparative Studies in Class Analysis.* New York: Cambridge University Press.

Yalnizyan, A. 1998. *The Growing Gap: A Report on Growing Inequality between the Rich and Poor in Canada.* Toronto: Centre for Social Justice.

———. 2000. *Canada's Great Divide: The Politics of the Growing Gap between Rich and Poor in the 1990's.* Toronto: Centre for Social Justice.

Contributors

HUGH ARMSTRONG teaches in the School of Social Work and the Institute of Political Economy at Carleton University.

PAT ARMSTRONG is a member of the Department of Sociology, York University.

PAT BARANEK is a doctoral candidate in the Department of Health Administration, University of Toronto.

DAVID COBURN is in the Department of Public Health Sciences, University of Toronto.

RAISA DEBERT teaches in the Department of Health Administration, University of Toronto.

JOHN EYLES is Director of the McMaster Institute of Environment and Health at McMaster University.

ALINA GILDINER is a doctoral candidate in the Department of Health Administration, University of Toronto.

JOEL LEXCHIN practises medicine in the Department of Emergency Medicine at The Toronto Hospital and is a member of the Department of Family and Community Medicine, University of Toronto.

COLIN LEYS is Professor Emeritus, Department of Political Science, Queen's University.

LINDA MUZZIN teaches at the Ontario Institute for Studies in Education, University of Toronto.

ERIC MYKHALOVSKIJ is a post-doctoral fellow in the Department of Public Health Sciences, University of Toronto.

DENNIS RAPHAEL is a member of the Department of Public Health Sciences, University of Toronto.

A. PAUL WILLIAMS is a member of the Department of Health Administration, Faculty of Medicine, University of Toronto.

Index